TIME IS ONLY AN INCH

TIME
IS ONLY AN
Inch

A SPIRITUAL MEMOIR:
The Universe Delivers (and Surprises) When Asked

ANYA KRU

Epigraph Books
Rhinebeck, New York

Time is Only an Inch: A Spiritual Memoir: The Universe Delivers (and Surprises) When Asked © 2022 by Anya Kru

All rights reserved. No part of this book may be used or reproduced in any manner without the consent of the author except in critical articles or reviews. Contact the publisher for information.

Paperback ISBN 978-1-954744-46-2
Hardcover ISBN 978-1-954744-47-9
eBook ISBN 978-1-954744-48-6

Library of Congress Control Number 2021923316

Publisher's Cataloging-In-Publication Data
(Prepared by The Donohue Group, Inc.)

Names: Kru, Anya, author.
Title: Time is only an inch : a spiritual memoir : the Universe delivers (and surprises) when asked / Anya Kru.
Description: Rhinebeck, New York : Epigraph Books, [2021] | Includes bibliographical references.
Identifiers: ISBN 9781954744462 (paperback) | ISBN 9781954744479 (hardcover) | ISBN 9781954744486 (ebook)
Subjects: LCSH: Kru, Anya. | Spiritual biography. | Kuṇḍalinī. | Hiking. | Adult children of alcoholics--Biography. | LCGFT: Autobiographies. | BISAC: BODY, MIND & SPIRIT / Ancient Mysteries & Controversial Knowledge. | TRAVEL / Special Interest / Adventure. | FAMILY & RELATIONSHIPS / Love & Romance.
Classification: LCC BL73.K78 A3 2021 (print) | LCC BL73.K78 (ebook) | DDC 291.4092--dc23

Text design by Colin Rolfe

Epigraph Books
22 East Market Street, Suite 304
Rhinebeck, NY 12572
(845) 876-4861
epigraphps.com

With love for PPC, BTMC, PAR, RLO, ERH, JDK, CRF, SMD, HSP

"Only great pain is the ultimate liberator of the spirit…I doubt that such pain makes us 'better,' but I know that it makes us more profound."

NIETZSCHE

Contents

Author's Note   xiii

Part I
Awakening Prelude

Asking   3

Part II
Nepal

November 1994	11
Dad	19
JFK to Kathmandu	23
Interrupted at Karachi	29
Yoga Group	30
The Universe has a Plan	36
Riding Elephants on Halloween	39
Solo Trekker	44
Mother Goddess of the Universe	49
Expelling Shadows	51
A Sound Prayer at Taksindu Monastery	58
Tuche Rinpoche's Plea	64
Corpses	67
Are You Breathing, Honey?	71
Silence Without, Silence Within	74
Muktinath's Eternal Flame	78
Mind's Eye	83
Absorbing Energy	88
The Kaligandaki Gorge	93
Slipping into Accord	97

Balcony of Death	100
Anger's Tutelage	105
Synchronicity on Poon Hill	115
Double Rainbows	119
Trekking the Edge	123
The Annapurna Sanctuary	126
Reattached to the Universe	130
Night Goddess	135

Part III
India

Varanasi	141
Lucknow's Guru	147
Sitting Satsang	154
Rishikesh	162
The Enlightened Beings List	165
Elephant Dung	170
Santa Claus in India	175
Keoladeo Ghana National Park	178
Siberian Cranes	180
Ministry of Home Affairs, Delhi	187
Encountering Cobras	191
Taj Mahal	192
Tying the String	195
Fiery Sari	200
Purge	205
Mundgod	209
Camp One, Gaden Monastery	215
Doeguling Tibetan Settlement	217
Kalachakra Initiation	223
The Leper's Touch	230
The Mandala	235
Decision	238
Avinashilingum College for Women Coimbatore, Tamil Nadu Southern India	243

Across Southern India　253
Aurobindo Ashram　259
Madras to Bombay　266
Keeping the Promise　270
Carnal Satisfactions　277

Part IV
Egypt

Melting Ice Cubes　283
Luxor　288
Walking into Time　291
It Wasn't Accidental　295
Singing Bowls　303
Cairo　307
Great Pyramid of Cheops　313
Yet Another Eternal Flame　323
Budapest　327
Panama　329
Art Camp　338
Arriving Full Circle　341
Love Letters　343
Each Other's Arms　347
Transits　354
Gdansk　360
A Stonewall　365
Living the Opera　366
The Letter　371
Don't Flee　373
Mission　375
Vision Quest　376
She Who Sees Through Purple Eye　384
Cleaning Drawers　392
Alignment Postlude　397

Post Script   401
Epilogue   399
Acknowledgements   403
References   405

Author's Note

Books come from the interior of individuals, often the soul, as does mine. Before writing this memoir, it ran like a movie for decades through my mind, rich in eidetic imagery. This is how I think; this is how I write; these pages look into my consciousness. Most names, professions, identifying details, and some locations were changed to protect the privacy of individuals. Any mistakes in the accuracy of dates, geographical and cultural facts, or historical background information are mine.

PART I
AWAKENING PRELUDE

Asking

I never expected to get a cobra riding over the roof of my head. Never. But when I asked the Universe for help, I got it big time.

It all started after being accepted into a doctoral program, and I realized I'd gotten myself in over my head academically. I'd struggled through college for a variety of reasons. When the heavy-duty, abstract workload poured in, I felt under a cerebral avalanche, and I begged the Universe for help. It delivered in the form of a Kundalini awakening. It delivered because, for my entire life, I had wanted, had asked, "to know."

Kundalini has a long, complicated history reaching back 3,000 years into Hindu scripture. In a lot of ways, it's scientific. It's an energy system identified with seven physiological centers in the body called chakras: the perineum, sacrum, solar plexus, heart, thymus, pineal gland, and the crown of the head all lined up streaming spiritual energy. Our bodies are vessels of electro-magnetic and biochemical dances—so research tells us.

Picture the energy as a translucent snake (sometimes two) coiled three and a half times at the base of the spine, waiting to be awakened so it can travel up two pathways called Ida and Pingala. Ida (the female representing the moon) and Pingala (the male representing the sun) comprise the yin and yang of divine energy. Or visualize them like the DNA molecule, the spiral helix with its two branches. Under certain circumstances, Kundalini awakens in the form of a light-filled cobra—its symbol—which rises through the seven chakras energetically, creating a Mind/Body connection with Universal forces. That's what happened to me.

How did I get this...gift? Kundalini can open spontaneously, although usually, it needs the help of either an experienced guide (a guru) to assist its release or a near-death experience—none of which I qualified for directly. Its awakening is often an extreme physical shake-up—electrical currents surging up and down the spine passing through the major physiological hubs causing body spasms, mood swings, strange sounds, intense bliss, orgasm, or those near-death experiences.

But some awakenings, the spontaneous sort not asked for, require austerities and are atypical—a form called abnegation. Self-denial surrounds abnegation and automatically affects the heart, lighting a spark of spirituality in the soul. It opens under the belief, in New Age terminology, when there is "nowhere to go and nothing to do," the Universe picks up the slack. My opening more or less fit this form because, although I asked for help, I didn't ask for a Kundalini awakening. Nor did I expect it despite carrying an underlying network of beliefs that did fit the bill.

The priming of my Kundalini awakening boiled down to an amalgamation of four things more or less in this order: a childhood trauma, a bonding to the planet's energies, an affirmation of my integrity, and a college friend who made sure I wasn't a novice to the esoteric power systems of the Universe. All composed members of my cadre that pushed me forward. *Had something been recognized in me early on?*

This whole thing began around money, or maybe I should say security. I had a job that provided unprecedented freedom, but my salary stank. Misbelieving I was at the top of a stagnant pay scale and wanting more financial security, I'd listened to a trusted colleague. She said I could increase wages by getting a Ph.D. just as she did by doing a distance learning program via the computer. I could continue to work at the same time. It appeared ideal, and it wasn't until I dove into the program that I discovered what a farce that was.

When the letter arrived, something in me must have known I was in for a big ride. My hand shook, the letter shook, and my spirit must have shaken as I opened the letter reading the acceptance. Shocked, I thought, "What have I done to myself?" I'd struggled through college, not having been adequately prepared by my high school or family background. Yet, there was some kind of quiet joy, some unknown anticipation spilling out of me.

I don't think you choose a cobra as a spiritual guide; I think it chooses you. Or maybe it has nothing to do with choice—it's more on a path with no other option. The Universe had a plan for me, and it didn't take long to feel I was scaling a mind-bending Everest without an oxygen tank. I was sitting for hours at the computer, pushed out of my comfort zone—stretched beyond my mental capacities. I read abstract articles three times to get their gist; all papers were written in several drafts to make sure my point was clear. I was stressed.

Rarely do I ask for anything, especially help. But the hurtles of the doctoral program, along with my less than satisfying marriage, served as the last straw pushing me over the edge. Realizing it took more analytical smarts than I thought I had, I knew—despite my relentless efforts—it was time to ask the Universe for help. So, I did.

While I waited for my help to arrive, I continued to grind away at my studies but figured I'd do two things to assist my progress. First, I began a daily meditation using mental imagery. I chose a technique learned in the Silva Mind Method course taken years before with my friend Dori who plays a significant role in all this. The course taught how the brain pipes along using all kinds of brain wave levels—gamma, alpha, beta, theta, delta—to integrate mind/body/spirit. It trained us to enter a meditative state, visualize and send pure light through the body, ours and others, for relaxation and healing. I'd consciously chosen imagery as central to my meditation—streaming golden light through my chakras—because I'd discovered long ago that internal sound mantras did little for me, although external ones were different. So, the second thing I did to help myself was to buy a cassette tape of the Gayatri Mantra by Vyaas Houston from the American Sanskrit Institute.

The tape's cover described the mantra as "The Sound of Light"—a divine poem in the Upanishads and the Bhagavad Gita—the "sacred of all the Vedic mantras." First referenced in a Vedic manuscript dating between 1100 -1700 BCE—this was old sound, very old. One of its translations included these words: Om, earth, heavens, the ultimate reality, illumination, intellect, who, ours, requesting, urging, prayer. Its chanting was supposed to ground the mind in earthly energies allowing the person to carry out work they were destined to do. It got better. The mantra was said to kindle the intellect 'bequeathing true knowledge' that could illuminate the darkest caverns dwelling inside the soul. It all sounded good to me; after all, I was primed. I popped the cassette tape into the recorder and pressed play.

These things, meditating with imagery and listening to the Gayatri Mantra, might actually have been the Universe helping me, but ultimately there was to be no more gentle nudging. The Universe gave me a big shove. I must have been ready for it because I survived. It planned to start by unblocking my second chakra, associated with mental energy, located at the base of my spine, getting that wheel spinning full speed ahead, opening me up for what was to come next. My back went out. And I was in pain.

Pain crawling on my hands and knees to the bathroom, pain twisted into a corkscrew, pain that went on for weeks. Finally, I knew I needed to take action to relieve my suffering and joined a yoga studio to stretch my muscles out. But it wasn't enough. I needed more. And that's when I found a pool where I went to align my back and where I began to pray, streaming prana through my body. But the Universe had more in store for me than basic physical therapy. A stringent alignment began to take place under the surface of my auric body. I have to admit I was genuinely ignorant of all that was going on at that time.

Each afternoon, I destressed by meditating. One bright day, sunlight filtered through the window I sat by. My eyes closed. And for some reason, I began to visualize a bluish light materializing over my head. *What?* I thought, but I was captivated. It started as a couple of inches, then slowly, over the weeks, it eased upward—soft, deepening blue. Curiosity surged up my spine, wondering what was going on. As I continued my daily routine, the light changed into a filmy marine blue, gently pulsing further upward, soon extending to four inches. Fascination is the only word to describe it. No fear, no negative emotion, no thinking I'd gone nuts. No.

As the weeks went on, the blue glow shifted into a pale golden light as if shedding skin. A diaphanous, radiant-filled cobra flowed above my head. I sensed its effortless aura interlacing my chakras and calmly emerging through the crown of my head. As I watched the snake pulsated: I wasn't afraid. I was in awe. I knew what it was. My Kundalini had awakened.

Yet, having a serpent guide gave me pause. A cobra riding over my head felt beyond the boundaries of so-called everyday normalcy, boundaries now breached by mysticism. I felt vulnerable. And I was puzzled.

I dug into the books (information on the internet was limited back then). So, I researched Kundalini's manifestations and meaning; and found that although in most cases it required the aid of a guru, Kundalini could still be unleashed spontaneously. But the body needed to be "subjected to austerities and purification through celibacy." That I qualified for: (my marriage to Tim was celibate).

From a different angle, Western medicine had borrowed the Rod of Asclepius (God of healing and medicinal arts) from Greek Mythology which depicted a serpent entwined around a shaft. About twenty-six other health agencies, including the American Medical Association and the World Health Organization, used a snake in its logo. I also vaguely recalled that belief in Kundalini paralleled mystical practices in other religions—the Jewish Kabala, the Christian belief in a personal God, and the Islamic faith in Sufism—all purporting direct access to God via contemplation. Whatever it was, I was ready, and it was no wonder the energy awakened. I'd been rehearsing for this spiritual shift my entire life.

I'd never known anyone who personally had a Kundalini opening which made it impossible to discuss. I didn't tell a soul. I was tightlipped, not sharing my experience with anyone—not my dearest friends—not with Cathy or Karette, not even with Dori —all of whom would have understood. It was my private stuff. Stuff I had yet to come to terms with.

My cobra energy opened in a hush rather than a crash-bang—a gossamer conduit that penetrated my *being*—arriving to guide my *doing*. This was a different neighborhood, and I wasn't about to be thrown off balance when I had a job to do, no matter the benefit.

Too bad, I thought, *unique mystical zone or not, I am not falling over some numinous edge.* I needed my feet planted firmly on the ground, not wavering, not straying into la-la land going off course, and not being stupid. Me? I stayed grounded to Mother Earth, a stance that didn't seem the way Kundalini operated, but a bearing that always helped me survive. Unbeknownst to me, for my work, I had taken up a practice of Jnana Yoga—the yoga that gives rise to knowledge and ultimately wisdom.

I said nothing. It didn't matter. This was *my* stuff intended only for *me*. I was held captive by my process. I clutched my secret close to my chest—locked in my heart, or in this case riding over the top of my head—its potential a minute sequoia seed waiting.

During my cobra's spontaneous appearances, I remained present, allowing it to shepherd me. I came to realize it was the result of the power of asking, but sparingly so. The truth was, and is, I accepted there was a resource of grit within me, and that as uncanny as it was, and it *was* truly uncanny, it was my inner truth. It fit with my reality—one my father had ingrained in me—a viable connection to the earth and an understanding that I was lovable and capable. And having believed him, I believed in myself, and it was that understanding that made the tangled world I was living in begin to untangle.

As I accepted the cobra for what it was, an awakening within my consciousness that opened a spiritual channel to my work on this planet, I consented to its advance, and I sensed its flow not so much a torrent but a tender brook. My back slowly healed, papers I wrote were published, my dissertation received 'most innovative,' and Tim and I swept our problems under the rug putting the marriage we both knew was failing on hold until we finished with it or it with us. What I didn't know was that there was a lot more to come.

PART II

NEPAL

November 1994

That was the year I finished my Ph.D., sold my house, quit my job, divorced my husband, and jumped a plane to Kathmandu. Slamming the door on responsibility was new to me, yet here I was begging Time for one delicious year to release me from all the 'gotta-dos' in my life. One year—just a pinch of Time's perpetual reach—to put away my devotion to work for a dose of serious play.

I wasn't angry. I wasn't depressed. I wasn't sick. And I wasn't in an existential crisis. *Doing, doing, doing* had fried my brain, shredded my heart, and soured my prana. I was empty. And somewhere inside of me, an exhausted child cried, having gotten lost in a maze of duty. It was time to dry her tears, and I knew exactly how to do that. Precisely where to take her to soak up living energy, reawaken her heart. I set my sights on the farthest reaches of the planet and bid farewell to family and friends. One year was all I asked. One. I promised. Truth was, I was homesick for a spiritual journey. An inch of time was all I wanted.

*

I gazed out the window fascinated as the small plane swooped low, plaiting the spine of the Himalayas. I was going to Jomsom, a remote village teetering on the edge of the Tibetan Plateau, the jumping-off point for my trek. Below to the north, the Tibetan Plateau uncoiled its reptilian crust—the earth's most prominent and highest table floating three miles above sea level. To the east, the planet's tallest mountains—old giants that had growled from the earth's center fifty million years ago—shook hands with the stars. I'd come to trek the Annapurna Circuit's western flank wanting to take in the high desert, and the mountains held sacred by Nepalis.

It was 1994. There were no roads, no cars, and no cell phones. The trail would be sparsely populated at best only with locals and other trekkers climbing through several ecological zones—and in the end—several numinous zones as well. The Himalayas held the world's premier power points.

I had just spent the last two weeks of October acclimating at 10,100 feet in the Mount Everest region with a yoga group from back home primed for more adventure in the Himalaya's vast emptiness. As the plane flew, I didn't know the words to the Halleluiah chorus, but my heart shouted with its joy. Play took control of me, and I was ready to trek the "Roof of the World."

The plane bumped to a stop on a short runway overgrown with weeds seeping up through cracks in the pavement. The other trekkers and I scrambled out of its belly. A short distance away, Jomsom, composed of a few low stucco buildings, crouched on the margin of Nepal's Mustang District. It was set against a backdrop of snowcapped mountains, and a dull November sun lit their white summits into pink flames. The air chilled my face. I'd heard the others on the plane wishing for good weather, noting the area's unstable terrain and climate as unpredictable. I hoped for favorable conditions, too. This was the threshold of my trek.

Thud, thud, thud. Backpacks were tossed from the plane by a shiny-faced crew member grinning broadly. I grabbed my sack, hefted it to my shoulder, and looked back at the isolated village that seemed barren of people. I thought of the yoga group I'd left back in Kathmandu a short while before. I'd trekked with them as an inaugural, in the Mount Everest Solukhumbu region, during my first two weeks in the country. The group had bid me farewell after the leader had directed me to the Annapurna Circuit for more trekking. Snapping the front of my jacket up against the chill, I thought to myself, if nowhere was somewhere, this was it. But I quickly brushed the thought aside because my immediate task was to hire a guide.

Out of nowhere, thirty or so Nepali men materialized, rushing toward the plane. Each was dressed in various states of attire from hiking pants to formal Nepali dress—all would-be guides. I heard English muffled along with French and some German. The plane's arrival meant jobs, and we were inundated with offers.

One man dressed in a traditional Daura jacket and Dhaka topi hat closed in on me, vying for my attention. "Madam, Madam, Hello! Welcome to Jomsom," he smiled, showing an array of white, straight teeth as he took me in. For my part, I wore an orange, gold, and blue patterned cotton skirt that reached below my knees and a long-sleeved shirt over a tee. I'd tucked my hair under a floppy, canvas hat. According to the yoga group leaders, this garb was culturally appropriate gear for women hiking in Nepal. I never deviated.

"Hello," I said, taking him in.

"Welcome to trekking Annapurna Circuit. You need a guide, surely. And I will safely get you along the trail. Not expensive. Are you alone?"

"Yes, I do need a guide. And yeah, I'm alone," I said, hearing the level of competence in the man's voice, his air of smoothness.

He glanced over at the others bunched together in small pairs negotiating prices, then back at me, nodding self-assuredly.

"OK. We start down Kaligandaki River, stop at Marpha—a beautiful, old village—pass through deepest gorge in the world, then to Tatopani hot springs where you will get a good soak there, loosen up muscles. Then trek Poon Hill, excellent view, and end in Annapurna Sanctuary. Yes?"

I don't know why I hesitated, why I stalled, or why I glanced about at the rest of the men. But my mind went into pause mode for a moment. I could hear the murmur of other trekkers and guides briskly finishing up their business. I couldn't figure out where the guides had come from. How had they gotten here? We stood in the middle of a vacant runway on the lip of a high desert. Had they flown in? That didn't seem possible given the flight's cost. They'd evidently walked up the trail to Jomsom looking for jobs. That appeared desperate to me, but these men—some dressed the same as the ragamuffin porters who'd carried my yoga group's bags and set up our camps—all knew it was the high season and wanted work. With only about a dozen of us standing in the middle of the windblown airfield needing guides, many of them would be left out.

"Not too expensive," white, straight teeth repeated, firmly smiling. "Is this your sack?" He pointed at the small black backpack I'd bought before leaving at REI in Seattle, along with my hiking boots. I studied the guide before me, his crisp Daura jacket, noting his almost perfect English, his self-assured demeanor, and said "Yes," but didn't bite.

He continued to talk. "I would be happy to guide you. I have ten years' experience and will get a porter to carry your bag. You, Madam, will not get yourself lost up here in the mountains—sometimes dangerous. Falling rocks, you know," he said, pointing out something I had not thought of before. He was polite and glib. Too glib for my liking.

I glanced over the crowd. Standing at the back outside the circle of guides, I caught the eye of a dark-haired man about thirty years old, hatless, dressed in a dog-eared, brown jacket with orange stripes running along the sleeves. *A castaway*, I thought. His clean-shaven face was quiet, and meeting my gaze, he moved watchfully through the group coming up behind the chatty guide who was still coaxing me to book with him, saying, "Yes, Madam?"

Ignoring him, I moved toward castaway guy asking, "Do you speak English?"

"Yes, English," he said shyly, heavily accented.

"What's your name?" I asked.

"Go…." he mumbled inaudibly.

"Go…what?" I asked, squinting at him.

"Gome. Guide for trek?" he asked upping the volume of his tone.

Something in his voice triggered a crazy, instantaneous recognition in me. Two seconds with him, and he drew me in. Gome's tone reminded me of the inner-city kids I'd taught in Connecticut, the minority kids who came from tenements with street smarts galore and smiles that lit my heart. His voice kicked off the teacher in me, the public servant who I thought I'd left behind. Anyway, what I wanted was a guide who'd get *me* safely down the trail, not the reverse of my helping *him* get down the track because he needed a job. Yet, there was a poignancy that held me.

"Gome, I want to trek to the Annapurna Sanctuary. Do you understand?"

"Yes. Trek. I carry bag."

That gave the impression of being tenuous, so I asked again, "Do you know the route to Annapurna Base Camp?"

"Yes. Annapurna…mumble, mumble."

"Teahouse to teahouse?"

Gome's throat garbled something that sounded close to an affirmation. His English was limited. Glancing at the other guides—spiffy, clean, seeming to speak fluent English—I knew if I wanted someone to take good care of me, along a trail billed as a serious high-altitude hike, one of them would fit the bill, not Gome. Gome's threadbare appearance told me he'd probably walked for more than a week from a god-forsaken village in Nepal to find this inaccessible spot to get work. After all, his sneakers looked as if they'd been assaulted.

I surveyed his open face. Could I trust him? I needed him to help me for about twelve days to keep me on course and in one piece hiking from teahouse to teahouse before the final climb—13,550 feet into the Annapurna Sanctuary. My body felt sound, and because I was acclimated to the altitude, that wouldn't be an issue for me. But I *was* sporting a half-dollar-sized sore on the bottom of my butt that had developed during the long plane ride to Kathmandu.

I'd gotten it lanced at the hospital in Pokhara and was taking antibiotics to make sure it wouldn't get infected. I had to be careful because I knew only too well how easy it was to get sick along the trail. While hiking with my yoga group, I had vomited my guts out and shit into the bushes after eating some shoe-leather, salmonella-contaminated chicken. By this time, I knew that in this no-man's-land, if the weather or a rock slide or a microbe didn't get you, knees or ankles could betray the sturdiest of bodies, plunging a hiker over the edge into physical jeopardy.

Still, I trusted my body to hold solid. In the past two weeks, I'd learned a few simple survival skills: I had a stash of Pepto Bismol and Imodium, wore a skirt for easy expel-lation of nasty organisms if needed, and was now a vegetarian for the rest of the trip.

There was one more matter. Did Gome speak enough English to get me from start to finish? I was in an immense—out-of-the-way, unforgiving place. I knew from the guidebook there were only a few turn-offs here and there, and essentially one trail straddled the river. So somehow, I wasn't worried about getting lost. I just wasn't. I was forty-eight years old and had spent a lifetime hiking in forests and had built what I think of as a sense of security in forgotten spaces. Any space, in particular the far-flung, felt like home to me in more ways than one, making me confident to trek alone with a non-verbal guide.

I was feeling can-do. I was feeling "nowhere to go and nothing to do." It would be easy, being in the *now* on this dusty plain with essentially someone who didn't talk my ear off. That's what I wanted. To be virtually unconnected while trekking. As I stood there, on the rim of the Tibetan Plateau, I was precisely where I wanted to be. I knew why I was there, ready to slip into each moment to savor its *breadth of being*.

It was decision time. The other trekkers had negotiated fees and were dispersing. I thought of the yoga group's scruffily dressed porters, who had carried the luggage and prepared our meals, speaking little English, who'd done a great job. I took in Gome's noiseless face and liked it. Liked it like I had liked my disadvantaged students, their bright eyes filled with a knowledge rooted there that I could only imagine—but never know—an oxymoronic mixture of independence tangled with a need for mothering. Gome's low register face would make no demands urging me to march quickly through the terrain or, more importantly, to converse continually as my group had done. I was there for a different purpose. I was there to absorb the hush of the Earth.

"How much money per day?" I asked slowly.

Gome held up four fingers and said hopefully, "Day."

Four dollars a day didn't sound the going price from all the background noise I was hearing. Gome was cheap. OK, I thought. He seemed to understand what I wanted. Without hesitation, without any bargaining (the money didn't matter to me), I held up four fingers and said, "Gome, you've got the job."

I'm not sure why it wasn't crisp Daura but Gome leading me—but something told me Gome would care for me while at the same time I'd care for his economic welfare. But for sure, his eyes—which mirrored all the ghosts of my past inner-city students—clinched the deal.

Gome hefted my pack onto his back and pointed north, asking, "Muktinath?" I glanced south where the other trekkers disappeared down the trail toward Marpha. Then, I focused north toward the open expanse of the plateau. In my *Lonely Planet* guide to Nepal, I'd read that there was a temple in Muktinath revered by Buddhists and Hindus, one that housed an eternal flame that had burned for two thousand years. It was dedicated to Vishnu, a Hindu god, the Universe's known preserver that kept it going full steam ahead in the right direction. The temple sat at 12,467 feet below the Thorong La Mountain Pass—the highest in the world, scraping the sky at 18,000 feet. Trekkers doing the entire Annapurna Circuit struggled to surmount it—altitude and unpredictable weather getting in their way—giving it a reputation of frozen bodies caught in blizzards recovered by the Nepalese Army.

I'd skip the pass. I wasn't interested in counting coup bragging about how high I'd climbed or how many passes I'd conquered when chances were it might conquer me. Instead, I wanted to feel the Himalaya under my feet, press my boot-print to meet the dirt at its most uncomplicated level of existence. There is nothing rational, nothing linear about hiking, not for me. This dirt had nothing to do with ego.

Pushing through spatial dimensions that connect me to the Earth, that's where I'd find liberation from past duty and mission, that's where I'd get a sisterhood with the genius loci of the mountains—the quiet. Getting to Muktinath Temple would be enough. I wanted to see the flame that symbolized an enduring spiritual awakening. The time had come to start, and Muktinath promised an auspicious starting point. Maybe Vishnu would grant me a propitious direction. After all, he held the cards of the Universe. The late mid-day sun cast bottomless purple shadows against the high desert floor. As the known world fell away, I turned north and said, "Muktinath."

Trekking. Cap to skull. Shades to eyes. Boot to trail. Gome and I hiked along. Here I was alone, on the most isolated plateau in the world, with a guide who barely spoke twelve words of English, and I liked it. I imagined that most women might not have. They would have dragged along a husband, a boyfriend, or at least a girlfriend to keep them company in a land where it wasn't possible to get a daily hot shower or find a laundromat to wash dirty underwear. Most women would have wanted someone else to talk to. But most women hadn't begun their trekking adventures in kindergarten at age four and a half as I had. The day I split from school.

In the fifties, kindergarten was half-days with parent-pickup at noon. Kids waited out front of the school. On that day, one by one, the other children disappeared into cars. As usual, the teachers retreated into the building for their next class with the expectation that folks would retrieve their kids. The strays, like me, were left outside unattended. I waited. *Where was Dad?* I waited and waited, but the maroon Hudson never showed up. Finally, after everyone had left, I figured out he wasn't coming and that most likely he was in a bar downing afternoon drinks, and I decided to walk home.

The route home still runs a movie in my mind: Past the school, right on Rochester Avenue, by the Catholic Church with bright red arched doors, and up a highway overgrown with grass and not much traffic at that time. I walked for two miles, almost getting to the turnoff for the hill I lived on when a black car pulled up alongside me. The dark-haired man behind the wheel peered down at me and asked, "How about a ride home?" and he opened up the rear door of the car. I looked at him and crawled into the backseat. Officer Freddy, a town cop who my parents knew, as did I, drove me up the hill and dropped me off in front of my house. With a quick smile, he was gone without another word. Had he been searching for a short child who'd wandered off from parent-pickup left at the school's front, or was he just patrolling and recognized a newly minted hiker who shouldn't have taken her inaugural trip on a two-lane highway alone? I never found out.

In the house, Mother was listening to Backstage Wife on the radio, leaning over the stove stirring a pot of chicken soup. She glanced at me and asked matter-of-factly, "Hungry?" I plunked myself at the table and gobbled up a bowl of soup with an extra helping of rice. I'm not sure how Mother thought I got home that day. There was never a discussion or recrimination or a rant toward Dad about not picking me up at school.

But the second time Dad failed to show, the school put its foot down. There was no second chance for me to practice my strong sense of direction. The second time, the teachers caught me before I could do my walk-about and made me an all-day kindergartener. Agnes, my older sister in second grade, escorted me to the afternoon bus to ride home with her. This put a halt on my budding spirit as a trekker but not my growing sense of independence and confidence in taking charge of my world. Dad, with his neglect, was actually teaching me to be who I would become.

Dad

Dad was wild-minded. He felt and fed off the woods. One late November day, Dad and I stood overlooking the pond, the one below the house he'd built for us. "Those out there, Honey," he said, pointing toward tall, green blades knifing from the water's edge. I waded out up to my knees in chilly, mucky water heading for a patch of iris. A stomach ache had plagued him for a couple of days, and we were on a healing mission. "Get me a couple of small roots."

I sloshed deeper before digging several tubers. Two crows overhead cawed shrilly, swooping low above us. Dad squinted hazel eyes and tipped the brim of his ball cap with his clawed, left hand revealing a sweaty bald head. The crows landed in a nearby maple. Dad's nostrils flared, a dog sniffing up a distant message in the breeze.

Nodding his head toward the crows, he smiled, exposing stubby teeth, and said, "Yeah, yeah. I hear ya'. So, it's gonna be like that then. OK. OK. I get it."

"What's up, Dad," I asked, not surprised but always slightly amused, knowing Dad wasn't shy about communicating with the birds—crows in particular—who were regular Walter Cronkites delivering trustworthy messages to him on maneuvering through the woods and the world.

"Oh, just this and that going on. Something is always going on, Honey. You know *it's* goin' on; you absolutely can't trust them." And, yes, I did know. I knew what Dad meant, that "them" meant people out "there," not the birds.

"Yeah, they're chemicalizing us again," he said. "They started big time during World War II, and now they're doin' it again! Those bastards are killing us with all those preservatives and white bread and sugar they're feeding us. And look here in the pond. There are maybe half the fish there used to be when I'd go fishin'. I'll tell ya what we're supposed to do about this. Live close to the earth, that's what." I never had a retort to any of his convictions that there was something, some entity out there hostile to him and the earth. People tainting our foods, dumping rubbish into our streams and oceans, and killing us with chemicals in general—the soil and the air. Growing up with Dad, there was always "They" lingering in the background. "They" were always out to get us.

We left the pond and bushwhacked back to the car. Dad claimed never to get lost. "It's my inner gyroscope in my brain, Honey. It's like the birds and butterflies have," he said, looking up at the sky to orient himself in a tangle of overgrowth. "I'm piloting through. I'm picking up the magnetic forces that drive the earth. I can feel the woods. Let's get home so I can liquid-dize these roots up and heal myself."

At home, Dad washed, cut, and threw the snarly iris roots into his blender, grinding it to a brown mush before he guzzled it down, a bitter smoothie, grinning widely. The times when Agnes and I had gotten stomach aches, and Dad had tried to get us to eat some liquid glop that came out of his blender, often there were no takers. He'd default to a glass of water with baking soda or an Alka Seltzer, the only medicine besides aspirin and mercurochrome in the house. Still, he was constantly searching for remedies from the chemicals spewed in the atmosphere from automobiles or the poisons that "they" put in his food, so he ate herbs to heal himself. He ate wild.

After devouring the iris pulp, Dad grabbed a bottle from the shelf that contained a long narrow carrot-shaped tuber and said, "I'm going to finish up with this later." The jar had a snarly tuber, a burdock root. "Honey," he said, "this is the best, *the best* blood purifier ever. Whatever you have—acne, gases in the lungs or blood, something with your liver, you name it! Why this might even cure syphilis. Want some?" I'd hem and haw. Dad couldn't pass a burdock plant heavy with its Velcro seed balls without digging up the root for later grinding in his liquid-dizer.

"Just take some home and boil this burdock root up with a little bit of baking soda, and you can eat it as if radishes. Get those toxins out of your blood. They'll just drain right out in your urine. You'll see." And although I said "Not today, Dad," I was being drawn into Dad's pre-herbal smoothie, pre-Celestial Seasoning tea, pre-artificial food-stuff bans, pre-air pollution awareness, pre-recycle—his pro-environmental movement understandings. He knew the secrets of the plants. Not the magic of photosynthesis that I learned later in school, but their medicinal power, their wisdom.

I must admit, I avoided imbibing any suspicious-looking smoothies that came out of his blender, but at the same time, I began to follow his advice. I had developed a large wart on my finger, and when Dad spotted it, he found a milkweed plant, tore off a leaf that oozed white latex out of its petiole, and he smeared the goop on the wart's crusty surface. After a few weeks of applications such as this, the wart began to shrivel. Soon I was searching out milkweed plants and applying their milky goo to my wart along with cutting off chunks of it with scissors; it never reappeared. Each plant had something to say to me, some healing power. Gathered in by Dad's half-crazy herbal expertise, half-over-the-edge understandings of how Mother Nature operated herself, an imaginative pulse inside of me opened to the veracity spoken by the Earth, its wisdom, its protection.

When the drinking and arguments erupted between Dad and Mother, I ran to the woods wanting the protection of the trees, and the scrawny pink azalea bush dripping dewy nectar, and the lone tiger-lily standing by its side. I waited to be hypnotized by their poetry. Hypnotized by the woods, its paint box of greens: pickle-green fuzz of mosses, blue-green scales of lichens, yellow-green tendrils of cat-briar, chartreuse stripes of jack-in-the-pulpits, and the olive-green slime of seaweeds in the pond. Hypnotized by its rhythms and patterns: spring's caress of rain erasing the icy tempos of winter calling out buds that knew how to pull vigor from soil and reach for the sun making shapes beyond human imagination—all predictably. The plants triggered something deep in me. More than just pretty. More than just soothing. More than just logical. They stimulated something profound inside of me where I wanted to know—to know! What? I wasn't sure, but I truly wanted to know whatever the Earth had to tell me.

Tramping with Dad through the woods grounded me in the Earth; well, it addicted me to the healing solitude in nature, gave me a special bonding. This is where I went to mend, where I was held—by nature, a parent, a mother—by Mother Nature, who pushed out my bad dreams, real and imaginary. Where I felt harbored. The first of two emotional—no, spiritual—"life preservers" Dad tossed to me.

Now, standing on the fringe of the Tibetan Plateau, I was ready for the trek. Yes, I'd taken on a guide who was rag-tag and barely spoke English, but was there a problem? No, not even though we were heading into a barren prairie. True, the landscape possessed an outrageous stillness and unpredictability that felt as if it might swallow me up. But I'd been suckled on a thousand volatile moments during my childhood, marriage, and the Ph.D. process. All those things had taught me to expect the unexpected; accordingly, whatever I faced out there, I was ready for it. Those two life preservers, tossed me by Dad, gave me emotional strength, which in turn provided the nerve to do whatever I pleased, including trekking a plateau that stretched 1,600 miles long and 620 miles wide from Nepal to China. I felt no trepidation.

The other trekkers had disappeared south down the trail. I stood there alone with Gome. If I'd wanted companionship, I would have joined another group or stayed home. But I didn't. Maybe I purposely chose Gome as a guide; because I counted on his silence during the following days to help rid me of responsibility's albatross I'd been carrying for the past nine years. And I was counting on the mountains to clear out the remnants of my monkey-mind chatter, counting on the river to let me wander without intent, counting on each boot step to grind miles of sharp pebbles into a poultice to soften my toughened heart. I looked forward to crawling inside myself to find fresh haven and reground in the earth's rhythms. I was used to existential loneliness. I'd grown up with it. So as Gome and I turned north to Muktinath, I knew what I was looking for. I was ready to take in everything offered me and everything not.

JFK to Kathmandu

It was October; the autumn trees burned red and gold along the Merritt Parkway as my friend Cathy drove me to JFK to catch my plane to Kathmandu. An epic chapter of my life had crumbled into dust, but I had a plan. I'd finished the arduous labor of a Ph.D., divorced Peter Pan after a sexless marriage, and sold my house of eighteen years which had ended up located on a small, noisy highway. In addition, I had quit my job in a school district where one administrator attempted to strangle his vice-principal, and another was accused of flashing in a men's restroom on the highway. I was happy, yet I was feeling—if I corrupt my favorite Zen proverb—I'd been chopping too much wood and carrying too much water. Not just during the dissertation, my job, or the breakdown of my marriage, but during a lifetime holding my nose to the grindstone.

I had my sights set on traveling to Nepal and India because of Cathy. I'd met her in graduate school while getting our master's degrees to become teachers. Meeting her made me come face to face with a perspective on life I'd never encountered, one that would take me a lifetime to understand. She knew all about the world's political system, a complexity never discussed in my family. Dad would pile the family into the Hudson on voting day, drive to the polling place and vote for Eisenhower. Neither my High School nor college courses ever debated any social or partisan issues. I was dumb politically, and meeting Cathy opened my brain, but more importantly, it opened my heart to the world.

Cathy—tall, clipped brown hair, clear skin, Coke-bottle glasses—carried a paradoxical air of strength and vulnerability, the mixture of an old soul. She, like me, could sleep on a rock in the middle of a forest and was a long-haul swimmer. She'd grown up living in various places around the world, including Nepal and India. Her father had served in the diplomatic corps for the USA government and grown up in Allahabad, India, along with five brothers and sisters, son of a doctor/missionary.

Cathy educated my blank-slate mind in politics and world affairs. She told me stories about her life in Nepal and India, tales that held me spellbound. That made me *see* images of faraway cultures, peoples, and places—the magic of the Himalayan Mountains in Nepal. The exotic lure of India rooted in my mind. As a hiker and lover of nature, the Himalayas quickly got stuffed into my travel bucket with the asterisk: Dream Trip.

The year I was finally finished with the Ph.D. and everything else, Cathy was there, instrumental in helping me to cast off the story I'd been telling myself for my whole life. The story that I had to work work work to survive in this world. True, there was no one to support me; I didn't marry Tim till I was thirty-nine, but in all honesty, achievement hooked me. In a way, I believe this Japanese proverb sums it up: *A Day without work is a day without food.* For me, work provided not only physical security; it fed my soul. I was happy when I was working and working hard.

After landing my first job as a teacher of gifted and talented, I created programs that taught students how to be independent thinkers. Maybe I was making up for something, but I loved to work—still, during the past nine years, I had to admit that I'd developed a psychic hole that needed patching up. There'd been too much doing and not enough being. I'd split myself into too many identities—wife, student, wage earner, family member; and I desperately wanted a year of respite. A simple truce. At this point, I felt stopped in my tracks yet moving ahead at the same time, but to where?

As my life pivoted that year, a brochure arrived from a nearby yoga center. It announced a trek to Nepal that combined yoga with hiking in the mountains. My doctoral courses had focused on human consciousness, where I'd read articles that described the Himalayan Mountains as one of the many places on the planet holding power points. Joseph Campbell called mountains "zone(s) of magnified power" hidden in the unknown. And I was not going to miss this opportunity—to become an apprentice of the planet's energy system that could help me purge a backlog of *shoulds* and *woulds* and *coulds*. Not miss an opportunity where, somewhere in the back of my mind, I felt I could banish outworn parts that had helped me survive until then—solid, strong, determined, persevering—but were traits that had pushed and pushed, causing an imbalance in my spirit.

The brochure said, 'sleep in a tent under star-filled nights, wake up to find nothing but to trek.' Trekking and yoga. Yoga and trekking. Meditating in the presence of earth's magnified power points. I was aching to re-connect with Mother Nature, her wild pulse beneath my feet as the mountains marched inch by inch imperceptibly through spacetime, taking me with them. Cathy had made

Nepal feel like home to me a long time before, and now its mountains were calling me. Holding the brochure while thinking about this, I saw a familiar place— a morning pond below my childhood home with ethereal vapors rising to meet chilled air as dawn opened a new window on the day. There was no doubt where I was heading. Hiking the Himalayas was precisely what my soul needed. I signed up.

This move was not without opposition. My dear friend, Karette, who did her doctoral work the same time I did, challenged my going to the other side of the world alone. She asked, "Aren't you afraid of getting sick?"

"Sick? Why would I get sick?"

"The water, the food, the long-distance, the jet lag…."

I was dumbfounded. My health had always been an asset. Except for seeing the dentist diligently, I'd rarely seen a doctor.

"I'm healthy. I can swim a mile and hike for hours." Traveling was oxygen to my lungs. I trusted my ability to navigate the globe and my body to stay healthy, so I dismissed Karette's objections. I'd just finished doctoral work, slicing through hard to construe brains of top US inventors, unscrambling thinking processes to discover how a mind accessed future ideas. And no one was going to tell me that traveling to the other side of the world held snares for me.

Besides, the major challenge in my life had never been my health, getting a job, or having a place to live. It was finding a partner, a lover—a task I'd failed at time and time again. Had I sent a message that I didn't need anyone to take care of me? Well, going to Nepal, I certainly wasn't looking for a partner having had enough with Tim. I was simply going to re-bond with nature, going to find the profound quiet the Earth had always provided me—I was going to walk to mend.

Another friend, though, Dina, who I'd taught with and who had helped me survive the emotionally difficult time of my marriage break-up, cheered me on. When her family heard I was going to India, she asked me, "If you get anywhere near Bombay, could you find the Sewri Christian Cemetery and check out the condition of my son-in-law's great-grandmother's grave?" I'd said, "Sure!" That promise would turn into an adventure, just like hanging out with Dina.

At JFK, there were no lines at the check-in. Cathy and I eyed each other quizzically. The Universe was giving me the green light, a supernova that was going to shine deep into the trip. The travel agent had booked me on Pakistan International Airlines (PIA). I had a bunch of open-jaw airline tickets that would take me from Nepal, then on to India, Egypt, Greece, and finally to Poland, where I would visit my relatives before returning to the States. The agent had explained that these tickets would provide maximum freedom of travel with no specific travel dates imposed. When I was ready to leave a country, I'd go to the airline office listed on the ticket and book the next flight to the following country on my list.

The PIA attendant smiled, took my bag, and threw it on the conveyer belt, pointing me toward the gate. Liking to travel light, I had bought the smallest backpack that would take me around the world. This one converted from pack to suitcase using a collection of straps that tucked in here and there. It contained a year's worth of clothing: a culturally correct hiking skirt that fell below my knees, two cotton dresses with mandatory sleeves covering shoulders, a pair of sweat pants, a couple of T-shirts, a long-sleeved shirt, sneakers, flip flops, three pairs of socks, a sun hat plus an extra dayglow-green Yankees baseball cap. I had put a few toiletries in micro-bottles, had tweezers to keep my errant unibrow at bay, and had broken a small mirror out of a cosmetic case. I'd stuffed in three books: *The City of Joy* by Dominique Lapierre, my favorite novel *Moby Dick* for a re-read, and a copy of the 2,000-page Lonely Planet guide: *India a travel survival kit*. Along with all that, I stowed several pairs of hard-won grit, a dearth of guilt over the marriage, and a box of forgiveness. But I wasn't going to look at that yet.

Time to depart. I hugged Cathy, not ever realizing in a million years how soon our paths would cross again. I went to the gate and boarded the plane. About a hundred Pakistani men wearing white or blue dress shirts sat quietly inside. None cast me a glance, the only Westerner and only one of three women on the plane. The cabin felt organized and calm, and I sank into a wide, comfy aisle seat. As the plane taxied down the runway, white plastic TV sets dropped from the ceiling reciting prayers from the Koran in English. I took a deep breath, joined in the prayers, and mentally shoveled the past years of my life into an enormous black hole I conjured.

As the plane flew across the Atlantic Ocean to my first stop in Frankfurt, Germany, for refueling, I thought of how I was following in my family's footsteps, their love of travel. How Babcia, my paternal grandmother, had left her home in Poland to take a voyage that had changed her life. The grit it took. Babcia, who might well have been better called Choleryk (Spitfire in Polish), at sixteen had immigrated to the US in steerage at the turn of the twentieth century. I can still see her thick mop of auburn hair, and her ruby cheeked face (from drink) frowning in its demeanor bent on argument. A trait she parlayed into a knack for negotiating real-estate deals building farmland-ownership despite her lack of English-speaking skills. Nobody ever told Babcia what to do. She was tough. If a blizzard was raging outside, and her cows needed water, she sent one of her daughters to the barn with warm water.

Remembering Babcia, there in the quiet of the plane's cabin, I was content with what I'd inherited from her. Her hair color, eyes to match, plus her desire to hit the road to see whatever was out there. But of course, over the years, I'd learned to mask my temper, best I could.

I thought of Dad and Mother, too. How they had crisscrossed the globe. Mother had immigrated from Poland just before World War II at age nineteen. And Dad—who'd quit school to help Babcia raise his siblings after the early death of his father—had ridden the rails as a hobo during the Great Depression of the 1930s.

"Girls," he'd tell us, "I was working my way through Mexico as a lineman picking up the language heading for South America when...Dios mio! That pulque was good! Anyway, I jumped this small ship hoping to get to Columbia, but no! Those customs guys searched the whole boat and found me stowed away behind some barrels sending me back home!" Later, I found Dad's deportation papers: white male, 5 foot 2, hazel eyes, bald, scar on left nostril.

It seems Babcia, Mother, Dad—and me included—all had type TFA blood: Travel for Adventure. So here I was, in a plane, hurtling through spacetime. And, as much as I thought my adventure was about trekking in Nepal and roaming cultural sites of India and Egypt, in actuality, I would end up bushwhacking the edges of reality, immigrating through apertures into yet a deeper understanding of life and myself.

Interrupted at Karachi

I woke up surprised. The plane was landing, but not in Kathmandu. I was in Karachi, Pakistan. It was 2 AM. Coming to a stop, I, and everyone else, were told to deplane. Confused, I had no choice but to follow the line of Pakistani businessmen into the terminal, where I fumbled to find my open-jaw tickets to see what had happened. I'd bought them over the phone where the issuing agent had held them till the last minute, sending them only after anxious yelling by me. I didn't have time to scrutinize the itinerary. Groggy-eyed and exhausted from the twenty-hour flight, I stood before a customs official who surveyed me and took my passport. He examined it, flipping through each page before looking up at me to pronounce the verdict, "You're staying the night, Madam."

Incredulous, I stared into his stern face while he gripped my passport. Then, I inspected the nearly empty terminal. I was the only Westerner, Western woman there. Was I out of my mind?

"What? Why?" I asked, tamping down my apprehension as best I could.

"The next plane to Kathmandu is not until tomorrow at 10 AM, Madam. We take you to a hotel, give you room, breakfast voucher, and bring you back in the morning. We keep your passport."

Keep my passport? I weighed this bleak option. The few

remaining arrivals scurried out of the sizeable vaulted hangar into the night. Sheepishly, and probably because I was exhausted, and because it sounded like I had no other options, which I didn't, I relinquished my passport to his keeping. I was escorted from the terminal to a van that held a pilot and two flight attendants. I crawled in.

The two-star hotel designated for the airline staff was located about fifteen minutes from the airport giving me a good look at Karachi's abandoned streets and back alleys. Checked-in, the bell boy dragged my small bag up the stairs to an un-scrubbed room with a private bathroom whose faucet leaked water casting green stains in the shape of a circular mandala in the bowl.

I was glad the lock on the door was decent. The busboy gave me a breakfast voucher and told me to be ready for a 7 AM return to the airport. This shoestring ticket was turning out to be uncertain. Still, I set the alarm, managed to sleep, and, in the morning, bounded out of bed, washed my face in the stained sink, brushed my teeth, and rushed to the van, skipping breakfast. True to their word, the Pakistani officials handed me back my passport and put me on a plane to Kathmandu. I arrived several hours later in the dark of the night. The word "Adventure" comes from the Latin for "about to happen."

Yoga Group

The moon, from the plane's window, brimmed almost full when I arrived in Kathmandu. The city, located in the Himalayan foothills, is situated in a valley 4,675 feet above sea level. The Basmati River runs through—venerated by both Buddhists and Hindus.

The entire city was dark. The dimly lit airport was on a generator casting sharp shadows throughout the airport hangar—Nepal was conserving electricity by turning off the electrical power grid several times a week.

I got through customs, exchanged money, and entered the main hall swarming with cabbies. I grabbed one and gave him the name of the hotel where I'd be meeting my yoga group in a few days. As we drove, a low mist engulfed the city. At the time of my visit, the population had not yet exploded, and the town felt passive, except for the endless beeping of car horns. Once at the hotel, a suited-up manager greeted me politely. "Hello, madam, welcome to Kathmandu. My name is Basta."

"Hello, I'm Anya Kru," I said, "I'm here to join my yoga group arriving in two days."

"Yes, Madam. We have that all arranged for the group. Can I get you a cup of tea?" he asked. His English was fluent, and we sat drinking tea in the reception area. Basta asked about my trip, and when we finished the tea, he explained that his hotel was full for the next two days and that he had arranged to put me up across the street before the group arrived.

He carried my bag across the road, walked up a narrow staircase lit by small votive candles up the steps, and unlocked the door into a small, clean room. That night, overtaken by exhaustion, I slept soundly until the feral dogs that roamed Kathmandu began to bark. I was awake. But prepared with earplugs, I stuffed them tightly into my ears as had been advised by the group's leader.

The following day, head cleared and rested, it was time to see the sites. With map in hand, I asked reception how to use the buses; and I went off to see Bhaktapur's Durbar Square, a UNESCO World Heritage site. Leaving the hotel, I cut my way through the streets, stepping over piles of rubbish and around construction debris that filled the streets. Adults and children walked barefoot through the lanes. Their faces carried a childlike quality that lifted me up. Stray dogs roamed scavenging through three-foot heaps of garbage. One dog with hunks of hair missing sprawled on the broken walkway. Was it even breathing? Other mongrels lurked nearby, growling low and probably rabid. Taxi horns blared at rickshaws. Bicycle wallahs, their skinny, brown legs pumping rusty bicycles, wove in and out of traffic. Overhead, snarls of electrical wires suspended between titling telephone poles creating sprawling games of *Untangle*. The round-faced people beaming their gentle demeanors, with hands folded before their hearts greeted me, "Namaste, Namaste (I salute the God within you)." And I responded, folding my hands before my breast and repeating "Namaste" as dust invaded my nose, lips, and throat.

The bus to Bharktapur passed through stands of eucalyptus trees flanking the roadside where hundreds of fruit bats hung upside down like Christmas ornaments bellies bulging. Forty-five minutes later, I entered Durbar Square. The Square consisted of a small village of historical wooden buildings stained with age, burnt sienna and tan. The structures of layered bricks and timber dated back to the late 17th and early 18th centuries. Archways pierced extravagant wedding cake-tiered pagodas that led to inner chambers through latticed doorways ornate with skulls and multi-armed deities that promised protection by wrath. Who had passed there? The King? The Queen? Who had sat in the windows supported by square columns lifting intricate roofbeams to the sky, elaborately trimmed with crown moldings carved in networks of geometric shapes of cubes and knobs and fringed with blood-red cloth flounces? Who?

I was lucky. Hardly any people walked among the ancient stupas. A sign, written in English, said the Germans were renovating the place. I roamed through taking it in. To one side of the plaza, sculptures of elephants and lions guarded the base of a steep, stone stairway timeworn by thousands of footfalls polishing its surface over the centuries.

On another side, yellow, red, green, and blue prayer flags hung from the rafters of a temple while grass grew there, without a breeze to nudge it. As I went along, at times, I couldn't move. I felt surrounded by cosmic fire oozing from the edifices of the temples radiating...what? ...something special buried with the past inhabitants? What *doings* had taken place there? What sufferings? What joys and sorrows? What loves and jealousies? I felt a hidden familiarity, ease. A home.

Several hours passed. I was envious of people who had booked rooms to stay the night. A scheduled blackout would make it impossible for artificial light to mar the beauty of Bharktapur's Durbar Square in the dark lit only by candles. So, I sat and sat and sat, taking it all in. To my right, a narrow flight of steps led to a shrine at the top. The steps were lined with fu dogs, lions, horses, rhinos, and a statue of a bejeweled woman dragging an errant child by its skinny arm along the way. Finials topped several temples. Erotic figures of women swayed arms and hands beckoning sweetly. Carvings of monkeys crawled overhead. Ganesh, the Hindu elephant god, peered down on me. Pigeons whirled—confetti up from the pavement—covering the roofs in a spin of dark wings.

A deity sat on a tall column with his hands folded in "Namaste": I salute the God within you. And *I in you*, I thought. To my right, a large ornate bell hung in a wooden armature. If only I had a mallet, I could strike it, hear its…errr-rangggg…its voice calling a mantra over the ancient facades that I felt occupied by cosmic forces dancing before and through me. I never wanted to leave.

I thought of how my friend, Dori, who I'd met in college, would have liked to sit there with me, picking up the cosmic vibes. How, as an undergraduate, she had become one of the gatekeepers of my spiritual quest. Our meeting had been improbable but perfect, and I recalled it now.

The first thing Dori did in the morning was to put on long, silver earrings that dripped Aphrodite's hand mirrors from her earlobes. Raven hair, creamy skin, polished hazel-eyed— beauty was her modus operandi. Every day, Dori signaled ease in her young goddess persona. She, similar to me, was short on money and was working her way through college as a resident advisor where we met. Each of us was in charge of a girl's floor in the dorm in exchange for free room and board.

Lonely one night, I rapped on her door to get some company. She called out from within, "Come in." and I entered to see Dori bent over a pile of books and sheaves of paper and pencils.

"Oh, am I interrupting your studies?"

"No, no, no," she exuded, "I'm calculating my astrological chart. Come on in, Anya."

"Astrological? What's that all about?" I was thinking of three-sentence newspaper columns predicting daily occurrences in affairs of love, finance, and everyday living. But I could see complicated mathematical configurations on a piece of paper in front of her. Dori shuffled through the pile of papers, rulers, and books, "I'm putting together my birth chart with the sun, moon, and ascendant."

"Oh?" I asked.

"Yes, the math isn't so easy to figure out, but I've managed to get through most of it by now."

"Oh!" I said, "What then?"

"Look here, what happens is you've got to calculate the degrees that each planet.... well, first you enter your birth time and date to find the positions of the sun and moon then you.... Do you want me to do your chart?"

"Sure," I said. I'd been feeling alienated from all the mind work needed to succeed at college, and this sounded fun. "Why not?" I repeated. "I need a good news prediction. Do you think you have one for me?" I was curious to see what the stars had to say, hoping they'd shine brightly on my coursework and grades.

"OK. Tell me when you were born," Dori said, applying her slide rule mind and doing my chart. I could see the math wasn't for mental lightweights, and there was something more to it other than just fun. After several minutes of figuring, Dori gave me my reading. I had a cardinal T-square, several trines, and retrogrades...things that weren't easy but weren't too bad either. It was all too cool, and a lot of it felt accurate.

Over the weeks, Dori's good nature drew me in, and we binged on astrology. She threw open the gates ushering me into all things New Age...all of which hit a nerve in me...something very subtle that made me want to know more. Not merely all the stuff in the astrological charts Dori had in her room—but all about the mind/body connection and human consciousness buried in her collection of books on esoteric sciences. Dori was an epicure of all things New Age, and I was feasting at her table of Spirituality 101.

Dori also had a set of wheels, an old Hillman that got us off-campus. It took us to workshops that plunged us deeper into understanding the cosmic nature of the Universe. Courses like Hawaiian Mysticism with its Shamanic Huna healing system. Another study, in particular, had to do with dream interpretation with Kilton Stewart and Clara Flagg, international experts. All this dream stuff wasn't new to me. I was familiar with dream analysis. As a child, Mother would describe her dreams to Agnes and me each morning at breakfast. This triggered my brain to remember my dreams. I had read books on the subject, recorded my dreams, and ended up with volumes of dream journals. At times, the Hillman's sticky clutch challenged us to get from place to place, bucking us along while we laughed hysterically.

One day after college, we were both teaching, I got a call from Dori, who was going to another workshop. "Hi! Anya, my family, and I are taking the Silva Mind Method course. Want to come?"

"What's it about?" I asked.

"The course teaches how to use mental imagery as a tool for self-healing and remote sensing. Jose Silva developed it during World War II when he taught the Army about brain wave levels." She went on to talk about its problem-solving skills. I was impressed by the science part, thinking it would fit into my teaching. I wanted to understand more about how the brain worked. So, I said, "I'll be there."

During the course, the brain's cleverness unfolded. The group was shown how it piped along using all kinds of brain wave levels—gamma, beta, alpha, theta, delta—to integrate mind/body/spirit. Large charts graphically illustrated all this. After several hours of lectures, the instructor taught us how to enter deep relaxation, a meditative state. That is, he guided us to slip into those brain wave levels to reach a point for self-healing. As we worked our way through the training, we learned to send healing to others by visualizing pure light. I gobbled this up! Dori, again, had brought me to an experience that gave me an invaluable tool, one that laid the foundation for its application to my teaching and my future research.

Dori took us from workshop to workshop, where we gorged on everything the Human Potential Movement of the seventies and eighties had to offer. At times our path diverged. When Dori asked, "EST?" I said, "No, thanks," and never took it. Nonetheless, Dori's schtick for New Age never ran out of gas. She was comparable to a deity in Greek mythology who presides over a particular threshold (mine) and who is allied to a person (me), who needs to cross a boundary but has trepidation and needs convincing or assistance (maybe some arm twisting), to get into new territory.

From our first meeting in the dorm, Dori served as my indefatigable gatekeeper. She opened doors that led me on an endless journey focused on spiritual growth that stretched my psyche toward rich cosmic understandings. Once she got the ball rolling, it didn't stop. With me in tow and her at the latch, Dori directed my life and hers in pursuit of everything mystical. She unlocked door after door, ones I would never have passed through otherwise. As a result, the floodgates of the New Age were released, and I dove vigorously into its currents both personally and professionally.

The Universe has a Plan

Back now in Kathmandu, I tossed a banana peel onto a garbage heap in the street. I became inured, loving every moment of the town's musty smells, the honking horns, the ancient wooden facades. I still had a day to myself before my yoga group arrived from the States. So I wandered the town's squares teeming with temples, peaceful people, and grime.

When the group finally came, I moved back across the street and joined them. Vani and Upendra were the leaders. Plus, there were two men and seven women in the group all my age. My assigned roommate for the stay in Kathmandu was Ava, a very tall woman who loved to talk. Upendra spelled out the itinerary. We'd begin each day doing yoga either in a room in the hotel or outside our tents on mats once we got into the mountains. The first few days in Kathmandu, we'd visit cultural spots before going on safari to

Chitwan National Park, a World Heritage Site. It was located in south-central Nepal in the subtropical lowland jungles of the Terai, where we'd see rhinos and possibly tigers. From there, we'd bus to the Solukhumbu, the Mt. Everest region, to start our trek in a place visited by few tourists.

The group sat having tea. It was clear to me that everyone had tightly bonded on the plane. "Anya, tell us why you came to Nepal," asked Bella, who was one of the two therapists in the group. Smiling, I relayed how I had recently finished my degree and had just divorced the week before. She asked, "You mean you were just divorced and flew out here by yourself?"

"Yeah," I said, laughing. Bella looked at me questionably. Dead silence in the group. I felt chilled by their faces, but then again, they hadn't been married to Tim.

And I thought, if there'd been more time to think it over, the marriage never would have happened. Tim had been my high school sweetheart. He knew my secrets. Tall, good-looking with liquid brown eyes, he possessed an easy charm and was a Jeopardy-intelligent guy. His voice could quell the cries of a baby or sell the Brooklyn Bridge twice over. From high school till our marriage, he'd first spent a stint in the Air Force and then in the Navy, having an "almost" career. That characterized him. He always left the services before he was eligible for retirement, which left him short of income.

But the marriage had been in the cards. The year before Tim and I hooked up again, after years apart, I dreamed that a large sailboat with billowing sails came charging across the ocean, making a sharp turn into a harbor. I woke up knowing I was in for something big emotionally. Tim's name was buried in the dream imagery. Dad had recently died from liver cirrhosis, and Tim, just out of the Navy, came to extend his condolences.

From that point forward, it was a whirlwind romance that stumbled over itself into a fire pit. I was thirty-eight, and it took a shove from Cathy. She'd served as yet another existential gatekeeper in my life, one who knew I needed a partner and that I'd been both wanting and shunning finding a mate. She knew that perfect someone was never coming, knew I was reluctant to risk the pain in other relationships. Agnes, for one, had been married twice; and Biscute, our cousin who was more our sister, was now strapped down with a slew of kids, not my cup of tea.

Cathy, not knowing Tim, yet understanding that it was time for me to take this plunge, threw me under the wheel of life. It could have been the Universe was involved in all this as well, having a plan for me. So, I guess my marriage to Tim had been the right path—seeing that the Universe was involved. For sure, the dream had pointed to the marriage's inevitability even though I'd forgotten Tim's need for someone to take care of him.

When Tim and I got married, I expected it to be a storybook marriage; but it wasn't. Instead, Tim lost job after job ending up working in a pawnshop selling guns. Despite expertise in many areas, including munitions, he managed to practice being less than he was, constantly rebelling against who he really was, his real self—smart, articulate, witty—someone who had skills to spy on Russian submarines for the Navy. Somehow, he couldn't pull himself together outside the stringent confinements of the military, its strict enforcement of uniformity and regimentation, to motivate himself on the outside world.

There was no sex in the marriage. It was devoid of caressing, sensual playfulness, seducing. To Tim's credit, he agreed to go to therapy. The short stint of couple's therapy, before the insurance ran out, opened up childhood family stuff for him. Shrouded in guilt, he told me his father had made him feel guilty for the Great Depression. Yet, Tim was tender.

When his mother found and gave him his old teddy bear (Teddy Boon), it went in with my doll and collection of stuffed animals I held dear. Somehow the group kept Tim and me connected to our childhoods. One morning, I came downstairs from early work at the computer to find him making us pancakes along with tiny pancakes for the dolls and Teddy. Another time, after I'd sown one of his tattered discarded Patagonia shirts into a shirt for the bear, Tim came home, saw it, and had a tear in his eye. Later, I found that he had fashioned a necktie out of a ribbon for Teddy.

Still, I saw him as indolent, not holding up his end of the bargain; I was working my butt off and felt financially deserted. The gross imbalance in the marriage didn't help matters. I owned the house, had a college degree, had a good job, and even though my accomplishments gave him a sense of pride, they also seemed to crush him. It didn't take me long to feel alone in the marriage.

As time went on, I kept tricking myself into believing my marriage was OK that everything was right when my heart knew differently. I was ashamed that I had made a mistake in choosing a mate. I kept my disappointment a secret for a long time, feeling I had failed and growing bitter as the years went on. It felt as if I was moving forward with my academic life but sinking into a pit of despair at the same time. Tim didn't seem to understand how to undertake the business of everyday life and marriage. My assumptions about marriage had amounted to a fairy tale. I didn't cry, yet I didn't laugh either. It came to an end.

But I didn't tell Bella that, although her eyes were still on me. I curled the edges of my lips up, sipped my tea, grateful that my roommate, Ava, pulled the conversation away, incessantly chattering about her own life back home.

Riding Elephants on Halloween

Monkeys scampered over the stairs, their sharp, little teeth flashing. "Oh, I love these monkeys, aren't they cute?" Ava said. *No, I thought, they look nasty.* Kathmandu's exalted Swayambhunath Stupa was the first stop for the yoga group. Avoiding the animals, feral dogs included, we walked around the 2,000 year-old Buddhist temple stepping over dog excrement. Two enormous eyes painted on its golden pinnacle watched. Its white base was decorated with arch patterns as if it wore a lacy collar. Red, blue, white, green, and yellow prayer flags hung from the top in a breezeless, blue sky.

Next was the Boudhanath Stupa, a massive spherical mandala

revered by Tibetan and Nepali Buddhists alike. A thousand pigeons sat on its curved white-domed face. I stared up at its piercing blue eyes that stared at me. Upendra told us, "It symbolizes Buddha's path to enlightenment. The base represents earth, the dome water, and the tower fire." I couldn't ignore the stupa's vast energy field while crowds of people milled around offering prayers both vocal and silent. Ava hung at my elbow, talking my ear off.

Before returning to the hotel for dinner, we stopped at a rental place where I rented a sleeping bag, and some women got coats. Ava put on a coat and came over asking me, "What do you think, too big?"

"No, it'll keep you warm," I said. Then she put on another and asked, "Do you like this color?" "Fine," I said, "Works well with your eyes," but this was getting silly, and as hard as I tried to extract myself from her, she was the wad of gum you can't get off the bottom of your shoe. Back in our room, she prattled on—frustrations and complaints about things I couldn't figure out and can't remember—and by this time, I'd had enough and tried to get away from her by walking into the bathroom. I said, "Excuse me. I really…"

"Then what happened was…" she droned on, ignoring me. It was clear this woman was not going to hush up. I wasn't quite ready to stuff my fingers in my ears, same as I'd done when Dad and Mother had fought. Yet, it was beginning to irritate me, striking a chord that I thought had been banished and was gone from my life, an old family chord.

Alcoholism tormented Dad and Mother. And not the prissy four-o'clock cocktail type—privileged— tucked away in some closet. No, they promised an almost weekly swearing bout, fist-shaking, passed-out drunkenness of the Shakespearean sort. To their credit, Agnes and I were spared the slam-down nasty punching or brandishing of knives type of alcoholism; but not the name-calling part: bastard, whore, son-of-a-bitch, and something in Polish that sounded to my young ear akin to "curve-va-sen" … all of which might have become a standard idiom for us but didn't.

Although Agnes and I had a complete scatological vocabulary by age six, we never used it. School during the fifties Americanized us into well-mannered little girls who tacitly understood that cursing was strictly the jurisdiction of our home. When the arguments started, Agnes hid in a series of Zane Gray books or managed to escape into the neighborhood where there were girls her age to play with. For me, when drunkenness flooded the house, I fled through the back door to the pond below the house. At times, I'd comfort myself by carrying an imaginary family in the palm of my hand. Now, Ava was strumming this discord in me once again.

I had come to Nepal for peace, so I said: "Ava, excuse me. Right now, I need to do some quiet thinking. Would that be OK with you?" She looked hurt, her excitement squelched, but her endless babble had exhausted me. My left brain was packed with no more room for her gossip. "I need to think for a bit," I said. "OK?" Ava was going to be a hard roommate to get used to.

Leaving for Chitwan National Park two days later was delayed. The yoga group had lined its bags on the sidewalk outside the hotel when Upendra told us that our transportation had broken down. Ava got irritable, and another woman joined in expressing her frustration. I moved away. Vani suggested that we shop to kill time. She said, "I know of a great place to buy thangkas and mandalas. Come on!" So, Bella, Ava, TexAnna (a tall woman from Texas), plus the rest of the group and I followed her to a line of tuk-tuks.

At the shop, Bella was by my side leafing through small paintings. "Oh," she said, "Look at the gold leaf they've used and these tiny buddha figures." Sure enough, the mandala shimmered in a luster that took our breath away, and I said, "Beautiful. All the deities are moving in the wheel of life."

"Your life certainly has changed dramatically in the past week, hasn't it?" she asked, looking at me. I glanced at the mandala in my hands, then back at Bella and said, "It has."

"How long were you married?"

"Nine years," I said.

"Any children?"

"No," I said.

"Oh?"

"My husband didn't want any," feeling more and more I wasn't fitting in. And thinking: *He was the baby I took care of...* regretting where my thoughts took me and Bella's questioning. Finally, I said, "I'm leaving all that back there for now." She nodded and turned toward Ava's loud ooohs and aaahs. A mandala was held up for everyone to see.

I pored over the array of thangkas, Tibetan scroll paintings. Many depicted mandalas to be used during meditation to disintegrate the ego and reintegrate the spirit. Each was constructed in a series of circles and squares within triangular points reaching toward the four corners of the Cosmos. The store owner told us they could represent different aspects of the Universe. Their symbols included fire representing the burning of ignorance and diamonds representing illumination. Some had lotus leaves signifying spiritual rebirth. All were used to enter the cosmic eye of the Universe, or the womb-world, also known as the thunderbolt world.

The thangkas were beautiful and expensive. One painted in gold and silver on a black background portrayed a bodhisattva named Guan Yin. A bodhisattva is a God who hears the cries of the world. And out of depthless compassion, she holds those in anguish close, rendering ceaseless solace before she steps over that cosmic threshold into enlightenment, leaving the world behind. Guan Yin was surrounded by eight symbols on that thangka, including the Wheel of Dharma representing knowledge, an Endless Knot standing for harmony, and the Lotus for purity and enlightenment. I took out my credit card, and I bought two. Rolled into a tube for safe travel, they stayed with me throughout my trip.

Finally, in the late afternoon of the third day, we loaded into a van to travel for five hours over rutted roads to the entry point of Chitwan Park. There we transferred into jeeps. It was 10:00 PM on October 31, 1994. A waning crescent moon hung in the sky. We still had several hours to our tented campsite far inside Chitwan. The jeeps tore through the jungle over dirt roads kicking up plumes of dust. A pack of one-horned rhinos ran from the bush, galloping alongside the vehicles. One stopped thirty feet away and flicked its ears before veering off into the undergrowth, joining its group. Then shortly, another pack stampeded alongside—a crazy National Geo movie! We were thrilled. TexAnna's melodic voice called out, "Oh! Look at these magnificent guys! Look at the baby!" Bella shouted, "What a sight!" I joined in with a "Wow!" "How many are there?" asked Ava, counting loudly, raising her voice above the others.

The drivers drove through the jungle for over an hour. Then, abruptly, the jeeps stopped at the riverbank of the Rapti River. Buzzing insects undercut the dark silence of the night. We loaded into several dugout canoes resting on the river's muddy banks crossing over toward our campsite. Knobby eyes of crocodiles floated soundlessly around us, dark weapons waiting for prey. "Is that a croc?" asked Ava.

Upendra whispered, "Yeah, but it's tame." We snorted nervously as the oarsmen poled through the gently flowing gray waters gliding us across the river. By now, it was midnight, the night of Halloween.

On the other side, two smiling men dressed in white shirts, hair combed neatly, faces scrubbed, stood behind a makeshift bar offering us soda pop and bottles of water. It was eerie. They had waited late into the night for us to arrive here in the middle of the jungle crocks swimming nearby. *How had they gotten there?* The look on my face gave me away, and they said, "Oh, no, Madam, our job. We are happy to greet you. Soda pop? Ginger, coke? Orange?"

"Orange, please," I said, shaking my head in wonderment. Behind them stood several elephants with their handlers waiting expectantly. After the drinks, we were helped atop the elephants and began a ride through twelve-foot-high elephant grass toward our campsite tents. By this time, it was 2 AM. The grasses brushed against the elephant's sides with a swish, swish sound. I don't know if things we might have feared hid in the grasses, but it didn't make any difference because it was a Halloween night to remember. By the time we got to our camp, we fell into our tents dog-tired.

The following two mornings, the yoga group was up early, did yoga, breakfasted, and left the campsite silently, riding elephants through the tall grasslands. The birds were abundant: babblers, ruddy shelducks, spotted forktails, sandpipers, grass warblers, and egrets. But really, we were looking for Bengal tigers. We had heard them roaring in the night and had been told one female had two cubs. The ride was bumpy, and I noticed a sore had formed in the crease between my leg and tush. It was probably from the hours on the plane, but I ignored it because I was looking for tigers. At one point, we got off the elephants and walked under a canopy of Sal trees over a rock-strewn stream. Tiger's footprints but no tigers. One group member, Fran, twisted her ankle on the rocks, and Upendra had one of the Sherpas carry her back to the elephants to be taken to camp.

We had no luck with the tiger spotting except for Bella, who claimed to have seen one in the grasses, but I figured her claim was mythical. It didn't matter. I was here, had come solo to the other side of the world to join this group, and was now standing in the middle of a jungle with dangerous animals rampaging around a croc-filled river. The adventure was storybook.

Solo Trekker

My yen to travel solo after my kindergarten jaunt grew because Dad and Mother were lax in medical care. One day coming home from Michigan after visiting Mother's Uncle, I bawled from a toothache.

I laid down on the backseat and held my jaw. Mother dug into her purse and gave me an aspirin thinking it might help, and murmured, "You'll be OK,"; but I wasn't. My tooth pained me for hours. Once home, Dad took me to the local dentist, Dr. Wood, who had an office on Main Street in town where we lived.

Dad, looking as if he had more pain than me, faced Dr. Wood sheepishly, shrinking into the shadow of his authoritative white coat, embarrassed I was crying. Dr. Wood put me in his chair, worked the strangle of silver drills and wires, and fixed the tooth.

When Dr. Wood was finished, he pushed aside the equipment

and asked, "There. All better?" "Umm," I nodded shyly, it being my first encounter with a dentist.

"OK, then," he said. "Come back and let me check the rest of your teeth soon, OK?"

"OK," I said. I realized that Dad and Mother weren't going to pick up the slack, but if I took charge, I would avoid pain. Dr. Wood's invitation had seeded a plan in my ten-year-old mind.

The plan focused on the CR & L bus line that stopped at the bottom of our hill. Mother had taken Agnes and me to town on it, and I figured I could manage the ride by myself to get into town to see Dr. Wood again. Although I was ten, those were times when a fairly young kid could ride the bus alone into town without too much worry—or at least I wasn't aware of it. When my next dental appointment came, I didn't hesitate to ask Dad for change to take the bus into town.

The jingling of coins falling into the throat of the farebox became music to my ears as I went to the dentist. By the time I was twelve and earning money from babysitting, I rode the buses to the other towns in the valley. I shopped for clothes, eventually venturing farther and farther away from home into New Haven. Ironically, the toothache had laid the foundation for self-reliance, me mothering myself instead of being mothered. I wasn't afraid of venturing out alone, but there were things I was afraid of, afraid to my core.

The day Mother got raped is branded in my memory. I was four years old. Mother had immigrated from Poland in steerage, at age eighteen, a month before World War II. She spoke no English. Still, she had high cheekbones, clear skin, full dark hair, and slicing blue eyes. Foreign and vulnerable in many ways, she was soon taught to be an alcoholic by Dad's family. I remember that day.

A neighbor, and his brother, took Mother and me to an isolated wood, plied her with liquor into a drunken stupor, and raped her. One of the men walked me up and down the road as I wailed, "I want my Daddy." When it was over, the men dropped Mother and me off close to our home, blood-streaked her torn silken pink slip;

she'd had her period. Sober by then, Mother raised her arm in the air cursing the men, "You dirty, dirty bastards." Her raised fist shook violently. We walked home.

Do things always start with mothers? I don't know. But on that day, a pernicious thread ran into my psyche, pulling me to places isolated—social, physical, and spiritual. Maybe the Universe had a plan for me. Part of my Kundalini awakening? I wasn't sure. But maybe, just maybe, that emotional earthquake—seeing Mother raped—made me eligible for that special blast of energy—Kundalini—which usually comes with a physical or spiritual tremor. Maybe I'd been made eligible by a robbery inside of me. Or maybe something important killed off—an innocence, a trust in the feminine, in the *mother within me*—a "near-death" necessary for spiritual kindling. Just maybe, that laceration served as a passport, allowing me to embark on a lifelong journey searching not so much for bliss but freedom and balance, kindling a universal life force. Just maybe, Mother might have played a role in my Kundalini awakening.

I don't know what my father knew. The rape was never reported. It could have been Mother felt her rights were few. Probably because during those times, there was little retribution against men abusing or assaulting women. It could be she felt broken and trapped by her weaknesses and vulnerability. Her shame. She hid in drink and True Romance Magazines, changing her view of the world looking for happy endings.

And me, already frayed from drunken arguments, my peace of mind shattered by witnessing two sexual hyenas hurting Mother—the terror sank into my bones. Who could I trust? Dad, yes, Officer Freddy, Dr. Wood? Yes, but not men in general. It made me look closely at people to try to figure out who could be trusted. Several of my aunts lived with mean, stupid men, and I couldn't figure out why.

Mother? Could she be trusted? Mother, it seemed attracted men who wanted to abuse her, including Dad when he was drunk. They both yelled and screamed, berating each other in a crazy frenzy, eating each other up when smashed. Could I trust Mother? My honest answer was "no." She hadn't protected me, and my contempt simmered. I rejected her and my femininity, developing an abhorrence of anything weak. Helplessness or needing rescue was not an option for me.

I'd undergone a robbery. Of innocence? Peace of mind? Forcing the door of my consciousness open too soon, too wide? It felt I'd awakened too early in my life. I hid in extreme shyness and mistrust of men.

Mother and I never spoke about the rape. She was reticent when sober, and I rarely remember a conversation with her except to be told, "Be a good American girl!". I was alone, living under a raw shadow, feeling shame. I never told anyone, not Dad, not Agnes, not my cousin Biscute. Not till much later in life. I grieved in silence behind a thickly built insulating wall. The song that stuck in my head was "Smile though your heart is breaking…" and I wore it, a smile that masked my reality for a long time, longer than necessary.

The ugliness of events between Mother and me took an eternity to reconcile. Still, during that alcohol-drenched childhood, some things overrode the drowning expected from it. There was a second spiritual life preserver, one Dad tossed me that kept me afloat.

Dad was also an original motor mouth. Along with ravings about medicinal uses of plants, or against the world's pollution, and bonding me with Mother Nature (my first life preserver), Dad bombarded Agnes and me with positive programming. He skipped the ego-deflating messages a lot of kids our age got to keep them in line: "Don't get a big head." "You're not so smart," or "Why aren't you like so-and-so down the street?" Instead, Dad, in his unrelenting grindstone nature, repeatedly told Agnes and me: "Girls, you're just as good as boys, even better." This became a critical affirmation that shaped my psyche and built the truth of my reality.

An affirmation essentially programs the bundles of neurons in your brain by sending signals to the unconscious mind as a declaration of a desire, a seed for manifestation. Maybe it's better thought of as an argument for positive thinking, better yet, positive *being and doing*. When planted and watered with attention, an affirmation contains all the instructions needed to blossom its particular message into spontaneous fulfillment. It displaces worries and negative thinking by using consciously chosen language aimed at your inner Self that represents the best of what you wish to be. This notion aligns with the Buddha's teachings on *right speech*—the impeccable use of words that bring the listener healing, transformation, and joy. In my case with Dad, *the listener* (me) *was* constantly being affirmed and reminded of the unlimited potential I carried within myself. Reminded of my wholeness.

Dad then, besides making me feel I was better than any boy (and I did swallow that whole), he told me: "You're Special. You're 'It.' Honey, You're really It." And, I guess because my psyche was at least fifty percent malleable at that time, my subconscious grabbed onto this affirmation. It planted penetrating mental grooves in my brain, not as a goal but as a truth. Being Special set the stage for my ability to take charge, organize the power of my intention, my purpose in the world. I was already getting approbation for being a cute, freckled-faced, red-headed girl, even though I was short and scrawny.

Dad delivered his affirmation argumentatively with passion. It conveyed a profound existential message for me—one that rose above the circumstances of my immediate, untidy life—and served to wire my brain and drive my mind. Mother played a role, too, never imposing rules, leaving boundaries fluid for Agnes and me. In some ways, even though living with one alcoholic was enough (living with two was exponentially more ludicrous), I felt my psychic wiring never got messed up when it came to feeling lovable and capable. There was evidence that Dad's constant, positive programming worked to unlock the "wholeness and unlimited potential" that I, and Agnes, carried inside us.

Agnes could out-read anyone, was a member of the National Honor Society in school and took charge of her life. Her scientific mind pushed ahead. She collected science stamps through the mail, which she pasted into booklets, fish stamps especially, and shared them with me. She was also busy buying up real estate—one square inch of soil in the Yukon Territory— when it became available for sale on a kid's television program she watched. Yet, for me, Dad's affirmations were more subtle and went further.

That seed Dad planted in me rooted into a sequoia that managed to grow through the family turbulence and my shame over Mother's rape—rebalanced it somewhat. Dad's words 'Special, Special, Special' repeatedly rang in my cells, making me know I was good enough and that I'd be OK, regardless.

Mother Goddess of the Universe

The sunshine in Nepal cast cool yet warm light. Navy-blue shadows sharply framed the clusters of two-story, white-washed houses lining the dirt road by the make-shift airfield where the Yoga Group had just landed. The buildings had thatched roofs with window ledges sporting mini gardens in gallon-sized olive oil cans growing marigolds and radishes, and by now, early November, dried weeds. An emaciated ox, hipbones sticking out of slick black hide, eyed us as we passed. Smiling Nepali came from behind buildings greeting us, "Namaste," which we returned in kind, placing folded hands over our hearts. Groups of curious children, barefooted and ragamuffin in old shorts, sweaters, and caps, clustered on stone walls. Some gnawed on the bottoms of corn stalks like lollipops. They grinned expectantly. The other women and I were ready, reached into our bags handing out candy and pens.

The yoga group had left the jungle in Chitwan and flown to Rumjatar into the Solukhumbu (Mt. Everest) District in the North-Eastern part of Nepal. During the flyby of Mt. Everest, I craned my neck, as did the others, admiring the mountain's ermine-robed crowns thrusting over 29,000 feet into the sky. The magic of Everest is best characterized by the locals. The Nepalese call it Sagarmatha, "The Forehead (or Goddess) of the Sky," while in

Tibet, it—or shall we say "she" — is known as Chomolungma, "Mother Goddess of the Universe." The plane had swooped in circles, so everyone got a good look. I felt gathered into the earth's energy fields, those of "Mother Goddess." I was sure she watched us float by, beckoning us to her bosom, and, of course, for some … holding forever.

The plan was to trek the lower elevations for the following ten days visiting monasteries and stopping at markets along the way. When the yoga group disembarked the plane, our guides—the Sherpas—included a young woman porter, all who met us with shy, smiling faces beaming gratefulness. They were dressed in jeans, sweatpants, formal pinstriped pants, shirts, sneakers, and flip-flops. Except for our small day backs, the porters would carry sixty-pound sacks, erect our tents, and cook our meals. We spent an hour organizing before the yoga group began its trek under "The Forehead of the Sky."

The group hiked for hours through the patchwork quilt of rice, millet, and barley fields. Late in the afternoon, the porters pitched our tents in an area where dusty miller plants perfumed the air. The headman, Kamal, came over and asked, "Does anyone want chicken for dinner?" There was a pause, but then I said, "Sure," not entirely knowing why, but maybe I was polite accepting a generous offer of food which was part of my upbringing. We were guests in the neighborhood. Kamal walked over to the farm next to the campsite to secure a chicken for dinner.

The group settled into the tents. I patted myself on my back for diligently hiking the first day at high altitude. Dinner arrived a combination of vegetarian dishes of dal bat (curried lentils), stewed vegetables, and the rice and chicken I had asked for. I stared at it—a pale, gray stringy mass that swirled in a pot. My mind shot back to the day I found Dad standing at the stove stirring a sizzling, pink glop of flesh laced with delicate transparent bones in a frying pan. "What's that?" I'd asked, looking at the unrecognizable heap and wrinkling my nose against a pungent aroma. "Oh, this?" Dad said, "Best thing to feed your brain, Honey. Squirrel. Want some?" "No," I said, declining the skillet of fresh road-kill.

Now, with politeness overwhelming me, I studied the mass of chicken sitting on my plate and thought: *Oh, well!* And bit into its leathery flesh. I took a second bite chewing the old, desiccated bird— chewed and chewed and swallowed it. This was not your Stop and Shop variety roasted chicken; still, I ate out of courtesy. But the stringy hide was inedible, so I planned to spit it out somehow discretely. I watched the group carefully. They dug into their bowls of dal bhat and chatted away. It was my first time in Asia, a newbie among veteran travelers, and I was afraid that the choice of chicken for dinner was pushing me farther out of the group. Finding a paper towel, I raised it to my mouth noiselessly spitting out the pitiful creature, deciding that dah bhat would do from then on.

After dinner, the group sat around talking about the upcoming day's hike. Then I noticed that Bella and TexAnna had dug small packets of something out of their bags and gave them to the woman porter, encouraging her to swallow their contents. The porter seemed sick. Bella said, "She's not well, and we're getting her to take ginger and charcoal to calm her stomach."

Expelling Shadows

Early the following day, the group trekked a steep four-hour uphill hike, this time to the village of Torke situated at 7,900 feet. "This is where we'll camp the night before continuing to the Jantre Pass to get a view of Mt. Everest," Upendra said. The ridgeline took us through old-growth rhododendron forests before it ascended to a view of the entire valley below. Lichens dotted the shrubs. Four monkeys played in the trees. As we hiked, I could see the tops of evergreens dropping and dropping into eternity.

The group did not have to share the trail with other hikers for our excursion. Upendra and Vani had trekked in Nepal many times and had chosen remote courses. The emptiness captivated me. I breathed in the clean air with each footfall. I felt drawn deeper and deeper into the pulse of the Earth, walking over the mountain's granite roots buried in the ravines.

I was getting to know the other women. The night before, I had tented with the Massachusetts therapist, Rhonda. She had told me she did yoga every morning at five AM, which she did in our tent upon arising. TexAnna had sung us awake that morning. Ava kept chatting, and the other women in the group pushed back on her in subtle ways. And although the single women in the group rotated roommates throughout the tour, when it came to the final draw, I ended up with Ava during most of the trip, probably because I hadn't complained about her incessant talking.

As the morning wore on, the mountains grew steeper, gaining elevation. The group surged ahead of me; two men hemmed in by seven non-stop women with non-stop hiking, non-stop energy, non-stop talking, just plain old non-stop. I was at the back of the pack with Kamal. He was playing the sweeper for the day, patiently walking behind the last person in the group, which by afternoon was me. He said, "You are very slow, Madam."

"Yes, Kamal, I know," I said, crawling along the pathways. I was taking in, sensing, admiring whatever bush or tree or flower, whatever orb spider or yellow and black-crested bulbul or even the scats on the trail.

Yellow butterflies flitted here and there, avoiding the woven cities—silvery two-foot geometrical webs—spun by five-inch long Golden Orb spiders with knobby knees. Fruit bats hung in tree shadows, their bellies bulging from the night's feed. I wasn't going to miss this—connecting to the power of the Himalaya, to its beauty swaying above and beside me. An abundance of purple asters grew along the trail. And I thought *The aster slips into the mountainside as the mountainside slips into the aster.*

But there was something else going on in me. By mid-afternoon, I was aware that my pace was getting slower and slower. Kamal was encouraging me to walk faster, but I was falling further behind. I kept moving my feet up the hill, but my slowness became different, making me lose my connection to flora and fauna. My stomach was feeling funny too. It was twisting into knots. Finally, I realized my slow pace wasn't just appreciation of nature: I was sick.

Was it from brushing my teeth with the tap water in Karachi or the old chicken flesh I'd eaten? Had the cock been loaded with salmonella? Then I was in the bushes calling for Kamal to stop and look away. I grabbed my skirt hem, pulling it aside while pulling at my underpants, grateful to be partially hidden. I defecated, wiped myself with tissue, and stood up beneath an enormous golden orb spider's web arching over my head, hoping not to get entangled. My throat seized, vomiting the contents of my stomach. I held my belly, and back on the trail, I rinsed my mouth out from my water bottle, spitting on the ground. Somewhere, I had Pepto Bismol and Imodium. I found the Pepto Bismol and popped it into my mouth.

Kamal looked at me and said, "Not OK, Madam?"

"No, not OK, Kamal," I said.

We went on, me dragging us further and further back from the pack. Somehow, I felt I had created my disaster by being polite. It didn't matter. I saw Upendra coming back down the trail to check on me. When he saw my face, he asked, "Are you OK?"

"Something I ate. I think the chicken might be catching up with me. It's a little belly pain." I've never been good with pain. With pain, I always wanted to crawl into bed and let my body heal itself with rest. That wasn't going to happen here—crawl under a spider's web and rest. I knew I was slowing the group down.

Upendra said, "Kamal here will help you. He'll carry your daypack, OK?"

"Yeah," I said. "I just took some Pepto Bismol, which I know will help."

When he left us, I was trying to convince myself that I was OK. I continued taking footstep after footstep as my stomach lurched and churned—an old, cranky washing machine with all the inner junk inside collapsing and wanting out.

As my distress increased and my momentum slowed, I recalled the mental imagery work of Bolivian-born philosopher Oscar Ichazo at the Arica Institute. Part of the Human Potential

Movement during the 1970s, he had trained his students in "cosmic consciousness-raising" by using visualization techniques to empower their minds to perform physically arduous tasks. I was desperate, and this is what I needed now—the visualization used when running spirals up the sides of the Andes Mountains. Ichazo had taught his students to picture a rope of golden light, an energy source that sat coiled in their cores, one he called a "kath". Once visualized, they would mentally throw it (like a grappling hook) to the trail's top, then imagine this power cord pulling them slowly up to their goal.

As my stomach bullied me with each step, I pictured my own kath coiled in my core, and visualizing, I threw it up the steep inclines, but it didn't matter; I was still moving at a snail's pace. Sweating and beginning to smell, my confidence shredded, I vomited some more. Was there a full enough bush to hide behind? I unloaded another pile of feces.

I wasn't supposed to get sick. I rarely got sick. I thought back to what Karette had said about getting sick halfway around the world, and I groaned mentally. I told myself to stop being weak. I was slowing up the group. My eyes brimmed.

After about ten minutes, Upendra was there again, jumping down the hill to check on me.

"How are you?" he asked.

"Sick!"

"Do you want us to stop at the top of the rise and set up camp so you can rest?"

"How far is it to the original campsite?"

"We still have a way to go to the planned stop. About forty-five minutes, an hour, it's your call."

All I needed was rest. If I could get to the next stop, I'd feel better. I said, "I think I can do this."

Upendra asked, "Do you want Kamal to carry you?" I smiled. I was feeling rotten. *Carry me*, I thought.

The last time someone had carried me, I was in agony. And I recalled it now, that summer Sunday morning, Dad and Mother had piled Agnes and me into the Hudson and headed to the river where he fished, and we picked blueberries. Mother packed a lunch, and Dad loaded the car with his slim ochre fishing rod and a shovel he used to dig nightcrawlers from the swamp below the hill. When we got to the river, Dad slipped over the bank to fish. Then Mother, Agnes, and I headed for the wild blueberry patch growing in the meadows.

After a couple of hours of picking blueberries and eating lunch, Dad was still fishing. I went over the embankment to the river to get him. I didn't see a broken beer bottle laying on the rocks with a jagged tongue of glass. It gouged me right behind my left ankle. Blood spurted, and I howled. Dad came running yelling, "Goddamit, Goddamit," at the top of his lungs, not so much at me, but at the circumstances—as if he was the one who'd gotten cut. He pulled out his handkerchief, wrapped the ankle, and carried me up the hill. Once in the car, we didn't head for the doctor or the hospital. Instead, Dad drove us home, where the gash was washed, swabbed with mercurochrome, and rewrapped with one of Dad's clean, white tea shirts torn into strips. The laceration probably required medical care, yet it was never sewn up and left a sensitive untouchable scar.

Upendra repeated himself, "Do you want Kamal to carry you?" My helplessness was holding up the group. I glanced at Upendra, then at Kamal, "No, not yet. Let's go on to the campsite," I said.

"You're tough," he said and skedaddled back up the trail.

Oh sure, I thought as I tried to put my physical sensations in a lockbox.

Kamal and I trudged on. By this time, I was contemplating the Imodium; and I sat down, dug it out, swallowed it, and pulled myself up from my perch, moving my legs counting each step. I threw my kath to the top of the climb, marched up the mountain, and willed myself to keep moving. Kamal and I walked for another twenty minutes. I felt like an anchor dragging the group backward instead of forward. I was still crouching behind bushes, disgusted with the mess I had left behind. I was upset, feeling I had failed or been failed. I was having a hard time accepting my humanness. I felt the Universe was taking me for a big cleansing ride. The Pepto Bismol and Imodium weren't kicking in. The kath helped some, but I knew a better way to trigger my healing than this and over-the-counter drugs.

My poisoned stomach demanded my attention, and I gave it. It was the same as the time when I was in over my head with academic work and had asked the Universe for help…and received it in a form that had surprised the hell out of me. And now I needed it again.

At this moment, a thousand miles from home vomiting and shitting on a backwoods trail, there was only one thing I could do. Shunning yet more over-the-counter drugs, I pleaded with my inner resource to synchronize me with the energies of the place to heal my belly. After all, I was trekking in the shadow of Mt. Everest— Mother Goddess of the Universe. I took charge.

In my mind's eye, I visualized energy flowing from the earth's center up into my legs into the base of my spine…pure light rising through my organs, through my chakras… out the top of my head in the form of a golden, diaphanous cobra. It streamed over my head— healing prana. Step, step, step. Focus, focus, focus. Me begging for a return to health as I pictured my body being flushed of its ugliness, a dark ashy sludge shedding from my system. I awakened my Kundalini for help.

Gradually I inched forward, dragging myself up the hill. After twenty minutes, I came to where the rest of the yoga group was perched on rocks waiting for me. I sat gratefully for a rest.

TexAnna came over smiling and said, "Hey, you alright?"

"So-so," I said it was impossible to create an illusion of myself as OK when clearly, I was wrung out like a soaked tissue caught in a tsunami. The others closed in on me in a tending flurry.

Rhonda came over with a small plastic bag in her hand and said, "Take these. You'll feel better. They're charcoal tablets that'll absorb the toxins in your belly." Fran held out ginger, "This will soothe your stomach." I chewed it hoping to mask the sour taste in my mouth.

I wanted a toothbrush. Warm, encouraging faces surrounded me. As I accepted their offerings, I found an unfamiliar place inside me, that of a naïve child as now the women of the yoga group mothered me.

I hadn't bonded with them, thinking they'd bonded on the plane, making myself an outsider wanting to break in. Or was this precisely my deficient social identity blurred by belly aches tipping me toward the paranoid? TexAnna and the others nudged me to abandon my stiff upper lip. "Look, it's happened to all of us while traveling. That's why we carry this supply of stuff," she said. After resting several minutes, with the women's compassion encouraging me along, I felt well enough to walk to that evening's campsite.

I slept well that night. In the morning, outside the tent, I noticed my belly had ceased fire. I thanked my body for springing back so fast after purging its toxins. With help from my yoga group, and my Kundalini, things had kicked in—and I was ready to go on.

Heading up the trail, I thought about how hard it was for me to own my vulnerability— seeing sickness as a form of weakness— opposite to the persona I put out. I'd been taken down a notch and felt humble. I had spent a lot of my life creating…or was it hiding?…in a tough identity—and I was tough—but there I had been, the real me…at the end of the pack puking and defecating behind the bushes with the prospect of Kamal carrying me up the hill.

Yet, my Kundalini had anted up when needed. Doing that physical/psycho cleansing expelling some shadowy obstacles buried in me …What were they anyway? …a resistance to connect, a need to let go? What? Things that had been gumming up the works but now, after this, had delivered me a spiritual release? It had reminded me to ask for help, making me more human, letting me know more of whom I really was.

The women in the group had nursed me. I took in the compassion and accepted I was the weak link—me, the not so fast, not so special hiker. It felt unfamiliar though I was abandoning a vital part of myself. Yet somehow, I grew stronger by admitting, caving into, succumbing to my weakness, and letting the women buoy me up.

I realized I needed to overcome keeping to myself toughing it out alone while sick. The women had come to my rescue, and I needed to share their mutual back-scratching to check in with the gossip of the other women's lives. I needed to tell them my story— about Tim, my sexless marriage, his pot-smoking, the target practice in the house's basement. They listened and were kind. And I learned that there is a wholesome vulnerability that relies on trusting other women to soak the drought of feminine remiss. They gentled me along, teaching me to release my power persona, submitting to utter vulnerability, and letting go of smiling while my heart was breaking.

A Sound Prayer at Taksindu Monastery

Cameras snapped. I posed on the Jantre Pass, standing at 10,100 feet, Mt. Everest hanging in the background. The sun splashed over the neighboring prongs of the mountains, a King's crown. Ships of clouds circled the metamorphic towers—schist, migmatite phyllite, gneiss, amphibolite, quartzite, shale, and marble—all authoritatively pushing up from the earth's epicenter where once they slumbered in a volcanic bed. The air chilled, and I zipped my ski jacket tight as I turned round and round, taking in the giants, hoping they were taking me into their own accounts.

From there, the yoga group hiked downhill into steep terrain, then charged through a forest of pines crossing a small bridge by a waterfall: a short rest, another uphill climb. Shorter than everyone else and with a shorter stride, I was still at the end of the group but happily so, feeling fine, not suffering from the altitude. Soon we came to the spot where the porters made us lunch: chapatis, cauliflower, small hot dogs, greens, beans, and tangerines for dessert.

Everyone was upbeat. We came to the village of Lower Garma and checked into a hotel that belonged to medieval Nepal. Patterned black rugs with green and red floral designs hung over the walls under carved wooden beams running across the low ceiling. Small statues of Ganesh and Shiva tucked into niches. After settling in our rooms, TexAnna, Vani, Ava, and I grabbed our purses and headed for the Saturday market.

The market was an endless prism of colors—the stalls decorated in golds, reds, blues, and purples —an abstract Kokoschka painting. As we walked through the street, one Nepali agreed to be photographed; his Gurkha knife slung in his white sash. He stood proudly while a woman with nose rings dressed in orange pantaloons, a long string of beads draped around her neck, grinned nearby.

The smells of spices and teas wafted through the air. Kiosks were filled with glass beads, carved wood, jewelry encrusted with semi-precious stones, thangkas, puppet dolls, felt articles, and Gurkha knives. Soon, we came to a carpet shop that overflowed with rugs. I dug through the piles, spotting one with a black background and swirling patterns of green and red lotuses similar to the ones that hung on the walls at the hotel. "How much is this?" The carpet seller rattled off a figure in rupees. "OK," I said, "Will you take…", and we went back and forth bargaining, laughing, and chatting about where I was from in the States and enjoying each other's company. Finally, we settled on a price, and I lugged the rug back to the hotel and gave it to my porter to carry on the rest of the trek.

We sat outside the hotel for a while. Three kittens played nearby. A group of women rolled ears of corn that had dried in the sun. I wrote in my journal and realized I'd been sick the same day Dad had died. I jotted a postcard to Dori. A woman came over, sat next to me, smiling. When I closed the journal, she reached over and opened it, pointing to the postcards. Several other villagers gathered around us, wanting to see them. Fran showed her cards as well, giving her one. I gave the woman a pen which was promptly appropriated by a young boy. At dinner that evening, we danced to drums in a smokey restaurant.

The group began a three-hour hike through Lower Garma/Phera. We now trekked at 8,200 feet, passing through small villages lined with fields of mustard. Again, the houses sported window boxes spilling with orange nasturtiums from dented oil cans. The trail was empty of other hikers. Along its sides, I recognized sedums, a few composites, and cinquefoils. TexAnna's singing lilted back from the front of the group, and I joined in, "Valderie, valdera, valderie, valder-rah-ha-ha-ha, not quite breaking into a yodel-lay-he hoo but laughing up the mountainside. It was easy to get caught up in her aura.

The camp, this time, hung on the lip of a mountain. The porters had set the tents against the side of a shed with the opening flaps facing a steep chasm that dropped a couple of hundred feet below its rim into a dark pit. Without much room to spare when stepping from the tents, our sure-footed Nepali guides trusted us not to fall off the mountain. "You'll have to be really careful in the night if you get up to pee," Ava said. We all laughed nervously.

Inside the house, our home-stay hosts for the night—a short man, his wife, and child— greeted us warmly. He had prepared dinner of dal bhat and vegetables, and we sat at a rustic wooden table in the middle of the room and ate. Battered aluminum pots and pans lined shelves against one wall. I could see a hole high in the corner of the ceiling directly above the fire pit where smoke slowly crawled up to find its way out to the roof. The smoke occasionally wafted back into the room.

After dinner, others lingered inside chatting, but I needed a breath of fresh air from the smokey room and went into the yard. The night was moonless and black. Billions of exploding stars, silvery eyes of God, sequins strewn across the sky. Catching my breath, I lifted my face to take in the astonishing emptiness of the Universe. I drank in the dimensions of the Milky Way that stretched in an endless, glittering, velvet scroll above me. I felt a shift.

Something was being erased. All that had gone on during the past years. That had brought me here, slipping away, leaving me with a clarity unknown before. I stood there under the eyes of the Universe—its stars watching me—me gazing at its cathedral, perfect and holy—imagining a conductor's wand directing a harmonic song—vast and fine and ungraspable. The Milky Way playing its melody right into my soul.

The following day, the group was up early. All accounted for. No one had fallen into the chasm during the night. We packed up our things while several children from neighboring houses looked on. The November sky was overcast, the undersides of clouds gray-blue but still holding their rain. The assent to the Taksindu Monastery was steep passing houses pivoting on the sides of the mountain, prayer flags flapping in the wind overhead. As we climbed, a little boy approached us carrying a huge bundle of sticks, his pants falling around his hips, tripping him. Falling flat on his face, TexAnna and Upendra rushed over to help him up, getting him on his way.

Three hours later, we went over the Taksindu Pass to the monastery that sat on an isolated knoll, ringed by high jagged peaks, at 9,600 feet above a valley. Smoke rose from cottages below. Clouds above, clouds below. A flock of crows coughed overhead. My feet were warm from trekking. I felt my Kundalini beneath them, a thread of intention surging from the mountainous earth, and I made a wish: *Heal me through the strength of light. Heal my heart and spirit.* I was just going along, but that's what was in my mind spiraling through my body.

Arriving, the porters pitched the tents in a broad field between the gompa and newer housing being built for the monks. A pit toilet was dug about 100 feet from the campsite and surrounded by a little blue tent to ensure privacy.

I walked over to scrutinize the newly constructed building, one receiving financial assistance from the Japanese. Oddly, the workers who'd glazed the windows weren't doing a good job. They needed Tia, my friend, who I'd visited earlier in the summer before taking off for Nepal. Tia was restoring a house, and it seemed they needed her admirable construction skills—carpentry, painting, plumbing, and mainly fixing the windows. *She could give them a lesson or two in window glazing,* I thought.

At dinner that night, there was cake. The cake: pan/ raw dough/cover—all placed over smoldering coals equals a spice cake. Anything is possible. After dinner, the monks invited us into the gompa to observe their ceremony. The interior walls of the building had colorful thangkas depicting Buddhist gods, deities, and myths. Pillars painted in red, green, and gold patterns held up the room. We sat whispering to each other in the gompa's back rows, delighted to have such a rare opportunity.

Soon a swirl of maroon and saffron-robed monks entered the gompa and took seats on low benches covered by maroon cushions. Chanting commenced. Deep voices resonating and alternating with prayers repeated against the backdrop of a ringing bell… uuurrrhing, tonggggg; then their voices…OOOhhh yeeeee…the bell… tonggggg; … voices again belly rich…aaahhh, eeeeee…and the bell…tonggg…tongggg…tongggg…in a combined intensification with each note traveling through spacetime, traveling into my spine. The monks pressed their lips to the mouthpieces of six-foot-long Tibetan horns, dungchens, vocalizing sounds of whales or elephants trumpeting their harmonic messages. The long horns moaned and groaned, whirring in and out of the temple's rafters. I inhaled the sound, otherworldly and dense, into my lungs. So remarkably ethereal, its thick beauty vibrated and deposited itself in my body. The monk's voices rang out insanely ethereal. How could it be described? The sonorous sound carpeted the air rumbling into every corner of the gompa into my body passing through the threshold of my skin into my bones—where there was no more room for any other thing. Each of my chakras was amplified, filling my chest, throat, and mind with their life force. The sound vibrated from pebbles to the stars—a sound-prayer for the World.

The monks' singing devotions carried me in and out to the peaks of the Himalayas and back again so that the room became a womb—capturing the essence of the Universe and making me feel aligned with it. My cobra rose. I felt harmonized.

Suddenly, a commotion broke out at the other end of the pew. It was Ava scuffling and crying out. She'd broken the spell, her craziness disturbing the ceremony. Upendra and Vani moved toward her, trying to soothe her and quickly removing her from the gompa. What had happened? Ecstatic ecstasy? Or a rat or mouse of some sort? I never asked. She wasn't my tentmate that night, and I didn't ask, knowing it would result in an endless venting of her stresses. Still, I did blast her with healing light as I slipped back into the zone of magnified power created by the monk's voices traveling beyond spacetime. The Milky Way was yet more spectacular that night.

On the sixth day, we trekked on the crests of the Himalayas, heading for a two-night stay at a hotel. As we went along, the group divided, with Vani going one way and Upendra another, which I joined. He got us lost. Realizing his misdirection, we bushwhacked up a 45-degree mountainside to find the right trail. My legs had grown strong, and I enjoyed the challenge of climbing off the path through the grasses. Reaching the summit of the ridge, I was happy. My body had carried me out of a sharp valley to a high rise. And as I gazed into the valley, the top of a small plane flew by, its fuselage glinting in the autumn sun casting a shadow far below in the gorge.

Joining the other half of the group, TexAnna sang on; Ava yakked on; and Kamal swept the last person who, by now, was not always me. At the end of the day, the group hiked to an upscale hotel by a river for a two-night stay. Comfy beds, hot showers, smiling faces. Namaste, Namaste. A well-deserved two-night rest.

Once settled in, I strolled to the river and sat on one of the massive boulders hunkering at its edge. Birds flew overhead. A black and white fantail, a tiny chocolate brown wren, a slate gray flycatcher, and a saffron orange-tailed bird. *Power points*, I thought. Joseph Campbell was right. The mountains held "zone(s) of magnified power," with power hidden in the unknown where the planet's energy system could feed the soul and rebalance it. This is how I felt just then as I sat watching the icy water jump and leap over gray rocks as a brown bird flew into a small pool. It bobbed up and down, skittering back and forth in the rushing stream, picking its way, working skinny legs while I rested mine gratefully.

Tuche Rinpoche's Plea

THE YOGA GROUP visited a second Tibetan monastery. At this one, we would have an audience with the Rinpoche, the monastery's incarnate lama, who had been a prominent teacher of the 14th Dalai Lama. When we arrived, about one hundred maroon and saffron-robed monks and nuns gathered in a courtyard. Large, flat baskets were laid out before them filled with pepper seeds and white strips of what looked like eggplant or turnip drying in the sun.

Inside monks painted, others made sculptures of barley paste clay. Through an open doorway, another hundred monks sat chanting quietly. I was transfixed by the incredible energy. Holy ground. The Thupten Choling Monastery sat 8,775 feet from Junbesi, its prayer flags streaming in the wind. On the way up the mountain, we had passed boulders carved with Om Mani Padme Hum—hail to the jewel within the lotus.

From the courtyard, we climbed a narrow, pitched set of steps up into a kitchen. Drying socks draped its windows, and a butter churner stood in one corner. A nun scooped sliced apples from a pot. And the smell of cedar, potatoes, and barley percolated through the room. The group sat drinking yak-buttered tea. When done, we stooped along a corridor past a doorway where a masked monk, preparing for a ceremony, rolled sacred balls of butter, stacking them into a pineapple shape.

Once gathered outside Tuche Rinpoche's door—who was also known as Trulshik Rinpoche, His Holiness—we reverently crept into his meeting room where we sat, waiting for him to receive us, an audience planned by Upendra and Vani. Sunlight poured through rainbow decals pasted on the windows. Soon, a plump, bald man with a sunny face entered, holding a white Lhasa Apso under his arm. He sat on a cushioned dais and placed the dog by his side. Smiling he said, "Welcome to Thupten Choling Monastery. It is with gratitude that you are here as our guests today."

Upendra said, "Thank you for this visitation. Please, if you could, provide us with a few words of wisdom which we would appreciate." And Tuche Rinpoche did. Can I remember what he said? Not really, but it didn't matter. Sitting at the feet of a Tibetan incarnate lama was comparable to sitting in a movie set. Tuche Rinpoche held an elevated special rank among the Buddhist community, and he generated warmth and exuded kindness. He also coughed incessantly, turning his head to his left and spitting a wad of phlegm over the dog's head into a brass spittoon.

All of us, including Ava, clammed up, not daring to whisper or show disrespect. When Tuche Rinpoche finished mini-lecturing, Upendra chatted with him, and some asked questions. The meeting drew to a close. Each had bought a gauzy white prayer Khata scarf for twenty rupees. One by one, we kneeled before Tuche Rinpoche. He wrapped each scarf around our necks, touched a medal he held to our foreheads, and tied a red string around our wrists to remind us to be compassionate toward others. The scarf represented purity, auspiciousness, and prosperity. *Did the scarf hold something for me?* I wondered. I looked from it back to the Rinpoche. He had coughed his way through the hour we'd spent with him, and it occurred to me he might be tubercular. So, whatever the meeting, or the scarf, brought me in the way of blessings, I knew it would be a good idea to get tested when I got home. A French team was there doing triage and testing for TB.

As we left the room, I bumped my head on the low door sill. I was thinking about Tuche's words. He had said, "I will pray for your mission, vision, wish." I felt an internal heat, and a mother-giving nature ignited in me. So later, I shared water from my bottle with Fran whereas I wouldn't have otherwise. And I lent Rhonda my polar fleece.

Endings hold a lot of things—sadness, relief, and the incentive to move forward. The last night was paradise. We stayed at the Hotellerie des Sherpa in Phaplu. It had a grand sitting room with a fireplace. It was decorated with several large, dancing Shiva statues flanking either side. Thangkas hung on the red walls painted with dragons and flowers. The carpets were rich and lush. After visiting the market, where I bought tangerines, and a few other souvenirs, TexAnna and I returned to the room. We changed into our swimsuits and went to the sauna where we sang a duet, making it up as we went along. It should have been taped. She massaged my shoulders, and I hers.

The following day, the group trekked to the helicopter pad carved from the mountainside. This is where we'd catch a flight back to Kathmandu. The trek was over. We still wore our red strings, and we took pictures smiling and hugging as the trek drew to a close. Being in the Himalayas, I had heard a bell ring in my spirit, one that wanted me not to stop soaking up its power. And I said to Upendra, "I'm staying in Nepal. Where can I trek next?"

"People often head for the Annapurna Circuit where there are longer and shorter treks."

"How do I get there?"

"From Kathmandu, you can take a bus or fly to Pokhara. From there, you fly to Jomsom where you can pick up a guide or maybe even a group."

The helicopter arrived, and we loaded on. It was my first ride in a helicopter, and I watched the mountains pass below. I felt giddy with my accomplishment, having trekked at 10,000 feet through mountains. I felt strong. An electric joy ran through me, lifting me up. And I thought of walking through the woods back home where I'd learned to respect each bit of bio-structure, and I was grateful. Being in the woods at home or being here, it was never just a plant or just a tree or just a mountain—each was more than that. Each was a piece of energy engaged holistically, reflecting the planet's aura, fulfilling its role, the fullness of it. And more. This is where I was coming from. This is where I had come to heal my spirit, come into the mountains…so remote, so green, so quiet…where I had opened and didn't want ever to close up again.

Back in Kathmandu, my yoga group left for the States. TexAnna, Rhonda, Fran, Vani, Upendra, all of us hugged and said goodbye. I told TexAnna that I would never forget eating dinner under the white Tara at Taksindu Monastery after bowing three times. Ava cried bitterly, vowing to come back again next year. It was farewell to two unrepeatable weeks— riding elephants in the middle of the night, charcoal and ginger, endless dal bhat, pit toilets, shopping sprees for thangkas and rugs, the Milky Way's diamond eyes, and the nourishing resonance of the Monks…uurrhing. Left in Kathmandu, I was happy for the security I'd received from the Yoga Group, free to travel solo again.

Corpses

Alone in Kathmandu, I needed a rest from trekking the Mt. Everest region before I flew to Pokhara to start my next trek on the Annapurna Circuit. I booked a yoga camp through my hotel that would start in a couple of days and decided to take in the Pashupatinath Temple where Hindus burn their dead on the ghats. Once at the temple, I took out my *Lonely Planet Nepal* guide, which provided background. It said the Hindu God Shiva, who grinds out the cycles of creation and destruction, had leaped over the Bagmati River at the temple's location marking it as sacred. Visitors were advised to view the rituals from the opposite side of the river, which I did.

The day was cool and bright. Long shadows lay bluish ghosts

beneath the trees in the park overgrown with weeds and strewn with ancient ruins. A passerby or two strolled through the park, but mostly it was just a troupe of monkeys cavorting overhead in the trees and me. I watched them cautiously for signs of aggression, but they stayed put in the high branches. A chorus of pigeons cooed quietly in the background. At the park's edge, I found a place sitting high up on a bank of the steps overlooking the Bagmati. I peered down on the ghats.

Three pyres: concrete platforms near the water separated into three sections—one for the wealthy, one for everyday individuals, and one for the impoverished. Remnants of an earlier cremation sent wafts of gray smoke whimpering over the river. Then three people arrived carrying a corpse wrapped in a white shroud. They placed it on the far pyre, the one for the poor. Next, a tall, skinny attendant draped in a white robe came out of the temple and walked over to greet the mourners. The guidebook described the attendant as a member of a particular group known as Dom. It was his job to cremate the bodies on the ghats.

As the mourners stood aside, he began to stack wood in crisscross patterns over the body. Then, he bent, lighting a fire beneath the wood. The mourners, hands crossed over their hearts, stood silently watching the wood burst into a blaze as the smoke swirled in bluish-gray spirals rising into the air. The only sound was of the monkeys swaying in the trees, swinging from branch-to-branch grunting. A flock of doves swooped low, a regimented formation skimming the river twirling up over the burning ghat.

After the mourners had left, the attendant circled the platform balancing a long bamboo pole in his hands. He walked in slow-motion, a dutiful dance, around the burning body, gently, yet deliberately, poking the rod into the fire, encouraging long tongues of orange flames to hug the deceased. The fire's warm grip took the corpse…all details of death's welcoming compassion at work: Life filled and emptied, given and taken, impermanent and resistant, pitiful and ruthless. All the yeses and noes of life. Taken now.

My own solemn thoughts seeped into the moment. For me, burial rituals were a part of life. I had no fear of death; I'd had lots of experience with it. Although I had cried for two years when Dad died, it was Mother's passing that was the hardest.

Mother had collapsed during my second year of college and was taken to the hospital when I got the call from Dad. Agnes and I had rushed to the hospital. The attending physician told us that Mother was in a coma in serious condition. I tried to explain that she was an alcoholic, convinced that was the cause of it. He kept shaking his head, looking away with a grim look on his face. Two days later, at the age of forty-five, Mother died of a cerebral hemorrhage.

Life became one hell of a mess. I don't recall anyone consoling or helping Agnes or me. In shock, I continued to take my finals, getting a couple of D's. We all drew within ourselves. Agnes was pregnant and taking care of her firstborn, and buried in her grief. I took charge of the funeral and had rushed to the priest to beg him to bury Mother in the Catholic cemetery. "What? Bury her in our cemetery?" he said. "I don't remember seeing her in church. Did she come to church?" I was terrified at his response but couldn't lie to a priest and said, "No."

"Then have her buried in a nonsectarian cemetery," he said, slamming the door on my grief. My mother had just died, no consolation, instead I was told more or less to go to hell. It took Tim's father, a funeral home director, to negotiate burial in the Catholic cemetery with the priest. The pain wrenched me. I can't even remember if the man gave her a mass. Still, when it was over, that's when I, a religious church-goer, stopped going to church, although it left a gap in my spiritual life. When the bill came for the funeral, I got a waitressing job and paid it, ashamed of what Tim's father would think otherwise.

Now at Pashupatinath Temple, I watched the attendant circling the corpse. A leg eased out of the flames. He pushed it back in ever so deftly. Hours went by. I sat in the park, witnessing a sacred ritual taking place on a holy river. I was reminded that as a guest in my body, at some point in my life, I, too, would step through a window of Time to release my space on this earth. I'd already trod over the remains of my everyday life coming here to this timeless world, not knowing what a year of traveling had to offer. Still, I trusted that my choice was right—as everything back home had come to a close. Now, would my unconscious provide me resilience for the next step? My cobra help? Its rootedness in Earth's available power?

Somehow, I felt I had enough of whatever I needed cached somewhere inside me. Whatever to propel me forward in the right direction, on the path I needed to take. Or the one I was destined for. I hoped so. Of course, I didn't know for sure; no one really knows… knows whether those middle moments or even that last moment will be polite or not. Yet, I felt that here, each drop of my life was soaked in the *now of being. A being* which demanded great physical and mental determination—just replenished by the Himalaya, its power points, soundlessly shouting through Time at me!

Two more corpses arrived, one placed on the rich man's pyre, the other on the middle platform. Wood was layered, fires lit, bluish smoke rose drifting across the river, smelling of unfiltered death as bodies reduced to ashes. The mourners didn't stay long, and the attendant working the long bamboo pole stoked the fires stirring the flames with care. An arm from one corpse rose from the blazing woodpile. The caretaker reverently poked it back into the fire, walking back and forth and back and forth stroking the burning body. Then with no longer any remains, he poured water from a metal jug over the smoldering embers and brushed them all—ashes, debris, and what I imagined were bits of bone into the Bagmati River flowing below the ghats. Then unceremoniously, the metal jars, too, got tossed into the river.

I shook my head, reminded of Dad's irreligiousness. When he was getting older, I'd asked him, "Dad, when you die, how do you want your remains disposed of?"

"Aww, Honey," he said, tipping his baseball cap up over his bald head, "Just bury me in the backyard. That'll do." I had figured that was illegal. Instead, when the time came—after all the hard-drinking caught up with him and he died of cirrhosis of the liver, I had him cremated—to the chagrin of his sisters—and went to Long Island Sound where he had loved to fish and cast his remains into a clear cold tide beneath a tall holly tree. Placed him there to swim with the fishes, which in effect was our backyard.

Are You Breathing, Honey?

The Ananda Yoga Center's yogi was a young man in his thirties, Batsal. He had an assistant, Arjun, billed as the naturopathic doctor who offered facials and kept guests supplied with tea and biscuits. Batsal smiled, Arjun smiled, Tina and Colley—two friendly women in their late twenties—smiled, and I smiled. The place was next to icefields and set in banana trees. It was upbeat, clean enough, bright, and quiet, with just the three of us there. My body needed a stretch, and I was glad I had found a yoga camp outside of Kathmandu. So that now, the world smiled.

For the next four days, Batsal led us through vinyasa flows—forward bends, backbends, the plough, the fish, the cobra, and the cosmic dancer Nataraja Sana. Our vegetarian meals were served sitting on the floor in the kitchen. Then, one morning, Batsal came in and told us that Arjun would be along to do a session of hand yoga.

"Hand yoga?" I said, skeptical.

Tina and Colley were altogether doubtful. "Let's see what's up with that," said Colley wrinkling her nose. Tina mumbled quietly, "Sounds like a waste of time." But by this time, Colley and Tina had run through the facials, and we'd had excellent massages, so there was no escaping. We sat patiently on our cushions, pretending to be captive yoginis. In came Arjun.

"Good morning," he said.

"Good morning," we replied politely.

"Let's begin. Close your eyes, soften your gaze. Inhale…exhale…pay attention to your breath…." Arjun crooned in a soft voice. "Relax your shoulders. Inhale…exhale. Hold palms out, shoulders loose, relax your jaw, turn palms to the right, hands out, pull each finger (he demonstrated on his hand) …inhale, exhale…." He went on, "Focus, now, on each ligament…each digit of each finger, your wrist, your right hand, the left…now sending energy up the arm to the elbow." Arjun's voice became hypnotic. "Focus on your right hand. Breathe. Breathe into your fingertips, into your knuckles, into your palm. Breathe deeply into the bone…the muscle…see the glow of your nerves…and breathe, breathe, breathe…."

Arjun chanted…yet more… "Breathe, breathe, breathe," …and I slipped back in time, recalling Dad asking me constantly, "Are you breathing, Honey?" …when we were out in the woods going fishing or foraging for mushrooms. "Breath is your life," he would say, "The Chinese knew it. Breathe with purpose." Somehow tucked in his brain, Dad knew about pranayama, that yogic tradition to cleanse the body with deep, belly-rich breaths.

"Breathe, breathe, breathe…" hummed Arjun, but I was chuckling to myself, sensing Dad's spirit, there in the yoga camp outside of Kathmandu so many years later, curious as to how many fathers ever, ever asked their kid if she was breathing? And I sat there and found a spot of laughter in my soul. Found a spot where I was home.

I focused on my hands spread before me, flexing and stretching them. I visualized golden light flowing through the skin of my fingertips, discharging pent-up stiffness from each finger, thumb, index, pinkie—stiffness held on for over seven years with the computer now softening. Inhaled through fingerprints, exhaled through palms; I inhaled through palms, exhaled through wrists imagining each muscle elongating and relaxing, each bone inaudibly alive nourished with blood and breath. This hand yoga went on for quite a while, each minute trickling a release. Arjun said, "There is intelligent awareness in your body, in your hands…."

Yeah, I thought, knowing this to be true. My research into inventors' thinking had taught me how hands play a critical role in creativity. They'd told me how their hands took on a mind of their own, went into automatic pilot translating knowledge from their brains into tangible three-D models.

Hands were intelligent. I got that. The odd thing was, I should have known this long ago…that even one hand was smart—known it from Dad's paralyzed claw which was crippled after he fell fifty feet to the ground when being struck by a sheet of ice while working for the CL&P as an electrician in the nineteen forties. His month-long stay in the hospital had never resulted in compensation, but it hadn't mattered. With a clawed hand, he'd built us a house, a sound Cape Cod by a dense forest that had nourished me so deeply—its woods, its plants, its prana.

Arjun continued, "Your hand is nothing more than your brain…inhale…nothing more than your heart…exhale…look carefully at your fingertips…". A bulging knuckle was on my right index finger—was that Mother's slightly arthritic finger or Dad's? I focused more intently, held spellbound, examining the loops of my fingerprints. It was as if my prints opened with eyes into this small temporary home of my body, reflecting its higher cleverness right here and now. Arjun went on, "You are a guest in your body…give thanks." And I felt a moment of balance—perched high suspended yet secure at the same time— unconditionally accepting the presence of my body, sensing its intelligence.

In the night, I had a dream. A doctor friend meets a woman for the first time. He plays a passionate concerto for her, then runs away, and the passion is left seething off the keys.

When I got up to make the bed the following morning, I found an Ace of Hearts card lodged between the mattress and the wall of my room. I tucked it into my journal. An omen?

My cobra was calm. I felt filled. I wanted more, more centering, and more supercharging of my hara. Hara being the purifying power of destruction that paves the way for renewal, both personal and universal, because that's what it felt like not to be in gear. Giving up the order of things. That's what I was looking for now during this year—drinking in the spirit of the land, slipping into neutral, coasting along to whatever, wherever, whenever, and with whomever.

When Tina, Colley, and I were ready to leave the yoga center, Yogi Batsal sat with us, thanking us for coming. Then, he handed each of us a list of names of gurus in India who he said had extraordinary abilities. They were enlightened beings. He suggested we make note to visit them. I had made no specific plans for traveling in India except to visit Varanasi and the Taj Mahal. Now, it seemed, the Universe had a plan for me when I got to India. But first, I flew to Pokhara to prepare for my trek on the Annapurna Circuit.

Silence Without, Silence Within

Gome looked at me, pointed north, and asked, "Muktinath?" All the other hikers on the plane had disappeared in the opposite direction.

"Yes. To the eternal flame," I said. I was in Gome's hands, and we left Jomsom trekking toward one of the highest and most sacred temples on the planet. Alone on the Tibetan Plateau with only one human contact, I felt OK. I liked it. With Gome to carry my backpack, I could imbibe the terrain without distraction. Gome's limited vocabulary would slowly unfold (OK, no, here, eat…) along with a lot of hand signals. He was not company of any sort, nor did I want or need him for company.

I was here to soak up the energies of the trail, its stark beauty, first to the temple, then the Annapurna Circuit's western flank straddling the Kaligandaki River. Eventually, we'd pass through the deepest gorge in the world. I was looking forward to the endpoint, a climb into the Sanctuary at 13,000 feet. About twelve days.

As we walked, everything became more open in its flatness. An ice-blue sky balanced over a scrubbed-down spatial skin of fields.

The quietness of the plain, no wind, was broken only by the soft crunch coming from my boots. We trekked toward the Kaligandaki River's headwaters which began a 506 mile journey towards the Ganges River before flowing into the Indian Ocean. I felt attached to the immediacy of the moment.

Gome had no hat or sunglasses. His job was to get me from point A to point B, and I needed him in good condition. So, I signaled for him to stop and dug into my bag, pulling out my extra dayglow-green Yankees baseball cap and a pair of canary-yellow rimmed reflective sunglasses. He accepted them gratefully and put them on only to resemble Johnny Depp. I was glad he wasn't wearing flip-flops, although his shabby sneakers were only marginally better.

Soon I had to pee, but there wasn't a single bush to be found anywhere, only smallish boulders, and not even many of these. Dressed in a gauzy calf-length skirt, still maintaining the cultural norms of modesty, I used hand motions directing Gome to look away, facing forward. At the same time, I walked at a distance and pretended to crouch behind a rock discretely. When I caught back up to him, his face was twisted in disdain; but I'd had no choice.

Gome and I walked for two hours, gaining altitude to 12,300 feet before reaching the small medieval village of Kagbeni. The town stood like an abandoned Hollywood stage set with a Tibetan flare, which had landed in the middle of nowhere. We entered unmarked streets paved with flat stones. Gray stones. Stone walls, stone steps, stone embedded in white stucco two-story buildings made ashen by the Plateau's blowing granitic dust. Firewood was stacked high on flat rooftops while smooth-worn staircases traveled up the sides of the houses to accommodate winter snows. The buildings' doors and window sills were painted a dull sienna faded by a remorseless sun. It was late afternoon, and the declining light cut sharp, burnt umber shadows in entryways. All the windows were shuttered.

The wooden structures felt prehistoric as they supported life in calm loneliness holding the whole place together against the harsh hand of the weather. Overhead, faded prayer flags hung in arcs from poles. Kagbeni appeared abandoned. No breeze, no sound, no goat, no dog, and not a soul in sight. I thought if someone wanted to be alone, this was the place. The town cast a mood of vast emptiness. Then from a dark doorway, a young child appeared timidly smiling and tugging at his hair.

"Namaste!" I said. Gome added a few words in Nepali. Then, he motioned to the buildings and said, "People…work," trying to give me an explanation for the place's desolation.

"Can I give him a pen?" I asked and dug into my daypack, offering the kid a pen which he took awkwardly. Pointing to my camera, I asked, "Can I take a picture?" The boy shook his head. We went on.

Out of Kagbeni, the trail opened up steeply. Gome and I made our way through the village of Jharkot where we stopped to have lunch and met two Canadians. I was trekking on the highest mesa on the planet, the Tibetan Plateau, which had heaved its subterranean plates three miles up from a prehistoric ocean's floor. It was over four hours more to Muktinath.

Occasional pairs of trekkers passed Gome and me heading toward Jomsom. A Nepali woman materialized out of the horizon, walking toward us carrying a bulky basket filled with branches on her shoulders. Where had she gathered them, and where was she going on such a desolate trail? We'd covered miles without seeing any houses. The high desert was emotionless. It lacked trees, shrubs, and even weeds. Yet this stony mesa, blanketing the area for a thousand miles, held the constancy of millions of years of space-time. And, it felt fresh with its touch of cool air on my face and its voice of clean sunlight. The Plateau drew us along, drew *me* outward and in.

Gome had pointed me in the Temple's direction, and I led us up the trail. By now, we had gained altitude. The surrounding Himalayas sky-scraped the space. I pictured the mountains parading across Nepal marching toward India, Afghanistan, Pakistan, China, and Bhutan. As the hours went on, my focus became unfocused. Each step, heel/toe, heel/toe streamed energy up my ankles, calves, thighs, flowing into my core. Something was staking a claim in me. Finally, I stopped and stood, letting my forehead absorb the rays of the falling sun. I felt like a homing-pigeon guided home to this empty place to fill some emptiness inside of me.

The moment reminded me of crossing through the Iron Curtain when I was twenty, just after Mother had died. I had wanted to go to Poland to tell my grandmother, explain to her what had happened. I'm not sure what got into my head; Poland was controlled by Communists at that time. But, on the other hand, it was the end of the spring semester, and I felt the job needed to be done. I wasn't even sure how I was going to do this; I only spoke a few words of Polish, although, to my credit, I understood a lot more.

I guess I was driven by shared grief and a sense of duty. However, I was also in a state of mind where I thought nothing of jumping on a plane by myself to Europe, where I had never been before. And I also thought nothing of taking a twenty-four-hour train ride through the Iron Curtain in East Germany to get myself to Poland.

I'd be meeting my grandmother for the first time, the only time, to comfort her. But mostly, it must have been to comfort myself by doing the expected, the right thing, the responsible thing to fill an empty place inside of me. That's what my march across the Tibetan Plateau was now. Trekking with no trepidation, no hesitation, just a need burning inside pushing me forward.

Each footstep harmonized with the eons of dust below the sole of my boot. I felt connected to all that went on beneath the earth's mantle—the blocks, the slabs, the rocks, the nuggets, the pebbles, the gains of sand that anchored me to the planet—the grainy blood of the living plateau. With each step streamed into my ankles, calves, thighs, flowing into my core, out the top of my skull. I could taste the sweetness of autonomy in my mouth, drinking in the genius loci of the land.

My focus unfocused connecting me with the nothingness that surrounded me. The hush. There was no commotion. I took it in, and I couldn't drink enough of it. My cobra rose from the top of my head, gliding. There was no communication or exchange between us. However, it grew a bit higher and brighter than before, casting its radiance upward and inward. I inhaled the sweet narcotic of the air.

The land was reshaping me, letting me reclaim an inner stillness that got lost climbing that intellectual mountain for the doctorate—that had, indeed, stretched my head in a thousand different directions giving me a new world view with a new identity but had not provided the hush I craved. Step by step by step, I was beginning to settle into the silence that shaped the mesa. My nervous system declared a cease-fire. Step by step by step, my sole re-visited my soul. Silence without, silence within.

Muktinath's Eternal Flame

After hours of trekking, Muktinath Temple came into sight. It was a small white building that shouldered a two-tiered pagoda structure on its roof. At the front, several bull-faced spouts discharged water from underground springs. A half dozen East Indians up from India milled around the shrine dipping their hands in and out of the water, touching it to their foreheads and hearts.

First, I found a room for the night. It wasn't easy. The woman at the hotel deferred to a young boy standing by her side who said, "No rooms." We haggled. Then, a woman, Barbara, sitting in reception, overheard the conversation and came over saying she'd seen several doubles still available next to her. And she'd share her room with me if I couldn't secure one. But I was determined not to be treated so rudely for what seemed like no reason. I had been in Nepal long enough by now to know how to handle the situation. Finally, I went into the kitchen where the Nepali woman had disappeared. I plastered a smile on my face and handed her thirty rupees asking, "Please give me a lock for a room." At that point, the young kid had no choice. I got the lock.

Before seeing the eternal flame, I checked the boil that had been lanced at the hospital in Pokhara. It was oozing. During the three weeks in Nepal, a half-dollar-sized sore had begun to fester in the crease of my butt, the one I ignored in the jungle with the Yoga group. The twenty-four-hour plane ride from the States had caused a pimple to form. With the lack of proper sanitation on the yoga trek, it had exacerbated into a boil. The pressure built as I walked, and I knew it needed checking before starting this Annapurna trek. I was afraid the lack of sanitation and daily showers would be sparse. So, I'd asked the receptionist at the Pokhara hotel if a clinic was nearby. He said, "Yes" a hospital was located nearby, and I went. I told myself if I didn't like the looks of the place or the doctors, I'd leave and deal with the gash myself, although I wasn't sure how.

The hospital's white facade was bigger than I expected, but my paranoia had already kicked in. I was doubtful about the care I could get in a poor, third-world country. I was about to go out into an isolated area. I pictured someone in the hospital not washing their hands properly causing more harm than good.

I went to the main window to explain my circumstances. The Nepali receptionist spoke English informing me they had a British doctor to treat me. "Go down the hall to the right and knock on the door," he said. So I did. When I turned the corner, I gasped, seeing at least forty Nepali crowded around the entrance of the door. *This, I thought is going to be a long wait.* And I stepped to the back of the line, not wanting to jump it. Shortly the door opened. A nurse peered out, saw me in the back, and quickly motioned me in ahead of everyone else. *Privilege!* I thought, feeling a shock of unfairness, a *white woman from the West—and forget everyone else!* Still, I followed the nurse into a large, dimly lit room where she took my information and said, "Wait here, Madam. The doctor will be in soon."

"OK," I said, glancing around the room up into its high ceilings. It looked like the old kindergarten classroom I'd attended as a child. Except here, a single beige curtain hung precariously from a rod partially covering a large dust-streaked window filtering pale morning light. A dented, aluminum pitcher stood on a gray-legged, metal table in the corner. There was little else in the dingy room;

the whole place was slightly soiled. It felt like a bad dream—akin to standing inside a Rene Magritte painting with everything out of context. That I was in a faceless space disjointed from reality while I was waiting for help to come.

A foreboding rose from my belly into my chest, and I knew I still had time to bail and run from the hospital. Quite suddenly, the door flew open; and a tall, clean-shaven, dark-haired man (white coat and all) briskly entered the room introducing himself.

"Hello. I'm Dr. Winsor." He did not hold out his hand, but he did smile.

"Hi! I'm Anya Kru," I said, instantly relieved by the competence of his manner. I explained my dilemma.

"Let me see it," he said. I bent and pulled down my pants.

"Humm, yes, I see. We can take care of that. It'll need lancing."

"OK," I said, relieved to hear the lack of concern in his voice. He scribbled on a pad of paper, handing it to me.

"I want you to go to the pharmacy and get these supplies we'll need." He pointed the way out the door calling after me, "The pharmacist is from New Zealand." He'd seen the concern on my face.

I left the room, trying not to make eye contact with the swelling group of Nepali I had jumped ahead of in line. I imagined their far greater need than I was in or could ever be. I felt guilty. I'd fallen into a dream clinic run by foreigners. But I needed to take care of my lesion or suffer the consequences later. I found my way to the hospital's pharmacist.

The New Zealand pharmacist stood in a well-organized sterile dispensary. He was from Christchurch and had come to service the needy in Nepal. I gathered my supplies, quickly went back down the hall, and shyly approached the crowd before knocking on the door. Let in, I went to a smaller room filled with sunlight pouring in from an inner garden courtyard. Soon, Dr. Winsor and a nurse came into the room. I handed them the supplies.

"We have a boil to lance, do we?" He said as he quickly peeled off his white coat, putting it aside and guiding me toward the courtyard for better light. "Bend over, take a breath," he said. Gritting my teeth, the lance sliced through the swelling, relieving the pressure. The deed was done except for tending.

"OK," said Winsor. "The nurse will return with bandages telling you how to care for the incision."

"I'm taking a second trek up on the Tibetan Plateau."

"You'll be fine. It'll take time to heal. Get some antibiotics from the pharmacy and keep it dry and covered."

The nurse came back, handing me the supplies. I kept my mouth from dropping open when I saw the newspaper wrappings encapsulating my sterile dressings. Or *were* they sterile? I was in Nepal. The dreamscape hospital I had fallen into had afforded me top-notch treatment under the best sanitary conditions available; because of that, I had to trust.

Gratefully, I gathered up my supplies and headed back to the pharmacy for my drugs before paying up. The bill came to forty dollars US. A light bulb went on in my head as I discovered the reason that I'd been pushed ahead of everyone else. Out of forty dollars, a princely sum in Nepal, I realized I was charged accordingly to support the hospital as a Westerner. I anticipated my travel insurance would cover it, and I grinned at the staff's logic.

Now in Muktinath, getting ready to see the eternal flame, I took out my small mirror and examined the wound. It was OK at this point. My thoughts darted back home, and I thought: *I'm here, alone, in the belly of Mother Nature with a ragamuffin guide, no available medical advice—What would Tim think or Agnes or Biscute?* It was almost a year since I'd finished my Ph.D. and just a few months since I'd quit my job, sold my house and divorced Tim, which already disconnected me from reality. But it didn't matter what anyone else thought. I knew why I was here in this remote area.

It was because I no longer had to be a student, or a teacher, or a homeowner, or a wife. I was free of all that. Roles carried for nine years. Things that had weighed me down, given me a sense of accomplishment and security, and hurt me at the same time. That was it. It felt strange to be so free, but it also felt good. I didn't own anything up here except the contents of my backpack and my boots…and my soul.

At the shrine, I removed my shoes and entered the enclosure that protected the flame. The flame itself was unremarkable. Yet its magnetic ability drew pilgrims, including me, from all over the world. I knelt on the floor, peering into the blue flicker coming out of a small opening from the earth. The flame fueled by natural gas had burned for thousands of years in this isolated location—a place on the planet where all four elements merged: water, fire, earth, and air. Like other eternal flames (the one I'd seen in Delphi years earlier), it symbolized enduring spiritual awakening and liberation.

Sitting at 12,467 feet, the Muktinath Temple is held sacred by both Hindus and Buddhists. Each religion sees it differently. The Hindus have it as a place of release, where freedom from ignorance can be gained by opening up to self-knowledge and self-realization. They seemed concerned with the proverbial question that burns in our souls (or for some that sputter) where we search for the answer to *Who Am I?*

At forty-eight, I, too, had asked that question, spent a lifetime fanning a spark of curiosity about the workings of higher consciousness, my spiritual world. A spark that had grown so bright, so hot—now looking into the heart of this flame—well, its symbolism wasn't lost on me. All those workshops with Dori and others, all those books had taught me finding meaning wasn't easy. Sure, I'd managed to get some insight by asking for help, by tapping into a source of the infinite—God? Mother Nature? The power of the Universe? And had received a Kundalini awakening. But then again, even though I'd always wanted to know more about the meaning of things, about the meaning of me—and especially at this turning point in my life—still, it was a question I thought I'd put aside for now, at least consciously so.

The Buddhists saw the meaning of Muktinath another way. They revered it as a place where bodhisattvas manifest. A bodhisattva is a person who personifies compassion and performs commonplace actions of kindness to relieve the sufferings of others. Like the two pictured in the thangkas I'd bought in Kathmandu. A bodhisattva's heart has a flame of bodhi—consciousness— which she uses to light the heart-candles of others before accepting liberation for herself, before accepting Nirvana.

In the tenderness of this place, staring into the flame, I thought of TexAnna and others from the yoga group, how they'd mothered me a bit after I'd fallen sick on the trail. And because it was the beginning of my journey untethered from them, I wondered what this time held for me, if anything, what the flame portended.

The flame flickered delicately. Yet, there was something strong, something ineffable in its pale blueness that spoke to the rebirth of my inner light—my own flame flickering in me—conceivably identical to the flame burning in everyone else. I am not religious, well, maybe a little. So, I said a few Our Fathers and Hail Marys learned in Saturday morning catechism classes years before.

Later at dinner, the young boy, who had been so rude, came over and sat next to me, looking at my postcards.

Mind's Eye

Gome and I snaked our way back along the trail to Jomsom, where we would stop for lunch. The clouds kneeled low, growing thicker and grayer. And thin gloves of frosty ice hung in shaded areas, clutching rocks. The wind picked up, at first gentle, and I pulled my hat tight against my ears. Soon a gauzy curtain of powdery dust blew skittering grains of sand across the track. Gome started to mumble, indicating that he was telling me something about the wind. He said two words in Nepali that I made out from his hand motions. One was hava—wind. The other amdhi—gale. Within an hour, it howled, sandblasting fine granules that blistered their way into my nose and down my throat. I gripped my windbreaker around my body and pressed into the squall.

Angled against the biting grit, Gome and I bound kerchiefs around our faces and crouched onward for two hours. The hands of the wind tore at us. Hair, nose, lips, shirts, pants, boots gilded with grayish dust…particles of stars connecting with us…our yet to be released personal dust…still very much alive and wanting to stay that way.

The sandstorm continued its choking, seeping into everything. I wondered how long the turbulent push and pull would last. A horseback rider made his way across the plateau. The Kaligandaki's voice blotted out by the wind. Dervishes of dirt danced around us. Gome charged on without comment making it seem an ordinary day on the trail. His unworried face gave me a sense of assurance. I had hired him, trusted him, and when I glanced into his canary-yellow rimmed reflective sunglasses, I knew we'd be OK as we strode through the blasting silt. I let my cobra reach out to gather up the stillness I sensed in him, learning to appreciate the wind's strength. Gradually the curtain of grit began to subside, giving way slowly to a cloudless afternoon. When done, my skin felt reptilian.

Jomsom gave me respite before trekking on to Marpha. I found a place for lunch and got out my camera only to find it jammed. It had sucked up the dust from the sandstorm, becoming a useless piece of junk. I was never so disappointed, but what could I do? I had rolls and rolls of film with me, yet I realized there would be no photos of this trek, only the rolls I'd taken with the Yoga group earlier. In future years, I would replay the steps of trekking the Annapurna over and over again, running my journey in my mind's eye as an eidetic movie. This living movie would take me back again and again and again to where my boots had trod a worn gray trail kicking up fragments of ancient stars around my ankles and more. Nature had found a way to make me utterly present on my journey.

Finished with lunch, Gome and I made our way toward Marpha.

Having encountered few other people on the trail thus far, I was baffled when, after an hour, an old man approached us out of the blue greeting Gome and me, "Namaste."

"Namaste," I said. Like the woman the previous day, he had appeared out of thin air. I searched for a house or shack or cave, something, wondering where he'd come from. He opened a large burlap sack with aplomb and plunged his brown, wrinkled hand to the bottom. He pulled out a bell and Dorje. I immediately recognized them as sacred Buddhist objects I'd seen in Cathy's house. The old man's hand rang the bell while its voice vocalized uninhibitedly over the land. Then, he showed me the bell's companion, a Dorje, or Vajra (the shape of a brass rattle with baskets at both ends) which he twisted back and forth in his wrist.

I took the bell and Dorje in my hands. Poor, cheap substitutes. I'd already purchased thangkas and five singing bowls in Pokhara. But, holding the bell and Dorje, even in the coolness of the air, there was a heat in them. *Where had the old man come from? A trickster,* I thought. A Coyote Trickster of the Southwest Native American sort who carry sacks on their backs containing any number of good or bad events to stir the pot of a person's life. A person who was about to receive a redirection (or misdirection depending on your perspective).

Anyway, right now, there was a chortling in my ear telling me to buy these holy objects. I was getting the message that maybe they were good omens backing me on my way. But I also knew tricksters could agitate the course of events in people's lives, such as that doctorate which, at the time, had turned me in a direction I never would have consciously chosen.

My life up to that point was defined by work. I had stumbled into the doctoral program, which had felt like a headlong plunge into the hidden parts of my personality. The darkest places buried in my unconscious mind…that depository of images, memories, desires—in short, the shadows. Shadows that didn't take long to manifest primarily within my marriage. As I'd settled into the academic program, Tim, my high school sweetheart, arrived on my doorstep. Within six months, we were married. In retrospect, it had all fit together. So now, with the old man appearing out of nowhere selling symbolic objects of sacred intent, what was the message out here in the middle of nowhere?

I turned the bell and Dorje over in my hands, knowing I wouldn't have to worry about losing them or having them stolen. "How much are they?" I asked, still wondering how the old man had found me in this emptiness. The man gave me a price. I considered his brown, lined face and, without haggling, dug for my purse.

Gome stuffed the objects into my sack, and off we went. Later, I discovered the bell and Dorje stood for the underlying nature of the Universe. The Dorje (the male principle) for a lightning bolt of power and the bell (the female principle) for wisdom and compassion leading to a path of enlightenment. Somehow, these symbols—now stuffed in my sack—had found me in the remotest place on the planet.

A large sign on the side of the trail greeted us: "Marpha—The delightful Apple Capital of Nepal." Gome and I stepped around holes in the narrow stone-paved main road. A herd of long-horned goats bleated as they bustled along the street surrounding us, escorting us through town. Prayer flags lifted by the wind made whapping sounds against their poles. Whitewashed buildings shuttered by wooden doorways hid alleyways revealing sets of empty tables and chairs, laundry hung on lines, bushels of fruit stacked in corners—the trappings of Nepali life mingled with the scent of pine, juniper, and apples crimson red.

A short, toothless woman dressed in traditional Tibetan garb scurried by. Then another appeared from her dimly lit shop. I peeked in, seeing shelves lined with necklaces, trinkets, woolen mittens, socks knitted from yak's wool. The old Tibetan village exposed a medieval past, and I slipped back in time.

I checked my *Lonely Planet Nepal* for a teahouse and found its sign hanging over the roadway: Paradise Guest House. Its entrance was an ornately carved doorway graced by hollyhocks.

The reception's host gave me a simple, clean room with a thin but comfortable mattress. The shower cost a few extra rupees. After all the stone dust I'd swallowed, I luxuriated in the semi-warm water washing the residue out of my hair and nose, tending my wound, and scrubbing the soles of my feet. As usual, once I settled, Gome disappeared. I wouldn't see him again till eight AM.

After dinner, where I spoke with several Peace Corps workers, I sat in the dining room lingering over tea. Shortly before sunset, a troupe of French trekkers, nine in all, poured into the teahouse laughing, joking, and talking loudly. Plunking themselves beside me, they told me they had taken off from Besisahar and described their hike over the Thorong Pass. "A touff pull, our calf muscles straining. Vee breathing, and breathing hard like heart attack!" We all laughed. "Not funny! Fight for breath! Determined to get to Muktinath!"

I told them about getting caught in the dust storm and the broken camera. They cocked their heads and murmured, "Pity, pity." They ordered dal bhat and ate. Then one shouted: "Marpha iz'ome of Apple Pie! Two apple piez. We feast! No? You, too, Anya!"

The apple pie was set before us, and I inhaled its aroma checking it against Mother's cooking. Mother had been the master of stone soup cooking in large soup pots as if to feed the Polish army. With her at the stove, there had been no such thing as leftovers in our house. And, her desserts from apples from our trees out back were incredibly coveted. So, biting into this apple pie proved disappointing. But the French wolfed it down, continuing their rowdy behavior long after I had left the table and turned into bed.

I fell into a deep sleep. Soon a dog was barking. Bark, bark, bark endlessly into the night. I'd been listening to dogs barking at night from Kathmandu on up into the mountains. Strangely, they never barked during the day! Cursing, I dug out my earplugs and stuffed them in. Dogs barking in the night never did stop except for one night, and on that silent night, I couldn't sleep a wink.

Absorbing Energy

Each day's schedule was the same. Up early, breakfast, out by 8 AM. This morning, Gome and I straddled the Kaligandaki River heading for Tukuche. The 'Gandaki' starts her descent at an elevation of 20,546 feet from the edges of Tibet and flows for 1,600 miles before spilling into the Ganges River to traverse India.

The river is named for the Hindu goddess Kali, a goddess sometimes personified as the Divine Mother of the Universe. The Mother, it seemed, was revered everywhere in this part of the planet. I'd already encountered this reverence at Mt. Everest—called Mother Goddess by the Tibetans. Goddess Kali is said to be in charge of the powerful forces of nature; and, at times, is also seen as liberation's protector. Knowing this, as I trekked alongside the Gandaki, I still found myself with mixed feelings about past mother abandonment that had once dwelled inside me—and maybe still did.

Seeing Mother raped had driven me to look for mothering elsewhere. First, I thought I found it in the neighbor woman next door whose three little girls I babysat for. I became their big sister while their mother, a teacher, became a role model for me. A model of what, in the end, became what not to do— three squalling kids, heaps of dirty laundry and dishes and bills, and an alcoholic husband—that ended in divorce and multiple marriages for her. And even though she and the kids did become extended family, it wasn't enough for me. I wanted the semblance of a Norman Rockwell family. And I found one when, as a teenager, I met a new friend, and I adopted her Old Yankee family of seven who appeared ideal, especially her mother. They adopted me, becoming a family to me, feeding my spirit and sense of normalcy.

Now trekking this ancient artery along the Gandaki, its gray-green surface waters swirling and pulling over what I imagined was a rock-filled bottom, my footsteps echoed silently among the millions of other footsteps gone before me. And I let Kali's forces, her divine mothering, carry me along, detaching me from the past the best I could—so much was gone anyway it didn't matter.

About an hour after departing, Gome and I crossed the river's broad sandy plain. I moved at my usual snail's pace. Then, just barely at first, then louder, I heard the chatter of voices approaching behind us. Within minutes, the French group, apparently having slept-in, powered by calling out their "Bonjours" and "Vaz goot pie last night! Bien, bien!". It didn't take long for them to sweep us up in a plume of dust as they raced by.

Soon after, I could see the group a half-mile off as they flew across the river bed as if marching in the service of a Napoleonic war waged through the heart of the Kaligandaki. I would never meet up with them again. By the time I got to the Annapurna Base Camp, where they too were heading, I expected that they would have trekked back to Paris, laughing, drinking, and eating pie along the way. As the French vanished from sight around the river's arm, they left a stillness behind. Yet, their circle of mayhem struck a hefty dose of merriment into my mood.

At the same time, I was grateful I was setting my own rhythm. I was thankful I no longer charged from point A to point B as I had done with my yoga group. The difference between hiking and walking, two different animals. Now, I could take in the river, its roiling milky waters sprawling across the delta, the nourishment of the empty landscape, its living geometry, its implicit power. Grateful to be brought back home trekking alongside Divine Mother Kali, single-minded in her bed. I absorbed the places' energy, and I was glad to be there and nowhere else.

The miles emptied behind us. Once the French had passed, the trail was vacant of other trekkers making it impossible to hook up with anyone to hike or chat with. Gome, the silent partner that he was, continued to walk either beside me or a few steps behind.

During the trek, he and I had gone back and forth with my name, with him twisting his mouth about, finally calling me "Onna," the best he could do.

I fell into my own pace, Gome adjusted to its creep. We went along the Gandaki's naked shoulder hemmed by gravelly banks fenced by mountains of pine forests asserting themselves into hoods of hoary snow. My ears filled with the water's churning movement against half-sunken rocks. All my steps, step by step, tripped a switch in me—that I can best describe as "in the moment"—where nothing mattered except moving forward. Whatever the future brought, good or not, I was here, and this was the only place I needed to be.

As time went on, I visualized a clean light drawn up from the earth's core flowing into my body—my backbone, my heart, my lungs out the top of my head—my Kundalini gathering the energy fields of the Earth. It spiraled through my physiological hubs into an elegant cobra dance. I was tasting a moment of surrender, a hard shift for me. I'd always taken charge, gotten the job done, directed the course of my life. But here, it didn't matter; nothing mattered out here. Nothing. I tried to cede control to let the moment carry me along. Walking, walking, walking…waltzing on the banks of the Kaligandaki River, a pure meditation of walking. I began to purr the Gayatri Mantra:

> "Om
> Bhur Bhuvah Svah
> Tat Savitur Varenyam
> Bhargo Devasya Dhimahi
> Dhiyo Yo nah Pracodayat"
>
> (Houston, & Snow, 1996. [Cassette tape]
> American Sanskrit Institute).

As I did, I recalled how it had opened me up to help me get through those difficult years of doctoral studies. How after popping the tape into the player, it had never stopped playing. And by the time the dissertation was done, I had memorized it, chanting its Sanskrit message over and over again, letting it enter my core.

Now, I snorted; because initially, I had been blind to the mantra's power—this sacred prayer—that called for final liberation through the awakening of true intelligence—my true intelligence—something I needed and desired at that time to help me with those studies. And I shouldn't have been surprised— because I wasn't deaf—the chant's vibrations had taken me firmly up into their hold, embracing my mind, body, and soul bathing me in its compelling sounds.

I chanted as I trekked. Each syllable nursed my core. I let my personal, narrow, material world merge with the entire cosmos. I was a drop of dust in a place where rules didn't apply. Where permanence gave way to limitless change. Where earth and water welcomed whatever prayers I had and grounded me in the pulse of nature. Where I could pray without promise—old prayers giving way to bigger hopes and dreams, if…I could only let go. I *was* simply a drop of dust—negligible, riding a matrix of dirt with millions of others swirling through the lower left-hand corner of the Milky Way—linked to *this* gorgeous pebble underfoot.

Miles, miles, miles. To my right, the cherished river busied herself. A streak of mountain sunlight polished my face. I hummed *Om bhur bhuvah svah…* absorbing the Gandaki's grace, its watery turbulence, yet its calming space. I felt detached and attached at the same time—felt flooded with the delta's genius loci, a sense of I/Thou…my personal wholeness vibrating in relationship with the wholeness of the Tibetan Plateau. I felt Special, the land felt special, the world felt Special, everything interfacing through dust and spirit felt Special. Miles passed beneath my feet as I felt one with the Earth.

Gome and I moved steadily across the churning riverbed, a flux of watery rapids swirling downstream around boulders, serpent tongues biting into the base of the mountains. We left the lip of the high desert behind, trekking uphill for several miles through cedars and pines. Soon, isolated groups of houses began to dot the hillsides. Gome stopped. "Ona" he said, pointing to the ground signaling for me to wait on the trail. Then he disappeared behind one of the houses.

I waited and watched a man who was tending a year-old girl playing in the pile of corn he was husking. An older man joined him and sat down to husk. A woman, happy and smiling, came out of a house and took the baby off. In a few minutes, Gome was back and held out a staff nodding for me to take it. "You," he said, handing it to me. I was pleased. "Thanks," I said. "How much is it?' He shook his head. "No," he said, not returning my smile, but I could see that he was pleased that I had accepted the staff, a gentle prodding to improve the speed of my pace.

We gained ground. The river's voice muffled below— "step gently, step gently." I climbed through the thinness of the air, glad the altitude was not affecting me. I wasn't even thinking of my knees or ankles at that point, never having injured or twisted them. I was proud of my body.

Gome and I pulled up the mountainside. Soon I found myself trekking between two of the tallest mountains on the planet. I called out, "Gome," to get him to stop. He turned, saw my face, and pointed to the massifs naming them. To the right: "Dhaulagiri," to the left: "Niligiri." Two snowcapped vertical thrusts heaved upward, establishing their imposing geometry in the icy blue sky.

Speechless, I was intoxicated. Two primordial giants thrust their power before me, and I saw them, not merely slabs of rock but living systems in their own right. The Nepali believed, and I felt the same, that I was in the home of Shiva—the Himalaya designated as sacred—where rivers and waterfalls and mountains, or even the most unremarkable scrap of stone contained a spiritual essence. Spellbound, I spun—a human whirlpool—rotating between them…Dhaulagiri, "white beautiful mountain" and Niligiri, drinking in the moment of meeting them, and their meeting me.

It was impossible for me to get enough. Dhaulagiri and Niligiri. Stone-faced above, fire swirling in their gut. My soul was pulled into the mountains. In turn, they fell into my soul. That's how it felt facing the rock, snow, sky under the stare of sunlight. I watched them; they watched me. I breathed them. They breathed me. I listened to their silence. They silenced me, yet there was a dialog. Had I consciously chosen to come to this spot, or had the spirit of the mountains chosen me? Called me? Now, striking a chord in me ever so deep? I was no longer walking through the mountains; they were walking me. Like Dad had always told me: Special. Special. Special.

Words, photos, poetry, music —none can capture the beauty of this spot! Of being here! I don't know how to better describe the two mountains. I was hearing Beethoven's 5th for the first time. Accepting the agony of Picasso's Guernica. Seeing the world "in a grain of sand." This was real. It was prayerful. I turned round and round, bathing in it—a liquid life of stone thrown up like an Andrew Wyeth canvas. One he'd painted with a single-haired brush capturing each detail—infinitely awake—its texture, its color, its composition, its line capturing the invisible hands of the massifs holding up the roofbeams of the sky. The two mountains hauled at my heart—the thickness of their wild beauty—and became rooted in my mind's eye.

The Kaligandaki Gorge

The following morning, I left the teahouse, as usual, to wait outside for Gome to emerge at eight from somewhere he'd slept the night. It was clear to me that he knew how to take care of his own needs. Each afternoon after arriving at our destination, Gome would deposit me in a teahouse and disappear. I assumed that guides and porters had some kind of arrangement with teahouse owners where they slept and ate in the same teahouse as their trekker. When I asked, "Gome, where do you eat and sleep at night?" he mumbled something unintelligible and signaled his hand behind the teahouse. I never got the whole story. But each morning, Gome was at the front door waiting for me, a solid frumpiness about him, ready to escort me ghostlike through the most unspoiled wild places on this trek.

On this day, the Kaligandaki Gorge lay ahead of us. Before

leaving the room, I had checked my wound with the tiny mirror I'd brought, catching a sliver of light coming through the cracks in the door I'd set ajar to assess its healing. The sore was reddish in the center and still weeping. Using my water bottle and gauze, I washed it carefully and redressed it.

Gome hefted the backpack onto his shoulders, and we hiked out to the main track. Each mountain was draped in a robe of snow covering sedimentary conglomerates of shale, sandstone, basalt, and quartzite. I walked and walked and walked partnering with the Annapurna Circuit's tempo—her low, still, muted, undulating pulse—my boots keeping my feet secure to the trail and blister-free. I sent hugs to the REI clerk who'd encouraged me to put aside my ego to buy a pair of boots one size larger than usual. That allowed my feet to breathe while fiercely gripping each particle of topography on the hard-bitten trail.

Leather on dirt. Dirt on leather. I surrendered to the trail, to every crag ever walked upon by thousands of ordinary Nepalese and thousands of other trekkers. I felt a part of all there was along the way.

That morning was marked with the same stubborn soundlessness that Gome and I had kept in our non-chatty relationship throughout the trip. I'd heard few birds along the trail, and the noiseless landscape disappointed me. At home, I was a member of a birding group regularly taking walks to catch the spring and fall migrations. I had not brought binoculars, but I still hoped to see the region's birds, but they amounted to mostly crows.

Then the trail's emptiness interrupted. I thought I was imaging it, a clinking of bells chiming through the air. The view was blocked by the track's twists and turns before a line of five tiny horses loaded with heavy packs came around the corner heading toward us. Each pony wore a brightly colored red, yellow, and blue yarmulke braided above its harness. Each wore a leather neckband of bells announcing its approach. There wasn't a soul in sight, no man or woman or child. I laughed as the animals confidently footed their way up the trail without shepherding. Gome and I smiled at each other, letting the ponies pass before we continued working our way toward the Gorge.

The Kaligandaki Gorge, the deepest on the planet, is also called the Andha Galchi by the Nepali. About seven miles downstream from Tukuche, this vein of life hangs low between the sharp peaks of Annapurna I, at 26,545 feet, and Dhaulagiri at 26,795 feet. At 8,270 feet, Gome and I gradually moved along the thin collar that circled the Gorge's neck.

I heard the river's throat swilling below the corridor's rim as it kicked its way through the narrows to the Indian Ocean. I felt shaky. A misstep could be easy, falling carelessly into the ravine below. I trod carefully over each loose rock while concentrating on the space ahead of my boots rather than on the drop-off.

The air was dry. The wind still. No birds called in the sky. A single damselfly flew by. I focused hard on the narrow trail. Trekking the edge was different. I felt something reaching up connecting me—earth, water, sky, air—in a moment, making me feel supported. And I felt I was moving from normal reality into yet a deeper personal reality. That I was able to slip between two states of consciousness, being in them simultaneously without effort, without stress, without panic, without doubting myself as normal. It made me think about my stint on the Earth—how vulnerable I (and everyone else) was to Time, what a stranger I still was to that entity.

The research I'd done on Time showed me the mind can manipulate its layers, pass through them, weaving their pieces into a tapestry of new realities. From that, I knew it was possible to have one foot in the past and one in the future, where those two domains of knowledge could collide either into a present moment of Eureka! or one of those strange moments of "been-there-before" that come from the incomprehensible past waiting to be reclaimed. Reliving the past, that sort of intimate relationship with Time that moves things forward can create a whole new meaning to someone's life.

Now, as Gome and I passed through the Andha Galchi, my

cobra undulated from the top of my head, a prayer flag cocooning my body. But it was different. Leaving the river's edge, the image reached higher and higher branching into a glowing candelabra, a multiple of cobras rising over the crown of my head. Amazed by this shift? Yes, but I shouldn't have been. Everything I knew about Kundalini said I'd been prepared for its development, so why should I be taken aback by this change now?

During its initial opening, when I'd asked the Universe for help and had received my Kundalini awakening, complete with a lucent cobra which I felt had symbolized a meeting of myself, a wholeness happened inside my soul. Yes, at first, it *was* disbelief, but it was clearly there. Still, I took no pride. I didn't attribute special qualities to it and didn't expect or ask anything of it. I never named it; how foolish would that be? It came with a profound, empathetic understanding— a "beyond-ness" that called for alignment, for order.

True, right now, I no longer had Dad to encourage me to master my "child's mind" or Dori with me to discuss the symbolic nature of my journey; but what I did have right then was time. Time had given me this trek, a bottomless quiet, a walking meditation powerful in its ability to offer me a subtle transformation. The very edges of physical reality along this journey softened, allowing me to sense the rewards of a numinous reality.

Here—in this immense, exposed space—the river and the mountains—watching my cobra branch, I felt, in its own way, Time was tracking me, asking me to surrender to its inevitability. That there was stuff waiting for me, something new…but yet, I resisted shedding so many layers that had protected me.

And I thought: *Me? Surrender? Hard* …being solidly anchored in physical reality, but was I? After all, I had a cobra riding over my head—easily thought of as an altered state of consciousness, oftentimes thought of as irrational. Was I willing to place everything in Time's hands, accepting each moment to unfold as true? *Hard for me to do*, yet invitingly rich. After all, I *had* asked Time for one precious year, and here it was unfolding under my boots… over my head…still more so streaming through my chakras. Could it possibly hold something more? I was grateful for having received this spiritual gift—the energy unleashed in me during my doctoral studies and more so here in Nepal! But I realized that I hadn't really put the meaning of my cobra into words. One thing I was clear on, though, I was glad my Kundalini was polite with me. The physical and emotional problems that initially came with my opening were in the past. And I had to accept that I was in it for life, like it or not.

Gome and I hiked out of the Gorge.

Slipping into Accord

In Ghasa, our next stop, I found a teahouse perched on a hilly slope. The whitewashed stone buildings looked like small, sturdy ships beached on a crag. After settling into my room, the lanced boil on my rear recaptured my attention. It worried me. It was still draining. The lack of hot water and robust showers in the teahouses didn't reassure me that it was healing. I was dirty. I had been unable to shower despite booking rooms that advertised hot showers, showers that froze my hair to my head. My clothes, unable to dry, stank with a sweetish smell of dampness. Urine was on my skirt from peeing behind a rock on the trail, plus I'd stepped in human offal in a latrine.

In one place, I had paid thirty cents for a bucket of hot water to sponge bath my body only to see that it had a ring of grease inside it. Usually, I can tolerate a certain amount of dirt trekking unwashed. But not able to see the incision properly—it would have taken a pretzel-ized yoga pose—my confidence was eroded, and I was anxious. Who knew what kind of germs awaited in Asian soils? What I did know was that layers of grime added to my bottom daily. Each night, I bought water in plastic bottles to thoroughly wash my wound before re-dressing it. But my nursing skills were nil. And I was running out of dressings and antibiotics. Something I'd have to look into.

I unpacked my gear and went out to get some water to wash my hands and tend my tush. A slim, young woman dressed in a pair of wide blue and white striped leggings was standing at the spigot, a brown wool cap pulled over her strawberry blond hair.

"Hi!" she said with an accent smiling widely.

"Hi. Where you from?" I asked.

"Australia. You?"

"The States. East Coast. Where did you start your trek from?"

"From the beginning at Besishar. My husband's a bit lame from it all by now, but we're carrying on. It's easy to injure yourself out here."

"Yeah. I'm tending a wound on my tush. I had a boil lanced in Pokhara, but I can't see the damn thing to check what's happening."

"Oh? Does it need to be checked? I'm a doctor. Name's Martha."

A little sigh escaped me. I couldn't believe my ears. "Yeah, OK. Please. I'm Anya." I grinned back.

"OK. I'll be back in a minute." And Martha went off to her room, returning with a bottle of Betadine. At the spigot, she scrubbed her hands surgeon style, took the Betadine, and coated them a bright burnt sienna. Then turning to me, she grinned, holding up her glowing palms, a mad scientist. "OK. Let's go to your room and have a look."

In my room, I bent over, exposing my rear. Martha fingered the area gently.

"Hurt?"

"Still a little," I said.

"Hah!" she laughed. "Looks good to me. It's healing, not bad. But, it's like museli on which germs will breed unless you change the dressing regularly. Are you still on the antibiotics?"

"Yeah, but I'm almost out of them."

"I want you to have another round of antibiotics. This time double the dose. OK?"

"OK," I said doubtfully. *What the hell*, I thought. *We were in the middle of nowhere. I mean nowhere! Where could I get them out here?* I was chagrined at having gotten myself into this situation, but here was Martha doctoring me.

"OK. I want you to go up the road about ten houses where you'll find a place with a blue door. That's where you're gonna get 'em. They sell antibiotics and get yourself some new dressings to keep the wound covered."

I really paused at this point. Really paused. This *was* the middle of *nowhere. Nowhere!* How on earth did Martha know this? Know that there was a stash of pharmaceuticals in one of the shabby shops lining the dirt road that ran through the center of teeny-tiny Ghasa out in the middle of the Annapurna Circuit? But it didn't matter. I didn't ask. The Universe had coughed up Doctor Martha, so I shut my mouth.

After her exam, I thanked her profusely and headed up the track looking for the house with the blue door. When I found it, the door stood wide open. I stepped into a darkened room. No one was there. I called out "Hello," and waited. I glanced over the room. Behind the counter, shelves were piled with bottles of pills, small boxes of what must have been other medications, and rolls of tape looking more like duct tape than anything else. Then, I called again, "Hello," and waited. In a minute, a woman with a melon-shaped face wearing a white babushka wrapped around her head came out of the back smiling through a gapped tooth.

"Yes?" she asked cocking her head to one side.

"I need some antibiotics and dressings."

"OK," she said, nodding. "What you need?"

I held out the old package and dressings showing her. She took a box of antibiotics from the shelf placing them on the counter. She grabbed a big roll of the duct tape off the shelf and rolled it back on itself into a small wad. The saleslady—pharmacist?—went into the back room coming out with gauze dressings and reached under the counter for a piece of newspaper, quickly wrapping the whole kit-and-caboodle into a bundle. She sold it to me for under eight dollars.

I walked back to the teahouse, dazed. The medication had been stacked behind an opened door. *All this trust.* Then, just as quickly, I counted my blessings. I had needed help. Hadn't even asked for it this time…well, maybe subliminally…and the Universe had kicked in by delivering up Dr. Martha along with the nowhere pharmacy filled with meds. Feeling confirmed, and one with the functions of the cosmos, I simply said: *Thank you, God.*

Back in my room, I cleaned my wound, dressed it in new gauze, and hoped there weren't too many germs on the duct tape now secured to my bottom.

Balcony of Death

The following day, I stood outside the teahouse as usual and waited for Gome. And waited and waited. We had a seven-hour trek ahead of us, and I was anxious to get started. I was looking forward to Tatopani's hot springs. The guidebook described them as a trekker's paradise where weary trekkers stopped to soak their bones after days of exertion. The springs, large and tepid, poured from the ground into shallow enclosures. I planned to book a two-night stay where I could soak and do yoga. I wanted to hang up my boots that hosted the dreams of my feet, the feet that now didn't so much need but wanted rest. Now waiting outside the teahouse, where was Gome? I got antsier and antsier as Ghasa emptied out of trekkers.

Thirty minutes later, Gome came around the corner jacket disheveled, collar askew, looking sheepish. His hair tussled out from under his Yankees ball cap cocked to the side of his head. He looked as if he'd been up to no good during the night. I frowned and began to interrogate him.

"Gome, where have you been? It's getting late."

He mumbled something guilt written on his face.

"We've got a long haul ahead of us. You know that," I scolded as if he was one of my students gone amiss. His eyes were dilated, identical to Tim's after smoking pot. But unfortunately, Gome and I hadn't progressed much with the English language, so there was no way of grilling him further and feeling disgusted; I didn't bother.

In a few minutes, we'd be on the trail, and it wouldn't matter.

Gome's usefulness was more than apparent to me. He was leading the way, schlepping my bag and not complaining about my slow pace. I'd never questioned him as to directions. Nor had I asked any of the teahouse hosts to see if he was going the right way. It had never occurred to me to doubt him. Gome was a good man. I had arranged my playing cards in a flimsy manner by hiring him, but I wasn't about to lose the round, so I surrendered to his guidance. As he bent over to pick up my pack. He was wearing a new pair of sneakers.

"New sneakers?" I asked.

He garbled something, unable to give me any details I could understand. Then without further explanation, he hefted my bag onto his back, and we headed to Tatopani.

Gome and I walked through the morning. Above, a clear cerulean bowl encircled us, a sole eagle punctured its porcelain glaze. Below, the trail to Tatopani was disrobed of vegetation dusty and gray. To the west, the mountains wore a veil of autumn snow. If I'd had a video camera, I might have caught the Gandaki's vast extensions, her gray-green skirts spreading her damp fabric of life weaving their way to the Ganges. But still, it was wonderful being there for me.

Sounds along the way were scarce and precious. So precious that when the eagle shouted a mile away, the sky felt broken, shattered falling to the ground. No sounds. Just a walking meditation. Mountains married to air. Air married to sun. Sun married to earth. Earth married to water. Me...willingly married to all.

Several hours went by. Gome and I pulled away from the river and came to the flats opposite Annapurna South. Across the expanse, I could see a kettle of vultures, rotating over the earth's belly, riding the thermals low above a rock balcony jutting from a high ledge. Something dead was there, something sending the perfume of bereavement—a nourishing death smell—calling the scavengers to service.

I stopped to stare up at the wake of black marauders wheeling over the shelf. Gome did the same. The vultures tightened their circle, carving smaller and smaller death sickles above what I imagined was a corpse. By this time, I'd learned the Tibetan custom of sky burials, where human remains are placed close to mountain tops as offerings to vultures. With the birds thought of as angels whose job it is to pick the bones of the body clean and carry the soul to heaven.

As we watched, the black orbit of out-stretched wings began to settle, ready to perform its rite of passage—pick apart the cadaver, make it relinquish its flesh and blood, disassemble its pieces of life—only to reassemble the body's nutriments back into the marauder's unsympathetic throb of life. Gome's face was pulled tight into a solemn expression, as was mine.

Standing below that funeral balcony, I looked up prayerfully. There had been plenty enough death and dying in my life to make me learn early on that death—Babcia, Mother, Dad—takes your history with them, only too soon. The bad times and the fun times. The times when the family loaded into the old Hudson heading for Uncle Sam's to fish, swim, pick blueberries and run free in the fields.

Now, watching the rim of the ledge where the vultures worked over some pitiful remains, I recalled how death had almost taken Tim in its hasty push. How I'd come face to face with Death, who had stood in my bedroom handing me a premonition that Tim's life was in danger.

That night when Death had come to me, I'd been sleeping alone upstairs to avoid Tim's snoring. And I awoke to a powerful dreamlike image, or was it even a dream? A hooded specter materialized before me. It stood four feet tall with a band of red light glowing under a corner of its hood. There was no mistaking what I saw. That image is plastered over books, cartoons, and movies galore. I gaped, my throat frozen. It was soundless, not moving, not pointing, not anything, just silently standing before my bed. I looked at the faceless thing.

Death had come to deliver a message, and somehow slowly, I understood the message—that it wasn't for me, that I was the messenger—open enough to receive the facts—and that it was for Tim, not a healthy person. His ills had ranged from arthritis to tinnitus to chronic digestive problems. He was always constipated. The specter was foreshadowing Tim's death.

In the morning at breakfast, I wasn't about to tell him what I'd seen. Instead, I put on my best wifey smile exuding as much unconditional love as I could (I did love him) and said, "You know, Sweetheart, you haven't been feeling well lately, right?"

"Yeah, you're right," Tim looked at me over his omelet.

"Well, maybe it's time to find a doctor, just in case something comes up. What do you think?" I asked…smiling, smiling, smiling.

He looked up, and I'm not sure why he replied the way he did—but he took in my sober message, took in my message of love (which is not always the case when trying to tell your husband what to do or anyone else for that matter); and he said, "OK. Sure. As a matter of fact, my cousin Bruno just got a new doctor who he was telling me about. I'll ask him."

Timing, I thought. *Good timing.* And Tim did make an appointment to see Bruno's doctor that week. When he came home from the doctor's visit, I was hopeful that the doctor had found whatever was wrong with him, and I asked, "How did it go?"

"Oh, he's a great guy, Dr. Goodman. I like him a lot."

"And…what did he say?"

"He said to come back to see him the next time I have a problem," Tim replied.

My heart sank. I'd just seen the shadow of Death signaling Tim's health was in grave danger, and Tim was waiting for "the next time" whenever that was going to be.

OK. OK. I thought, *Relax. Don't nag him. Something will come up soon.* And, I don't know why I didn't tell him about the specter, but I didn't. I kept it entirely to myself, hoping his body would tell him that something was drastically wrong.

But it didn't tell him. It took Tim's body six months before speaking up. Finally, on the afternoon he got its message, he called from work, said he had terrible pain in his gut and was coming home. He'd made an appointment later that afternoon to see Dr. Goodman. When he got home, he was bent over, holding his side, and crawled into bed. Later going out the door to the doctor, I was driving him; I wondered if I should grab his toothbrush. I sensed he wasn't returning with me that night but chose not to inflame him. At the doctor's, Goodman poked Tim's abdomen, making him yelp in pain.

"Come to my office," he said to me. "You lay right here, Tim." In his office, he grabbed his phone furiously dialing the hospital's admitting office, telling me, "You've got to get him to the hospital fast." On the phone, he told the hospital he had an emergency coming over. Back in the examination room with Tim, he said, "I'm rushing you to the hospital. Get going."

"No way, I'm fine," said Tim.

Goodman pursed his lips at Tim. Then he cocked his head sarcastically and said, "Here are your choices, Buddy. You go, *or* you die!" Goodman, it seemed, had assessed the truth of Tim's condition, the truth I'd known for months while waiting for the other shoe to drop.

At the hospital, Tim went through several hours of tests, his pain increasing steadily. Finally, the doctors reported to me they thought it was a severe intestinal problem. I waited through the hours, calling Tim's mother and Biscute asking her to call Agnes. I read the newspaper while I waited. A front-page article described the nasty effects of a condition called peritonitis that could result in a death knell once the intestinal wall was punctured. At one point in the night, I went outside into the hospital's parking lot to get a breath of fresh air. It was December 9th, and a full moon had risen overhead, casting sharp shadows.

Tim was diagnosed with diverticulitis. He had a baseball-sized pocket ready to burst at any time. After a course of antibiotics, nine days later, the surgeons took him into surgery and removed eleven inches of his colon. It was not a happy time. After the surgery, I sat by Tim's bedside, pumping a morphine drip into him to relieve his pain, both physical and psychological. Tim said, "They didn't give me enough anesthesia. I felt every initial incision they made. I tried to wiggle my pinky to tell them, but then I passed out." He'd been through excruciating trauma, but I realized he'd be OK. By this time, the specter was nowhere in sight. I sat by his bedside and pumped morphine.

The vultures on the ledge settled their affairs feasting on the corpse that lay on the mountainside. Two flew off. Gome and I took a last look then we moved on.

Anger's Tutelage

I stopped at several teahouses where I was told, "No room. Full." It didn't seem possible. It was late in the afternoon when we arrived at the Tatopani Hot Springs, and yeah, it was high season for trekkers, but this wasn't a luxury resort in Tahiti overcrowded during the holidays. So why couldn't I find a room?

Gome proved himself to be the best guide, but he was of no help now. Speaking little English, he couldn't really explain to me why I couldn't get a room. After going back and forth, up and down the main drag, I went back to the second teahouse where I'd been offered a third-floor garret over the kitchen, the one I'd vetoed as totally inadequate. But now, I had no choice but to take it. I checked in, and Gome disappeared into the shadows with the understanding that we'd be spending a couple of nights in Tatopani.

I dragged my sack up the stairs. The room was dark, cramped, and shabby with walls-stained black smelling of smoke as if a thousand pots of dal bhat had been burnt immediately below its floorboards. Its pungent odor clogged my nose. I hefted my sack onto my back and went downstairs, handing the host the key telling him I wanted another room.

"No other room," he said, eyeing me dubiously.

I stared at him incredulously. The place looked empty. *He's lying*, I thought.

"There must be. I need another room. That one is...."

He cut me off. "No, Madam. All filled."

The Nepali teahouse hosts along the trail had treated me

decently. I had no reason to doubt this guy, but you could hear a pin drop in the building. The man behind the counter handed me back the key, and I dragged my sack back upstairs, trying to tamp down a paranoid suspicion that I was being duped.

I stuffed myself into the 5 x 8-foot enclosure and collapsed on the lumpy mattress. Arranging my stuff, I pulled out a package of biscuits and ate them along with an apple for dinner, too tired to search for a restaurant. Finally, I fell off to sleep. In the middle of the night, I woke up coughing, the smell of smoke gagging me as it wafted into the room from a stovepipe straddling one corner. Through a small crack in the roof, I could see that the line emptied out a hole in the ceiling. Coughing still more, I angrily covered my nose with a handkerchief feeling humiliated at being treated like a beggar. I'd been in a great space all day only to be submitted to this dirty trashcan of a room. I wondered if Gome slept in quarters like this.

I managed to get through the night inhaling a smokestack of pollution, barely sleeping and vowing this would not be repeated. After all, I had a half-dollar-sized wound on my tush and wasn't about to get myself infected by this filthy place. The following day, I packed my bag and stalked the road looking for a better room; no, the best room in Tatopani. I knew that trekkers had left that morning, and there would be rooms. I went to several other teahouses only to be told every room was full. Impossible. It was nine o'clock in the morning by then. I felt confused. OK. It was the hot springs, but I still didn't see that many hikers on the trail or even here in town that would overcrowd the place booking every room in the joint. I bumped into the two Brits I'd had dinner with previously up the trail and stopped to say hello. I was unable to stop myself from complaining. "I can't find a decent room. I checked half a dozen teahouses, and nobody will give me a room." I grumbled.

"Yeah. They fill up because it's the hot springs, and we're all stopping to kick back," said one of the Brits. While the woman said, "But you've got another problem."

"What's that?" I asked.

"You're single," she said.

"What difference does that make?"

"People are usually hiking in groups or pairs and eat at the teahouses they're staying at, so they pay for food—two meals at a time, not one. It's not about the room's price; it's about the profit on the food."

A lightbulb went on in my head. "Oh, for Pete's sake! Why don't I simply pay more for the room? I'd be willing to do that!"

"It doesn't work that way," said the guy. "The hosts stick with their charge sheet and won't do an overcharge."

I shook my head in frustration. I was pissed. I wasn't about to spend one more night in that pigsty of a room and get COPD. I wasn't going to be robbed of my rights. These men stood in the way of my fair treatment, and I was having none of it.

Being angry was not outside my modus operandi. Dad and Mother had taught Agnes and me its ins and outs. I'm not sure many people would call them good role models in this regard, but we'd been kids raised to sleep with fingers plugged in our ears. That's how I learned anger's complexities—that anger is either short-lived or has the capacity for long-term-muscle-memory, like veins of ore buried deep in the ground—maybe, in my case gold.

Short-lived anger takes place in the moment; once vented, it's never revisited. Dad modeled that one summer when the family traveled to upstate Michigan to visit Mother's uncle. Babcia was loaded into the car along with all of her belongings. There was a sack of pots and pans, a thick pierzyna (feather quilt), and two large 18" X 24" religious pictures—one of Christ's crucifixion and the other of the Virgin Mary holding baby Jesus—all stowed neatly in the Hudson's trunk. That year, Dad (big on shortcuts) wanted to get us to Detroit by cutting across Ontario, Canada via Buffalo.

At the Canadian border crossing, a Canadian guard had a different idea. He looked into the car and asked, "Where were you born, sir?" "Connecticut," Dad replied. "And you, Ma'am?" he asked, nodding to Babcia in the backseat. Unfortunately, Babcia, who only spoke a few words of English, was not a US citizen and had no green card. When this became clear, the guard turned us around, pointing us back to the US. Dad angrily drove away only to stop at the nearest liquor store to buy a bottle of wine. This he gulped from a paper cup poured out by Mother as he drove into the middle of the night, speeding along the northern edge of Ohio. Then, going through Cleveland—I awoke—the car bumped and jumped over the tangle of railroad tracks that filled the city streets.

Dad, well-oiled by then, jolted us across one set of tracks after the other. Then, suddenly, the car let out a grinding sound as it lurched to the right. Dad shouted, "Goddammit to hell!" as we rattled to a stop by the side of the road where the thing refused to budge another inch. He got out to see the drive shaft hanging under the car. He stood in the street and swore.

Somehow as the night went on, I don't remember exactly how; the car got towed to a garage where we slept in the backseat waiting for the mechanic to come in the morning. A U-bolt had broken, and the repairs set us back an entire day. Dad quietly cursed his way through the ordeal, plus its cost, making for a glum atmosphere in our little group huddling in the backroom of the gas station eating baloney sandwiches.

Later that afternoon, leaving Cleveland behind, we entered Southern Michigan, and Dad spotted a Burma-shave sign yodeling out its message at the top of his lungs. Soon, he broke into "Red River Valley," then into "You Are My Sunshine," singing it for Mother dissolving the dim mood in the car and in my heart. He never revisited that incident. That was short-lived anger. Yet there was one incident that he did revisit, that we all revisited time and time again.

And that incident was an entirely different animal—what I learned as long-term muscle-memory anger. That anger arrived home one day with Dad holding his stomach, his face contorted in a foul scowl. Groaning, he dove for the toilet. He emerged face flushed and headed to the kitchen to fix himself an Alka Seltzer, this time skipping the herbs.

"My stomach's killing me," he said, dropping into a chair. Soon he was up again to rush into the bathroom, puking a veritable Niagara Falls. "Goddammit! I've been poisoned," he yelled, his bald head hovering over the toilet, glowing red. "They've poisoned me, the sons-of-bitch-bastards! They put stuff in my food trying to kill me!" he boomed on accusing "them" whoever they were…over and over again. And because Dad was never sick, something about that incident pushed him over the edge. For three days, his volcanic anger raged as he groped between bed and toilet. A strange fervor ignited in him. One that cycled round and round, rooting the incident deeper and deeper in his psyche—and in mine—turning it into *a thing* that belonged to the whole family. Making it (*his* food poisoning) burrow into *my* muscle memory because he refused to give up that initial anger, dipping into it time and time again.

The anger lessons were hard. A lot got wired to my jaw, and I practiced them in school. In fourth grade, a kid cut the water-fountain line only to get the sharp edge of my tongue. This flare-up got me a report-card check "needs to control anger." The teacher obviously didn't see the injustice of the kid's behavior the way I had. Hard-wired by Dad's responses to the things that bugged him, I expressed my anger too but with different intent—I wanted fairness. And that's what now drove me to act to get myself a decent room in Tatopani.

I wasn't going to die of black lung disease in a revolting attic just because hotel keepers wanted to make a buck on food instead of giving me, a single woman, a decent room to sleep in. I set my jaw.

I combed the street, surveying the teahouses deciding on the biggest and nicest one closest to the hot springs. I'd passed two Danes standing by the roadside and went back to take in their demeanors. The man was tall, blond-haired, while the woman had the looks of a model—a classic blond-haired, blue-eyed Scandinavian Venus. They both looked congenial. *They will do*, I said to myself. I stopped and smiled at them, and they smiled back at me. We began with the usual conversation of who, what, where, when: "I'm Anya," "I'm

Paul." "I'm Helle." Was she wearing a scent? What was it? Citrus? No, musk.

Then I let out my frustration and told them how I couldn't get a decent room. They sympathized. I asked, "I was wondering if you could help me?"

"With what?" Paul asked as he looked down at my 5'3" frame.

I explained. "I've been trying to get a decent room here since last night, but I'm being told there are none."

"What do you mean? There are plenty of rooms," said Paul.

"Well, last night, I slept in an attic that filled with smoke from the kitchen below."

"What! Poor thing!" Helle exclaimed in accented English.

"Oh. Ha-ha." Paul laughed, not unsympathetically shaking his head. I squinted my eyes at him and explained my dilemma that I was single against the economic framework of the teahouses.

"That's not fair," said Helle.

"Will you help me?" I asked and spelled out the role they would play to get me a decent room.

Amused, Helle and Paul agreed to assist me.

For me, it became simple math. To get a suitable room, I'd create an illusion where one guest equaled three. Now, I'm not a liar. Dishonesty wasn't part of Dad and Mother's culture. Living with their brand of alcoholism meant that Agnes and I parented our parents, so there was no need for the protection that lies give. I'd learned, living in that untidy reality, lying was not to be used lightly (if done at all). I believed lies were an avoidable device resulting in bad karma. But, struggling now to get a nice room, a part of me refused to be discredited, and I *was* mad. Anger's fists shoved me across a boundary that was important to me—fairness and honesty—making me lie to get the treatment I deserved.

Helle, Paul, and I headed for the teahouse I had selected—a two-story with several separate buildings. We entered it and approached the host standing behind his desk. He was neatly dressed, dark-haired, with unemotional eyes set above an unsmiling jaw.

"Namaste," I said, folding my hands in front of my breast, "Is it possible to book a room for two nights?"

The host eyed us, glancing at Paul and Helle. I had instructed my two tall, blond cohorts to merely stand behind me mute. I wondered if they wore smiles on their faces. And I counted on pretty Helle messaging the host with the same feminine eau de cologne vibes that I'd seen pass between herself and Paul.

The host looked back at me, then again at Helle and Paul, taking his time sizing us up. It was nine in the morning, not the usual time hikers came for rooms. Did it feel suspicious to him? I wasn't backing down. Deciding I needed some big guns, I visualized my cobra streaming from the top of my head, spiraling with Helle, Paul, and the clerk. I accepted that he, as well as I—and everyone else alive on the planet—had this magnificent energy within them—and that my visualization might help me with my predicament.

"How many rooms?" he asked, his voice cool.

There was no movement behind me; I glanced back at my companions to see the edges of Helle's blue eyes turned up. Then calmly, thinking of the stinking night I had spent, I gave the host a measured smile and said, "One room. Do you have a large one?"

He paused, scrutinizing—was he calculating rupees, or did he smell the lie of omission? Shamelessly, I eyed him steadily and purposely magnified the cobras embracing each of us as I kept breathing inch by inch closer to my goal.

"Yes," I nodded, "One nice, spacious room will do it. Can you show us one?" I asked. He hesitated then slowly turned to grab a key off the backboard. Finally, he motioned for us to follow him. I didn't dare look at the Danes as we walked through the buildings to enter a large, clean, bright room with three beds.

The host looked at Helle and Paul, asking, "You like this one?"

They grinned widely and nodded approvingly. Helle said, "Very much."

"Oh, yes. This is good," I said. "Yes, we'll take it. Thank you."

We went back to reception, where I paid for the room and board for two nights.

Helle, Paul, and I walked to the road grinning at the math scam we'd just pulled off.

"Thanks for helping me," I said.

"Helle laughed, "We needed the entertainment." "Yeah, it was good!" Paul said. They gathered up their backpacks from behind a wall, and we shook hands. Gratefully, I hugged them, inhaling Helle's scent. Paul said, "Bon Voyage, maybe to meet you again down the trail." I knew that would never happen—their long legs and agile bodies would propel them faster than I could ever go. And I never did see them again, but I never forgot their generosity helping me fashion an illusion to get what turned out to be the best room I was to stay in on the circuit

Lying to the host that day was a strange breakthrough, a dipping into shadow parts, a "biting through." Or maybe it wasn't a lie, more a sin of omission. I was not a liar. Living with two alcoholic parents, Agnes and I never had any rules to go against. So, maybe, that morning, I'd dipped into a dim reality propelled by anger to create a bit of fairness in the world... for me, a woman traveling solo in a land controlled by men. And it occurred to me that there was no way I was ever rejecting those shadow parts if that's what you call anger birthing a lie. No! Those were valuable parts, parts that got me what I needed to stay happy.

As far as Gome was concerned, I knew that he would find me. I was sure there was a network among the guides and teahouse hosts, and he'd get the message where I was staying. I'm not sure if Gome ever told the host that I was a single traveler without two buddies, but I didn't care. I was in. And a time, that year, never came again when I was on the road and had to lie. Still, the insidious pattern of denying me, a single woman, a decent room would repeat itself over and over again throughout India.

The following days in Tatopani, I enjoyed the hot springs. Once settled in my room, I slipped into my bathing suit and flip-flops, ambling to the hot springs. I did my laundry and got into the pool to soak my bones. Too shallow to swim in, I still submerged, coming up with my hair clinging to my neck, droplets rolling down my back. A sigh of relief escaped me. Golden butterflies moved in and out of nearby bushes. Sun rays glimmered through the clear water rippling my shadow cast at the bottom, breaking it into parts, then reassembling it back into a whole. I welcomed the soak, my muscles appeased.

As I melted into the warmth of the springs. I imagined all past hurt, marital pain draining from me, sending its dregs into the mothering flow of Kaligandaki River, rushing below the bank. Emptying, cleansing, letting go…wounded particles of me…no longer holding taint for my future. More butterflies rose.

Two women joined me in the pool, and we chatted. A dark-haired woman said, "Hi, I'm Monrova, and this is Paula," pointing to the bikini-clad woman with her.

"Hey," said Paula.

"I'm Anya. Where have you been?"

"We came up from Ghorepani and did the Poon Hill climb. You?"

"Flew to Jomsom and went up to Muktinath. And here I am."

"Muktinath! Did you go over the pass?"

"No. I've been hiking for a couple of weeks now. I was in the Mt. Everest region with a yoga group from back home.…"

Monrova, Paula, and I struck up a friendly conversation sharing the details of our trips. Then, I invited them to join me for dinner at my teahouse.

After dinner with my new buddies, I went back to my room and got into bed with a book. I thought of Agnes and what she would have said about the whole deal of me "biting through" getting a room in that way. She'd been in the thick of it with me scoured by Dad and Mother's conflict—in the same ring of anger that had permeated my core—maybe even my soul.

And I recalled that the phrase "biting through" came from the I Ching, the Chinese Book of Changes (Wilhelm Translation, 1950 86-9). Dori, of course, had introduced me to it a long time ago. It involved asking a question (money, career, love) then tossing three coins six times (combos of heads and tails) to form a hexagram that rendered a judgment, plus a metaphor, whose lesson was provided in the book. And it was Lesson 21 that charmed me now. A reading that called for action to "bite energetically through the obstacle." The metaphor for the obstacle was perfect: "The obstruction is due to a table-bearer and traitor who is interfering and blocking the way" (86). And best, the lesson said: "Biting Through has success" (86). I thought of all the obstacles I had bitten through to gain entrance to things I wanted in my life. Agnes and I would have laughed together. Especially over the part that said, "No Blame." (87).

The room I'd secured was truly a suite. The sun washed through the large window, and I turned it into a yoga and meditation studio before heading to the pools. During meditation, my cobra rose over my head, a silent guiding light. There was no dialogue between us, never had been, which I appreciated. After all, I was seeing things (so to speak) but didn't want to start hearing things, too. But, although its image gave me a certain amount of comfort when it appeared, the cobra wasn't a personal God I prayed to.

I had time now to think about my relationship with this luminous spirit within me that was shifting. At times, it was golden, then iridescent, then a rich bluish red. The imagery of singing bowls spun fast through my chakras—my pelvis, throat, and in the center of my brain. Although I recognized it as a profound energy system, it was still something I had to come to grips with. *Where was it taking me?* I really didn't know, but I did know I didn't want the journey to be radical or traumatizing. I wanted it—I guess a bit naively—whatever *it* was, to be beneficial and maybe even somewhat mundane. Which might have been an indicator that I had some fear of its power, or perhaps a good amount of respect. My imagery on the trail was changing; its candelabra branching mystified me.

Synchronicity on Poon Hill

Dawn, in pinks and blues, rolled out of its eastern bed, yawning warmth. The trek to Ghorepani would take several hours and pass by small villages. The trail became a steady ascent that turned away from the Gandaki—moving from the feminine to the masculine energy of Shiva. As we went along, the terrain changed, revealing sharp drop-offs.

Gome perched his day-glow Yankees cap high on his forehead and attempted to describe the Poon Hill climb. "Poon Hill…" he sputtered, using many hand gestures, but again a lot of it was lost on me.

From *Lonely Planet*, I knew Poon Hill really wasn't a "hill." It was listed as an ascent to 10,500 feet which tourists climb for the view. And similar to any other sightseer, I wanted to see "the best viewpoint of spectacular mountain scenery on the Annapurna Circuit." It was doable because steps had been built into the side of the mountain to assist climbers in getting to the top with relative ease to see the sunrise.

Gome and I met other trekkers on the path. Two young guys, in particular, caught my attention. The taller, about thirty years old, was hobbling along while the other encouraged him, groping at his elbow. Gome and I stopped. "Hi," I said. "How's it going?" knowing very well from the look on the guy's face, it wasn't *going*.

"It's his knee," said his partner. "He twisted it yesterday, and we're trying to get to Ghorepani to a teahouse to rest."

"I have some Advil in my bag. Do you think that'll help?" The guy with the knees looked at me uncertainly and said, "No, thanks. It'll be OK. I just have to get off this fucking mountain." We left them, and I whispered: *Thank you, my knees. Thank you.*

At noon, we stopped at a cafe loaded with trekkers. A menu board nailed by the door listed spaghetti, and I drooled. I sat at a table with other hikers, and after introductions, I took off my boots and rubbed my ankles. It felt good to release my feet. A large sociable, black mongrel roamed the dining area, sniffing guests, getting pats, and looking for a handout. Unlike the half-dead, boney dogs I'd seen in Kathmandu, this one looked well fed.

"How has it gone?" I asked a woman called Karen, sitting at the same table.

"This whole trip for us is about getting to the Sanctuary in one piece. John's ankle is starting to kill him, and there're only so many drugs I can give him out of my stash before knocking him out. Drugs at this altitude can make someone go over the edge literally, and I don't want that to happen."

"Can someone carry his backpack?" This had been my way out to avoid strain.

Karen said, "Maybe. But I don't know. I'll have to check with the restaurant owner," and she looked at John nodding her head. *Good, I thought. She's taking charge.* But John said, "I can manage."

A large bowl of spaghetti covered with sauce came from the kitchen and was set before me. I almost inhaled it after so much dal bhat. Karen, John, and I chewed the rag some more, but then it was time to hit the road. I got up to find the bathroom and mistakenly walked into the kitchen. I was greeted by a battered collection of pots and pans piled high on shelving behind the cook, who stirred a pot with steam roiling to the roof. We exchanged smiles.

At that moment, I heard the sound of dripping water at my feet and glanced down. (There are mistakes I've made, not serious, not critical, not earth-shattering, not anything, but this one burns in my memory fueled by the sharp contrast to Mother's tidy, always Lysol scrubbed kitchen, and Agnes's kennel.)

The dripping was coming from a water faucet protruding about eighteen inches off the floor from the wall where dishes piled haphazardly. In their midst, a colander brimming with steaming spaghetti drained into the sink's basin. And lap, lap, lap. The big, black mongrel…pink tongue extended…slurped up the spaghetti from the strainer. My gut wrenched. I gagged. Groaning, I snorted in disgust before bursting into laughter. Plainly, a cosmic joke on me! Because from that, it didn't take long for me to recall the day that Agnes and I, as kids, came across Dad cleaning fish behind the shed.

"Come here a second, Girls," Dad had said, his eyes sparkling. He groped in his baggy trousers for his pocket knife unfolding its thin blade. "Open your mouths." Agnes and I acquiesced, watching him jab the knife-edge into the trout's eyes, popping a glossy eyeball into each of our mouths. We chewed and swallowed them without any great reluctance—pre-sushi—Dad being thirty years ahead of the times. Now, I wondered, had this dog here shared my spaghetti, or was it *me* sharing his?

Ghorepani is one of the largest villages on the Annapurna Circuit. Its buildings hang on the sides of hills at 9,429 feet. Located at the base of Poon Hill, its draws hikers and tourists from Kathmandu like magnets, people wanting to see the unobstructed views that include the peaks of Annapurna South, Annapurna III, Dhampus, Dhaulagiri II, Hiunchuli, Machapuchare, and others. This time, I had no trouble finding a room, had dinner, and settled into bed early to prepare for the 5 AM climb.

Before dawn, Gome was at the Snow View Lodge to pick me up. I put on my headlamp and got in line with him behind about a hundred other people. We climbed up the 35,000 steps cut into the mountainside. The predawn was moonless, and headlamps twinkled in the dark as the group filed slowly upward-moving in one rhythm toward the summit. The big dipper seemed to hang upside down over Machupachae.

My feet, my ankles, my knees, my hips all held—*Thank you, God*, I said. I felt like Wonder Woman, my body serving me, a biotic miracle. Still, it wouldn't hurt to throw my kath to the top of Poon Hill, like I'd done when falling ill with my Yoga Group. I visualized a golden stream of energy—coiled in my belly. I mentally unfurled it, imagining a grappling hook at one end, which I hurled to the mountaintop. I anchored it there with the other end secured to my body's core. Step by step by step, I allowed the golden stream of energy to draw me to the summit.

The climb, a good 1,000 feet, took forty minutes. A heavy frost coated the steps. The light from the east tiptoed over the mountains just as we reached the summit. Its glow cut across the pale sky, holding grayish clouds marring the view of the surrounding skyline. The ground was covered with yellow grasses and the remnants of wildflowers. A falcon glided by the ridge. Like a pack of Druids, we all faced East waiting for the sun to rise over Annapurna Mountain. When it finally did, it peeked out brilliantly but ever so briefly. I was disappointed. Clouds occluded the mountain. I had been brushing shoulders with these giants for the past week. Now they were touchable, and I wanted to be held in their arms, not at bay. I experienced a bewildering reserve even though I was standing at eye level with the mountains. The others on the hill milled about snapping pictures. I felt alone, but that didn't last for long. I turned to see Tina and Colley from the yoga camp outside of Kathmandu coming toward me. We fell into each other's arms with hugs.

"Hey, you guys! Tina, Colley! My God. You're here!" I almost cried.

"Anya! I don't believe it! We found you again!" Tina said.

"Where have you been?" I asked.

"We hiked around the Kathmandu Valley, hung out in some villages, and now we're here," Colley said.

We laughed, unable to get our stories out fast enough. We'd all ended up at the same place simultaneously—uncanny synchronicity—one that played out throughout the remainder of my trip in Nepal, reaching into India and Egypt. When it was time to go, Tina, Colley, and I hugged, saying goodbye, not knowing if we'd ever meet again. They were also going to India, as was I, but India is a big place.

Double Rainbows

Gome and I took the trail to Chhomrung in the direction of the Annapurna Base Camp. Junipers, pines, and bamboo grew along the track. No flowers or herbs were left in bloom. Only rhododendron bushes their green-purple leaves gracing the hillsides.

As we ascended the track, the sun-bleached light gave way to heavy clouds, and the temperature dropped. A heavy quilt of damp moisture permeated the air, and I felt chilled. Dressed in my skirt, I called Gome to stop. "It's getting cold," I said. Then pointed to my backpack, "I need to change into my pants." He handed me the pack, and I dug through, finding my sweat pants, rain pants, a polar fleece layer, and jacket. I slipped into the bushes and put them on. Orange lichens clung to the surrounding rocks. Marijuana grew wild in the shrubs.

The weather was changing fast, and we quickened our pace. I'd been hoping it would clear and come in dry. A hot spot was developing on the ball of my left foot. There was nothing and still more *nobody* on the trail. We were gaining elevation and moving slower than on the flats. The rain amplified the land's earthy smells.

After two hours, I heard footsteps coming up behind us. A porter carrying a large pack passed then stopped and greeted us, chatting briefly with Gome. Five minutes later, a Japanese man followed up the trail.

"Namaste," he said. "Namaste," I said. He was carrying a green hooked staff used for working out knotted pressure points. I was amused.

"I have one of those at home," I said, pointing to the staff. "How's it working?"

"The body has pain, and this hook keeps me going."

"I hope it helps," I said.

He nodded agreeably and continued on his way, turning back, saying, "Better get moving. Might be a storm coming."

As he disappeared around the corner, I felt relieved that my body, feet, and brain were running like a fine-tuned Ferrari. I was glad I had gotten over the food poisoning from the Yoga trek, glad my stomach was cooperating. But I was worried about my tush. Each evening, I'd been carefully washing the incision Dr. Winsor had made. I planned to check it more thoroughly when I got to the teahouse, but now I was getting hungry.

"Gome, eat?" I motioned toward my mouth.

"OK," he said while pointing up the hill and holding up his fingers, indicating twenty minutes to go. Within a half-hour, we came to a house on the trail, and we stopped. A Nepali man came out and spoke to Gome, who ordered dal bhat and rice, still the only thing I was willing to eat after the stringy chicken episode.

I sat at an outside table. Several children played in the area. Thirty minutes later, there was still no food. I felt chilled and put on my gloves. The sky promised to open up at any minute. I knew cooking at high altitudes was a challenge, but I wanted to be on our way, thinking we were wasting time. I grew more and more impatient. Finally, after another twenty minutes of waiting, I peeked into the kitchen. The man preparing the food squatted on the floor, squeezing an unrecognizable mixture in his hands. When it came out of the kitchen and set before me, I frowned, tasted it, and called the children over. I was not remotely interested in eating anything that might get me sick again. Still, I knew that living in this setting, the children's digestive systems could handle anything. One girl, about seven, fed the three and one-year-old toddlers in the group. A boy about four or five was picking scraps out of the garbage box—apple peels—eating them. This was not a trip for foodies. I could wait to get to the teahouse. I wasn't starving. Gome and I hiked on.

The mist thickened into the afternoon. The wind picked up, growing steadily. Sleet soon pelted, pocking my face with tiny stings. I crouched into the wind wiping my forehead from a layer of crusting ice. I raised the hood of my jacket and zipped it tight around my chin. Gome and I trudged over the roots of gnarled rhododendrons that stood thirty feet high. Dark panels of wetness formed across his back from melting sleet. Pine tree branches overhead began to sag under the sleet as the cold wrenched its knuckles on us. Footing got slow. We picked our way for another hour through rivulets of water. By this time, I'd had enough. We'd been hiking for eight hours.

But it took yet another half hour until we rounded a bend to the back of the mountain. As we turned that corner, the sleet stopped, and the clouds began to break. Several houses were built into the angle of the hill, hovering over a slice of the valley below. Fifteen more minutes, we arrived to see a sizeable two-story tea house perched owl-like on the side of the gorge. Gome pointed to it. I grunted in relief.

The teahouse's host gave me a room on the second-floor balcony. All faced the opposite mountain. The room's walls were rickety thin as tissue. The bed had a mattress about three inches thick, clean, and surprisingly comfortable. I settled in and checked out the wound on my butt. It was doing fine.

The late afternoon sky still held light. I put on a jacket, hat, and gloves and plunked my drained body into a chair on the balcony. I inhaled the brisk air. The storm had passed, and the sun began to find breaks in the clouds to shoot rays diagonally across the valley, streaming its last minutes of fire through a crystal mist. I put my feet up on the railing and sipped my water bottle. Gradually, the sun rode to the bottom of the western sky, throwing patterns of scattered light on the wall of dark pines growing opposite the teahouse.

A rainbow shimmied into view. Colors bent, reflected, and arched in water droplets suspended over the mountain. Within a few minutes, a second ribbon formed above the first. I gazed at the sequined arc, the double rainbow—red, yellow, green, blue, indigo, violet—which reversed its reflection in the top. It went on for an hour, intensifying.

How intelligent Mother Nature is! I thought. I watched her hand script her signature across the sky, an illuminated Chartres Cathedral. I took in the transparent prisms imprinting the rainbow's image into my mind's eye, a forever snapshot of contentment. Calm jaw, calm hands, calm legs, calm feet, calm brain…a place within me taking a deep breath free of struggles—the past, the dissertation, the house, Tim. And I gave thanks for the endings and to Tim, who had supported me financially through the Ph.D. process, barely, but nonetheless. Who, in retrospect, I had to admit had transformed my life, pushing me forward in the direction I needed to go—yet another gatekeeper giving me a shove toward transformation—cracking my shell, making me face reality, releasing new growth. I felt the breath of the Earth cradling me, and I laughed, marveling at my luck.

At dinner that night, I sat with two Brits and a group of four trekkers from Australia. We exchanged stories and shared hopes of having our legs hold out till we finished with our treks. Afterward, in my room, I lay in bed reading with my headlamp. Soon I heard the couple next door entering their cell whispering softly, cooing to each other. I could hear them roll into the bed, wedged the same as mine against the thin paper wall dividing our spaces. More cooing. Breathing. Heavier. Low giggles building into moans, building into sounds of passion trying to be quiet bare inches from my head. I stifled my giggles, putting my hand over my mouth, not wanting to disturb them… but would they even have heard me? I laughed to myself, cheering them on.

Darkness fell, and the teahouse quieted except for a woman coughing non-stop at th end of the hall. After about thirty minutes, I dug out my lone Alka Seltzer Plus Nighttime cold tablet, went out, and knocked on her door.

"Hi," I whispered, "I'm Anya."

She opened the door and said, "Hi," turning to cough back into the room.

"I have this cold tablet that'll help you with your cough. Do you want it?"

She looked at me doubtfully. "Do you have another?" she asked.

"No, this is it."

"No, I can't take it then."

"Yeah. Please take it. You need it, right?"

"Yeah, but what if you need it some time?"

"Hey, right now, you need it, so take it. If I need something, it'll show up." And I thought of Dr. Winsor in Pokhara, and Dr. Martha in Ghasa. "Trust me on this one. If I need, I will find," I said.

She eyed me reluctantly, taking the tablet.

In the night, I got up and went to the toilet to pee at the end of the balcony. As I approached, holding my tiny three-inch flashlight, eyes glinted at me from the corner of the floor. I stopped dead in my tracks backing away. *What kind of animal could be up here*, I thought? Did they have skunks or raccoons in Nepal? I didn't move. It didn't move. I could see by its shape that it was too large to be a raccoon or even a deer's head. It was still. Approaching it, I bent to get a closer look seeing a mound of black, shaggy hair on a creepy severed head. The dead eyes of a yak glared up at me. I covered my mouth, not wanting to laugh out loud. In the pitch dark, I used the bathroom. There was no sound coming from the coughing woman.

Trekking the Edge

The Annapurna Base Camp (ABC) was not a long haul but a steep one. We'd be gaining 9,613 feet from the lowest point on the circuit at Tatopani to 13,000 feet at the camp. There were several routes to choose from and to get there, we'd need to spend a night at a place called Hinko Cave.

Trekking along the flank of the South Annapurna glacier is risky. Choosing this route, we were on the narrowest of trails dangling on the side of the mountain. It was gambling with Mother Nature, who always held the last card when hiking in the mountains. Plus, out here, the weather was law. The danger was palpable. My core told me: *Careful. Be aware. Make each step count. Reach into the energy system of the earth and draw its electro-magnetic currents* into your core. *On this trail, you need to be held by the earth as if in the arms of a lover.*

Step, step, step. Boot on dirt, dirt on boot…step, step, step… Gome and I picked our way, navigating the mountain's sharp embankments that dropped hundreds of feet into the valley below. I tried to keep my eyes away from the downhill pull, my feet engaged in prayer while hugging the trail. I recited an Our Father, a Hail Mary, and then just *Please!* Trying to visualize a strong *energy kath* holding me steady like I'd done with my Yoga Group. Still, the tips of my toes had awakened to the possible nightmare of falling off the mountain, so I had a hard time.

Gome, ahead of me, marched on for forty-five minutes like this, crossing numerous slides of fresh gravel. Sand and rocks drained over the trail's rims. The narrow ribbon of the track, scarcely wide enough for one person to pass, was not wide enough for me to cram down my growing unease. Glancing into the abyss, there was nothing but an unrecoverable drop. The electrons in my body tingled, a charge I didn't like. With several hours to go, I felt anxious and ungrounded. Was the altitude getting to me? I stopped to take a breath to look up the mountain. Areas of loose rock hung suspended on the overhead slope. I gasped. We had been crossing avalanches!

My nerves felt frayed. Could a landslide come tearing down on us? Taking us with it? I kept walking; there was no turning back. My shaky hands almost reached out to grab Gome's coat-tails for support. Instead, I took another deep breath, used my staff for balance, and pulled myself together to center on the gritty path.

For a half-hour, Gome and I snuck over slide after mini-slide. Nobody else was on the trail, and now I knew why. Picking my way across the face of the mountain, my feet felt numb, and I realized their brief, tenuous connection to the earth. My gut understood the meaning of my own temporary moment rooted in this planet. It was easy to recognize that we each have an expiration date, and I didn't want this one to be mine. True, I *was* just a drop of dust, but this drop of dust had made a promise to cycle back, and this drop of dust wanted to stay intact.

We picked our way on the thin, suspension-bridge pathway edging the cliffs. Rounding the face of a craggy outcropping, I heard bells tinkling. Within minutes, a tribe of goats came toward us. There was no choice. I stepped gingerly to the upside slope, yielding the way on the narrow promenade for the goats to stream past bleating, their shepherd not far behind smiling broadly.

Not long after that, the trail leveled out, and I felt relief being on better footing. Gome and I trekked for another ten minutes. Then, all at once against our backs, the mountain thundered, sending a rolling vibration beneath our feet. I froze, as did Gome. My mind screamed, *"Avalanche!"*. Stuck in my tracks, my whole body shook as the sound crashed around us. And I imagined the earth's skin lacerated, debris being thrown across the mountainside that took us with it. The crack echoed throughout the valley and hung in the air. My heart pounded, then quiet. We turned to see thirty-foot-long chunks of muddy ice torn from a ledge sprawled fifteen feet behind us. We stared blankly at the clumps of earth, avoided looking at each other, and said nothing. It would have been effortless, I thought, to have moved through the mantle of Time just then. We went on to Hinko Cave past Kuldighar and Dobang to spend the night.

That night I dreamed. Hooded skulls surrounded me. One appeared over the sun as its rays poured out from the thing's interior. A thick mask peeled off my face while my whole body split in two except for a toughness cinched by a daypack buckle across my heart which, as I dreamed on, suddenly sprung loose.

The Annapurna Sanctuary

Gome and I climbed. The altitude went from 11,000 to 12,000 to 13,000 feet. The air thinned. Cold burrowed into my lungs. A few inches of snow covering patches of russet grass crunched beneath our feet. The trail's fingertips barely clung to the sides of the mountain, which was suspended above a cavernous valley shaped by eons of Earth's labor. I felt like I was passing an invisible entry point guarded by two giants, Machapuchare and Hiunchuli, who beckoned me into the Annapurna Sanctuary—a coliseum of rock, ice, and snow.

Now, encircled by mountains, I struggled to take it all in *There! There! There!* I found myself in the center of a singing bowl—a soprano sun humming its harmonic hymn round the frosty lips of the highest peaks in the world. I felt empty and filled.

Gome pulled me away to reception. I got a room in one of the dormitories; the camp had fewer than thirty guests. Dinner, I was told, would be served in the communal building at seven. We walked to the dorm where Gome deposited my backpack in a sparse, unheated room; and, as usual, disappeared. I took out my sleeping bag, filthy by now, but it no longer mattered. I'd reached my destination, and I was glad. I settled my things in for a two-night stay, after which I expected a downhill climb off the mountain to catch a bus back to Pokhara. Outside I took in the Himalayas.

In a nearby doorway, a woman—in wide blue and white striped leggings, a brown wool cap pulled over her head—was bent arranging her pack. Martha, lady doctor, glanced up, a grin opening her face.

"Hey, Anya!" She yelled.

"Martha!" I hugged her to me. Hugged my healer.

"How's your butt?" She laughed.

"Almost healed. Your therapeutic henna hands did the trick!"

"Glad to hear it. How's the bod?

"OK," I said, and I meant it.

"You? Your husband?"

"Good. He survived it with a little help from his wife's expertise, of course." We laughed and chatted.

"See you at dinner," she said. "We need to bulk up for the descent."

"OK," I said. And I couldn't be happier for the sweetness of seeing Dr. Martha again to thank her yet one more time for ministering to my wound.

There isn't much light in the Annapurna Sanctuary in late November. Maybe seven hours at best. Gradually, the sun faded behind the western mountains. I walked toward one of the glaciers to take in the panoramic view. A group of famous massifs who'd risen from the ocean floor ages before surrounded me. They included: Lachenal and Tilicho Peaks, Nilgiri Himal North, Annapurna I, and South, Annapurna Fang, Tarke Kang, plus Machapuchare, and Hiunchuli. The tallest reached over 26,000 feet. They took my breath.

It had been a long time, but at that moment, I was intoxicated by the drama I saw. This time not by a leafy New England woodland harboring lone tiger-lilies—but from Earth's superstructure— the Himalaya— beyond words, opulent beauty. Looking from Machapuchare to Hiunchuli then back again at the surrounding Annapurnas, I was a greedy moviegoer binging on a film themed "Eternity," one animated in towers of granite. And I was unable to get enough of its actors, its dialogue, its plot still thickening as the mountains pushed toward the heavens each year inching upward.

Yes! I understood! I could feel the presence of Shiva or God or Divine Mother Kali. Feel it in my core. Feel centered and happy at once as I repeated: *Thank you, thank you, God!* And not just for my body's strength getting me there, but for Gome's guidance, for the weather holding, for my cobra, for every breath I took. And still more... *Thank you God!...* for all the refusals of my life that brought me to this treasured place. *Thank you* for the endings of past years—all of it; because I, like they, these mountains before me, had stood up under pressure.

As I watched the scene play out around me, I memorized their script... grandeur and might... eleven Goliaths on Mother Nature's stage. Gradually, she brought in low wisps of clouds curling over the actors' heads, brushing their peaks occluding the scenery. The light drained from the bowl. Finally, a breeze began to whisper, drawing the day's final curtain on the massifs.

And I felt at peace with myself, at peace with everyone I loved and who loved me. A backlog of *shoulds* and *woulds* and *coulds*—no longer needed to survive—were swallowed in the thin air. And that smile, that false smile plastered on my childhood face so long ago signaling that everything was OK when it wasn't, was no longer needed. Because now everything *was* OK. Composure. I was falling in love again—and again and again and again—falling in love with Mother Nature—and maybe the mother or the feminine hidden inside of me. And there wasn't anything more to say or be: It was simply *Thank you!* for having reached this rare stop in my life where the mountains held my hands and my heart and my soul. I was full.

About thirty of us gathered for dinner in the dining lodge. There was, of course, no central heating in any of the buildings. We all wore our coats and hats. Heavy blankets draped the long rectangular tables we sat at. And every so often, a server came from the kitchen with a bucket of smoldering charcoal embers, and he shoveled them into scuttles under the table. Heat radiated around our feet—a delicious system!

Dinner came. Dal bhat loaded with potatoes and beans and vegetables. The group was jovial. It included Australians, some French who sang loudly after dinner, and a few Germans who talked among themselves. The only ones missing were my Danish saviors, yet I was sitting next to a friendly Aussie. "Name's Bert," he said. "Where you been?"

"I'm Anya. I hiked from Jomsom down."

"Man, my joints are killing me, but I've got a few more days to Pokhara than back to Kathmandu. You?"

"I'm in one piece. I had a guide who carried my backpack."

"Good for you. Saved your buns," Bert laughed.

"The only problem, Bert, was that we got into a sandstorm on the first day, and it ruined my camera. I have no pictures of my trek."

"Me? I ran out of film."

I said, "I've got plenty of film. You can have it. My camera's a goner."

"You sure?"

"Yeah. I'll try to get a couple of disposable cameras back in Kathmandu. But first, can I borrow your camera in the morning to shoot a roll of film for myself? Then, you can have the rest of it after that. It's useless to me."

"Deal."

At dinner's end, when the tea came, Martha held up her tea glass, we all followed suit.

"To arriving in the Sanctuary in one piece!" she beamed.

"To trekking!" We all shouted, raising our tea glasses slurping the hot liquid.

"To getting the job done…to the finish line…to personal victories….to make it off the mountain in one piece…" The merriment of dinner was a kid's birthday party incredibly warming. But I knew the temperature in the night was going to drop well below freezing in the dorm; so, I ordered a liter of hot tea. I'd learned early that fuel in the inaccessible mountains was dear, making it impossible to ask for hot water for my water bottle. But to prevent my feet from becoming blocks of ice in the night, I could buy hot tea. When the tea came, I poured it into my water bottle, planning to also brush my teeth with it safely in the morning. I tucked it in my parka and walked to my room. By this time, the night sky was occluded, but I knew beyond that blanket of clouds lay the radiance of a billion twinkling stars.

In my room, I took off my boots, adjusted my coat, pulled my hat over my ears, and nestled into my sleeping bag, where I'd tucked my water bottle. As I fell off to sleep, a reverie from the family's annual journey to up-state Michigan slid through my consciousness. And

I re-dreamed the time Dad had tied a mattress to the top of the car before we had started off.

After driving for twelve hours and reaching northern Ohio, the time came to a stop for the night. Dad pulled the Hudson onto the edge of a field. He untied the mattress and threw it down on a slight incline, making it look like an adjustable bed. Exhausted, Mother, Babcia, Agnes, and I snuggled under a pierzyna, curling up to sleep. Dad crawled into the car's backseat. Stillness overspread the fields of the lush grasses. The summer sun gradually retired on the hem of the horizon, laying a carroty quilt.

It was the fifties, and reliably what little traffic there was soon ceased to a trickle. Then, slowly, darkness gathered up the five of us sleeping on the old mattress thrown by the roadside, a canopy of lacey stars overhead. As I fell asleep that night, long ago, I could hear lone cars passing by, their tires sizzling on the asphalt whining far into the distance.

In the morning, Dad pulled the mattress up from our makeshift open-air bed-chamber. It had left a rectangular imprint in the grass. Mother looked at it quizzically, nodding her head in its direction, and said, "It's like there's been a wedding here."

And that night in the frigid dormitory of the Annapurna Sanctuary, as I fell into a bottomless dream—cocooned warm in my sleeping bag, resting my head in one of the most sacred spots on the planet—I realized it was a marriage for me—one of mind, body, and soul.

Reattached to the Universe

The following day, I was up early. Bert lent me his camera, and I walked over a thin layer of snow away from the camp to take pictures. Deeper in the Sanctuary, I stopped to inhale the biting air pulling my parka around me. The sun's wintry light spiraled across the face of the glacial basin striking the massifs scraping their heads at 26,000 feet. They shouldered four blue-eyed glaciers. The Nepali had it right, calling the Sanctuary "The home of Shiva"—a colleague of Space and Time. The place issued staggering, dynamic power.

Being there that day, I still couldn't help but be moved...again... just like at Dhaulagiri and Niligiri. And I spun around, a human top, connecting with some magnetic helix I was sure emanated out of the earth. But more than that...being in that place...it was hard to ignore its seductive connection to the cosmos where the mountains reached toward billions of stars, toward miles of Universe that had no edges, none. And so, feeding there for that fragment of Time, the Universe (whom I felt to be an ally by now) held me captive in its palm—though insignificant— making me bigger.

At that moment, I believed yet more deeply in myself, a drop of dust now standing in the Annapurna Sanctuary, which was God's answer to the Grand Canyon, different but the same. Both used uninhibited vocabularies to write us Mother Nature's love letters. The Canyon in a calligraphic script, the Sanctuary using bold type. I felt humble. And as I took pictures collecting memories, an important current bore an openness in me, one that was unrestricted. I welcomed it, and I didn't care what happened: Who, what, where, or when? I was grounded, yet at the same time, I felt a fluidity surrounding me.

I finished my roll of film and walked back to find Bert. I gave him the camera and all my remaining rolls of film. If there was one thing that would burn forever in my life, it was that day. I'd come to receive what the mountains had to give, and I was in a space of quiet, of composure. Each breath I took intersected with the light of the stars hidden behind the curtains of blue sky, and that day, I banqueted on joy in the Sanctuary. The only thing left was for me to walk out in one piece.

Later that morning, Gome found me and began to babble, pointing in the direction of the dining hall. He was struggling to tell me something that sounded important. Pointing to the snow-covered ground, he said, "Ona, chopper here. Movie—tomorrow."

"What? A helicopter coming here?" I pointed down.

"Yes, Kathmandu. You go Kathmandu—chopper."

I stared at him. Was this right? If so, it sounded as if I could get a lift back to Kathmandu. My yoga group had done that returning from Eastern Nepal. Was there a chance I wouldn't have to trek the mountains out of the Sanctuary?

Gome tilted up his cap on his forehead and pointed toward the lodge.

"Right! Gome," I said, "Let's go to the dining hall to get the lodge manager to explain." When we found him, I asked, "What's up? Is a chopper coming tomorrow?"

He confirmed what Gome had said, "Yes, Madam. Tomorrow a movie crew comes. Bossman here already waiting for them."

"Bossman? Do you think I can hop a ride back to Kathmandu?" I asked, excitement rising in my throat.

"You talk to Bossman at lunch," he said.

"You go, Kathmandu chopper," Gome said, and I hoped he was right.

At lunchtime, Gome came to my room and motioned for me to follow him to the lodge. Inside, a guy—obviously the crew leader dressed neatly in casual sports clothes—sat at a table. I went over to him, putting on my best face, and said, "My guide here tells me there's a helicopter coming tomorrow. Is that right?"

"Yeah. It's coming in from Kathmandu to drop off supplies. We're here filming a Hyundai car commercial." I couldn't believe my ears. "Do you think I can hop a ride back to Kathmandu?"

"Let me check with the pilot in the morning when he comes in. I don't see why not."

"What's he going to charge?"

"I dunno. Maybe fifty US?"

I had been trekking for a total of twenty-one days. My legs, knees, and feet had done what I'd asked of them, and I was ready to go. When Bert came into the dining hall, I went over and told him what had transpired between the filmmaker and me.

"You're kidding? We can get our tired asses out of these mountains tomorrow?" I could see that he, same as everyone else, was finished with weeks of trekking. Sick of dirty clothes and weary of sleeping in bags that had fast become smelly overused potato sacks.

"I'm not kidding. I think it's going to run us about fifty US bucks each." His blue eyes twinkled. Later in the lodge, I pointed out the filmmaker. Bert, his buddy, and a few others asked him if they could also book a ride out.

I spent the rest of the day taking in as much of the Sanctuary as I could before departing. That night I bought another liter of hot tea for my water bottle, but I could hardly sleep. Nevertheless, this was going to be a boon, and I said a little prayer.

The following day after breakfast, Bert, the others, and I huddled near the narrow landing strip beside the buildings. The helicopter engines roared against the sides of the mountains, shattering the quiet as it dove into basecamp. When it landed, Bossman got in to ask if the pilot was willing to transport us back to Kathmandu. Then, exiting the chopper, he came over to us nodding his head. "Fifty bucks each. Pay the pilot in US dollars, and you're good to go. You leave in one hour." My happiness quotient jumped one thousand percent. I went to my room, gathered up my backpack, and dragged it to the helicopter. Bert and several others had secured seats as well.

Gome was standing with the other guides, and I motioned him over to pay him. What words did I have for him now? I'd depended on him. He'd been a silent escort guiding me safely and patiently, letting me align the whole of my being with the terrain, and myself, as I passed through the highest, most revered mountains on the planet into the belly of the Annapurna Sanctuary. He'd allowed me to slip into a zone where I felt one with the Earth.

"Gome, I'm leaving on the helicopter."

"OK," he nodded, "Good."

"I can't thank you enough. You were the best porter and guide I could have asked for." Of course, he garbled something I couldn't decipher, but it didn't matter. We smiled into each other's eyes and shook hands. I handed him the staff he'd gotten me and a pile of US bills. I knew Gome would walk home out of basecamp, probably taking days to get back to his family. Or would he go back to

Jomsom for another gig? He'd told me his home was somewhere at a distance, buried in the hills of Nepal to the west. I was never sure what his family was comprised of or if he had a wife or kids. Our vocabulary never got that far. I wished that my tone of voice conveyed all the gratitude I felt for his work that had allowed me to connect with the miracle of the place.

They called us to the helicopter. "Goodbye, Gome. Thank you so much!" and I folded my hands to my heart, "Namaste!"

"Namaste," he said as we bowed our heads together.

The helicopter took off, veering swiftly out over the basin's edges, taking flight—a fledging falling free of its nest. Out the window, Gome's figure shrunk in size—his neck sticking out of his shabby coat, his hat shading his inexpressive face. He was holding the staff in one hand and in the other a payday, what I hoped amounted to a princely sum. Although we had agreed on four bucks a day, I'd given him eighty US dollars hoping it was generous. As Gome faded—and to this day—his figure is still stamped in my brain… Yankee's baseball cap and all…never to be forgotten, never. He'd been one more gatekeeper in my life who'd helped me journey in the right direction.

As the chopper roared toward Kathmandu, my trekking circuit raced beneath me. A path laid down by fire and ice millions of years before. A space where I'd found grounding, reestablishing my sense of grit. Deep inside of me, in a corner, so yearning I couldn't access it consciously, an aperture of happiness opened to define the moment I found myself in. Resolve. I was shouting *Hello!*…to my body as resilient, my mind as empty, my heart as reaching for the future toward a world I knew was there calling me. All those power points, all of them! Outside and now inside me. At that moment, detached from the Earth, I felt re-attached to the Universe.

Night Goddess

After weeks of trekking, I was ready for a change. It was early December, and back in Kathmandu, I went to the airline office and booked my departure to Varanasi, India. I had two days to kill before leaving. I spent the time walking around town to take in yet more of the ancient wooden architecture and the bustle of its people for one last time. I was going to miss Nepal terribly. Ava had been right to cry her eyes out when she left. I wasn't crying, but I knew I wanted to come back someday. To soak it all in even deeper…into a part of me that felt like home.

On my last night, I went out to dinner. By now, it was the end of November and pitch black by late afternoon. With most lights turned off to conserve power in the city, I couldn't find the restaurant I was looking for. Searching, I bumped into a woman dressed in a baggy, lavender dress with gray hair tumbling to her waist

"Excuse me. Do you know where The Third Eye restaurant is?" I asked.

"No, I don't. But I'm dining there." She pointed a short distance down the street. "Want to join me?"

"Yes!" I said grateful for some company after leaving the other trekkers at basecamp. She entered a small, candle-lit cafe with a few tables lined up against the walls as I followed. The atmosphere was warm and welcoming. We settled in and ordered food.

"My name's Lydia. Where have you been?"

"I'm Anya. I just finished hiking the Annapurna Circuit from Jomsom into the Annapurna Sanctuary. You?"

"Oh, wonderful! I'm coming from the Mt. Everest basecamp. Boy! Was it cold!"

"I saw Everest from a plane when my yoga group flew to the Jantre Pass area. How was it up there?"

"I froze a bit in my shabby sleeping bag, but it was worth it."

She described her trip, the details of surviving the altitude. Lydia's exuberance took me in, and as I listened, I got the picture that she knew the ropes. I shared how I reconnected to the earth after the strain at home. How I felt I had been walking with the heartbeats of the planet. Then the conversation turned to where she was heading and where I was going. For her, it was to Thailand. For me, it was India.

India had been on my bucket list since I'd met Cathy in graduate school. At that time, she'd painted a picture of its exotic romance twenty years earlier. I hadn't quite thoroughly worked out in my mind yet where I was going exactly, but I did have that fat Lonely Planet guidebook to lead me on my way. And also, I remembered, I had that list of enlightened beings, so I had a plan beyond just seeing the Taj Mahal and the other cultural sites.

There was also that visit in the south to Avinashilingum College for Women. Again taking the bull by the horns, Cathy had arranged a visit to Dean Fatima, who'd known her relatives since the 1940s and '50s. Cathy's father had served in the diplomatic core and her aunt as a public health nurse in India. I'd previously taught at the college level, and Cathy had suggested I do a stint at this college of home sciences for women. I had agreed to do a bit of service, not so much because I was anxious to teach while on my trip, but because Cathy thought it was a good idea— so it was a good idea. And, why not? After all, I loved teaching. Moreover, it could be like a home visit, a taste of the culture.

"I'm going to Thailand first," Lydia continued. "I need the beaches for rest before I can even think of going back to India."

"Why's that?" It was going to be my first time in India.

"India gives, and India drains. It's intense, not easy to travel through for very long. It's, it's…." Lydia looked at me quietly, studying my face, or maybe it was my aura she was studying. There was something about her I could almost put my finger on. Was it that I was sitting with a Dori chatting about her latest New Age workshop? Or her telling me there was a Saturn return coming in my astrological chart? It felt like it. Lydia had the same draw.

She said, "Hey, you should go to Mundgod while you're in India!"

"What's Mundgod?"

"The mini-Tibet of India."

"What do you mean?"

"Mundgod is a Tibetan Refugee Camp in central India. It's a huge encampment that India gave to the Tibetan people for relocation after China invaded Tibet. The Tibetans left their country, fleeing persecution, the Dalai Lama included. But here's what's happening. In January, the Dalai Lama will be there to give his Kalachakra Initiation Teaching. You ought to go, Anya!"

My mouth dropped open. I knew the Dalai Lama was the spiritual leader of Tibetan Buddhism. And that he had received the Noble Peace Prize as a promoter of nonviolent ways to liberate Tibet from Chinese rule. But I didn't know he gave teachings to the public.

"You're kidding," I said. "What kind of teaching is this? What is happening?"

"What's happening is, he's spending two weeks visiting the Tibetan refugees while he gives this special wisdom teaching. It only happens every few years. There's probably going to be thousands of Tibetan monks and families from all over Southeast Asia."

I was stunned. Tucked in the back of my suitcase was a list of enlightened beings from Yogi Batsal, but this—a chance to hear the Dalai Lama! A vibration hit me in my chest as excitement washed over me. Somewhere in the back of my mind, a child stood—me—, and I remembered that I had always wanted to know. And that I, never quite sure what that meant, knew now this was an opportunity to dip into a form of understanding, dive into a form of living wisdom, a *form of being* that the Dalai Lama was about to deliver in Mundgod.

"Are you going?" I asked.

"Yeah, maybe. It's in Central India. You'll need permission from the Indian government to get into the refugee camp. They won't just let anyone in."

"How do I get permission?"

"Go to Delhi and get your papers from the government office at the Ministry of Home Affairs."

"Are you doing this?"

Lydia grinned, "Well, maybe. But like I said. I'm heading for Thailand for a rest and then back to India for whatever comes up next."

Back at the hotel, I knew I'd met a night goddess. Someone who was truly pointing me toward one of the biggest events of my life. Could I get the papers to attend the Dalai Lama's teaching? I was going to Delhi, and I knew I would try. It was the end of November. I had plenty of time. *Chance*, I thought. Yogi Batsal and Lydia had prearranged my trip through India. A journey where I'd find myself in the presence of the most enlightened beings on the planet. I was ready.

PART III

INDIA

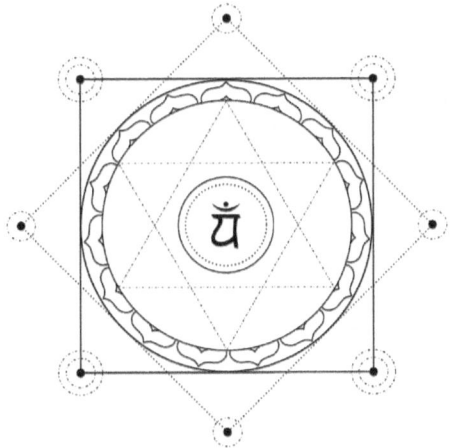

Varanasi

It's as if the rest of the world presents in black and white while India rages in technicolor. Its culture clammers through a private, kaleidoscopic warp that either happily ensnares travelers like me or miserably repels them to jump the next plane home.

My plane landed at Varanasi Airport, located in the Indian state of Uttar Pradesh, and I made my way to a hotel found in *Lonely Planet India*. A gray, barracks-like motel, the room walls were decorated with water streaks from last year's monsoon. As soon as I had settled in, I went to see the town—see India for the first time. Store-fronts lined the streets squeezed into flat-roofed buildings painted in sun-bleached mint greens, whites, yellows, pinks, teals. Hindi and English signs plastered the walls advertising Coca Cola, Hotel Ganesh, Shiva Restaurant, Silk Factory, etc., etc., etc.

Banners overhead pictured pretty models and politicians and fluttered above a hustle of men in neatly pressed dress-shirts rushing to and fro. Women in jewel-colored saris huddled under striped umbrellas bartering at stalls that sold every imaginable kitchen gadget. Racks of bottled water were stacked next to fruit stands heaped with oranges, apples, lemons…yet more.

Turbaned men peddled vegetable carts brimming with tomatoes, potatoes, cauliflower, and more. Bicycle wallahs pumped their brown, hardened calves skirting banana peels, crushed juice cartons while tuk-tuks swerved in and out of lanes. A hollowed-eyed, silvered-haired woman squatted in a doorway peering at me as I passed. Overhead, electrical wires crisscrossed the backstreet in a jumbled spider-web. Monkeys swung there low over two saffron-robed sadhus crouching on wooden platforms, seed beads twirling off their fingers.

I picked my way around three rib-skinny dogs nosing in piles of trash growling at each other's finds. They scuttled among the workmen out on the streets. A barber had set up a chair on the sidewalk shaving a client. To his right, a cobbler squatted, his white cotton robes pulled over his knees as his bony hands reached out to straighten and re-straiten again his tools waiting for a client. The air stank of exhaust. I held my nose against the smell of damp earth and urine. Yet, sweet fragrances of incense wafted from stores mingling with spicy pakoras frying in hot vats of oil. Surrounded by the humming commotion of sepia-toned people rushing along, I went along.

Cutting through a narrow alleyway, I avoided a set of twisted, rusted bicycle wheels, yet more banana peels, broken plastic washbasins, along with the stray flip-flop. I thought of Dad's junk piles. His collections of copper washbasins, old motors, sewing machines, boat parts, jars of screws, nails, washers… all broken, corroded, trashy pieces which for him weren't symbols of poverty like here; but recyclables… his "potentials" that he'd amassed after Mother had died and he'd moved into a trailer with no storage facilities. These "potentials" lay strewn over his yard, an original recycling center—his hive of activity the same as what I see before me. *If Dad were here*, I thought, *He'd see possibilities in every scrap of scrap.*

I walked the streets with the crowds. The spirit of the place was pulling me in like a gigantic magnet. Somehow, Varanasi—the human energy of its streets—found a quick way to trip some internal switch in me (maybe foolish), making me feel—*here* during my first day in India—I'd returned, I was welcome, I'd found home.

The following day, I took a tuk-tuk to the Dashashwamedh Ghat on the Ganges River. I wouldn't say I have a fascination for death. But still, honest respect and curiosity had taken me first to Varanasi, the spiritual capital of India, if not the world. Why do tourists, like myself, go? Why such allure? Maybe it's an opportunity to touch a bit of heaven or maybe hell. After all, don't we all wonder what happens after our personal piece of dust takes its last breath and crumbles through the tangles of life? I did. What *were* the dimensions of the soul anyway?

The cramped tuk-tuk, a noxious three-wheeled people mover, spewed bluish plumes of carbon monoxide into the atmosphere. It was the beginning stage of making my sinuses crash. The driver wove in and out of motorbikes, cabs, vans, trucks, and people. Then, at a roundabout, the vehicles jammed. A cow ambled through the din, its ribs jutting from an emaciated carcass. Horns blew, but the cow, treated as a sacred animal in India, was deaf to the blaring and claimed the right of the way in the center of the street.

When we got close to the Ghats, the tuk-tuk driver pulled over and motioned for me to get out, pointing to a passageway through a series of tall, tan buildings wedged one against the other. I paid him and passed by a group of mourners lowering a body wrapped in white sheets from the roof of a taxi. Three men carried the corpse to the narrow passageway toward its watery vault.

A crowd mobbed at the top of the stairway leading to the Ganges. I picked my way down hundreds of steps between the buildings scaffolded with bamboo poles keeping them from collapsing. At the river, hundreds of Indians and Westerners milled around the ghats. Cows, some with missing or broken horns, sat on the concrete terraces at the riverfront. Beads were tied around their necks, and red bhindi marks splotched on their foreheads.

To my left, an ancient temple tower teetered from the bank, listing half-submerged in the gray-green water. Men stood waist-deep, chests bared, bathing and brushing their teeth. Several women washed discretely, the wet fabric of their saris clinging to their bodies glistening in a rainbow of colors. Others washed clothing in the river's opaque, jade waters that crawled, flat and tranquil, toward the Bay of Bengal. To one side, under a ridgepole festooned with marigolds, a boy bent over a small collection of candles, selling them as offerings to be floated on the river.

Large faded umbrellas dotted the landings offering pockets of shade from the sun. Instead of hiding under one, I walked to the river's sandy bank and watched an attendant arrange a body on the ghat. Boatloads of tree trunks stacked six feet high in crisscrossed patterns were tied to the shore. The man gathered wood from the boat, returned to the corpse, and covered it with logs. Then, he bent to light the fire. It bit the wood, quickly flashing into an orange blaze. As the flames took hold, the attendant poked the wood with a bamboo pole, in and out, in and out, same as at the Pashupatinath ghats in Nepal. Both rivers were held sacred for the same intent.

The Ganges river—called Mother Ganga—is believed to be the domain of Lord Shiva, God of creation and destruction. And once a body is burned and the ashes tossed into the water, Shiva dances a dance of solace and liberation to welcome the soul into nirvana. Thousands of Hindus come each year hoping the soul of their dead loved ones can escape the cycle of rebirth (and its anguish). I wanted to see this.

The atmosphere was hazy. Billows of grayish-white smoke rose from the incinerating cadavers laid out on the open-air ghat. Hot air stifled my lungs. I tasted acrid ash in my mouth as the smell of burning flesh lamented across the watery cemetery—each of the river's molecules carrying solemn irreversibility.

Wooden boats carrying tourists glided by the pyres snapping pictures. Other vessels, over-loaded with Indians, drifted by, barely breaking the water's surface. Each face was heavy, observing the burning corpses. More bodies were brought to the ghats. My mind rushed back into the countless mortalities I had shared. And I joined with the bereaved community—mothers, fathers, sons, daughters, wives, husbands, friends— in their moment (sliding between past, present, and future), letting go. And I thought of Mother.

Her early death at age forty-five. And how I'd forgiven her after she was gone, forgiving her for not protecting me as a child, for letting me see her raped while drunk. And I thought: *Shame and Anger: I forgave*. And, it was good that anger could dissipate over time just like anything else —health, wealth, love. And that my anger toward her, buried in muscle memory so potently long ago, had ebbed by writing an essay. Words I'd written about that event meant to oust its hold, meant to begin forgiveness.

Standing at the ghats, I joined the mourners around me, and I found a calmness. Not merely in my personal history, but in theirs, as they delivered their loved ones to flames and the watery cycle of Time. I realized we were in a moment where *Self* becomes *Non-Self*. Where there's no changing of mind or matter or soul. It was too late!

And I felt I'd been brought here, as were they, to do a simple task of burying the dead. Yet, it was more than that. Somehow, we vibrated with the intelligence of this river—its clouded waters, its tranquil movement, its muddy brown banks—in part created by the ashes of dead loved ones. And we were there to accept the blessings of Mother Ganga's spirit that welcomed the countless souls into her protective flow.

The young boy who'd been selling candles approached me. He was about seven and wore a dirty, ragged shirt that hung open at the neck. He held out a small candle and smiled, "You buy candle? Good omen. Light and put on river."

"What's your name?" I asked.

"Ahkil," he said. "Buy candle, one rupee."

"A rupee?!"

"Yes. Cheap. You go to river, float candle, wash hands. Good for you." I laughed a bit at this—all the human remains filling the water! *Lonely Planet* had said not to even consider touching the Ganges. I offered Ahkil half price for the candle, and he took it. We went to the river where he lit it and handed it to me. I crouched and placed it on the river's current without too much thought except for a brief acknowledgment. I gave thanks for participating in the enormous ritual taking place at the river's edge—one that included forgiveness. And I had.

Later, I lay in my room meditating on what I'd seen at the river's edge. I regretted that I'd been unable to buy a disposable camera either in Nepal or Varanasi. They just weren't available back then. Sounds from the outside interrupted my thoughts as I overheard familiar voices and jumped up, throwing open the door. Karen and

John from the café on the Annapurna Circuit were walking across the courtyard.

"Hey! Karen, John!" I called out excitedly. They turned abruptly, and we greeted each other with glee.

"You're here!?" Karen said.

"Yeah, funny to meet up like this!" I said, but knowing synchronicity had kicked in again. We shared stories of what we had done since last seeing each other on the trail.

"We're going to see the Ghats now."

"I was there this afternoon. Breathtaking!" I said.

Then John asked, "Are you up for renting a boat with us in the morning to see the sunrise on the Ganges?"

"You, bet," I said.

"Good and dinner tonight, right?"

And they were off.

In the pre-dawn, as the oarsman paddled into the middle of the Ganges, a thick misty mirage engulfed us. Karen, John, and I now floated on the water's ripple-less surface. I kept my gaze on the east. Ever so slowly, the sun's reddish orb birthed from the horizon, inching higher and higher. Steadily, it turned from red to molten orange, placed its foot on the rim of the skyline, and pushed itself up into the sky. A rich agate glow cast over the building's facades that lined Mother Ganga.

Karen, John, and I were a bit overwhelmed. It was a Van Gogh painting equaling the intensity of his colors and brushstrokes. Karen snapped photos. *When I get home*, I thought, *I'll paint a picture of just that.*

The oarsman paddled us for miles past an electric crematorium and a couple of large waste disposal tanks. Women in saris washed clothes in the river. Men bathed. With no camera, I burned each scene indelibly in my mind's eye—images of burning ghats against the morning's stillness.

When we departed after dinner that evening, Karen, John, and I knew we'd never meet again. They were heading for Delhi while

I for Lucknow to visit the first enlightened being on my list. But still, we had shared Varanasi's transitory power, one that magnified the core of India's flux and flow. One that embraced the intimacy of death, and that was enough.

Lucknow's Guru

KABIR WILL TELL you the truth:

> I laugh when I hear that the fish in the water is thirsty.
>
> You don't grasp the fact that what is most alive of all is inside your own house;
> And you walk from one holy city to the next with a confused look?
>
> Kabir will tell you the truth: Go wherever you like, to Calcutta or Tibet;
> if you can't find where your soul is hidden,
> for you the world will never be real!
> (Kabir, The Kabir Book: Forty-four of the Ecstatic Poems of Kabir; Goodreads.com/quotes/119945. Accessed 19 August 2021)

I dug my earplugs out of my bag and jammed them into my ears. The overnight bus to Lucknow blared videos, and I threw my coat over my head, waiting for the torture to end—torment the Indians on board watched and listened to intently. Sullenly curled on a back seat, I told myself it would be worth it because I was heading for one of the spiritual heavies in India: H.W. L. Poonja, aka Papaji. Feeling like I had gotten myself into an impossible situation for sleep, I jammed the plugs deeper.

The following day in Lucknow, I staggered off the bus and found a taxi to Papaji's ashram, a simple white-washed building. Once inside, I went up to the man behind the desk. "Hello," I said. "I've come to hear Papaji. Can I rent a room here?'

The man behind looked up and said, "No, Madam. No rooms here. Sorry. We have only a meeting room and places for the staff to live. You look there," he said and pointed across the reception area at a small bulletin board tacked to the wall.

I went over to read the notices searching for a rental. A man in a dark business suit was watching me from across the room. He cautiously approached me, introducing himself. "Hello. My name is Mr. Depok Asan. Do you need lodgings, Madam?"

Uneasily, I took in his sedate manner. "Yes, I do," I said.

"My wife and I have two rooms at my house a short distance from here. Only a ten-minute walk. Would you like to come and see and perhaps rent one?"

I hesitated sizing up his reliability. He saw this and said, "I'm a businessman. I have a card here," holding out his hand. I glanced at the man standing behind the desk. He nodded his head slightly to indicate that Mr. Asan was legit. That convinced me to go along and check out the room. When we reached his house, he introduced me to a somber woman dressed in a dark blue patterned sari. His house was multi-leveled with the rental rooms at the top level—one large double, one smaller single, both en suite. The smaller room's window looked out onto a large courtyard facing a few trees and a ten-foot wall. The price was right. I could see that I'd fallen into a good deal—clean and safe.

"Take whichever room you want," Depok said.

"I'll take the single room. You just might get someone else for the big room."

That settled, and because no screens protected the windows, Depok pointed out mosquito repellent coils and a plug-in zapper that I could burn in the night to kill the little vampires. I took tablets to avoid coming down with malaria; still, I was thankful for the repellents.

I unpacked my bag. At the ashram, I'd been told that satsang took place in the morning and again in the evening. Translated from Sanskrit, satsang means "in the company of truth." By custom, people sit together with others who want to hear their guru's teachings about the ins and outs of *good* living. The guru lectures then takes questions from followers after they've reflected on the teacher's words. Enlightenment was the goal. Bringing it into daily life by living intentionally…or maybe thoughtfully… while finding personal happiness. Satsang, unlike meditation, used social interaction, discussion with others while examining one's soul. Pretty heavy stuff, but that's what I'd come for. To listen and partake of this…the power in groups to help personal vision along. Having practiced yoga and meditated since my late twenties, it all sounded good to me.

Satsang. We sat on the floor cross-legged, waiting for H.W.L. Poonja or Papaji to come. When he finally arrived, he swept into the room with an air of authority. In his mid-eighties and heavy-set, he wore a crisp, white kurta shirt. His bald head crowned a large symmetrical face that held beaming, dark eyes. He sat in the chair set on a dais. He looked down at the forty of us, primarily Westerners, sitting at his feet.

Papaji opened the session with a short lecture on something less than meaty that I can't remember. His words didn't seem to grab his audience either, who patiently fidgeted as if jockeying for position. As soon as his words ended, hands shot up with questions. One man, who identified himself as Herman, dove right in. "Tell me who I am," he appealed, his voice filled with tears. I gasped and turned to look at him. He was no more than thirty years old, blue-eyed with a shock of neatly trimmed blond hair falling over his forehead. He wore an expensive linen dhoti kurta, and I noticed the toenails on his bare feet glinted out from under him like newly polished pearls.

I turned questioningly back at Papaji. I conjectured how anyone, even a guru, could answer such a question for someone else. It was a question that sent me back to Muktinath peering into the eternal flame—a query I felt took a lifetime if ever, to decipher. The other faces in the group looked expectantly up at Papaji, rather more hopeful than me.

Papaji frowned at Herman. "Why do you ask me such a question?" *Uh-oh*, I thought. The moment felt suspended. I'd never sat satsang before and thought I better give it a go rather than slip into criticizing Herman for stepping in it.

"No, please, I don't know who I am," Herman said, seeming to beg from somewhere hollow inside him. "I've been searching for years…" he went on, giving us his family history of mental abuse and useless therapy sessions and broken relationships and… Well, it went back and forth between him and Papaji for quite a while till Herman cried, "What am I to do?" The room held its collective breath; I know I held mine.

Anxiety washed over my stomach. The whole thing, sitting there, became the crest of a gigantic wave rolling in about to break over my head. And I was struck, not at all fathoming, how another person, even a so-called enlightened being, was going to provide a reasonable solution or balm for Herman's pain. My left brain wanted to yell out that it was existentially impossible for anyone except the individual to answer that question. So, how the hell could Papaji answer it?

Papaji gazed at Herman, "You are the answer to that question." OK, I thought *maybe we're getting somewhere.*

"No, no …I've tried to look into my heart, to open and heal…". Herman stammered on to explain. "I've done yoga and meditated. I've fasted and given away my stuff. I'm vegan. I really need help…I came here to get help. Inside, I'm just…Please." My right brain did surge a bit in sympathy.

Papaji went on. "You have too much fear, you need to embrace your fears, and you will find yourself."

"How do I do that?"

"You must be honest with yourself. Then, facing your fears, you realize they're part of you. They are you. You are them. Then you resolve your problem."

"I'm not sure what you're saying?" Herman said.

I wasn't either. It was all too abstract. More was needed in explanation, a concrete example, or so I felt.

Papaji said, "Turn off your brain. You're overthinking. I don't want to merely give you a lollipop and send you away. Get out of your head and stop telling yourself a story that you should be this or that. Just be."

Hearing this, I was a bit more hopeful for Herman but not very when I glanced back at his twisted face. He persisted, "I'm a nobody. A piece of shit. There's nothing inside me. I need to have *you* tell me *who I am*." *Oh, no!* I thought, *does anyone else make your lungs inhale or your heartbeat?*

Papaji went on, "You are digging a hole that tells you that you're not good enough or not happy enough or that you need to be in *bliss*. Stop digging that hole, and you will get out of your head and the pain you cause yourself."

The air went from the room. Faces went blank. We'd witnessed a collision between guru and devotee. I identified with the idea that I was responsible for figuring out who I was and maybe even for my own pain. Accountable for thinking that I was one thing—strong—when I was really another thing—weak. Hadn't I recently just faced my own pitiful ego vomiting my way up a mountainside during the Yoga Group trek? It occurred to me that Herman, besides needing some serious therapy, also needed to think more with his feet, move his body. But then I pitied him. To me, it was clear; he'd missed out on early programming instilling self-belief. He'd missed out on how "Special" he was just by being on the planet.

The query continued back and forth between Herman and Papaji for five long minutes, with Herman validating his inner trash heap. Finally, Papaji became gruff, turning to others in the room asking for other questions. Questions came similar to Herman's, dealing with unresolved conflicts circling around self-defeating topics.

OK. I'd found myself smack in the middle of a plague of monkey-mindedness. That inner chatter that bickers and criticizes endlessly, telling us we're not good enough or should be doing this or that, impulsively twisting us into knots of self-stupidity or guilt. Despite Dad programming me, I hadn't escaped monkey-mindedness. I'd struggled with it like everyone else. But, I had learned to put mine in check using yoga, meditation, and mental imagery; so, I knew how hard it was. And I'd learned if I could switch my locus-of-control from that inner negative chatter—which dealt with self-absorbed crap—to an outward focus concentrating on a task or watching the world go by in detail (like I'd done on the Annapurna Circuit), I could find some stillness within, re-ground and find more of me.

Strangely, sitting satsang with that cross-legged group made me think I hadn't left trekking the Himalayas behind. I was in the thick of it—a desperate uphill struggle, a psychological climb—that felt like I'd made a wrong turn on the trail. Instead of avoiding the Thorong La Mountain Pass at 18,000 feet, I'd made a mistake going over it. And I had encountered the worse weather at high altitudes, finding myself unable to cope. Finding that my *psychological knees* were bad, failing me, and I was trekking in a painful, downhill pull. Sitting there, I imagined a group of fellow trekkers who were climbing steep emotional mountains, and I wasn't sure how they would get out of their personal, seemingly dark, psychic valleys to reach clear summits.

Satsang gave me pause. *Could a guru tell us who we were or heal our wounds?* I believed there was no quick answer to this vital question. But it did occur to me that Papaji was the real McCoy. And that reminded me of the time during my doctoral studies when I had gone to my local yoga center to hear a woman guru from Southern India, Shri Anandi Ma. Those of us at the yoga center had been told that she could deliver something called shaktipat, an awakening of spiritual energy.

A friend and I went. The yoga studio was packed, all of us anxious to hear what she had to say. But, as it turned out, Shri Anandi Ma had very little to say. Instead, she sat at the front quietly, generating a warm personality. At the same time, her translator did most of the talking, delivering a commonplace message of peace and love. But, for me, that wasn't all. Listening to her words had turned out not to be the point. Instead, being in her presence was.

When the event finished, and my friend and I rode home in the car, I asked her if she had seen a red glow around the picture of

Christ that hung in the yoga studio. She looked at me askance and questioned, "No?". Well, I had. And in retrospect, after the whole deal of my doctoral process had unfolded (over my head, etc.), I thought back. I realized that Shri Anandi Ma had non-verbally transmitted spiritual energy, shaktipat, to me (and maybe the others in the group that night, for all I know). She had probably (along with the playing of the Gayatri Mantra and all the rest) initiated Kundalini energy in me, my cobra, although passively.

Sitting here now in satsang, I questioned whether or not Papaji, whose ashram was filled with seekers, was capable of healing the insurmountable task before him. So many sounded steeped with self-rejection. Did he possess a unique spiritual oomph, like the lady guru I'd met up with? An ability to ignite self-healing through shaktipat or another esoteric form of spiritual power unknown to me? Or was it that he was dealing with his own stuff, or maybe ashram staffing stuff, or financial stuff. Who knew?

I looked around at the devotees and couldn't help but think *this will not be fun*. I felt a sense of spiritual bankruptcy pervading the room. Papaji was expected to use his wisdom to rebalance each devotee's over-drawn spiritual account. Well, as I took it in, and I'm not a skeptical person by any means, I believe in people, but here in this moment, I didn't think Papaji could make a big difference in their lives. Hand them a new PIN and say: *Go! Use this to draw out value from your deepest inner accounts, those born with...pure and whole... Spend those resources thoroughly and sensibly in each moment, and accept what you get.* But, as the dialogue went on, the amount of suffering in the room became more conspicuous. I thought that each person was searching for a level of consciousness that could only be found by living fifty lifetimes.

After satsang, I walked the ten minutes back to my room and stopped to buy fruit from a young guy in a street stall. His piles of bananas, mangos, and papayas, along with vegetables, were lined up in rows. I said, "I'd like two bananas, an orange, and carrots, please."

He smiled and asked, "Where are you coming from?"

"America. Not far from New York City," I said.

"Oh, New York! Tell me what it's like."

I did. The man was friendly and took in my descriptions of the tall skyscrapers, the streets' tempo, the crowds' rush on the wide sidewalks, and the noise of the cars and buses moving millions of people through its bowels. The underground subways fascinated him most. It was easy to dive into the warmth of his eyes, his wanting to understand New York City and the world where I came from. I smiled at him as I left thinking how I hadn't made one contact with anyone at satsang that morning.

When I got back to my room, I could hear women's voices chattering in the larger bedroom. I knocked on the door to say hello. Tina and Colley were there again.

"Tina! Colley!" I said, surprised. They, too, had found their way from Nepal, from the yoga studio outside of Kathmandu, to sit satsang with Papaji. My social group was forming around me, and I felt content, gathered up.

Sitting Satsang

India is hot and dry—airless during the winter months. The room was screenless. I kept the fan on and burned the mosquito coils during the night to keep the little, disease-ridden Draculas from me. The second morning at five AM, the sun glared through slits in the shutters; and although still early morning, waves of heat had seeped into the crevices of my room overnight. I got up and threw the shutters open wanting more air. Outside the window, a half-dozen women elegantly dressed in clean cotton saris milled about in a large field beyond the courtyard. Powdery clouds of dust eddied around their ankles as they came and went with large baskets on their heads.

Other women in the yard squatted on their haunches and used their bare hands to pick through cow excrement evidently collected from the streets. They mixed the muck with handfuls of hay forming patties. Then several got up, approached a stucco wall on the field's edge, and threw the cow pies against it. Each cake stuck to the wall—lined up evenly in a grid which reminded me of Dad's dog-eared multiplication table that he'd kept in his wallet. The one with a grid of numbers on a two by two-inch scrap of cardboard cut from an old black and white composition booklet. Except here, instead of numbers lined up evenly, rows of patties calculated the women's wages in the dung of sacred cows.

Other women peeled dried patties off the barrier at the wall's far side, leaving their surface pock-marked with giant, pale freckles. Loaded baskets were hefted to heads, the cakes on their way to be sold for cooking and heat in braziers. As I watched the women work, gracefully moving in their clean saris, their drama unfolded—a continuum from manure to nourishment and back again in a never-ending cycle. Again, I flashed to the seekers at the ashram. Something felt radically wrong between these two pictures.

Over the next several days, Tina, Colley, and I sat satsang. Satsang continued with narratives of broken families, broken relationships, broken health, and broken dreams. Papaji would come in, sit, and be bombarded with questions concerning emotional abuse; physical abandonment often centered on lack of motherly love. The pain I heard at times was shared by me, but different. For the first time in my life, I felt like a fake sitting there. I wasn't unhappy or lost or depressed. Yes, I'd suffered trauma, felt abandoned by Mother and Tim; but I didn't share the group's self-hatred.

It had taken a long time for me to come to terms with Mother, but I did. At thirty-two, I'd entered an essay contest that called for writing a critical moment in my life—seeing Mother raped. And when I was finished, I broke down sobbing, pardoning her for not shielding me from the ordeal that burglarized my innocence. At that moment, I forgave her for not mothering me the way I wanted. Then, I found my way to group therapy which helped purge the wound that had made me reject my feminine Self. It had begun the process where I could let go of fighting against my own closed-off heart. A heart that refused to be vulnerable and bore the consequences of not connecting with others, keeping me unhurt but keeping me alone.

Sitting with the group, I hoped they could see their way out of their pain even though I felt they were asking too much, asking the wrong questions of Papaji. For his part, Papaji repeated that insight was brought about by living without ego, letting go. The goal was liberation, of course…whatever that meant here. And I thought if they'd come to India to find liberation…I knew where it was happening. I'd seen liberation here in India. It was usually mingled with a pile of firewood and an attendant wielding a bamboo pole.

The questions continued, fired up at Papaji. When he asked: "Can you learn to no longer fear the unknown?" I winced. Somehow the dialogue was not focused correctly, not for me, my teacher's mind. I have to admit my teaching experience told me that, as much as I liked him, Papaji's message was getting lost in abstractions. His words butted up against childhoods that were full of angst, and I felt his words needed to be replaced by prescriptions of action.

There was no yoga or dancing or music or chanting at the ashram. I was getting to a point where instead of sitting satsang what I really wanted was a bag of Fritos or a glass of red wine to shift my consciousness. My cross-legged stance on the floor cramped my legs, and the narratives cramped my compassion which I wasn't happy about. I was bored, and I realized that I, like many others in the group, had not uttered a word or asked a question during satsang. What were they thinking? What were Colley and Tina thinking? "Guys, what're your thoughts about this?" I asked them later back at our rooms. Essentially, they shrugged their shoulders, saying, "So much for enlightened beings!" And after a few days, they packed their back backs and left, leaving me with several more days to go in Lucknow.

I was feeling guilty for not having more empathy for those crying out for help. But, to me, many in the group had no encouraging inner dialogue to get them through their torment. Maybe affirmations had been offered. Perhaps they had been sent an inner tape telling them they were lovable and capable—but those messages had gotten lost in a tangle of upbringing. And I wished, really wished, each had had a Dad who had tossed them a life preserver early on.

My cobra wasn't helping. It hadn't emerged during this time; instead, it settled into a mellow quietness, one I couldn't put my finger on. There was something it seemed to know or that I seemed to know but didn't realize that I knew. I prayed I wasn't blind to the suffering around me. I did understand how scary it was to confront the darkest parts inside of myself—the wounds, the angers, the inadequacies, the paranoias—the darkened corners repetitively rehearsing personal hurts. But in this group, in this satsang, something was missing. And I don't have a lot of patience for bullshit.

Each of us was searching for acquaintance with ourselves, a more profound awareness, finding where our souls are hidden. Yet, something kept creeping into the back of my head—a nagging practicality rubbed up against the Zen proverb I'd pinned to my computer during my doctoral studies. It had read: "Before enlightenment chopping wood, carrying water; After enlightenment chopping wood, carrying water." And I was betting that my crossed-legged colleagues in the room hadn't seen the sari-clad women up at 5:00 AM throwing cow manure against the wall to feed their families. What if that was *their* life or *mine*?

All of that made me consider whether or not the antidote to suffering could be found by leaving our angst at the door, along with our entitlements. That it was necessary here to have a good look at the underbelly of India—its spirit—which at its core sat coiled in an unrelenting hand-to-mouth existence for millions engaged in service.

Papaji needed to have us perform service, work. Why didn't it occur to him to assign us to scrub out the toilets or chop wood and carry water for the ashram? What was he waiting for? From where I was sitting satsang, it made sense that a good dose of labor could bulldoze through the dump loads of suffering many of us had as emotional foundations or thought we had. Over the years, work had kept my head above water, had given me purpose and meaning, and happiness. It was a good ego killer that led to finding where *my* soul was hidden. *A good dose of work,* I thought, *might put us all, put me in the company of yet more Self- truth.* But, of course, I didn't know what I was asking for at the time.

The struggles of satsang exhausted me. I needed a break. A trip to the National Botanical Research Institute in Lucknow listed in the *Lonely Planet* guide would do the trick. I needed to look at green stuff, absorb the plants' energy, and pretend I was back home walking in the woods to regain some balance. There might be birds there, too. The following day, I took a bicycle wallah into town to explore the Institute.

As I walked through the Research Institute's gardens, the plants drew me into their world. The place is renowned for its chrysanthemums, and they did their job lighting up the beds in gold, lemon, blonde, straw, corn, and amber hues. The flower heads had many shapes— pompoms, buttons, fireworks with petal edges either rounded or sharp or curled. Their earthy fragrance wafted the air. After an hour of imbibing, I sat in the shade, letting my inner chatter settle into a low murmur.

It occurred to me that satsang was a left hemisphere process recounting personal chronicles that analyzed hurts ad infinitum. But its real intent was to problem solve. Here I was attending an esteemed meeting but wasn't taking advantage of its approach. I searched my brain for something to add. Before I left Lucknow, I thought I should contribute. And slowly, a question formed in my head.

The following day sitting satsang, I shot my hand up. Papaji called on me, and I asked, "The Western educational system places heavy emphasis on developing left-brain types of verbal thinking like reading and math. But for enlightenment, do I hear you say that Eastern spirituality asks that we turn off this part of the brain?" He looked at me…I went on prepared, "…That our brains have to let go of all this kind of intellectualizing…the stuff that distracts our ability to tear down our desires? And, …and…if this is so, can you tell me how to use Eastern spirituality to improve the Western educational system? My goal is to develop the whole brain and hearts of my students."

Papaji's eyes flew open, and he shouted "Yes, yes!" almost springing from his chair. I'd hit a nerve and wondered if it was time for me to jump up and make a dash for it, but I didn't move.

His voice raised as he said, "You want to know how my teachings fit with the Western World's educational system? That's no question for the marketplace! The ultimate truth is not found in words…it's true! Come to my office tomorrow! We give you information that will instruct you to your goal. This is an important matter! Come to my office in town."

Had an enlightened being just given me a slap across the back—Zen-like—to wake me up, to focus my focus? It felt it! I looked at Papaji a bit sheepish, I must admit. "Come at ten in the morning," he said, "and we'll be there for you." I gulped down my excitement but felt the others in the group staring at my back. Papaji moved on to the following query. I sat there dumbfounded and thought: *Is that where we've been? In the marketplace?* There had been so much bargaining going on. Soul bargaining.

The following day, I found myself sitting satsang next to a good-looking, sandy-haired guy with a Dutch accent.

"I'm Anya," I said, craving some masculine conversation.

"Daan here. You American?"

"Yeah. What do you think of satsang?"

"A lot of weak people here. Too much insincerity. They need to get out of their own way." A bit taken aback by his directness, but in agreement, I nodded my head. *Maybe a like-minded guy here*, I thought, but still, there was something…

Daan said, "I'm sick of it. I'm leaving for Rishikesh in two days."

"Me, too. I'm going to town to buy a train ticket this afternoon," I said.

"I'm going later. I'll get you a ticket if you want. No problem. First-class, OK?" I was grateful I didn't have to make the slog into town again and was being taken care of, seeing that it would be my first train ride in India.

The following day, I took a rickshaw into Papaji's office feeling nervous, remembering his abruptness, his sternness. Three older men dressed in white suits wearing turbans greeted me with little ado. Papaji was nowhere in sight. The men gave me several books to read, not by Papaji himself but written by others. The books included *Papaji: Interviews* (A collection of Interviews with Poonja) by David Godman, published 1993 by the Avadhuta Foundation, and *Papaji Interviews & Reflections* (earlier Indian edition published 1992) Pragati. Both books discussed his philosophy.

"Is Papaji here," I asked. I had prepared several questions the night before and wanted to look smart.

"No, no, Madam. He's not here. You are to read these books and come back next week." Clearly, this was not going to happen. I told the men I was leaving for Rishikesh in two days—were they sure he wasn't in? Not in. I thanked them for the materials and left disappointed.

In the evening, I went to the ashram where I met up with Daan. I asked if I could pay him for the train ticket to Rishikesh. He said, "No. I only bought tickets for my friend and me. You have to buy your own." I stared at him dumbfounded. My mouth must have been hanging open for all I knew. He said, "Each on his own."

"What? You mean you didn't buy me a ticket?" I was incredulous. "But you said you would. You went right there!"

With an indifferent smirk, he shrugged his shoulder and walked away. I was stunned. Why hadn't he bought me a ticket? It didn't make sense. What was he doing here anyway? What he'd said about the group earlier applied to his own mindlessness. I was done with Lucknow.

When I left the Asan's place for the train, the bicycle wallah peddled past the fruit and vegetable stand where I had bought stuff during my stay. The young guy who had sold me produce caught my eye. He nodded in warm recognition. Daan shot through my mind—and I realized the fruit seller could have given lessons in the intricacies of mindfulness at the ashram. Could have expounded on its connections between people, to us self-absorbed tourists sitting satsang. That fruit seller's brief display of consciousness—one that would come my way from many souls throughout India—made me tuck Lucknow in my heart as one place I had truly found an enlightened being. The fruit seller.

As the train raced away from Lucknow to Rishikesh, taking me to my next enlightened being, I scrambled down the aisle toward my compartment. I opened the door to find five Indians—a husband, wife, two kids, and a grandmother—the Amble family—seated there. They stared up at me watchfully. Putting on my most expansive smile, I stepped in and introduced myself. "Hi, I'm Anya Kru," I said.

"Hello. I am Manu Amble, and this is…" introducing his family. Soon Manu pointed to the top bunk where I put my bag. They were shy about sharing a compartment with me. Because this was not an American train with a dining car, it became apparent that I was new to train travel. When they discovered that I had forgotten to bring dinner along for the ride, the Ambles kindly offered, then insisted on sharing their meal with me. I accepted.

The food was in silver steel containers with snaps that held the tops on tightly. There were various potato rolls, puri, and chapatti. Smiling, smiling, and more smiling, we ate—otherwise, I would have starved. I was learning the ways of train travel in India, which I was to find had its nuances. After dinner, I crawled to my top bunk. There was no heat in the compartment, and I didn't have a sleeping bag nor a liter of hot tea for my water bottle to warm my feet. Draping my coat over me, I kept my boots on, shivering through the night, but I was happy that, at least, I couldn't see my breath.

TIME IS ONLY AN INCH

Rishikesh

Rishikesh was pink. Not only the sunset glow coloring the wedding-cake-like buildings perched on the Ganges' shoreline but pink in its laidback atmosphere. Before I arrived, I'd checked *Lonely Planet India* for a place to stay, finding the town was saturated with ashrams. Yog Niketan Ashram, nestled on the outer edges of town, was not far from the residence of the enlightened being, a woman I'd come to see. It served breakfast and dinner, had yoga classes in the afternoon, and overlooked the Ganges River, all for fifty rupees a day.

It was late December by now. When I'd arrived, the receptionist, Girish, a quiet-spoken man of about thirty dressed in a traditional Indian dhoti, came out of an office and booked me in for a week. This included the Christmas holiday. Girish explained the only requirement was that all guests attend an evening satsang with the ashram's patron, a blind guru named Vikram. He lived next door with his wife. This satsang commitment took place at eight every evening. Even though Vikram was not on my enlightened beings list, I agreed. That's what I was here for.

My second-floor room was stripped-down-basic, clean with two twin beds. Water stains embroidered the pale green walls. A small bathroom dribbled a bit of lukewarm water in the sink when I needed it, but best of all was a long balcony that straddled the backside of the ashram. It gave a view of the Ganges River, Mother Ganga, that flowed below in her long, green sari.

Across the river, I could see a Bollywood-like stage-set of salmon-pink buildings tiered with turrets in the shape of pointy bishops' caps that scraped the sky. Sunlight bounced off the buildings where a few foundations soaked in the river's hem. I was thrilled with this view—shops and homes and offices nestled in the foothills of the Himalayas against a backdrop of magnificent dark pines.

Upriver, I could see the Lakshuman Jhula pedestrian suspension bridge spanning the river. It connected the two sides between the villages of Tapovan in the Tehri district and Jonk in the Pauri district. The bridge was alive with people. One man pushed a cart filled with fruit dodging a stray cow venturing across, while another strolled a motorbike under the thick steel cables. Below me, at the river's edge, I watched a swarm of rose-skinned pigs rooting. The scene took on feelings of an irrational juxtaposition of images—street theater replete with humans surging back and forth across the bridge, buildings sinking into the river's edge, and pigs ambling along grubbing for food. Sitting on the balcony, I imagined living here could easily slip into a lifetime.

My train-cramped legs begged for a good hike, and I chose to kill two birds with one stone by checking out the location of the woman guru's satsang. Girish had told me that the guru on my list had a meeting place located about a mile up on the other side of the river in Jonk.

Walking across the bridge and up the street was like stepping back in time. Men stood behind counters in small shops selling cheap bracelets, earrings, and sundry trinkets. Others sat in the cool shade. Women, bright saris gleaming, bustled about the streets. A sadhu dressed simply in a white robe perched atop a stone pedestal. His tangled hair hung in narrow, dull clumps framing his painted white face in which his buried eyes glimmered.

I reached the address I was looking for. The house appeared empty of people, and I called out. A young man came from the building. "Do you have satsang here?" I asked. He said, "Yes," and to return at seven in the morning.

On my way back, Daan approached over the bridge. I stopped staring at him as he came up to me and said, "So, you got here," his lip curled.

"No help from you."

He grinned, "I heard you in the next compartment. Cold, right?"

There was no reason to be courteous to this phony who presumed to seek truth while he needed a brain transplant. But just as quickly, I thought: *No*. He was another mirror out there, a message sent to remind me not to get caught in an illusion that someone else would care for my needs when it was my job in reality. And quickly, understanding this, I flashed back to a Thanksgiving when I was twelve.

That holiday, Mother was passed out in bed drunk, Agnes was hidden in a book, and Dad rummaged in the basement. I had wanted someone, my family, to take care of me like in a Norman Rockwell Painting. A fifteen-pound turkey lay defrosting on the kitchen counter in a puddle of pinkish liquid. There was no one else, so I took charge. Onions, celery, bread crumbs, boiled giblets—all chopped and churned into a stuffing which I rammed into the cavity of the bird. The gas oven turned on; I guessed at the temperature and put the turkey in before charging out the back door along the path to the pond. That was the day the woods could barely calm me, but eventually, they did.

Back in the house, I looked into the oven. The turkey's wings were charred, but it didn't matter. I took it out, made myself a plate, and ate, biting down my indignation and shame. I'd taken custody of a small corner of my own happiness, or so I thought.

Now, standing on the pedestrian bridge spanning the Ganges River, I stared into Daan's face. I realized he was just another aspect of myself that was out there in the world. Daan reflecting me; Mother reflecting me, Dad reflecting me, Tim reflecting me, the whole world reflecting me…and probably, I had to admit, reflecting my own blind spots back to me. And that my job was to embrace those spots, their flaws…and their beauty… and my own: I/Thou Daan, I/Thou Mother, I/Thou Dad, I/Thou Tim, I/Thou the World. And understanding that, I turned on my heel recalling a lesson from the I Ching: "No Blame" and walked away.

Back at my ashram, the yoga class was about to begin. It was held in a large well-equipped room with windows opening out to the Ganges. Light reflected back into the studio, washing over five of us, waiting for the teacher. Soon, a short, dark-haired man dressed in loose-fitting sweat pants briskly walked into the room to take charge. Without introduction, his voice resonant; he commanded us through a vinyasa flow. Child's pose, standing tree, downward-facing dog flowing through triangle, and warrior asanas. He directed us to pay attention to the details of each position, and he repeated them each three times. This opened and released areas of stress I didn't know I had.

"Have respect for your body," our instructor uttered sternly but prayerlike. "It learns slowly." Then to one woman, "Madam, do not force the position. If you need a block, use it. If you need a strap, use it. We are not all contortionists. You come to the form and make it your own. Find your strength in your weakness and look through its eyes to receive the energies of the Universe." I thought of Daan and of Mother.

He went on guiding us through the lion pose. "Inhale, exhale, breathe..." he said, and placing my hands on my heels and arching my back, I put my tongue below my chin and roared like a lion before peeling back into a child's pose. The vinyasas flowed. I was in the zone. The presence of my cobra was palpable. I sensed its auric branching.

As the session ended, the group and I pivoted into a half-moon kneeling asana with hips stacked. Then to the floor into a backbend with hands resting on heels opening my heart to the Universe. As we were leaving, the teacher said, "In a few days, I will show you how to use the ropes to stand on your heads—Salamba Sirsasana." I was ready.

The Enlightened Beings List

I walked over the pedestrian bridge up the river to satsang held by the lady guru on my enlightened beings list. It was 6:30 in the morning with little action in the streets. As I passed a small blue stand, the front panel dropped down to reveal a man who had slept in his shop—a six-foot by six-foot wooden box sans heat, sans running water, sans electricity—a box. I marveled at his clean, pale blue dress shirt and his grin. "Namaste," I said, and he nodded.

Satsang at this ashram was different than at Papaji's. Its space was a narrow, open courtyard already filled when I arrived. Twenty people sitting cross-legged on cushions murmured quietly. I found a place in the back, grabbed a pillow, and sat. After ten minutes, a woman wrapped in a white cashmere shawl swept into the courtyard and sat at the front. Her appearance was quite non-guru-ish. She had blue eyes, long blond hair falling around her ample shoulders below an attractive face that glowed without cosmetic care and with confidence. She adjusted her cushions, threw one corner of the shawl back around her shoulders, pursed her lips, and eyed us with bemusement. She was an American.

"I'm Sharlene," she said. "I see we have several new faces this morning. First, let me tell you about myself. My personal guru had spiritual powers which he passed to me to do my work with you." And she continued for several minutes, spelling out her resume, how being in her presence was special. How the world's mystical knowledge had been bestowed on her. She'd been imbued with holiness. How she could transmit that to others. I glanced around at the mostly young faces focused forward, absorbed in her story and maybe the aura of self-assuredness.

OK, I thought. *This lengthy background information doesn't hurt, even though Sharlene's self-assurance sounded like bragging.* After all, I had a cobra guiding me. So, why shouldn't she share what was special about herself?

She launched into a lecture on non-attachment, a subject I always found confusing. Where I was coming from, we had families to take care of, needed shelter, food, a job; and if you lived in the West, you had a house, a car, and let's face it, lots of stuff—that's how the economy ran. Lots of attachment, a lot of it necessary. But *yes*, some of it owned us instead of the other way around. On top of that, we had desires, often complex ones, to get rid of. It was only human. So non-attachment seemed a good idea, and Sharlene dove into it: "Give up control, stop clinging." And it sounded to me like she was saying, 'do your thing, let it be.' Wasn't that what the Beetles sang about after they'd been in Rishikesh?

She went on. "Stop being attached to your thoughts. This brings about suffering. Become mindful. Let your life unfold...be like a river flowing its course...this will lead you to your higher Self." But I still wasn't getting it. The conversation felt over my head—attachment, non-attachment, freedom from suffering—and I felt left out. I needed practical examples of how to "let go." But Sharlene offered none, launching into yet more abstractions, discussing the nature of liberation. And I got uneasy with the tone she was taking. Yet I listened.

The only thing I could think of was to fall back on fundamental religion, opening myself up to "thy will be done" —accepting whatever came my way. Still, somehow, here, that felt like throwing up my hands in despair, not a path to my higher Self. I think that's what I was looking for by visiting the enlightened beings on my list, but I wasn't sure just then. When Sharlene finally stopped talking, people asked questions.

"My name is Magda."

"What can I do for you?" Sharlene asked. *Sounds like we're now in the marketplace*, I thought.

"I'm not sure. I have everything I need in life, but there's no joy within myself. Thoughts go around and around in my mind. I feel lost and hopeless."

"You're groping," Sharlene's eyes seemed amused for some reason. "You're clinging to everything you think you want. Desire is the problem. Get clear and come back with a question. Don't waste time," she said. And she similarly rebuffed each question for the next thirty minutes or so. Still, the men and women in the audience were not put off. I listened, more or less dumbstruck by the verbal wall she surrounded herself with—the wall that left me out. And I recalled that Papaji had equally been bombarded by people who wanted "fixing," and here it was again. Could I stand another round?

Then, it occurred to me that this guru was engaging us in some sort of Socratic dialogue. That she purposely took an opposing stance to pry something out of us. After all, she was on my enlightened being list. That had to mean something. And hadn't she told us that *insight* had been passed to her by her guru? Couldn't she do that for us as well? Us sitting in her presence, sharing her light? Like Shri Anandi Ma had done for me giving me shaktipat? All of us wanting—I assumed—some vision of wholeness—just like the people in Lucknow? I was confused. Gurus were supposed to possess wisdom and want to share it, or so I thought.

The more Sharlene was questioned, the more she challenged each inquiry. She gave the impression that she enjoyed provoking those who asked questions. She was not bringing us together as a group but splintering us. Where was the compassionate understanding I expected from gurus, from holy men, and in this case, a holy woman? That's how she had billed herself! But something was missing.

And at that moment, it didn't take long for my mind to jump back to the parish priest who'd stolen an essential part of my religious beliefs right after Mother died. He'd refused to bury her in the Catholic Cemetery, ungenerous and spiteful because she never attended church. Sharlene's satsang had the same air of remiss about it. The same clinging to rules, to abstract concepts, to authoritarian control while she pretended to walk in her guru's footsteps, but for me, she had fallen out of them somewhere along the line.

After satsang was over, I needed a long walk back to the Yog Niketan to digest what had been discussed. I crossed a bridge not far from Sharlene's meeting house and walked along the Ganges' western bank. As I went along, four large tents made of black plastic garbage bag material crouched on the side of the river. Children played barefoot in the dirt around the shelters as a woman squatted by a brazier mixing a pot.

I squinted at the woman. *Was she getting water from the Ganges? Where else?* I felt my throat close up as I realized families lived inside the garbage bag tents. Here I was walking along in a shabby pair of sweat pants topped with a sixty-dollar fleece from REI—I felt wealthy. Looking at these people who'd been left behind, my heart hurt. I thanked God for my prosperity.

By the time I reached my room, I had decided I would go back to satsang the following day. I was booked into the ashram for a week and had no place to go and nothing else to do. Maybe I could figure out what this blond guru was teaching, wrap my head around the abstractions. Although I disagreed with her methods of instruction, I'd give it another go.

That afternoon, our yoga instructor swept into the studio and immediately led us through one asana after the other. I opened yet more to the flow with each pose—the camel, the eagle, the cobra. Next, the class moved into Natarajasana, the cosmic dancer of creation and destruction. The rhythm of the pose spawned my cobra, which arched softly above my head.

Soon the instructor was prepping us to stand on our heads using ropes attached to the walls. I stepped into a rope, leaned back at an angle, and propped my feet against the wall. I carefully released my arms to the floor to hang like a bat. I felt a release discharging from my body, untangling knots.

When the class ended, I went to thank the teacher. *He was wonderful.* Face to face with him, I was bowled over. It was Girish, the quiet, unassuming receptionist who I'd been interacting with for days, coming and going from the ashram. He had somehow remained unrecognizable to me, hidden behind a soft demeanor as a receptionist but intense as a yoga instructor. In the studio, Girish had shape-shifted, morphing from a yin personality into an unflinching yang yogi. I shook my head. *Gifted*, I thought. *Truly gifted.*

As part of my stay at the Yog Niketan Ashram, I was committed to attending satsang with the blind guru, Vikram, who lived next door. So, after dinner on my second night, I climbed a flight of stairs to a large airy room that opened out to the river. The ashram was mainly empty, and few people showed up for the satsang—me, a man, and another woman plus Vikram's wife who served us tea. Vikram greeted us almost shyly before his forty-five-minute lecture I can no longer remember. The night was cool, and I wrapped myself in the taupe cashmere shawl I'd bought in Nepal. A small fire burned dung patties in a brazier, barely heating the chilly room.

Vikram kept losing steam, yet he went on forever, his words filling the room. But for me, they didn't penetrate my head or my heart. Physically, he'd seen better days, and his dwindling demeanor blanketed the room, making it hard to focus on his words and message. Instead, my mind drifted back and forth from trekking the Circuit to staring into the brazier and seeing the sari-clad ladies of Lucknow throwing cow manure against the wall. Halfway through sitting cross-legged on a cushion on the floor, my back began to complain. I held myself as still as possible, shifting ever so slightly to gain some relief. The others politely mustered a few questions before we departed unceremoniously.

Each night would be like this—listening to Vikram lecturing in a gentle but unconvincing way. Most of it was a blur. A kindly man who exuded feebleness. Vitality drained from the room, and I felt bad that he lacked devotees. So many of us scrambled around India searching for enlightenment—yet the only ones who showed up here had paid for a room next door.

Elephant Dung

Once again, the following day, I went to the courtyard where Sharlene held satsang. Questions were rebuffed. Others challenged her. *She* was *right* in each exchange. I wondered what the others were getting out of it. I thought she was there to help, and I was befuddled by her approach. Why was I resisting all this *talk*, this satsang...sacred conversations...which I had traveled from Lucknow to Rishikesh to hear? Why when I genuinely believed that there were individuals, Shri Anandi Ma, for one, who had special powers to transmit to others? After all, I had Kundalini energy rising through my chakras—I believed—but this satsang sounded like, "Blah, blah, blah...."

I chuckled to myself, Sharlene's going to end up being reincarnated as a slug if she keeps this up! Then feeling silliness bubbling up in my throat, I hoped I wouldn't have to jump up and split the scene, my own experience with rebirth came into view out of the past. It had been a Stanislov Grof workshop I'd taken at the Esalen Institute.

During my summer school break of 1977, I spent a month at Esalen in Big Sur, California. I'd taken workshops and soaked in hot tubs. Those tubs were filled with sulfuric water coming from the earth's center and worked magic on my body. I'd gotten massages and enjoyed the company of like-minded people while working in the kitchen cracking eggs and slicing carrots for meals in exchange for room and board. The whole place hovered on the coastline of the Pacific Ocean. It was just gorgeous. And the Esalen Institute, at that time, was a world premiere humanistic psychology establishment. It was the home of Fritz Perls and Alan Watts, innovators in the field.

I'd found my way to Esalen after a series of teacher training in Confluent Education workshops (mind/body/spirit integration for students). I loved participating in consciousness workshops—and this re-birthing one, Stan Grof's holotropic breathwork, was the craziest. Stan laid us out on mats and cranked up the Balinese "monkey chanting" music. He instructed us to breathe rapidly for two hours. There was no discourse back and forth, no agonizing over past emotional problems or traumas. Instead, the music played, and I laid on the floor, allowing the process to take me where it may.

I inhaled, I exhaled…inhaled, exhaled…picking up the speed… heavy-duty pranayama… picking up yet more speed…dropping into an imaginary past world, or was it the present or was it the future? I didn't know or care staying in the process of Grof's breathwork—remarkably not fainting out cold. Inhaling, exhaling, monkey chanting drove my brain waves, shifting my mind's gears. Finally, I visualized myself traveling through a narrow passageway—squeezing and pulsing—to an entry point to be reborn.

At that moment, it wasn't so much that I was re-incarnated—the same me entering a body again to play out and resolve my karmic debts—no. Instead, I was being transformed—mind, body, and spirit renewed, re-energized—re-me-ed...in a package that was moving forward in my present life. That is, I wasn't sure precisely what was being "reborn." But I knew the course at Esalen put me in the "zone" (what some call the runner's high) —a continual, subtle meditative state that changed my life in profound ways.

I pulled myself back into the satsang courtyard in Rishikesh. Sharlene droned on, and for me, she was becoming a millstone grinding at my psyche.

Those afternoons in Rishikesh, I sat out on the balcony and read *Moby Dick*. I'd packed it as my all-time favorite. I knew there'd be time to reread the tome, this time savoring each line and metaphor—the quest for meaning and the haunting nature of death. The whale's symbolism grabbed me. It was a creature who sang soul songs, whose melodies traveled through watery miles to touch other living beings—fish, (and I was sure) the kelp fields, plus each molecule of the ocean I loved to bathe in. An aminal that could sense the moon's phases so that it could change its monthly tunes—it mystified me.

I watched the pigs slouching along the river bank, their rosy snouts rooting through the mud. At times, I strolled along the Ganges among the shops on the opposite side of the river. I bought a pearl necklace and a couple of zircons. I also purchased a set of steel containers for train meals: a covered dish, utensils, a metal cup, and an electrical heating wire to make a single mug of tea in my room. I was affluent.

At night, the shops were dimly lit, and the streets were without lights. I carried a three-inch flashlight making sure I'd miss the dog droppings on the pavement. One night, a few men standing outside their stores asked if they could see my flashlight. Fascinated by its smallness, they examined it politely, asking to buy it. I declined. It was my only torch, and I would need it throughout my trip.

One morning, wanting variety, I stole away to take an Iyengar yoga class at a different studio. By the time the class began, fifty people had crowded into the room. Each mat was placed about six inches apart. The yogi stood on a dais at the front and barked out instructions like a Sargent: Details on alignment, strength, and stability, exact positioning was critical. This was not my cup of tea. It felt like bully-yoga, not yoga-yoga. I soon realized I'd made a mistake.

Less than three minutes into the class, a late-comer arrived and glanced wearily around for a space. There were none. We were packed in— mat to mat. I turned to the door getting up on my knees, signaling the guy to take my place. I danced carefully between the mats, not looking at the instructor, and slipped through the door, walking gingerly back to Yog Niketan to wait for Girish's class later that afternoon. He'd spoiled me from that time forward. For many decades to come, this soft yet forceful instructor remained anchored in my recollections as a master yogi. It was he, there in Rishikesh, who had opened a breadth of sympathy inside of me where I accepted my weaknesses as inherent in my strength. Maybe he even could be called a yoga-guru, one undoubtedly enlightened.

I continued to go to satsang. One morning, a woman and I struck up a conversation. Sheila, from the State of Washington, was a forester. She was going wild elephant stalking in the hills that rose over Rishikesh. "Do you want to go with me?" she asked.

Anxious for an escape, I said, "I wouldn't miss it. My brain needs a hike after this...ah, intellectualizing."

"Yeah, I know what you mean. All the words begin to wear on you after a while."

That afternoon Sheila and I stocked up on bottled water and snacks. Then, we walked across the bridge to the back of the shops. Sheila found the trailhead, and we hiked up into the pine forest.

It wasn't long before Shelia said, "Look!" and pointed at a pile of dried elephant dung. "This is the trail." And soon, we were climbing steep slopes through thick overgrown woods, me wishing I had and knew how to use a machete. An understory of bamboo buried us. After an hour, piles of steaming elephant excrement littered the trail. We quickened our pace, climbing for another hour, but no elephants.

The humidity was high, and by the time we stopped, we dripped sweat. Coming up the slope, the trail had divided several times. Consequently, we placed markers on the path expecting the down track to be tricky. As the hours went by, the light slid from the afternoon sky. Finally, disappointed with nary an elephant to be found, Sheila agreed to turn back.

As we went along the trail, we relied on the few sticks we'd placed at the divides, but they were hard to follow through the thick brush and trees. We stumbled along for a while, and it was time to tap into my mental imagery to recall the way back. I thought of Dad, how I'd inherited a bit of his photographic memory, and now—groping toward Rishikesh—I remembered the first time I'd used it as a kid.

It was the early fifties, the pre-Eisenhower highway system era, and we were loaded in the Hudson to visit Dad's brother, Uncle Sam, who lived in upstate New York, farm country. Dad drove the backroads through the northwest hills of Connecticut. Those 5AM mornings were ripe with expectations for me. Gauzy veils of vapors rose over small vernal pools by the sides of the roads lined with miles of Queen Anne's lace, blue chicory, and carroty daylilies. The plant families always were calling me.

Every so often, Dad checked the map. Still, it was his inner gyroscope and his photographic memory that got us a thousand miles from home and back again without too much ado. But drink did impair it. That year, arriving late in the middle of the night at Uncle Sam's, Dad couldn't locate the vacant neighbor's house he'd been told we'd be bedding at—a place we'd stayed the summer before.

Dad had been drinking heavily during the drive and was now circling the dirt roads. I woke out of a groggy sleep as the car rattled along. Dad was cursing, "Where the hell is that house, Goddammit!? It's gettin' late!" His face was twisted into a scowl, and I could smell the booze. I looked out the car's window through swirling dust clouds just as we passed the neighbor's house we were looking for, but Dad drove on. Five minutes later, he circled back around, speeding past the same place again. "I know it's here somewhere!" Dad said driving on. At the third pass, I yelled out, "There's the house, Dad!" to which he slammed on the breaks cursing softly,

"Oh for Pete's sake! Yeah, Honey, there it is!" Alcohol and photographic memories probably don't mix.

But here now, with Sheila hiking down the elephants' footpath, I kept a close look at each stick on the track noting the ones we'd used for markers. When we reached the road and walked back to the town, the sun cast an amber glow, cutting long blue shadows against the wedding-cake buildings. And even though we hadn't found any wild elephants, the hike—putting boot to trail—had cleared my head.

Santa Claus in India

It's easy to lose time in Rishikesh, so mellow, so singular, so pink. That week, I spent hours sitting on the balcony watching Mother Ganga in her green sari flow beneath the ashram. I took in the sun's rosy blush across her lap. I read, meditated, did yoga, and basked in the village people's laid-back manner. As time went on, I felt pink.

Several days after my arrival, two young German women, Erika and Harriet, booked a room at the ashram. We immediately made friends.

"We are looking to visit the American guru," Erika said. "Do you know where we can find her?"

"Ah, I do. I know where she is," and filled the two women in on her location, agreeing to take them with me the next day. When the morning arrived, Erika and Harriet were anxious to be on time, so the three of us took a tuk-tuk to satsang. After the session (same old stuff to my ears), the women said they liked Sharlene's approach. No matter; we hung out and went to lunch at the same place I'd eaten the day before. The café that served dal bhat with nice chapattis, where they'd promised to make chapatti pizzas for me if I returned.

As the three of us sat in the café—well, the tables, the chairs, the plates, the food—all covered with flies. Where had they been yesterday? Off sitting satsang? I was disgusted, but evading flies was like escaping taxes or maybe even death in India. Impossible. The restaurants along the Ganges…questionable sanitation, I was sure…still, I loved it, every minute of it…the waiters always friendly and accommodating.

Christmas would be in two days. It was time to play Santa Claus. I walked into town and shopped. I spent twenty dollars buying several large bags of rice and lentils, plus bunches of bananas, children's horns, rattles, balls, and dolls. In addition, I purchased combs and red bhindi patches worn on women's foreheads to ward off bad luck. When I got back to the ashram, I found Erika and Harriet and brought them to my room, where the tuk-tuk driver had helped me haul my loot.

Harriet asked, "What are you doing with all this food, Anya?"

"Are you having a party?" Erika asked.

"No. Well, yes," I laughed. "I need your help to pass these things out Christmas morning after we finish satsang," giving them the details of my action plan.

Erika's eyes lit up, and she exclaimed, "Oh, yes! We are happy to help." And their faces broke into broad smiles, and they nodded vigorously.

Like anywhere during Christmas, it was a busy time in Rishikesh. India is primarily a Hindu country, but Hinduism embraces all the major religions incorporating them into their practice. The town was loaded with Westerners, and the local Hindu community planned a Christmas Eve gathering. We had been invited to come together for a service at the public hall not far from the ashram.

That night, I got my spot on the floor in the fifth row from the front of the speakers. The room was decorated with strings of tiny Christmas fairy lights that twinkled on and off. People kept coming in—Westerners, Indians, everyone. We were already wedged shoulder to shoulder when an Indian woman stepped carefully through the crowd and plunked herself almost into my lap. By the time the service started, there wasn't a hairsbreadth between any of us.

The service began. One Indian leader from the community greeted us and read passages of Luke and Matthew from the Bible. The story of Baby Jesus was retold. Others spoke of their commitment to world unity and peace. A harmonium played, and we sang Christmas carols till midnight. The fairy lights twinkled around us, and I remember…as close as we were sitting together…the glow of warmth that night drew us yet closer.

On Christmas morning, Erika, Harriet, and I went to satsang where they were content. I had managed to pay attention with one ear while thinking about Keoladeo Ghana National Park in Bharatpur, Rajasthan. It was a birder's paradise where I planned to go after leaving Rishikesh in a few days. I needed to intersperse all the head stuff with a dose of nature.

After satsang, the three of us walked across the bridge and hailed two tuk-tuks that took us back to my room. There we gathered up the pile of food and toys before heading back up the river. When we arrived at the garbage bag tents, I'd seen earlier when I'd come to town, several women dove inside only to stare out from under the flaps with kids peeking from behind.

Erika, Harriet, and I hauled the bags of rice and lentils across the dusty stretch to the tents. "Namaste," I said, dipping my head greeting a woman sitting on the ground by a make-shift campfire. There was no reply. She stared back in bewilderment.

Other women crept from their tents cautiously. An older lady with lines etched in her face came from behind the far tent. She began to say something I couldn't understand while gesturing toward the other women. I pointed to the bags of food, bowing my head to show they were gifts. The children crept in closer. I stepped toward the opening of a tent and placed a bag of rice inside indicating the rice was to be shared.

Ericka did the same with the other bags of rice and lentils. Harriet came handing out the bananas and the toys. Back at the tuk-tuks, I could see the drivers' astonished faces. The toys were divided among the children whose curious faces gaped at us.

I passed out the combs and bhindi patches to the women; not a word was spoken. The Germans and I repeated, "Merry Christmas" over and over—not that we knew it held any meaning for the listeners—but it did for us. It held giving, it held well-being, it held connection, it held home—sans words, sans sitting, sans head stuff. For us, maybe we were hoping (or maybe not even) that the gesture of rice and lentils and toys might just have shifted our own karmic reckonings one jot further toward the growth of human understanding.

Keoladeo Ghana National Park

Held up at the train station's ticket booth, I ran to the platform, got on the train, and scrambled to my overnight compartment. I had booked a ticket to Bharatpur, Rajasthan, because my *Lonely Planet India* had described the Keoladeo Ghana National Park as a birder's paradise. As a birder, this was definitely what I needed, communing with nature. I'd had enough head stuff, the endless talking in circles that got me nowhere.

When I threw open the door to the compartment, I was shocked. Four men sat there. The men stared at me. I stared back. "Are your wives coming?" I asked.

"No wives here tonight," one guy said. My hackles went up. I'd make a mistake. I'd booked a first-class ticket, but...Confused, I asked myself, *Why hadn't I been put in a section with other women or a family-like before? Sleep in a compartment with strange men?* I felt threatened. Heat shot through my body.

I grabbed my bag and jumped off the train to a platform empty of passengers. It was five minutes from leaving the station. Several cars down, a conductor talked to another man, and I ran to him, interrupting him. The fact that station masters and conductors on the Indian train system all spoke fluent English turned out to be a blessing. The British had occupied India for close to a century making English the country's universal language.

Breathless, I said to the conductor, "I've been put in a berth where there are four men. I can't sleep in a compartment with men. I need a sleeper with a family!" The train's engine revved loudly as it spewed volcanoes of steam into the dark air. The conductor glared at me expressionlessly.

"Madam, get back into the train. We are about to depart," he said, turning back to the other man.

"No! I need a safe berth with other women. Please!"

"Get back on the train to your compartment, Madam." I could see that he was losing patience with me.

"No, please, a compartment with women," I begged.

"Madam, we have no space like that," he said crossly, turning back to the man before him. Then, remembering that baksheesh was the universal language in India, in any culture, I rummaged in my purse, taking out rupees waving them in his face.

"Madam, back on the train! Go into your compartment," he said decisively. He shook his head, not meeting my eyes or the money I was poking into his face. "I will come shortly."

I realized taking the baksheesh in front of the other guy was like waving a red flag, making it look like he could be bribed. *OK*, I said to myself. *I get this. OK.* I turned back to the train and jumped on seconds before it pulled away from the station. I waited just inside my assigned car. The train picked up speed, and within minutes the conductor came along grabbed my bag, saying, "Come, Madam!"

I followed him through several cars before he stopped in a well-lit one. It was stacked with clean berths curtained off by cotton drapes behind which I could hear people murmuring—women, men, and children. The conductor pointed to a single top berth on one side of the train and motioned that it was mine. I thanked him profusely and handed him the baksheesh he tucked in his jacket pocket before turning on his heel and briskly leaving the compartment.

I pushed my bag up into the top bunk, crawled after it onto the narrow mattress, and arranged the folded pile of sheets waiting for me. I took out my lock and secured the bag to the railing. I drew the curtain down alongside the bunk, stretched out, and let out a sigh. The rhythmic clacking of the train wheels on the tracks took up my attention.

Soon I was chuckling at myself. I have to admit I'd been stupid about figuring out the Indian train system. To me, the whole ticketing system didn't make any sense—the classifications of first-class, second-class AC, etc. For example, to book a sleeper bunk that had heat in the winter (or AC in the summer), I had needed to book a ticket designated as "second class AC." Of course, first-class had no heat and no AC. But again, it had taken me getting angry to end up in a safe, heated berth—*second class AC!*

I removed my boots and got comfortable balancing my little silver food containers on my bag. I smirked at my little success. Too bad satsang had not examined the efficacy of anger. I would have had a lot to say about that. How a sober use of anger could propel you to not only stand up for yourself but change your whole nervous system.

Anger was part of me. I'm sure all that stuff that had gone on in my childhood had made my nervous system undergo changes, some brutal, some necessary. Still, it did push me to action without hesitation when I needed to look out for myself. As the train rattled on into the night, I fell into a deep, secure sleep. What I didn't know at that moment was there would be a yet more profound application of my anger when I arrived in Luxor, Egypt (still a long way down the road). It would be there on the banks of the Nile where my anger's application would change my life.

Siberian Cranes

Keoladeo Ghana National Park was no Bronx Zoo. A few families made their way along the wide dirt road under the kadam trees at the entrance. The day before at my guesthouse, I'd been told to search for rare Siberian cranes. Unfortunately, the cranes were almost extinct. Only a handful remained wintering over in the park, so they'd be hard to find tucked somewhere in the park's eleven square miles of wetlands.

According to Lonely Planet, Keoladeo had once been the hunting grounds of the Maharaja. He had diverted waters from a nearby irrigation canal to create the present-day medley of wetlands, woodlands, and grasslands. This action encouraged the winter migration of thousands of birds from all over Asia to its shores. When hunting stopped in 1971, the park was later designated a World Heritage Site because of its abundant bird populations, wildlife, and botanical diversity.

My birding skills were average. I'd been programmed first by Dad to appreciate the cleverness of birds, but also early in my teaching career, I'd fallen in with a group of international birders. I'd roamed the Connecticut woods with them. So, as far as the cranes were concerned, I wasn't looking for bragging rights or ticking off a life list—even though I had one at home for local areas. Instead, I wanted to see these remaining powerful creatures for their majesty. Using their gyroscopes, they could catch the thermals each winter to fly over 5,000 miles from the edge of Siberia then across the Himalayas to Rajasthan.

I walked for two miles into the park, leaving the families behind. It was a time in India that I was virtually alone wherever I visited, either natural or cultural sites. It was before the tourist explosion had surged, overcrowding the country's historic sites. And it was a time definitely when wild places were not heavily visited. As I drifted farther and farther back into the park, it was empty, and I liked that. Being alone in nature was where I felt most at home.

I strolled along and thought about my travels in India. I had come to see the Taj Mahal and experience the country's exotic culture described by Cathy during our college years. It had not disappointed. Not even sitting with the sat-sangees. Trekking the Himalayas had bolstered my ability to savor each day.

Every morning I felt the day belonged to me, to no one, or nothing else unless I chose it. No schedule, no task, just imbibing the energies emanating from the worn-out yet rich land I was in. Taking in the vitalities of the people who lived ordinary lives in a complex, stratified society—the sari-clad women making dung patties, the bright-eyed fruit seller, the tent dwellers by the side of the Ganges. And then there were people like Papaji and Sharlene, the enlightened beings.

I recalled satsang—Papaji, Sharlene, and Vikram, the blind guru, and wondered about the impact of their work. As a teacher, I knew they had something to give. Chances were, they'd encounter seekers (I guess that included me, too) who could take and connect with their messages even though I hadn't. I was looking for something else. I wasn't sure what that was, but it was something else. The other's pain during satsang had saddened me—what had appeared to me as their futile quest to find their true selves, to find healing. I sent the gurus prayers to encourage them in their work.

I penetrated deeper into the landscape before diverting off onto a narrow boardwalk. That structure was built over a shallow waterway. It straddled grasslands dominated by mesquite bushes and tall acacias I recognized from TV documentaries. Plants unknown to me populated the shallows. However, by examining their flower heads and leaves, I identified some of their families. The daisies belonged to the composites and grew alongside the rose family, which included a sort of plum tree along the walk.

Trees, shrubs, herbs, grasses, roots, tubers—all did their job in the freshwater marshland—all provided food for the chain of fowl, fish, and reptiles. Each plant rooted in the muck before reaching for the sunlit sky—a recitation of green and brown and yellow and red…a living rosary-beads-of-life. All spewed oxygen into the atmosphere, bathing the mosaic of wetlands in their graces. *Thank you, God, for each root, stem, leaf, bud, flower…for every breath they give.*

I stood under the tropical trees that I had no names for but appreciated the shade made by their ever-so-clear chartreusey-green leaves. And I watched. Birds flew overhead. Ospreys, bee-eaters, warblers, and others I couldn't begin to identify without binoculars or a bird book. All dive-bombing from treetops gobbling insect life, tiny packets of energy. Herons, storks, cormorants, ducks, sandpipers wading in the shallow water, eating duckweed, and hunting for crabs, frogs, and snakes. A small sharp horned deer picked its way through the far groves of trees nibbling vegetation. *Good*, I thought: *Keeping the shrubbery at bay*. Keoladeo Park was all about dinner—eat or be eaten—the cycle of Shiva—the supreme ecological creator and destroyer.

Then there they were—cranes. About thirty of them promenading elegantly through the weeds picking up each long leg placing it down precisely in a watery dance. Were they Siberians? I scrutinized the markings on their heads. These were red-hooded. I'd seen pictures of the Siberians back at the guesthouse, and none of these wore the red face-masks that identified them as such. Disappointed, I took note of their markings and later identified them as Sarus cranes. But pretty indeed, I watched their stylish feeding rituals.

The afternoon wore on, and having read the park's brochure, I knew there were snakes and big ones at that, and I wanted to see a python. I searched the tall grasses without luck. Then, as I approached a grove of acacias, I smelled a rich odor of rot. I rounded the corner and was startled to see a colossal vulture perched on the ground. Its wings spread cape-like—black, shiny, and six feet across— it danced the paso doble over a rotting carcass of a water buffalo. Arching its long neck over the carrion, the bird's head bobbed up and down, paused, eyed me briefly before turning back to its task, its talons tearing the animal to pieces. The vulture's beak was smeared crimson dripping putrid guts.

I froze, fascinated. *Forget the snakes*. For twenty minutes, I watched (this time close-up) the wheel of life grind on…molecules of flesh and blood from the dead water buffalo ripped apart to slip lifegiving nutrients into the vulture's throat, performing a rite of passage, stripping sinew—the surrendering of the dead animal's energy to nourish the bird. I witnessed. And as the vulture dined on, I thought of Gome, us standing below the sky burial balcony reverently so many weeks before.

TIME IS ONLY AN INCH

Brimming with this drama, I walked back to the park entrance, still looking for the Siberian cranes but came up short. Returning to my lodgings, I was determined to resume the search again. The men in reception told me the cranes were best spotted very early in the morning. The plan was to rent a bike to ride through the park and look for them mixed in with the numerous Sarus cranes.

The following day as dawn broke, I passed through the park's check-point entrance, showed my pass, and rented binoculars and a bike. Alone on the road, I rode along, not quite sure where to find the cranes but trusting that I would. Trusting that determined spot inside of me that never gave up, trusting it to deliver.

I peddled along, often stopping to use the binoculars. Then, about a mile in, I heard a bike coming up behind me. A tall Indian man dressed impeccably in a knee-length Baghal bandi jacket with a turban on his head rode up alongside me. His stately appearance was out of place; at first wary, I quickly sensed that he was connected to the matter at hand.

"Hello, Namaste," I said. *Where had he come from?*

"Hello. You are out early," he said in an educated voice.

"Yes. I'm looking for the Siberian cranes. Back at the hotel, they said to get out early."

"Yes, the cranes. Very beautiful. Do you know where they are?"

"No. I only have a general idea from the guards at the entrance."

"I can show you if you like. Follow me."

The road was empty; he'd come from nowhere. *Should I accept his guidance?* I didn't have many choices. Yet there was something more to it, more than him looking the reliable professor type in his pristine suit. More to it than his professorial voice. It was my own sense of OK-ness, something being decided from my gut to trust him. And I said, "OK."

My guide cycled down the dusty road for about five minutes before coming to a marshy area of tall green grasses where he stopped. The morning's young light glinted off the water. Seven Siberian cranes, standing nearly six feet tall, fed about thirty feet from the road's edge. Each wore a red face-mask, clearly seen as they turned their amber eyes to peer at us. I was spellbound.

Casually, they picked their way along, digging up roots, harpooning fish, snatching insects. Party-punch-pink legs scissored through the weeds, parabola-ing water slowly outward in concentric circles. Then suddenly, their waltz broke into a ruckus filling the air with sharp cries. Necks craned in corkscrew twists—true yogis—as the birds arched into backbends, anuvittasana. They hopped and skipped across the marsh—their grayish wingspans billowing eight feet out into black-trimmed ballroom dresses. Siberian cranes partying. Beauty and power dancing in the cycle of life.

My guide and I watched the Siberian cranes for several minutes before he took his leave. I never did ask his name or where he was going or where he had come from. The conversation had been about the birds—him telling me the cranes stood for symbols of marital fidelity, that they took a mate for life. After the man had left, it was apparent that I never would have found the cranes on my own and that the little wishes in my life were being granted. And I felt myself falling deeper into a zone of random guidance—synchronicity kicking in for me, getting this guide who helped me find this elegant bird of faithfulness. What if I wished for something big? Like what? I couldn't think of anything just then. But just *what if?*

That day, life in the Keoladeo wetland unfolded like a magnificent Japanese fan, folding, unfolding—refolding in and out of creation's cyclic rhythms. Each time I took in the egret-filled pond, Mother Nature gave me a blast of energy, gentle yet profound. Greedily, I needed more. And the next day, I put on my blue dress, and I took a bus to yet another bird sanctuary not usually visited by tourists. Mistake number one.

When I jumped off the bus at the bird sanctuary, I got a bad taste in my mouth. No guards stood at the entrance; few people milled around. A quick look showed a dilapidated building with paint peeling, probably abandoned. It was nothing compared to Keoladeo Ghana Park with its vast marshlands. Instead, it had tall trees patrolled by monkeys.

I wandered under the trees. Feeling hungry, I took out a packet of biscuits popping one in my mouth. Mistake number two. It didn't take long for a monkey to come down from an overhead branch exposing its teeth to me. "Shoo. Go away," I said, waving my hand holding the biscuit. But it came toward me. "Shoo," I said louder as I retreated backward from its snarling maw. It lunged at me. I kicked at it. "Getaway," I cried fearfully, thinking *all I need is to be bitten by a rabid monkey!*

Then it charged me. Realizing it wanted the biscuits, I flung them into the bushes. The monkey did a flip going after the packet, retrieved it, and gobbled its contents, eying me steadily. By that time, I hated the whole rundown place—the feeling of being in a ghost village, monkeys crawling in the trees, attacking. I turned on my heel and ran back to the bus stop. Mistake number three.

At the bus stop, I waited for about twenty minutes with a group of sari-clad women. While waiting, an adolescent boy came along and stopped sizing me up. I wondered what the kid was up to. In a minute, he yelled something at me in Hindi, pointing toward the road. I ignored him, turning my back. He came around, nudging closer to my side, continuing the harangue. I turned to step away and said, "Leave me alone. You're rude." More mean words from him in Hindi.

My neck got hot. I looked him in the eyes, "I said beat it!" His neck tightened like a cord. The women standing nearby cast their eyes down to their feet. I couldn't read their faces. The bully came closer, putting his contorted face into mine, unwilling to let up. Threatened, I moved closer toward the women who dipped their heads, refusing to make eye contact with me. I was getting the message it was none of their business. Boss-boy was in charge. With fists clenched, he came nearer.

By now, I was almost physically touching the circle of women but felt they were impervious to my plight. Then, one shifted to the right allowing me to step inside the group so that the bully stopped his approach and backed off. I stood inside the circle of women for several minutes, still pelted by the kid's nasty glances. To my relief, the bus finally arrived, the boy went off, and I crawled into a seat on the bus. It was a lesson for me. A sour taste of the culture. Women in India, which now included me, lived in a bitter reality: wearing a dress made us second-class citizens.

Ministry of Home Affairs, Delhi

It didn't take long for me to experience the caste system in India. Departing the train in Delhi, a gaunt, elderly turbaned porter approached me, signaling he'd carry my bag through the train station's jumble of platforms and multiple staircases. This sounded good to me, especially that he held up three fingers, indicating it would cost me about the equivalent of ten cents. I agreed. On the street, I told the porter to cross the road to a hotel.

I checked in while the porter waited with my bag. When I gestured him to follow me to my room to deposit it and pay him, that's when the clerk shook his head vigorously. And he spewed something in Hindu at old man forbidding him to take one step beyond reception. This needed no translation for me. By this time, the caste system had been outlawed in India; but I learned only too soon it was still practiced. Part of the untouchable class, the baggage carrier wasn't getting an inch farther into the hotel. Shocked, I stayed the night and found a different hotel the next day.

It was early January, over a week after the Christmas shared with Harriet and Erika in Rishikesh. I planned to stay about a week in Delhi. I'd see the sites, take a short day-trip south by train to the Taj Mahal in Agra, buy a sari, and secure my entry papers into the Tibetan Refugee Camp to hear the Dalai Lama give his Kalachakra Initiation teaching. He was the enlightened being I most looked forward to hearing, well worth all the uneasiness and weariness of sitting through Sharlene's lectures.

That afternoon, I took myself to the Ministry of Home Affairs, Jaisalmer House on Mansingh Road to get my access papers into the refugee camp at Mundgod. I crisscrossed the back streets of Delhi. They were jammed with people—sari-clad women, men in crisp dress-shirts—all rushing along narrow alleyways past men who sat cross-legged on stools in shops selling everything imaginable from bangles to spices to carpets. Car horns blared, cows roamed the middle of the street, the smell of frying puri wafted from carts mixing with the toxic perfume of Indian life—air pollution. By the end of my stay in India, I would be popping Sudafed to keep my sinuses open.

Street corners felt familiar to me, strewn with piles of rusting bicycle carcasses, old twisted machinery, broken wheels, tangled cables, algae-covered water cans all under snarls of electrical wires with the ubiquitous monkeys overhead doing their high-wire acts. Venders wheeled carts filled with bananas, cauliflowers, and carrots over cobbles obscenely awash with who knew what. I might have found it contemptible but didn't. There was no helping it. My mind rode with the culture's undercurrents. I had become inured to the trash, dirt, smells, crowds, poverty…all bundled up in a society with a hefty dose of sacredness, just like Varanasi.

Now in Delhi, my heart began to stretch through India's time zones and space zones and cosmic zones to tell me the same thing: *See these people? Smell this city? Touch this disorder? Then, listen to its humanity in your heart.* Something in me merged with the whole of the place, its genius loci, spilling out on the sidewalks down the streets. I slipped into its tide and began to eat, drink and think like India, joining its universal chaos. I/Thou India.

The Ministry of Home Affairs was in an imposing building. I entered through a once-grand foyer and found my way to the correct office. A clerk stood behind the counter.

"Hello," I said.

"Yes, Madam, may I help you?"

"Yes. I would like to obtain papers to enter the Tibetan Refugee Camp at Mundgod. I want to go to hear the Dalai Lama give his teachings."

The man behind the desk looked at me blankly. "One moment, please," he said. "I will get someone to help you so that you can please explain further." And he went into the backroom.

I glanced around the empty office. A large portrait of an official hung on the wall. After about ten minutes, I got up from sitting and walked around biting my lip. Although I imagined there was a possibility that this event I wanted to go to could turn out to be simply a grand religious instruction of Buddhist teachings, somehow, that didn't matter. I'd already run through several enlightened beings on my list, plus other gurus. And somehow, I knew the Dalai Lama was different. For me, he was a mega-teacher, a real guru who had something to teach not just me but everyone on the planet. So, I felt an urge to get to Mundgod to be in his presence.

As I waited in the office—unmistakably wanting to attend the Initiation—it reminded me of a time in grade school. This was when Agnes got wind of Saturday catechism classes, and we'd demanded that Dad take us. Agnes must have calculated it would give us a 'get-out-of jail' card from our circumstances so we'd fit in better with the other kids. Those Saturdays became the highlight of our week, with Agnes (and sometimes me) hauling home the loot, book winnings from the catechism bees.

But then again, going to Mundgod, there was also the possibility it could turn out to be wholly different, more than a religious event. It could be where shaktipat energy might be found. Having experienced that previously, I believed that if anyone could transmit shaktipat it was the Dalai Lama. After all, it was called an "Initiation," but somehow, that didn't matter either. Having a chance to sit in the presence of the Dalai Lama would be a once-in-a-lifetime experience—and I wasn't going to miss out.

After waiting for what seemed an eternity, an official wearing a crisp khaki uniform came from the back office.

"Where is it you are going, Madam?"

"To Mundgod to the Tibetan Refugee Camp to hear the Dalai Lama speak," I said.

"Can you tell me how you are going?" he asked skeptically.

"Yes, by train."

He asked me again, and then yet again to explain where I wanted to go and why. *What was there to explain? Who wouldn't want to hear the Dalai Lama?* I patiently repeated myself. After still more back and forth, the official asked me to fill out papers.

When that was done, I handed them over and asked, "When can I come back to pick them up?"

"They will take time to process, Madam. Not this week." My heart sank. I was leaving in five days.

"Can I have them approved now?"

"Now?" his face became puzzled.

"Yes, now, so I'll have them with me when I go." I dug in. "Is there anything you can do? Anything I can do to expedite the… permission?" I thought of baksheesh but afraid to get arrested in a government building and locked up who knew where for who knew how long.

"Expedite? No, Madam. We will take care of this for you for sure. It's in our hands." *That's what I was afraid of. It being in their hands.* "Madam, we are very busy here. Can't you see? You come back next week," he said.

I looked around at the run-down, gray water-stained walls, the thick haze on the windows preventing the sun from cutting through. I stared back at the official, into the face of Indian bureaucracy. He reminded me of Tim saying he'd get the job done when there was little or no chance.

"Sir," I asked hopefully. "Can you send those papers to Mundgod to the post office or to the train master where I can get them when I arrive?"

"Well, of course, of course," he said unconvincingly and waved his hand in the air. "Don't worry, Madam. We will get them to you." The official scribbled a note on the top of my papers and offered his hand over the counter; I extended mine getting a feeble handshake. As I walked out of the office, I wondered how foolish I was being. The thought of not being able to get into the refugee camp at Mundgod depressed me. Outside the building, I found a store selling Sudafed. By this time in India, my sinuses had clogged, so in desperation, I popped a few to keep them awake. *Breathe, Honey, breathe*, I thought.

Encountering Cobras

R<small>EAL COBRAS ARE</small> scary. And they live on the streets of Delhi. Do they ever escape? I didn't think about that as I watched the skinny cobra rise out of its wicker basket, eying me swaying back and forth. The snake's glittering silvery-gold scales and shiny black eyes mesmerized me. Still, I took a step back. The snake charmer, a turbaned, elderly man, squatted on his haunches next to the cobra's nest. He shot me a toothless grin, mischief in his eye, and a flute in one hand, motioning me in closer as he removed the lid from a second basket. I took a half-step to peer into the basket where another ring of scales coiled, and I wondered if the venomous little creature was defanged or whatever is done to de-tox them. It was strange, me knowing, or rather experiencing, what I had for many years, my cobra, now looking at a real, *no* actual, *no* a solid cobra face to face.

The snake charmer grinned up at me and began to play his flute. I thought of how snakes, for most people, hold fear and fascination. But for me, it was different. For me, cobras meant alignment with the Universe, my own internal energy flow. I dug in my pocket for a few rupees and dropped them on the rug near the charmer's foot.

As I walked away, down the busy street, my own Kundalini rose steadily over my head. Mentally, I watched it evolve, my numinous cobra rising higher and higher, branching into multiple candelabras doubling then tripling, cobra heads streaming golden light. I wasn't dizzy or lightheaded or faint, and I wasn't sure exactly what triggered it. Still, then again, maybe those live cobras had tripped this incredible iteration. Not knowing how to easily or completely explain the dramatic image taking me over, I felt respect for my own imaginative mind having given birth years before to my Kundalini opening.

I didn't care that this sort of experience was often seen as "fringe" or schizoid. For my Ph.D., I had examined the brains of some of the most creative outliers on the planet—inventors who used imagery and other unconventional methods to discover new ideas that changed the world. My brain had opened in an equally anomalous way—giving me a glimpse, no, a flow, no, a torrent of insight into the nature of reality just like theirs. I knew I was in good company. Knew that years of using mental imagery slipping between realities, slipping through openings of cosmic spaces into the "zone," I'd found my way of knowing and being in the world—that I was linked to something beyond myself. God? The Force of the Universe? All that and maybe more.

I walked on through the mayhem of Delhi. I reflected on how far I'd come from home, the time I'd spent in Nepal, the time now savoring India. I walked along in a confluence of energies—ordered and disordered— that were casting an old me aside, opening up a space for me to enter and take up a still stronger alignment with the Universe. I wasn't sure how to use it consciously, but I was grateful it was there.

Taj Mahal

The January sun ramped up, rolling heatwaves over the train tracks. The early morning platform to Agra was almost empty. Then two women stepped out of the station, Monrova and Paula from the Tatopani hot springs on the Annapurna Circuit. I was ready for some company, and here it was. They, too, were going to the Taj Mahal.

Several bear hugs later, Monrova said, "Come with us, Anya. We rented a car and driver in Agra."

"Do you have room?"

"Are you kidding? Wait till you see this vehicle."

Accidental movements of the cosmos were beginning to be the norm. My cobra was at work.

The vehicle, or should I say "the chariot," waiting in Agra turned out to be a shiny blue, 1936 vintage Plymouth touring sedan. It was grand. A hood ornament embellished the front surrounded by bulging fat fenders trimmed with metal bumpers that supported frog-eyed headlights. Inside, I fell into a cushiony, velvety seat that gobbled up my butt. Paula climbed in, plunked herself down and giggled. At the same time, Monrova gave directions to the driver before gliding herself into the backseat with us. The driver drove toward the Taj Mahal, and it was easy to pretend we were three princesses in a coach riding to a gala in style. The only thing missing was the champagne.

Once in Agra, Monrova, Paula, and I left the car and walked through a garden lined with fountains and cypress trees toward a tall sandstone entrance. Through it, I could see the Taj Mahal gleaming at the far end of long reflecting pools stretching back over forty acres. A double, pearled-white image—the Taj—floated one above, one below—in the pools that wore corsages of lilies.

The Taj overlooks the Yamuna River. Mughal Emperor Shah Jahan constructed it between 1631-1648 in honor of his favorite wife, Mumtaz Mahal. Mumtaz had died after giving birth to their fourteenth child in 1629. The Shah's grief was unquenchable. He employed twenty thousand artisans from India, Persia, and Syria who combined multiple architectural styles into a narrative that became a wonder of the modern world. It was now a UNESCO World Heritage Site.

Monrova, Paula, and I agreed to split up and meet again after two hours. I welcomed being alone with my own thoughts to take in every iota of the tomb without distraction. I wanted my artist's eye to observe it even though I didn't have paper or paints. I wanted to let my mental imagery snap and store pictures in my mind's eye—the luster of the pearled-white marble, the richness of its design.

It's easy to fall in love with the Taj Mahal. It laughs, it sings, it dances on reflecting pools while it grieves the inherent sorrow of love lost. From afar, the mausoleum's regularity and poise took me in. An onion-shaped dome, a gilded brass finial, was surrounded by four octagonal minarets at its top. The windows and doors, and turrets were evenly spaced, symmetrical and balanced. The monument held a geometrical composure of its own, a mathematical intelligence crafted in perfect scale. Each arch angled upward toward the heavens, a calculated elegy. Closer up, rays of sunlight glinted off the Taj's marble facades where the Koran's calligraphic passages etched in black prayers recited up its walls. Inlaid floral patterns repeated above and below, large to small, framing latticed doorways.

I went up the stairway that surrounded the building. Close up, it was palpable that someone's hand, each enlightened finger, had exacted a remarkable repetition of windows and doorways that reiterated over the marble's smooth face. I could almost hear the thousands of human hands chiseling and sculpting the stone, releasing its chill into the fire of the flickering inlaid gems bordering the archways. The craftsmen, honoring the religious ban on human or animal images, had carved numerous bas-relief panels of flowers. They ringed the tomb's base, forty-six different species—tulips, irises, anemones, lilies, more—blossoms, buds, and stems fixed in an eternity of stone yet swaying through a ceaseless, ancient breeze. The panels felt alive. Each sculpted in a botanical language narrating love's story.

I entered the dimly lit octagonal chamber of the mausoleum. A single lantern hung overhead shedding milky, yellow light on the white marble floors that tessellated with interlocking crosses curving and folding in and out in diamond-like star patterns. Filigree screens evocative of a woman's lacy handkerchief surrounded two cenotaphs in the middle of the room. One symbolized Mumtaz's presence, the other Shah Jahan, ensconced side by side.

The walls, the ceilings, the cenotaphs were ornate with yet more carved panels echoing the immortal garden portrayed on the monument's exterior. Arabesques of itinerant vines tiptoed up the walls. Their movement was imperceptible in uninhibited exquisiteness.

Still more florals—this time chrysanthemums, orchids, narcissus, asters, along with bulbous pomegranates. All flowed in leaves simple and compound, real and imaginary inlaid with delicate pieces of precious and semi-precious gems ruby, emerald, amethyst, carnelian, turquoise, lapis-lazuli, coral, onyx, cat's eye, jade, bloodstone, agate. The bas relief reflected Jahan's devotion, sorrow, and loss in a stony bouquet that grew exponentially more exquisite through the ages. I almost wept at the beauty of it.

I walked around and round the cenotaphs peering through the filigree screens lacing light and shadow. Inside, the hunger of love lingered, clasped by the wringing hands of death. I was in a jewel box entwined by passion and tragedy. I knew the history. After Mumtaz's death, Shah Jahan was overthrown by his son and placed under house arrest at the Red Fort—a distance away overlooking the Taj Mahal. From there, the Shah spent his final days gazing at his soul mate's tomb. And it made me think of Mumtaz Mahal, the volumes of love devoted to her that now surrounded me, and I wondered: *Where do you find a love like that?* Unending devotion, passion, loyalty? I had to admit that the big challenge in my life had been just that—finding love given fully. Not self-love that I had. Dad had instilled that. But to find a partner, someone who'd share the challenges of a relationship or marriage equally—work through the problems, that's what I'd be interested in, an equal deal facing whatever adversities faced. Tim had failed, but it could have been. He was in my life for a different reason. At that moment, standing inside the Taj Mahal thinking about love, I remembered what Dori had said before I left town, "The Universe loves a vacuum, Anya."

Tying the String

THE TINY RESTAURANT was cramped, clean with six aqua-colored tables. Monrova, Paula, and I sat, and a waiter with dreadlocks came out from the back smiling broadly to hand us menus. I read "spaghetti" —my downfall. I pushed the memory of the big black dog slurping the pasta-filled colander out of my mind and ordered it. I bet there was no dog in the kitchen lapping around the dishes from a sink on the floor. Or, if there was, I would avoid going into the kitchen to check.

"OK, Anya, you've covered Varanasi and Rishikesh so far. Where are you going next?" Monrova asked.

"First, I'm heading south to hear the Dalai Lama teach. Then on to Madras."

"Sounds cool," Monrova said.

"Want to join me? I'd like some company, but you need papers to get into the refugee camp."

"No, we're heading for Osho's mediation retreat in Pune. Why don't *you* join us?" asked Paula.

"Pune? Tell me about it,"

"There's good yoga and meditation…Osho died about five years ago, but his people offer a great deal of spiritual support and…."

"Some good times, too," Monrova interrupted with a hint of something hidden in her voice.

Paula changed the tone. "When I go there, well, I wanna be believed in, and they believe in me. I feel acknowledged. You know what I mean? There are good people there. This restaurant is run by the Osho community."

From that, I figured my companions were Rajneeshees. My head began to spin with bits of news concerning some sort of cult in Oregon. A quick inward qualm stabbed me, but I guessed that Monrova and Paula were not proselytizing right now; they, like me, were hungry.

Monrova munched on a chapati the waiter had brought. "There are a lot of cool people there like yourself who are interested in the mind and the soul. You know—get grounded through yoga and get centered by meditating."

"You'll get a chance to breathe with highly conscious people," Paula added.

"Sounds…sounds nice…," I mumbled, thinking about what I'd encountered in Lucknow and Rishikesh—a bunch of fruitless lectures to re-invade a corner of my brain that was fast rejecting this as an enlightened being option. Then I began my pitch, "This woman I met in Kathmandu was telling me about the Dalai Lama giving his special teaching every couple of years, so now he's on my list to visit."

"List?" they asked. And I explained.

Paula cocked her head and said, "These people in Pune are different from any other place we've been. They're evolved; they'll accept you for being yourself. Completely yourself."

"We met this one guy there," Monrova said, "from New York who is just the sweetest, kindest. He fell in love with the place because he didn't have to be afraid about who he was anymore. That's what he said! At Pune, he put everything that cut him up behind him and started to love himself, ridding himself of the shit that had piled up in his brain over the years. You'd like these people."

I understood what Monrova and Paula were saying about angst. In the past month sitting satsang in Lucknow and Rishikesh, I'd heard many cries for spiritual help, longings for wholeness. And I have to admit, I'd felt isolated from them even though I'd encounter troubled waters myself. But the difference was, they were sinking while I had been tossed a life preserver by Dad—one that kept me from sinking very deep (even when I felt battered like hell). I, unlike the satsang-ees (and what sounded like some of the people at Pune), never got swallowed up in a flood of self-doubt or self-hatred. Never got so submerged that I couldn't get myself out of those torrents. Pune sounded like it was throwing out life preservers to help people keep afloat emotionally. I considered Paula and Monrova, and I wondered if they had ever felt "Special."

"Sounds like people are being...being helped," I agreed.

The meal came, and we ate. I spun the fork around the thin spaghetti coated with a red-orange sauce and placed it in my mouth. Light, tasty, zesty, each forkful a bit of gourmet sophistication I'd not tasted before. A combination of tomatoes and maybe turmeric delicately added? Mother had made very savory spaghetti sauce flavored with green peppers. But this sauce melted in my mouth like butter on a hot ear of corn. When I was done, fully satisfied, the only thing I could figure was that I was eating spiritually. Did they serve food like this in Pune?

"So, what do you think? Pune?" asked Paula.

My new friends were tempting me. I thought about it. "I'll think about it," I said in a polite voice, but something was nagging inside, throwing up a red flag.

"Look, there are only a few things you have to do to get in. You'll have to buy a white robe; we all wear them. They want us to be, well, look compatible. You'll also have to get a blood test."

"A blood test?" I asked.

"They do 'em right there," Monrova interjected.

"For what?"

"To make sure you don't carry any sexually transmitted diseases," said Paula.

"It's more fun," said Monrova.

"Well!" I said. Now, it was clear. My memory coughed up a tidbit about the Oregonian commune run by a guru who owned a hundred Rolls-Royces and whose retreat was rife with sex scandals. Plus, there had been some kind of corruption charges before the guru, Osho, had been run out of Oregon by the authorities. How could I mention my qualms? Monrova and Paula's generosity, scooping me up into the lap of luxury for that day, had been like winning a small lottery. Plus, I'd just chowed down the lightest meal I'd ever eaten. Still, these two new buddies were luring me away from the Dalai Lama.

"What about it? Come to Pune after Mundgod, Anya. Do it," Monrova said. She sat back and rubbed her belly. "That was a great lunch!"

"Best food I've ever eaten!" I exclaimed.

Paula smiled broadly. "Cooked with love."

After lunch, Monrova, Paula, and I got back into our chariot and went to Fatehpur Sikri. This deserted sandstone fort was once the 16th century capital of the Mughal Empire. Again, we agreed to meet in an hour. I wandered off, following Indian tourists into the fort. It was hot. Abandoned red sandstone and terra cotta buildings that had accommodated harems and audience halls seared under the cloudless sky. I clambered up a flight of uneven stairs sans railings to get a view. Very few visitors roamed the courtyard below. I used my imagination to envision the guidebook's account of a court once populated by singers and poets and hundreds of people going about their business, men in turbans, women in gauzy saris.

One building, the Tomb of Salim Chishti, a Sufi Saint, captured my particular interest. The guide book described a legend of a marble screen inside the building where the court women had tied strings around its latticework, making a wish. I entered the tomb's cool shade and walked along its halls, quickly finding the Jali filigree screen.

The white marble was intricately carved like the screens I'd seen inside the Taj Mahal. This lacy stone curtain held a garden of daisy patterns where short, white strings were woven in and out. I gazed through the latticework into the courtyard beyond; a couple strolled by. My fingers went to the marble, caressing it along with the strings-wishes, and I decided to add my own.

The passion of the Taj still lingered on my mind; so, I knew what I was going to wish for, though I needed a string. And you'd think, it being India, there would be a string wallah out in the courtyard selling threads, but no, not one was in sight.

I glanced at my faded blue cotton dress where ragged edges had appeared from wear. Taking up my hem, I found the loose end of a thread and pulled it carefully, breaking it away. Having spent the morning in Mumtaz's and the Shah's aura, I exhaled a sigh: *What the heck? Why not? I'm young, I'm a woman, I'm human. Life's an adventure.* I reached up toward the filigree. Bright light filtered through the lattice tattooing designs on my tanned arms. The tips of my fingers carefully entwined the blue string through the smooth Jali filigree entangling a wish from my heart with a ritual harkening back to Mughal lovers.

And I whispered, "*Find true love,*" ...wishing at that moment, though unconsciously, to solve a pain that resurfaced from some lonesome corner of my heart, a pain I was unaware of. *Life's an adventure*, I repeated, having no idea where my wish would take me and not knowing that the word "adventure" comes from the Latin for "about to happen."

When Monrova and Paula left me at the train station in Delhi, Monrova asked, "Well? What do you say about Pune? We hate to leave you behind. You're heading for Mundgod and then onto Madras which makes Pune right on your way. We'll be there. Come."

"I'm mulling it over. Yeah, I'll be in that area for the Dalai Lama. I could come along. I have the train schedules. It'd be nice to meet up with you again," I said, thinking maybe I'd have no choice but to go to Pune after all if I got turned away from the refugee camp without papers.

When they were gone, and I was back at my hotel, I crawled into bed and studied my options. If I went to Pune, I'd be traveling with two women who knew the ropes. I pictured myself buying the white robe, getting free bloodwork, and enjoying myself in style, unlike my current celibate approach. As I fell into a slumber, I thought about letting go of my Mundgod quest. Thought of letting go of synchronicity's liquid flow to carry me in its tides to some exciting destinations described by my new friends.

Fiery Sari

It was my third day in Delhi, and I had a few days left before leaving for Mundgod if I followed my plan. I was at yet another cultural site, Qutaub Minar, which swarmed with people. I took off my sneakers and handed them to the shoe wallah, who placed them carefully in an ocean of worn sandals, flip flops, and trainers. These were my only pair of shoes, albeit dirty. Would I ever see them again? Not second-guessing the old wallah's visual skills, I reckoned he had the memory of an elephant. And that he'd match every pair of shoes with every owner here without fail—all for a penny's compensation.

I joined the milling crowd. Then, head scarfed; feet socked, I moved across an expansive, swept courtyard toward the tallest minaret in the world. The historical sites in Delhi were endless. This one, called the victory tower, was named after a long-lost battle. It was built of red sandstone bricks and marble. Closed to visitors at that time, I stood with the crowd staring up at it. Soon I retrieved my sneakers from the shoe wallah and hopped a tuk-tuk for Connaught Place, Delhi's main square. I was out for a day of errands, including buying an airline ticket to Bombay.

Connaught Place forms a big traffic circle frenetic with noisy cars and filled with stalls selling fruits, vegetables, saris, household goods, and statuary. I found a tourist's office and booked a flight for the end of the week to Bombay (Mumbai), where I could pick up a train for Mundgod. I also bought two half-day tours of Delhi.

Outside the office, I stood under the tall ring of Doric-capped columns making Connaught Place resemble a modern Ancient Greece. The columns were splattered with reddish-brown stains running down their sides, victims of the cultural practice of chewing and spitting a red nut that stained teeth, sidewalks, walls, and these elegant columns— betel juice.

The Delhi stalls were irresistible. As I browsed them, I thought about the synchronicity I'd experienced lately. Just an hour before, I'd bumped into Harriet and Erika, my friends from Rishikesh. The Universe, it seemed, was making sure I wasn't alone. It provided me a karmic family from all over the world. They were returning to Germany that night. I recalled passing through Germany when I was twenty on my way to see my Polish Grandmother behind the Iron Curtain right after Mother had died.

I went into one shop filled with Hindu and Buddhist sculptures-Ganesh, Parvati, Krishna, Shiva, and Buddha. One twenty-four-inch-tall brass statue caught my eye. It was of Lord Shiva, the God of Destruction and Regeneration cycling through eternity—the God whose grace I'd met at the Ganges River in Varanasi and trekking into the Annapurna Sanctuary. In this statue, Shiva was depicted as Nataraja, the cosmic dancer dancing over a dwarf-like figure who represented ignorance—a good symbol for a teacher. I liked the statue's benign countenance, and I liked the slim cobra that streamed over his right arm. I asked the shop owner, "How much is it?" He told me and said, "Shiva represents spiritual energy, Madam." The price was right, but still, I asked, "How would I get it home?"

"Oh, we ship it for you, Madam. No problem. No cost."

"I'll take it!" Later in the day, I found a phone store and checked in with Agnes, who agreed to pick up the statue at customs in Boston. That done, the next stop was to buy a sari.

When I stepped into Roop Kala, an upscale sari shop, the saleswomen eyed me askance, but they welcomed me respectfully. Despite being shabbily dressed and wearing a sloppy, canvas hiking cap, which I'd pulled off my head before entering the shop, I was a Westerner. They knew I was there to buy. Dollar signs scrolled in their heads, I'm sure.

An older lady approached me and asked, "Hello, Madam. May I help?"

"Yes, I'd like to buy a sari."

"Oh, yes, yes. One moment. We have someone who will help you, Madam." She hurried into the backroom. I glanced around at the bolts of material. Color! The reams of silks and brocades matched the blaze of a New England autumn—more color than the eye could hold.

A tall, dark-haired lady appeared from the back. "Yes, Madam, how can I help you today?"

"Hello. I'd like to buy a sari? A silk one."

"Of course, Madam," the sales lady said and led me to one side of the shop that held blots of silk. She unfolded the fabric that shimmered lustrous greens, indigos, reds, and golds like semi-precious gems. My eyes dazzled, flashing on the memory of the double rainbow hovering in the sky at the teahouse in Nepal. I recalled the romance of it all—rainbows and lovers.

The sales lady pulled out bolt after bolt. My choices were vast. The tints and shades of the fabrics, its array of patterns, were endless. I loved new dresses and blouses and skirts, having worn hand-me-downs throughout my childhood. I felt like a kid in a candy shop who had trouble narrowing my choices to two fabrics—one for the skirt (twelve feet of it) and a complementary piece for the bodice.

I wanted that sari. I deserved this expensive dress yet had no idea where or when I would ever wear it. Still, I knew a goddess was lurking inside me who desired to own it even if it stayed folded away in a drawer, forever sequestering its seductive nature. The saleswoman stroked the silks. My hands accompanied hers, playing the smooth threads—their fibers woven into strings like a textile harp that would dance around my body—maybe for a distant refrain.

In the end, I chose skirt material that was trimmed by a twenty-four-inch-high gold border against a black background. It was stitched in a multi-colored pattern of purple, green, and red horses marching above and below turrets reminiscent of the Taj Mahal. For the bodice, I selected an exquisite deep, fiery-red silk fabric that glimmered like a flame. I figured I'd feel like Mumtaz Mahal if I ever wore it, irresistibly attractive. At that moment, it filled some feminine corner in me that connected to Dori, her love of beauty, and all the other goddesses of the world.

The women's tailors beamed from ear to ear as they fitted me for the bodice, and they told me to return the following day to pick up the finished sari. When all that was done, I pointed to my shabby dress and asked, "Do you have any cotton dresses I can travel in?" A saleslady rushed over carrying a handful of folded dresses, and I ended up with a black and white print complete with pantaloons.

When I left Roop Kala, I didn't have a clue where I was going to wear the sari. I couldn't have imagined it would be to the Cairo Opera House and that in the ladies' restroom, it would be greeted with copious "oohs and aahs." Yet more important, I couldn't have imagined that I would wear my gorgeous sari to impress—no entice—a tall, attractive date—someone who barely spoke a word of English.

I kept shopping. In the afternoon, I took a cab to a workshop noted for craftsmen's wares. I wandered in and out of the shops, including one place that sold carpets. I had no intention of buying a rug. Still, after being graciously offered a cup of tea by a low-keyed salesman, I purchased two traditional hand-made cotton prayer rugs. One was brown with floral patterns, and the other navy blue, designed to represent a doorway into heaven. The salesman asked me to sign my name on the bottom of their hems before he shipped them home to Agnes.

The next day I went back to Roop Kala to pick up my sari. On my way out of the shop, an elderly woman was sprawled on the hot sidewalk. Was she sleeping, or was she sick? Men and women were rushing by, stepping around her body without a glance. I paused, not knowing what to do. *What could I do for her?* I thought of the people in Rishikesh living along the Ganges and felt India's burden of poverty overwhelming me. Mother had given few directives during my upbringing, but now her words shouted in my ears: "Be a good American girl." I stared at the woman. I stood there for a moment, considering what to do, and realized there was little I could do. People continued to walk by, and although I felt insane and shameful, I hailed a cab.

Soon the cab was stuck in traffic. I rolled down my window to get a breath of air. An elderly grandmother with a baby in tow came up to the cab and stuck the child's hand into the window begging for money. Peering in his rearview mirror, the driver became very gruff.

"Do not, Madam," he instructed.

The grandmother said something in Hindi, her voice softly meowing to me. The cabbie's eyes stabbed me from the car's rearview mirror. I searched through my bag for change when the driver barked, "Madam, roll the window now!" He enforced a rule supported by Westerners and Indians alike that commanded: "Not to give!" Agreeing that hand-outs encouraged begging.

"Roll your window, Madam!" the car jerked forward. I rolled up the window cutting myself off from the grandmother's desperate hand and the others in India—those sleeping on sidewalks, bathing in the Ganges, earning a living throwing cow manure against a wall—knowing every single one of them was just like me except with one titanic difference. I could afford to buy an expensive dress that I might never wear. Still, a bigger difference was that I could eat three meals a day if I chose, while they were smothered by need and scarcity.

Long afterward, I cursed myself for not letting my instincts take control to give something to the grandmother. However, I did realize, if I'd handed out money to all the pleading people in India, I would have ended up sleeping on the sidewalks myself. But still, at that moment, I had held a silk sari in my hands, she a baby.

Purge

The following day, visiting Mahatma Gandhi's home, I fell ill. The night before, I'd eaten at a nice restaurant and had eagerly drunk a cold lime juice, falsely assuming it was safe. Now, my belly was rebelling. I was learning that eating and drinking like an Indian was not an option for me.

Barely reaching the tour's end without mishap, I returned to my hotel to spend the night going up and down the hall to the toilet. Back and forth, I clutched the sides of the walls to stay upright. Vomit and diarrhea exploded out of me. The morning was no better. This wasn't like the food poisoning I'd had in Nepal on my Yoga group trek. This was much worse. I grabbed my guidebook, searching the medical section. It wasn't food poisoning; it was bacillary dysentery. This was beyond Pepto-Bismol. I dug in my bag for Cipro, the anti-bacterial medication I'd gotten before leaving the States. I gobbled a few tablets and ran back and forth to the toilet before falling asleep exhausted. But it didn't work, and by the morning, I could hear the hotel manager Yatin, a gray-haired, middle-aged man, hovering behind my door. He knocked gently, asking, "How can I help? Do you want food, Madam?"

"No, no, thank you. I don't feel well. Water, bottled water, please," I begged.

"I will get some and bring it." When he returned with the water, I opened the door looking into his worried eyes.

"I'm taking Cipro," I said. "I'll get better. I need rest."

Yatin gave me the bottled water and said, "I will pray for you."

"Thanks." *I'll need prayers*, I thought, because this bout felt different. It was not just a physical cleaning like with my yoga group. This time I was in for a purge like when Karette, my friend from doctoral studies, and I had participated in a shamanic drumming experience. It was part of our coursework, and Dr. Ruth Inge Heinz, a Berkeley specialist in alternative modes of healing and human consciousness, conducted the workshop. She came prepared, bringing a three-foot-tall, round-bellied drum which she straddled between her legs.

Karette and I, along with everyone else in the workshop, lay on the floor. Dr. Heinz's hands struck the drum's goat-skin head sending deep, African rhythms throughout the room. The sounds grew louder and filled my ears, throat, lungs, heart, muscles, bones, and central nervous system. Filling them with the force of the drumbeats that drove my brain waves and synchronized my heartbeats. Ruth guided the group with her resonant voice, "See an opening in the earth… walk toward the opening and enter it, go deep into its chamber."

Dr. Heinz's intensity engulfed the room. I visualized myself by an oceanside cave, then my body spiraled down through its rocky mouth deeper and deeper into the earth. I emerged on a semi-arid savanna very much like the Serengeti Plain. There, I walked through tall grasses coming to an open area to see a heap of human bones bleaching and deteriorating. There was a shock of recognition—me!

A dismembered pile—with insects greedily laundering my putrid flesh, ribs, pelvis, femurs, tibias, vertebrae, skull—me—timeworn, crumbling into gray-white ash, skeletal remains mixing with the volcanic sands of the desert floor.

The drumming beat in my ears. My heart found a partner in it as an image of a buffalo head poised above it. A tendril of light surrounded my remains lying there in the ancient landscape. Ruth's voice rang out, "Give over your hate, angst, and despair. Go behind it and remove its fearful charge." Then another image. A shaman adorned with animal pelts—beaver, fox, wearing a deer's head—danced on my neck, jaw, shoulders, back, frightening off a demon by shooting it through the heart. And it was all me wondering if I had the strength to transform.

But that wasn't all. After it was over, the drumming workshop's most thought-provoking part came when Karette and I drove to San Francisco and walked to Haight-Ashbury Street. Once there, nausea gripped us both, forcing us back up the hill to where we had parked the car.

"Are you OK?" I asked Karette. "What was that down there? I felt sick to my stomach."

"Yeah. Those streets were known as havens for drugs, homelessness, and crime in the '60s. Those lingering vibes got to us," she said.

"Do you think the drumming had something to do with it?" I asked.

"It must have," Karette said. "I bet the drumming caused a shift in our states of being and re-arranged our personal boundaries throwing us open to the past."

I asked, "What's it getting us?"

"Liberation. Union with God. Be prepared to open up to higher orders of the cosmos. It's spiritual stuff going on," she said.

I wasn't new to these kinds of experiences. I'd taken other workshops on developing higher consciousness and transformation—like the Grof workshop at Esalen. And it was evident that Karette knew her stuff and her way around the Cosmos. So I, for one—and maybe she also—had felt a shift in her core, a disturbance. And now here I was again alone in Delhi—trying to get to the Dalai

Lama—feeling like I'd penetrated into something that needed changing, and to get there, I was heaving out my guts.

Throughout the day, as I lay sick in bed, there'd be a knock at the door, Yatin checking to see if I was still with the living. The next three days took their toll. I vomited, and I tried to will myself to get better. Where was that cobra when I needed it? I had a plane ticket to Bombay for the end of the week—my ticket to the Dalai Lama—and I was determined not to miss it. Or was I going to end up in Pune instead? I prayed along with Yatin.

I kept drinking water—wondering if it helped or if it too, despite being bottled, was making me sicker. Yatin assured me the water was safe to drink, plus I had no choice. He'd brought me a bucket so I wouldn't have to run to the toilet to vomit. As I leaned over the side of the bed to puke, my head felt better hanging low. I stayed in that position. Small dust bundles rested under the bed.

As I dangled there, checking out the bed's underside, it hit me—the absurdity of it all! There I was hanging upside down like the Hanged Man Tarot card—suspended by one ankle from the tree of life with a halo encircling his head, looking serene. However, I didn't look serene. The card meant that the man had chosen his own predicament, his own self-sacrifice, his own aloneness. He had chosen his path freely.

And I had a weird moment just then—thinking that no matter what happened in my life—happiness or suffering, gain or loss—everyone I'd met or helped or taught or understood or loved—plus those who had encouraged or strengthened or inspired me—all had led me to my life's intended path and were blameless. Life was a deliberate mirror calculating and casting back our illusions into spiritual sums. And for sure, I believed this, because whether consciously or unconsciously, I had to accept, and I did, that I *was* being guided by the Universe. Had to accept my gift, my cobra, my Kundalini opening, and that I had no choice but to follow its counsel.

My body took its time. It had never failed to repair itself, and now I had to trust that some genuine healing sans cobra—or probably most likely "veiled cobra"—was taking place. In the middle of the night, I got up, went to the bathroom, and had a last good purging. The Cipro had kicked the germs out of my system. At eight AM, Yatin knocked on my door checking. I had spent three days in bed under his worried eye. "How are you, Madam? Better? Food?"

"Plain toast," I said and thanked him for his prayers. One more day of rest, and I could make that plane to Mundgod in the morning. A lot of toughness had broken down.

That final morning in Delhi, the sun slashed through the window early, and I felt my old strength return. I drank lots of water, paid Yatin, and thanked him profusely—another angel who had helped me bite through—and I took a taxi to the airport. On the plane to Bombay, I settled into my seat. The Hanging Man Tarot card drifted back into my awareness. Now that my head was cleared, I figured it could mean many different things depending on how it was pulled from the deck. The card, of course, was about being suspended in time and about ultimate surrender. To that point, everything in my life had been left behind and put on hold temporarily, so that made sense. What more could be surrendered or suspended? Had the cleaning I'd gotten been meant to prepare me for a shift in consciousness? I was on a plane heading for an opportunity of a lifetime…hoping to see the most enlightened being on the planet, the Dali Lama. Whatever the card held for me, it had to be good. Had to be.

Mundgod

At about 9 pm on the overnight train to Mundgod, I placed my flip-flops by the lower bunk and crawled up into the top berth of the women's compartment. Other women from Germany, France, Denmark, and India settled in around me. The clatter-clack of the train wheels against the tracks lulled me to sleep. In the middle of the night, the woman in the bunk below got up, standing by the side of the open berths waking me. She quickly checked around before slipping on my flip-flops to go off. Distasteful didn't describe how I felt about a stranger's questionable feet walking in my shoes. These were not public slippers, and sharing them offended me. When she got back, I scowled in my bunk but bit my tongue, falling back to sleep; promising myself to hide my flip-flops from then on.

In the morning, the train stopped to let passengers off and on. Young, turbaned vendors surged onto the train, their skinny bodies carrying baskets of food. One wallah came down the aisle, and I dug into my pocket for rupees to buy scrambled eggs rolled into a banana leaf. I ate the eggs hungrily and stowed the leftovers in the metal containers I'd bought in Rishikesh. Soon, another wallah came along carrying a steel jug shouting "Chai, chai, chai," a creamy, black tea boiled and blended with herbs. I bought some that he served in a small, unglazed clay cup. I swallowed the hot chai savoring its sweet, spicy flavor, tasting ginger and cardamom. After the cups were drained, the train's windows were opened, and hundreds of arms, including mine, shot out, throwing cups onto the train tracks. This was the norm back then and thought hygienic. During my entire four-month stay in India, I probably drank several gallons of chai out of those little nonreusable clay cups.

During the day, the train's wheels clattering against the tracks hypnotized me. The other women in my compartment told me they were going on to the beach at Goa. They chattered amongst themselves in German or French or Dutch or otherwise slept. I sat and sat and sat. When I went to the toilet, I carefully balanced myself in the narrow, rumbling closet, trying to hit the floor pit just right. I touched as little as possible. Back in my seat, I watched out the window, India's enormous flatness scrolling by under streaky white clouds filling the blue sky.

In the fields, men tended rice paddies that were rimmed with acacia trees. There was an endless palette of earthy browns, subtle greens, and shades of Naples yellow. If I'd had my paints with me,

I'd have mixed a dab of umber with a spot of sap green, taken a fan brush, and blended the sparse vegetation up into the azure sky.

I sat and sat and sat. And watched and watched and watched. Hours embraced the countryside as it opened up, dry fields into marshes, egrets visiting water buffaloes, scrolling and un-scrolling an endless horizontalness. Every so often, I glanced at the palms of my hands. They were soiled from merely sitting in my seat on the train.

Twenty-two hours later, the train rumbled into the tiny station of Mundgod. I was still two hours from my destination, the largest Tibetan Refugee Camp in the world, where the Dalai Lama was scheduled to give his Kalachakra Initiation Teaching. The Doeguling Tibetan Settlement in Mundgod, Karnataka was a 4,000-acre settlement given to fleeing Tibetan refugees as a safe haven by the Indian Government after China had invaded Tibet in the 1960s. It was here at the train station, or maybe I thought the post office, where I would find my entry papers into the camp.

I got off the train and thought, *OK. The stationmaster.* I knew that despite its remote location, the station master would speak English. A century earlier, the British had established the extensive railroad system that crisscrossed the subcontinent. Knowing this, and even though traveling to isolated parts of India felt like going into Neverland, I still hadn't really wrapped my head around Indian bureaucracy, nor did I fully understood what I was headed for. But just then, I was undeterred. I went up to the station master's window, expecting my entry papers to be waiting for me.

At the window, I said, "Hello. My name is Anya Kru. Do you have a letter for me from Delhi? From the Ministry of Home Affairs?" The station master squinted at me, "What?" he said. I repeated my request a bit more softly.

"No, I have no papers here for you, Madam. Why would you think that?" My heart sank.

"Because I applied for them in Delhi, and they said..." my voice trailed off.

"Madam. I have not received any papers from Delhi for you or for anyone. This is a train station, not a post office, and we have no post office here," he confirmed.

Maybe the papers are being held at the camp—a foolish thought on my part, but I was getting desperate. "When do I get the train to the camp?"

Again, he looked at me as if my head was not quite attached. "There *isn't* any train to the camp from here, Madam."

All this way, and I was stranded? Tears welled up in my eyes. "I need to get to the Tibetan Settlement."

The station master, wearing a cap that covered his dark hair, sat behind a shelf in a small room, peering out at me. He glanced at his papers, shuffling them about. I didn't move. He glanced up again and must have seen the desperation on my face. His voice softened.

"Madam," he said not unkindly, "Walk down the hill to the busses…down there," he said, pointing outside the station. "There is a man who is organizing the Tibetan refugees from Bhutan, and they've rented buses to take them to the camp. Ask him if there is room for you. Go now. Hurry!"

Something released a grip on my heart, and I hoisted my bag on my shoulders and ran several blocks down the hill where hundreds of people were milling around. Had they been on the train with me? It didn't matter. Somehow in the crowd, I spotted a short, well-dressed man talking to a large group. I sensed immediately that he was in charge. I pushed myself through the crowd praying he spoke English. Finally, reaching him, I asked, "Excuse me, Sir. Do you speak English?" He turned to me, his face with a friendly question.

"Yes, I do. How can I help you?" A moment of relief struck me. Perfect English! The man, Champa, turned out to be the liaison for UNICEF in Bhutan. He had organized a trip to Mundgod for the Bhutanese community to hear the Dalai Lama. I explained my plight that my papers had not arrived.

"We have room for you on the bus," he said. And, as the bus loaded, he ushered me to the back, where I slid into a seat while exhaling a breath I'd been holding for a week. None of the other

Bhutanese on the bus spoke English, but all faces beamed contently, and I beamed contently back. Then, as the bus took off, my heart swelled with gratitude that within minutes I'd gone from misery to utter relief despite the fact I had no entry papers. Luck? Synchronicity? The Cobra? I was for the moment happy, but I knew that within a few hours, we would be passing through the camp's checkpoint that was secured by Indian officials. And my happiness was struck by a pang of anxiety because I'd have to figure out what to do.

The bus drove deeper into the camp's interior. For miles, the vegetation of the starved fields was repeated over and over. The Bhutanese spoke quietly and passed chunks of pink watermelon around the bus. They handed me a piece of the juicy fruit which I ate greedily. It tasted like ambrosia.

After about ninety minutes, Champa came back to tell me we were approaching the checkpoint where the bus would be stopped by Indian guards checking transit papers. He told me to keep out of sight when we reached that point. Soon the entrance gate into the camp came into view, where a group of Indian Officials dressed in khakis stood holding clipboards. I buried myself into the seat and held my breath. Champa got off the bus to talk to the guards. A nervous knot that had been growing in my stomach tightened like a fist.

Would the official come on the bus, find and question me? I pictured myself in a small, dimly lit room, sitting under a single glaring light with my hands tied behind my back. What was I going to say? I'd been traveling through Nepal and India across borders and on trains and planes for two months. I knew the Indians took an authoritative stance, valuing paperwork as if it were currency, stamping and initializing documents thousands of times over, making it mean something important while travelers stretched in long lines waiting, waiting. If they found me hiding in the back of the bus and removed me, all was lost with the Dalai Lama.

Champa and the Indian official stood outside talking forever. Everyone on the bus was very quiet. Shallow breaths. Sweat. I could hear my heart racing like I was about to hurtle over the Berlin Wall—was I facing success or capture? Would I be caught lying to the Indian bureaucracy? This time by way of actions? I was trying to convince myself that this lie was critical for my spiritual growth. Were lies even allowed in spiritual development?

How had I gotten myself into this dilemma? Rules were rules. I was not a lawbreaker or liar, or was I? Lots of negative stuff crashed through my skull. Was meeting up with the primordial night goddess in Kathmandu a misguided coincidence? Was I putting Champa and his group in jeopardy by being on their bus illegally? I thought of the Hanged Man Tarot card, his sanguine expression of acceptance of what was. *Oh, Dear Cobra, if there was a time I needed help, it is now!*

I was hardly breathing. Thump, thump, thump. My heart pounded in my ears as I waited to be dragged off the bus, turned around, and shoved unceremoniously back to the train station to be left out. Time inched on. I waited for the official to come aboard, marching down the aisle to discover me kissing the floor. I wondered if there was a small miracle waiting for me. My Kundalini rose from my head, and I visualized it wrapping first around Champa's—a cobra I imagined he had—then around a cobra the official had, syncing us together in harmony. It was the best I could do.

Unable to stand it any longer, I edged up from the seat where I was hiding and peeked out the window to see three guards in front of the bus blocking the road. Champa was standing arms akimbo, talking and smiling with a uniformed man holding a clipboard. This official abruptly stopped talking and arched his neck to survey the entire bus from front to back. I ducked quickly but not before seeing a sharp air of authority on his face.

Then a loud squeak as the bus door opened and heavy steps came up the stairs stopping by the driver. Crouching, I turned to see alarm on the faces of the Bhutanese sitting across from me. I covered my head. The bus held its collective breath. A deferential silence filled the bus, so quiet that if a grain of rice had dropped, it would have shattered the repose. The guard's voice droned on against that of the driver's.

Then there was a collective exhalation as I realized the guard had stepped off the bus. I glanced up at the man sitting across from me, his eyes signaling acquittal. A thousand years of waiting for Godot had passed. Instead of waiting for papers that never had and never would have arrived, I'd taken action. Then Champa had taken action, but the guard had taken no action. I had been bold.

The bus door went cha-chink, locking behind Champa, and we drove through the checkpoint. Slowly, my face went toward the window, venturing a look at the guard who was waving the bus through the gate into the refugee camp, this bus that smuggled me in to hear the Dalai Lama. A tear, one of gratitude for Champa and then another for the Universe, hovered in the corner of my eye.

Camp One, Gaden Monastery

I got off and stood at a small stop on a dusty road in the middle of the four-thousand-acre refugee camp. I felt alone. Around me were flat, ranging fields, meager houses, and makeshift tents under an overcast sky. Champa's bus had driven through the Doeguling Tibetan Settlement for close to an hour. It dropped the Bhutanese off at various small villages. When we came to the camp where Champa and his family were staying, he walked to the back of the empty bus.

"Anya, none of these places are suitable for you to stay at. You must return to camp number one, Gaden Jangste Monastery, and ask the head monk for a room. I'm sure this will not be a problem," he said kindly.

"OK. Thank you for helping me, Champa. Thank you more than I can say. I have never been more grateful in my life." And I meant it. He and I shook hands, he got off, and the bus departed.

Several more stops later, the bus turned to head back to the camp's entrance. Sitting at the front, the driver somehow managed to tell me that I had to get off at the next bus stop because he was not passing through camp one. He indicated that there would be another bus to take me in the right direction. The worse that could happen was rain, and I wondered if I could hitch a ride to Camp One, but only motor scooters passed occasionally. Soon two women and a younger man came to the bus stop. I asked the man doubtfully, "Do you speak English?"

The look on my face told him how out of place I was. "Can help?"

"I need to get to Camp One. Gaden Monastery," I said.

"I help. Second bus," the man said.

"Thanks," my relief was plain.

By this time, it was late afternoon. The man and I boarded the second bus that came along, and we rode for about twenty minutes. It stopped to pick up and let people off. My guide said, "I get off. You…" he held up three fingers, indicating three more stops for me. Departing, he nodded vigorously, still holding up three fingers.

"Thank you!" I said and waved, thinking, *at least I'm here.*

By now, I'd been riding buses around the camp for close to two hours. My apprehension at finding a place to stay was snowballing. At stop three, I got off the bus and walked a short distance toward a cluster of buildings that included a monastery. I entered its front gate into a large courtyard. Feeling lost, I stood before the temple with no idea where to ask for a room. A round-faced, bald monk walked toward me from around the building's corner, picking up on my confusion.

"You need help?" he asked in clear English.

"Do you know where I can get room to stay?"

He pointed to a two-story annex a short distance beyond the temple and said, "Go there and ask for the Rinpoche. He'll give you a room."

I went up into the building where a man was sitting behind a desk, and I asked for lodgings. Without explanation or question, he had me fill out paperwork, told me the room included meals, handed me a key, and pointed toward a two-story building across from the temple. "Go there. Here's your key."

"How much do I owe you?"

He shrugged and bowed his head. "You are our guest," he said.

I hauled my backpack across the courtyard, up the stairs onto a balcony, and unlocked a door into a large private room. For a moment, I stood in disbelief before collapsing onto the bed, completely drained. There, I gave thanks to God for the tenderness afforded me throughout the entire day. For the grace. For the openness of the Universe. For gifting me. I'd found a humble monk's quarters with a comfortable bed and meals free of charge. I'd landed in Shamballa.

Doeguling Tibetan Settlement

The Dalai Lama's Kalachakra Teaching was first given in 1954 in Lhansa, the capital of Tibet. It was followed by seventeen others throughout India, the USA, and Europe. An esoteric practice of Tibetan Buddhism, it's a profound, complicated system of belief that is beyond me to explain in any detail. Essentially, "Kalachakra" means wheel or, better yet, wheels of time. In this system, three wheels are addressed. First, there is the Outer Wheel of the environment. Next comes the Inner Wheel of the human body (plus the elements and movement of the winds). And last is the Other Wheel which consists of a set of teachings, a pathway of initiations or empowerments taken by followers to achieve ultimate emptiness and liberation. It was this Other Wheel that I would be experiencing over twelve days.

Followers of the Kalachakra Initiation often desire to attain an awakening into Buddhahood—which simply put means to give "free and full play" to their unique talents. Joseph Campbell called this heavy mission "following your bliss." He meant to connect with a sense of *being* within yourself (a deep motivation). And then move out of that "push" into the world living fully (in work and play) regardless if the experiences are joyful or painful, which often, they are. Agnes was an excellent example of "following your bliss." She had always loved dogs and became a noteworthy national dog breeder.

The Initiation also included the building of a sand mandala by a troupe of monks. At the meeting's end, the mandala's fate was to be swept into a body of water as a symbol of impermanence. Fifty thousand Tibetans and about seventy Westerners had come from all over the world for this profound teaching.

Later that evening, after I came up from the dining room located in the same building, I stood out on the balcony taking in the temple directly across from the dormitory of rooms. It was a small two-story building ornately ringed by columns shouldering elaborate cornices like the ones I'd seen in Nepal. I wondered if it was unlocked and went to check. A short flight of steps led up to an open door where I entered. Elaborate art murals depicting Buddhist gods adorned the interior. No one was inside, and I stood for a while, giving thanks for the opportunity to sit with the Dalai Lama.

Returning to the balcony, a door across from my room opened, and a woman stepped out. She wore a dress, had curly brown hair, and had blue eyes trimmed with glasses. Delighted to see another Westerner, I said, "Hi!"

"Hi!" she said.

"Name's Anya."

"I'm Lilia. Back in a minute," she said, going off to the bathroom. When she returned, I found out she was a librarian from Chicago who was here for the sole purpose of seeing the Dalai Lama in person. And, it didn't take her long to see my ignorance about the whole thing. But she took pity and proceeded to fill me in on what to expect the next day.

"It's going to begin early, so you've got to walk down the road here about two miles until you see where the tent was erected. Get yourself a seat. You'll go toward the front, where they've set up a place for the Westerners. You can't miss it."

"OK. Walk down there, right?" I pointed, hoping she'd invite me to join her.

"Yes, about two miles, and bring a pillow to sit on. We'll be sitting on the ground for hours, and you're also going to need lots of water. It's going to get hot."

"OK. I have a water bottle I'll fill," I said, sounding yet more stupid as I took in her directions. I tried to continue the conversation. But as we talked, Lilia slowly backed into her room, holding her door. It was clear she was not going to invite me to tag along with her. I was alone.

That first day, standing at the perimeter of the tent, I was mesmerized. An assembly of fifty thousand people sat waiting. 'Awestruck' might cover part of how I felt, but it's hard to put into words what exactly was going on inside me at that moment. Monks, nuns, men, and women from all regions of the subcontinent sat under an enormous, white tent to hear the Dalai Lama teach.

Maroon and saffron robes blurred the space, bald heads bobbed, thousands of faces angled forward in rows. I'd never seen, never been in such an immense crowd. I was no Woodstock goer, no football or concert goer (well, yes, a Broadway theatergoer); still, I'd never been in a venue that opened into such a family of devotees. Palpable energy, taking the form of a flock of soft cooing doves, sat in utter anticipation.

A monk immediately came over to where I was standing and said to me, "There is a place for you in the front." And he directed me to cut to the back of the tent to find my way to where a Western envoy sat no more than sixty feet to the left of the Dalai Lama's throne-like chair. I searched for Lilia, figuring I could sit with her, but she was nowhere to be found.

I took my seat at the back of the group. Arranging my pillow, I turned my head to the left to take in the sea of round faces, thousands and thousands of monks. I was numb with excitement; I wasn't sure my heart was beating. There was no such thing as big screen TV in those days for events like this, but it didn't matter. I greeted the two men sitting next to me. The one sitting on my right pointed up over our heads. He told me the monks had rigged a speaker on a pole to translate the Dalai Lama's words into English for us Westerners. We all faced forward; it was almost time to begin. The temperature ramped up. I could feel a circle of sweat forming in the middle of my back and under my armpits on my new dress bought in Delhi. I sipped some water.

The Dalai Lama entered the tent and walked to the raised dais taking his seat. He was dressed in simple monk's clothing, a maroon and saffron robe reflecting his audience. His head was shaved, and his smile carved creases in his forehead like dove wings. He didn't mince words. His voice filled the tent. And, as he lectured that first day, I got his message.

Everything counted toward the goal of working toward selflessness and improving the lives of others. Being a teacher, that message fit with my philosophy. It was a message of loving-kindness and reminded me of what Depok Chopra had said about being "called to live the ordinary life in a non-ordinary way." The speaker squeaked out yet more. A good life, the Dalai Lama said, requires using the mind to make inner transformations that will lead to a good rebirth.

The Dalai Lama spoke for hours…about eliminating suffering. Is that why we were here? Why was I here? At one point, he said that prayer was not enough for inner transformation. More was needed…I strained my ears to take it all in. Was the translation coming through accurately? It didn't matter. The full bell of his voice vibrated to the edges of the multitude, the edges of my existence. He continued telling us it was essential to avoid unethical behavior. At that point, guilt shot through me as I recalled the episodes where I'd tricked the teahouse host and had illegitimately entered the camp. I no sooner got caught up in this monkey mind chatter when I was retrieved by the monks' voices reciting the Heart Sutras. Soon the crowd joined in chanting the Kalachakra mantra: Om Ham Ksha Ma La Va Ra Ya Sva Ha. All of us from

Bhutan, Nepal, Vietnam, Europe, and America—the far corners of the globe chanted in a demonstration of amity.

That night back at the monastery, I went to dinner. I had calculated it housed about twenty rooms all told, but few people showed up for the meal. I recognized one man who had a room at the back of the building, and I said hello to him. He greeted me then closed his body language down to imply he wanted to be alone. Finishing his meal, he got up and disappeared into the night. I wondered where Lilia was. Feeling the need for company, after dinner, I knocked on her door. I was eager to discuss what had happened that first day.

"What did you think of today's event?" I asked.

"The Dalai Lama has wisdom needed by the entire world," she said. I wanted her to come out and chat with me, but she blocked the doorway. "The Dalai Lama is coming to this camp in a few days," she said.

"Kidding!"

"I'm making an appointment to see him."

"Appointment?" Surprised, somehow, this woman knew the ins and outs.

"Yeah. This settlement is big, so each day, he goes from village to village, so no one feels left out. He'll be coming here, and he takes visitors who have questions, and I've lined up an appointment with him. This is why I came."

Impressed was not the word, and I bet *she* had papers to enter this camp. An audience with the Dalai Lama, the most famous enlightened being on the planet! "He'll see you privately?"

"Of course, but obviously, there has to be a reason that you want to meet with him," Lilia explained. She had questions about her work as a librarian back in Chicago.

An audience with the Dalai Lama? That sounded like a dream come true. But what would I ask him? What did I want to know from him? Certainly not the questions I'd contrived for Papaji in

Lucknow. I searched my brain. What? What? What? I couldn't think of a thing to ask him.

I could make up a question and make an appointment with him just to say I'd met and spoken with the Dalai Lama face to face, but that struck me as an outsized, insincere ego thing. I thought back to Lucknow, where people had asked Papaji, "Who am I?" questions draining his time and probably dulling his wisdom. Conjuring some excuse for a meeting with the Dalai Lama was opposite to what I'd learned in the morning teachings. Helping others, not using them to inflate my ego—I couldn't do it.

No. Meeting with the Dalai Lama was not an option; besides, part of it was my own shyness preventing it. Unlike my ability to use anger when needed, my throat had gotten locked up long ago when it came to schmoozing others. I didn't have the facility. It was hard for me to push myself in for no real purpose. I wasn't angry about anything here. I was happy and choosing to do something like that which lacked legitimacy didn't fit me. It was enough that I was in the thick of things, sitting at the Dalai Lama's feet listening to him. After all, he was telling me to act out of sincerity. Unless I could think of a genuine concern, I'd be content with nothing more than resting like a pebble among thousands of other pebbles and just take in his message. Asking for more was disingenuous.

Back in my room, I felt unsettled. Was I making a mistake? The Hanged Man card lingered in my mind's eye. I wondered which way I had pulled the card during my bout of dysentery in Delhi. Was this going to be a missed opportunity? Having moved from intellectual Anya into just being Anya—grubby at times trekking through the Himalayas and the streets of Delhi—had I turned my brain off? I badgered my skull trying to parlay an important inner struggle into a genuine question significant enough for His Holiness. Was my introversion standing in the way? I'd been in his presence, sitting a mere sixty feet away, absorbing his vibrant words along with 49,999 others. I'd watched his eyes dance over us with a simple truth seeming to accept us wherever we were on our paths. I was not about to manufacture a false query. I had no illusions as to who I was. I'd thrown my identity into the bin months ago. No barriers blocked my happiness. I felt free inside. Enough. My ego stepped aside…almost.

The following day, I knocked on Lilia's door again. "Hi!" I wrote my best smile on my face. "Lilia, do you think I can come with you to your appointment with the Dalai Lama?"

"You really need your own appointment," she said in her cool voice unable to hide its dismissiveness.

"What're you going to ask him?" I asked.

"It concerns my business back at home." Librarian business, I thought. Oh, well. The Dalai Lama was smart but was he prepared to answer librarianship questions? At that point, bewildered at the thought of talking to the Dalai Lama by myself, my ego stepped aside.

Kalachakra Initiation

They saw me coming. One man's brown arm, a shriveled stump, shot up at me. I had passed several of the same beggars squatting beneath some leafless trees the previous day as I had walked the road to the tent to hear the Dalai Lama. About a dozen of them now huddled under what little shade was available.

Passing by, knobs of fingers spun in the air, bent like dark wings hovering toward my face. The "no give" mantra echoed in my head as yet another man waved severely gnarled fingers at my knees. Arms, hands, desperate eyes reached up at me from all directions like car-wash brushes stroking my sides. I imagined terrible accidents the men had gotten tangled in. Pity shot through me, and I was glad my purse was back in my room.

When I got to my space in the tent, I was feeling disconnected. Thick insulation of language isolated me from the Europeans that made up the group. Nevertheless, I wanted company as fleeting as it might be. I began to chat with the guy sitting to my left. Polite enough, he exchanged a few words telling me he was Dutch before turning back to his buddy. Next, I tried the woman sitting in front of me. Making an excuse, I asked if she had enough room. She was from France and gave me a curt "Merci" before turning back to fluff up her pillow and continue her conversation with her seatmates. I had no idea where any of them were staying in the camp and when I tried to ask the woman sitting on my right, I got a mumbled answer that wasn't clear. I was clueless about the group's different languages. Making small talk with them netted me nothing, and I soon gave up. As for Lilia, was she in some sort of VIP section? Again, I didn't see her in the crowd. I felt surrounded by Westerners too busy seeking enlightenment to give me the time of day. I regretted not twisting Monrova and Paula's arms to join me.

The Dalai Lama climbed the dais to his chair. He began to describe the path to enlightenment by obtaining bodhicitta—the aspiration to attain enlightenment for the sake of all sentient beings. This lesson required working with the most subtle energies in the body, including food. I was taken aback to hear that the Dalai Lama was not a vegetarian. I'd grown up eating tons of vegetables and fruits along with ample helpings of Mother's homemade beef galumpkis, chicken soup, and Dad's catch of the day—truly part vegetarian but not. I felt vindicated by the Dalai Lama's appetite. His instruction included the Inner Wheel of Time—the body/mind connection here on Earth. Taking care of our bodies was crucial so that we, I, could respond to the subtle relationships we have with all other sentient beings on the planet.

It made sense to me. All the hiking, skiing, yoga, swimming I'd done over the years—especially the swimming. Swimming had always been my pleasure from childhood, and when I met Cathy, she was into it, too. We'd find secluded lakes and swim marathons. And those miles in the pool during my doctoral studies. It all came back. How my back had gone out, and pain had driven me to a local pool to get some relief. I recalled it now. How my Kundalini had awakened through pain that was both physical and emotional.

I'd married Tim soon after I'd begun my courses. With him

working, I stopped teaching and stayed home grinding out the academic work and sitting for hours at the computer. Then, my back went out, probably because I had scoliosis. I was in bed, icing it, taking Advil, and crawling to the bathroom with Tim looking more like a lost child than a helpful spouse. The pain persisted for over a week, and I knew I needed to take physical action to relieve my suffering. I'd done yoga starting in my twenties and joined a yoga studio to stretch my muscles out, but it wasn't enough. I knew I needed to swim to restore my back, so I found a pool not far from home.

In the pool, I did the crawl and practiced breath-control, a form of pranayama breathing. Instead of turning my head and breathing out of just one side like most people favor, I alternated my breathing out of both the left and right sides. Being a teacher and having taken the Silva Mind Method, I knew about brain hemispheres. And I also knew, if both sides of my brain synced in fine-tuned alignment, it would benefit my body and my brain, the effect of all that oxygen. Soon it became a meditation, a mind/body experience. But more than that, that's when I started to pray in the pool, a practice stimulated by Karette.

At that time, Karette (also doing her doctoral studies) told me she too had physical problems. She asked me to pray for her. *No problem*, I thought, and I could have shot her a couple of Our Fathers and Hail Marys during meditation, but I didn't. By that time, I'd reached a point in my life where I'd switched off using words for prayer. Instead, after taking the Silva Mind Method training decades earlier and understanding the power of visual thinking, I adopted dynamic imagery as my main form of prayer. It was keyed into my physical movement.

Walking in the woods, I had discovered that moving through spacetime generated a flow of light through my body, through my chakras. This is what I focused on in the pool while swimming laps to heal my back. So, when Karette asked me to pray for her, I did. In the pool.

Lap, lap, lap. Arms stroking, legs kicking, splash, splash, splash moving in a watery arena slicing horizontally through thousands of gallons of life-giving liquid. Back and forth, back and forth, kick turn heading up the lane, visualizing a thread of golden light streaming through my feet moving slowly up my legs—muscles, bones, organs—into my sacrum and gut, and through my heart pulsing the light's rhythmic energy into my brain cells amassed in my skull, the billions of cells I'd asked to do their job on behalf of my doctoral work.

Swimming like that, engaged in pranayama breathing—oxygen surging and pushing brain chemicals throughout my body, my neurotransmitters became flushed with endorphins—most likely hooked up with Dad's programming: "You're Special, Honey," which always buoyed me up. And probably—what I didn't realize, working with light that way—was also stimulating my auric body, reprograming my neurons.

A lot of things came together in my brain's electro-magnetic gray matter. Crunching the inventors' research data, their thinking skills…well, somehow that, along with all that bodywork…allowed the juice of the inventors' brains to seep into my own psyche. And that allowed me to absorb their esoteric problem-solving skills, or maybe it was absorbing me. And as I swam and flowed light through my body like that, the movement of crawling horizontally through the pool's watery womb, one day, Karette popped into my mind. And I began to pray for her using the same healing light I was using on myself.

I visualized Karette encasing her entire body in a transparent cocoon of protection woven by a ray of pure light. Lap, lap, lap. Back and forth, back and forth a prayer of light. I sent her healing energy. I superimposed her body with Christ, Buddha, Muslim script, and the Star of David. I plied her aura with spiritual love.

Eventually, every time in the pool, first me, then Karette, then family, friends, or whoever needed care, or didn't, got a dose of golden light. Got a dose of the spiritual energy embodied in the religions of the world. The pool morphed into a church for me, a cathedral. Yes, it felt like that where I flowed over a threshold of spacetime, into a dimension that threw open a door in me that connected my body/mind at a level, gentle yet powerful tempering a steely resolve in me for my work. Doing that extended my sense of intuitive knowing, brought me to the point that formed the nascent physical basis for the opening of my Kundalini. That's what was going on while I healed my back. As I sent healing messages and spiritual love to others, I was tapping into a channel of the Universe.

Using that torrent of energy, I have to admit, I was impressed with my own ability to sustain it, and I believed fully in its therapeutic properties. I had confidence in mental imagery as bearing the potential of psychic medicine.

The Dalai Lama brought the body/mind and the Inner Wheel of Time discussion to a close. The takeaway was: Our actions toward others required a big dose of compassionate understanding. And further, the body's subtle energies could be harnessed to allow the illusion of Self to fall away. It sounded like what I'd found in the pool, in its watery womb. That we all share a larger field of energy spread over the world where each person moves horizontally through its healing fuel. Or just simply, the take-away was: We are all in this together; let's make it work.

The long hours of sitting in the tent began to set in. I was glad the sore on my tush was healed and could take the heat and sweat accumulating in my pants. I paid close attention to the lessons, but fatigue blurred the message. As the speaker dangling overhead sounded scratchier and scratchier, I missed a lot of the translation coming out of it that day. Maybe my head wasn't grasping the multifaceted concepts of dharma (right behavior and social order). Yet, even though it was hard to absorb, I became fascinated with the Dalai Lama's voice, its sound.

His voice was a resonant mantra. Its tone reminded me of a brook flowing through the Appalachian foothills by my home. A stream passing beneath the hollow roots of oak trees drumming against the trunk's holdfast. Liquid against rock. The Dalai Lama's voice created a vibrational field that swaddled me and everyone in the tent in a living comforter sheltered and nourished. I'm not sure my brain was getting all his messages, but my heart was inhaling the meaning of his meanings.

During those long hours of teachings, I willingly slipped into the care of the Dalai Lama's voice. And I wished I knew more about music to pinpoint the chromatic scale of his vocals. Was that note an "a" or "g," or "c," or maybe an "e"? I'm not clever about music, but I'm sure he spoke the same harmonic language as the Universe. His tones entered my body, a thousand instruments that woke a far spot in me, casting light on a bit of darkness hiding in my psyche. Sitting profoundly humbled at his feet, I heard his voice go from a simple tune of 'do-ray-mi' into Beethoven's Fifth. It reminded me of looking at Dhaulagiri and Niligiri.

My monastery gave me two basic meals. Breakfast consisted of porridge, bananas, and bread. I can't remember if yak butter was on the table, but if so, I skipped it. But I did grab a hardboiled egg and some bread for lunch to take with me to the tent. Dinner was dal bhat or root vegetables with unrecognizable boiled meat. I thought better of asking what it was, glad that the food was cooked thoroughly and hot. Lilia never came to the dining area. Somewhere she had a circle of her own. And despite not hooking up with anyone and having long evening hours to myself, I was content. Maybe part of the experience was to be alone again, like on the Annapurna trail, not getting distracted by interactions with others. I spent the evenings walking the road digesting the Dalai Lama's teachings.

On the fourth day, I donned my fading blue dress, the only clean thing left and walked the two miles to the tent. The heat of the morning sun quickly promised to fry eggs by noon. As I passed, more beggars with dark, pleading eyes squatted along the road, bent limbs arching up out of their broken bodies. I kept imagining the scenarios of terrible car accidents and entanglements in machinery that resulted in such maimed figures. Finally, it was time to break the rules, and I dribbled rupees into maimed hands while I nodded my head at the men, not quite sure why I was nodding, but I did. Was it some sort of benediction? Or approval at my sorry generosity? If so, was it for them or for me atoning for past omissions that I couldn't quite remember or figure out?

That day, the Dalai Lama announced the monks were building a mandala. This sand painting would be dedicated to "individual and world peace along with physical balance." It represented the power of existence and the intricate alignment between everything large and small, male and female, being and doing, form and function, yin and yang on the planet. However, the sand painting would ultimately be cast away in a symbolic gesture of impermanence. This gesture was to remind us that all life—I had re-learned this at the burning ghats of Varanasi—slips away for all and only too soon.

That night in my room, I woke up to a ringing alarm clock that refused to stop. I put in my earplugs; I pulled the pillow over my head, but nothing stopped the buzzing. It was coming from next door. Angry, never good without sleep, I went out on the balcony peering into the monk's room across the hall. He was dead asleep with an alarm clock screaming a mere twelve inches from his head. I banged on the window to wake him. He snored away. I knocked, he slept. By this time, Lilia and others appeared in their doorways with wry smiles on their faces.

Finally, after five long minutes, my blood pressure rising, the monk opened one sleepy eye, got up, looked at me sheepishly, and turned off the alarm, mumbling before crawling back into bed. I fumed at him, thinking: *What a wreck of a monk. So dense, unable to wake up. This young bastard might never wake up*, but then I laughed, thinking *he had served to wake us all up*—which became an even bigger lesson for me the next day.

The Leper's Touch

The following day, going to the Initiation, I walked up the road dripping coins into stumped, fingerless hands. Giving alms mechanically had become my daily duty. I kept the same schedule passing through what became a deepening tunnel of beggars, their bodies twisted and deformed. That day, their numbers had swelled exponentially to form a subway of ragged heads and lost feet. One man was minus both legs—balanced on a trolly paddling along with the back of his crooked hands. By now, I was used to it, satisfied with myself, my service, performing by rote until one man's half-blind eye gaped out of his broken face catching me off guard. I was paralyzed in my tracks.

The rupees froze on my fingertips. The man's contorted glance sent a lightning bolt splitting a moment of recognition in me. My ears buzzed. I tore my eyes from the man, searching the road for escape from my own ignorance. What had I missed? Not seen? Ignored?

These men were not victims of accidents. They had no cars or machinery to smash them. These faces that stretched above half-eaten bodies, missing arms and legs and hands. They were lepers! My heart strangled my throat. I'd been handing coins to lepers for days. My brain swirled, trying to sort out what ate flesh so viciously—a bacteria? A virus? Contagious? Not pinpointing that bit of data, I remembered that a microscopic germ opportunely chewed up humans leaving mangled living lumps.

I looked back into the face of the blinded leper. I was a fool. *Who here was blind?* I'd been walking through a physical Chernobyl of ravaged bodies, and I'd been asleep. My pity had plundered the truth of what I saw.

I looked at the hand spinning below me. Looked at the man who each day dragged his body's remnant to this road, imploring me for pennies. And I searched, yet couldn't tell: *Was he in despair or not? Was there hope in his eyes?* My monkey mind, prone to wanting to see the glass as half full, tried to make it better for myself by imagining that his violation might be more physical than spiritual. *Stop lying! Right now, right here.* I was facing a human being eaten by leprosy. A human at the bottom of the bottom. Worse. And here I was—standing whole, or was I? *What was I missing?*

Think back. My own ignorance, doubt, fear —maybe my own strength and independence—stood in the way of me admitting I had damaged parts. Slowly, I crossed a threshold identifying those lost parts in me—times in my marriage when I could have done better and didn't. Times in my life I could have done more but somehow hadn't. It wasn't easy to sort out what was missing, things that had been pushed away, unfulfilled.

I stared at the leper. His eye held a fortitude I would never know. Staring at him, my emotional armor fell in pieces around my ankles as I met the leper within me for the first time— awakening from some amnesia I'd built around myself—awakened by a heap of spoiled flesh sitting at my feet, making me examine my own spoiled—my own hurt parts.

The whole thing felt hypnotic, like crossing back and forth over the horizons of two worlds, cutting through layers of ego, making me come face to face with myself, the leper in me, those imperfect missing parts, all the terrors of my past twisted together into verifiable resistances and liabilities, making me realize that this leper and I were living in the same world, divided by a single germ.

The moment wasn't lost. Over forty years of psychic grime washed away from my inner mirror. I saw things differently. I recognized that this leper ate like me, drank like me, slept like me, shit like me—carried hopes, desires, and dreams like me. Like me, he laughed and cried. He loved and hated. We were the same—carnal and spiritual. And by what I saw and what I felt and what had awakened in me, I was upended only to be righted by an existence shone bright in a leper's eye, some knowledge I could never know.

I pondered the leper's face. And it wasn't until later I learned that leprosy is not spread by touch, but now that didn't matter.

TIME IS ONLY AN INCH

My heartbeats synchronized with his and synchronized, not just with his, but with all the lepers lining the road in Mundgod and with all the sufferings of people everywhere. And, what was once a monologue of me was now a dialogue of Thou—with the leper, I/Thou the leper—with humanity, I/ Thou humanity—with the planet, I/Thou the planet—I/Thou… feeling yet deeper—yet more unprotected.

As I walked to the tent, I recalled during the past couple of days, the Dalai Lama had asked us, *asked me,* to reach for the *not-self,* the one inside that may be reborn in the service of all sentient beings. He'd asked us to wake up to utter vulnerability. That lesson had sunk in on the road, and I understood that I was here to see and re-own everything I needed to be for my spiritual survival. I'd met myself on the road, and the whole of my being waited to be healed.

The monks charged up and down the aisles to start the ritual of puja. Red arm and headbands were passed out across the rows of people, all fifty thousand of us sitting under the steaming tent. I donned my bands, ready to free (myself) along with all beings from "the cycle of duality"—body/mind, intuition/logic, dark/light. The point was to stay in balance, have our feet secure on the stepping stones along the paths of our lives. Puja is a purification ceremony conducted to ensure the realization of people's actions.

Next came Prasada, the distribution of food offerings. I had watched the food cooking over several nights at my quarters after getting up to use the bathroom in the night. I'd heard a minor commotion at the far end of the balcony and smelled frying oil permeating the air. In the courtyard below, a cooking party of monks worked over a six-foot vat of simmering oil. Crispy, golden twists bobbed in the fat—twists that reminded me of kruschiki, a Polish bowtie cookie my aunt used to make. For several nights, in the midnight hours, the monks cooked diligently, piling the kruschiki into a six-foot mound, giggling; and, I'm sure, cooking with love.

Now, hundreds of monks faces damp with sweat, baskets on

arms, rushed about tossing food into the crowd as part of the ritual to remove all obstacles—worldly, inner, or secret—that blocked freedom. And the pitching of food went on throughout the morning, a sea of kruschiki cooked beneath my balcony. When it was done, everyone removed their headbands symbolically shedding all negative thoughts; and at that point, ready to receive the Initiation, compassionate motivation, aimed at serving all sentient beings.

The Dalai Lama guided us to meditate on "emptiness," the Void. I pictured trash littering my mind turning to ashes, its remnants flying into the wind. Golden light swept through my chakras, cleansing, emptying, healing everything that needed it. I imagined my Kundalini entwined with the Dalai Lama's and each person in the tent, each leper on the road, and each person on the planet.

The Dalai Lama's voice rang out, sunlight flooding the tent, floodlighting our needfulness of his wisdom. As puja came to a finish, he told us to move away from clinging and cravings and desires. Move toward emptiness while embracing all reality, the world, others, and the Self. An ultimate purification. I have to admit, we were being asked to examine that same ontological question: *Who am I?* I'd butted up against in Muktinath…and Lucknow and…but in different words.

Now it was framed: *How do I empty my Self from my Self to see my Self? To see the world and others clearly without illusion? Without needing to control or change things before I became happy?* It was us examining us, our personal deceptions, not a guru telling us who we were. We were charged with the harder task of all—self-examination (self-truth finding)—the lesson I'd gotten from the lepers.

Days before the Dalai Lama visited Gaden Jangste Monastery, a flurry of monks ran back and forth decorating the temple by hanging strings of fairy lights over the gate and along the fences. I watched the activity in amusement, its joyful silliness. In one section, a garland of turquoise and yellow mini-lights was draped in the form of a peacock. Switched on, the lights rotated the bird's tail back and forth, open and closed glowing in the evening dusk. The monks were ready.

The Dalai Lama slipped in and out of Camp One without fanfare in some mysterious timeframe. I never saw him, but I'm sure Lilia had because she disappeared into the woodwork after that day. Had she moved to another camp? She had atypical connections and lived in an inner circle to which I wasn't privy. Yet I didn't begrudge her that because I was filled to the brim with insight sitting sixty feet away from a truly enlightened being each day. The only disappointment I had came *after* His Holiness had visited the monastery, the monks immediately took down the fairy lights. Their flickering had amused me and made Camp One seem like Christmas in January, where I'd celebrated my forty-ninth birthday.

I had sat and taken in the Kalachakra Initiation for eight days. Now hearing the Dalai Lama's laughter, I heard his mirth as verse that only Shakespeare could capture precisely. His laugh struck a chord in me. Made me feel in the middle of nowhere yet everywhere at the same time, everything spiraling inward and outward, bringing the stars from the heavens down into my chest throwing open a sash in my heart. I felt absolutely right…counseled by the Dalai Lama's medicinal joy as it handed down revered truths through penetrating sound.

There was no doubt I was in the presence of a powerful, spiritual entity. I wasn't sure what the others were getting out of the Initiation, but, yes, I felt the pull of a "Father" —an ultimate Voice on this planet. Parts of me rebalanced. Parts forgotten long ago, parts I couldn't even begin to name, but parts that needed to be re-found.

Alone as I was there, I never felt so bonded with everyone. I'm sure it was the Dalai Lama's laughter that did this—amplifying a thousand harmonic sounds of the Universe, sending out its own unique brand of shaktipat—bonding me with the fifty thousand souls in Mundgod, everyone in India, in Asia—everywhere with all sentient beings on the planet. Everyone was my sister, my brother, my mother, my father... I/Thou humanity. And I believed it. Believed in a sacred connection to everyone.

The Mandala

STEADY HANDS, CONCENTRATION, grain by grain, inch by inch, the mandala grew. A few monks held long, metal funnels and leaned over a six-foot under-drawing, dripping colored grains of sand from their tips. Blue, yellow, green, red, white, and black grains radiated out into patterns taking shapes similar to the rug I'd bought in Nepal.

I'd walked several miles to watch this process. The monks worked from the center outward. They formed a symbolic cosmic picture depicting the union of humans and physical reality, their time and cycles.

Grain by grain, movement by concentrated movement, the monks' hands buried the geometrical under-sketch formed by snapping strings to mark its boundaries. Jot by jot by jot, the mandala took shape. It revealed the Wheel of Time depicting the principles of compassion, humility, peace, and the wonders of death seen as a message of spiritual liberation. Continuous unbroken circles, protective rings, and squares indicated the four corners of the Universe. Hundreds of deities would be portrayed along with animals protecting the outer wall and gates.

I watched as they built the extension of time, inch by inch, in the two-dimensional space. The mandala was magnificent. Still, it would be dumped into the nearest body of water as a reminder of the constant flow of life's impermanence. And I thought, we're all riding this crazy Wheel of Time that was sometimes jubilant, sometimes abysmal, and I was glad I'd bought the Shiva statue in Delhi. It would remind me of the never-ending cycles of life and death before I, too, was washed down that existential drain with nary a trace. And it would remind me, moreover, that I had better make sure I did a decent job while here on Earth.

My stay at the Gaden Jangste Monastery was free. I'd been housed and fed without an expectation of remuneration. But it was time to tie up loose ends. The day before I left the monastery, Lilia reappeared. I went over and asked her, "Lilia, when I got this room, the Rinpoche said I didn't have to pay anything. But I *do* need to pay the monastery for my stay. How much should I give them?"

"It's all relative. You decide what it's worth, and give them a donation of your choosing."

I walked over to the Rinpoche's office and knocked on the door.

"Nothing is required of you, Madam. You were our guest," the monk demurred.

"I'd like to give a donation to the monastery."

"It is not necessary," he insisted. But it was for me. And I handed over two hundred dollars and said my goodbyes thanking him profusely for the accommodations. When I saw Lilia later, she demurred, "You've given a princely sum."

When the Kalachakra Initiation ended, did I get the "Initiation"? Was I spiritually healed in some way? Liberated? I don't know. Can I even put it all into words? No. Through sheer doggedness, by biting through, I'd found myself in the most humbling experience of my life—sitting at the feet of the Dalai Lama embraced by his very Being—the mudras of his hands, the deep-toned bell of his voice, and the verse of his laughter. Yet, I knew the Initiation had taught me something special.

I'd learned a profound equation: Knowledge plus compassion equals wisdom—a value hard to calculate; harder to implement. Nonetheless, my gut had taken in the Buddhist tradition of extending an open hand, my hand, to all sentient beings. And because, after leaving Mundgod, I was heading south to Avinashilingum College for Women, where I had a date to teach, that's where I could start on my personal path to enlightenment, if that's what I wanted. That's where I could give "free and full play" to my talents as a teacher giving back to a country that was giving me so much. I was in.

And although I'd made no lasting contacts with others during the Initiation, except for the lepers on the road with whom I shared a humble bond, I was sent on my way with an abundance of community. The lepers, enlightened beings in their own right, had freed a dark cavern dwelling inside my soul, making me feel a new coherence within myself. And because I had accepted the Dalai Lama's message to carry out the work I was destined for, I wondered: Was I ever doing enough for others? Enough in my teaching? Enough for my family and friends? Had I exerted enough courage in my marriage? Enough for Tim, who probably had needed a mega-dose?

Despite those qualms, I thought if I practiced the equation of "knowledge plus compassion" fully, I'd get an answer to those questions. And maybe, just maybe, it wasn't only about having more empathy for others. But instead, if I could reach a certain level of awareness, gather enough strength, then my average-sized heart hidden in my average-sized soul could find a way to transfer its full grace to those I touched. *That* was the quest.

As the train pulled into the Indian landscape away from Mundgod, my heart was filled with a lightness of being. I couldn't have been more thankful for all the randomness that had merged— Champa being there when I needed him or for meeting the Night Goddess in Kathmandu that dark night. And I thought, *Were those things even random, those accidental meetings, those rendezvous with Chance?* It was hard to know. But what I did know for sure was that I hadn't stumbled into the refugee camp by mistake. No, I'd chosen this journey (or maybe it had chosen me); and I'd fought my way in to have my spirit moved, and it was. I loved my fate just then. The Dalia Lama, the lepers, the thousands under the tent—I'd become a citizen of the world.

Decision

Over the next two months, I covered a sizable swath of the sub-continent kidnapped by a culture that is part beautiful, part punishing. One housing millions of people existing in a galaxy of needs, desires, and intentions. I saw a countryside stripped of sustenance that sustained the masses only in basics. I was pulled in by cities frenzied and alive at that time—still called Madras (Chennai) and Bombay (Mumbai). As I traveled the rails from archeological sites to Avinashilingum College for Women and yet another spiritual center, India opened a new view of the world in me.

Before boarding the train in Mundgod, I had been forced to make a decision. It was the end of January. Was I now going to Osho's ashram in Pune to join Monrova and Paula, who'd invited me to join them after we'd visited the Taj Mahal? After a dearth of company at the Initiation, Pune sounded good. Maybe it had something different to offer me in the way of spiritual practice.

I remembered what Monrova had said about "mingling with like-minded people." I pictured them, white-robed, lined up for the compulsory blood test, and my mind snagged. I conjured up a party scene that was too big and too free for me. I was, after all, strait-laced by any standards—no smoking, no drinking, no drugs, and no promiscuous sex. And after meeting a woman on the bus coming out of the refugee camp, I had another choice—Hampi. The woman described it as one of India's most compelling archeological sites, which might suit me better. So, now I was on my way to Hampi.

The routine on the train played out: wallahs got on and sold food, travelers boarded and departed. The train rumbled through fields of sugar cane, bananas, and other crops blurring by. I sat in the hot train staring out the window only to see my face shimmering on the glass watching the comings and goings, the transience of it all. I felt a little strange. A sense of hollowness had invaded my heart, one of those unsettled feelings that often comes with the end of essential yet incomplete business. I didn't know what was ahead for me for the rest of the trip, how my personal Wheel of Time would turn. I was expecting nothing more than the usual touristy experiences, but I was wrong.

The Wheel had a private lesson for me in store, and it would take its time. It wouldn't be until Egypt, weeks later, when Time would take me in its hands to shift the intention of my journey, begun in Connecticut, that had reached a zenith in Mundgod. Time, now, drove me forward toward an unexpected yet significant turn not even asked for—or maybe not even dared for. Time, as is its nature, simply punched my life's clock-of-impermanence doing its job. The train and I raced onward toward East-Central Karnataka to the town of Hospet right outside of Hampi, the medieval monuments I was about to visit.

At the hotel, two men stood behind the receptionist's desk eyeing me as I approached. I went up and checked out the assigned room and immediately returned to ask for another room. "Please give me another room. The walls of that room are not clean," I said. I'd seen tiny, ugly gestalts of blood stains from squashed mosquitoes stenciling the walls.

"No, that is the only room we have," the man in charge said. I hoisted my bag to my shoulder and left. I tried two other hotels only to be told that each place was packed. I couldn't figure it out. I was dressed, head, shoulders, and knees covered, per modest dress requirements and knew I didn't look like a prostitute. Forced back to the first hotel, the men behind the desk inspected me as I reentered.

I'd just spent time with the Dalai Lama learning compassionate understanding. When I went in, I bit my tongue and politely asked for another but different room. The men refused. "All full!" one said. "Only that room available." No one else was in the lobby, and there had been no one in the upstairs halls.

TIME IS ONLY AN INCH

I stared straight into the clerk's eyes, daggering him with the F-word. But in the end, no matter how much I tried to charm or push back against this misogynistic encounter, there was no other place for me to go. To dissuade myself from slipping into a negative space, I kept my focus on Hampi, the ancient ruins I expected to see. In the end, the men won the day. Tamping down my anger, I booked a two-night stay. When I got to the room, I attempted to scrub the scuzzy walls with toilet paper.

The sun in India is unforgiving. The morning I went to Hampi, I armed myself with my water bottle, guide book, and floppy-brimmed hat covering my slowly bleaching hair, which was getting brassy. I wished for a repeat of the warm, dry days I'd experienced for the past several weeks, days without a drop of rain.

It was a short bus ride to the ruins. Once there, I was struck by the surrounding hillside that sat on the banks of the Tungabhadra River. A greenery of palm trees edged the hills covered by giant boulders strewn across the area's nine square miles. There was something of Henry Moore's sculpture about these boulders. Their curvy organic forms, their smooth-surfaced invitation for touch. They weren't common everyday rocks. Instead, they were weathered geologies—10, 20, 30 feet across—holding eons of history.

The coral-colored stalwarts—they could be called grandfather rocks—balanced precariously, edge on edge, one risky dimension atop another. They hovered in the blue air. That might have been enough, Mother Earth showing off her heavies, but there was something more to these stones. Said to be sonorous, the stone had been carved into one of the temple's pillars inside the complex. The pillars were said "to sing." Looking at the boulders, I got the idea that they (solid as they were) held "the sound of light," a sound that rang out from the throat of the Earth reverberating through the heavens. A sound I'd been listening to throughout my trip.

I entered the central courtyard greeted by the Virupaksha Temple dedicated to an incarnation of Lord Shiva. The building, dating from the 7th century, was stacked with ornate layers of elaborately carved dancers and mythical animals shaped into a cone similar to a bishop's hat. A drum-like structure turned side-ways rested on the top. Once the Vijayanagara Empire capital city, Hampi had thrived for over two hundred years, starting around 1336 AD.

Few people roamed the site. I walked through the ruins stopping to take in the area's subtle flow of energy. *A power point here*, I thought, no, I *sensed*. The guidebook said half a million people had flourished on this spot controlling the region's spice and cotton trade, prosperous and wealthy. That day, the remaining shells of buildings radiated an unimpeded richness. I pretended the population still lived—their vital *doings and beings*. Women moved in bright saris, children cried and played along the lanes, men's voices bartered loudly in the Bazaar; donkeys, goats, geese scurried wild. All remnants of activity left behind that had been both ordinary and influential. Now, caught up in that expired liveliness, its dimensional energies, I imagined that it lingered still passing in and out among the buildings. And I was glad I was not prone to getting spooked because the place felt magical to me, and I wanted to keep it that way.

The Stone Chariot is Hampi's centerpiece. It was carved of granite slabs that bore intricate designs of battle scenes. Two small elephants at the front wore tasseled blankets. Its four large wheels spun floral tendrils along their perimeters. According to the guidebook, Vishnu's sky chariot was driven by Garuda (the half-human, half-eagle Hindu god), who knew the routes through the heavens. Sadly, his statue was now missing.

Circling around and around, I sipped from my water bottle and ate breakfast leftovers. Doing so reminded me that Vishnu was the same God I'd encountered at the eternal flame in Muktinath. That flame symbolized an enduring spiritual awakening. Vishnu here was the preserver god who kept the Universe bustling in its true direction. Back there on the Tibetan Plateau, I had wished that Vishnu, as I went on my way, might grant me a propitious direction, and, of course, he had.

I soaked up the Stone Chariot's magic. As I turned to cross the courtyard, I hoped if I had been an inhabitant back then, I'd have been bold enough to sneak up to sit beside Garuda and Vishnu. Then, simply take a ride through the Universe, full steam ahead in the right direction on a cloudless day.

Across the courtyard, the Vijaya Vittala Temple offered some shade. That temple had fifty-six pillars, the "singing pillars," carved from the boulders that surrounded Hampi. The building itself took the shape of a fabulous flower, stellate, day-lily like, or an angular star that had fallen to the Earth. Small sculptures of dogs, erotic goddesses, and other animate carvings nestled above and below the smooth-sided pillars crowned with delicate capitals.

The pillars rose before me. I sipped more water and gave thanks for such a clever place. I admired India's ancient artisans. Their ingeniousness had built this temple using the sonorous stone surrounding Hampi to capture sound. I equated it with the Rose Window in Notre Dame Cathedral that caught glowing light. Holding that image in my mind's eye, I stroked the pillars tenderly, hoping no guard would slip from the shadows to yell at me.

I gently tapped the columns realizing my fingers touched the same stone touched by Hampi's residents thousands of years before. Smooth and cool. The pillars gave out a ping! And a plunk! Similar to striking a drum or maybe the deeper notes of a sitar. Sounds you might hear in a Ravi Shankar concert. Notes filled with the lightness of sound entering beyond the ears into your marrow. And as I struck the pillars, their voices spilled as if from throats that could sing through time zones. The pillars were by no means inert.

In response, I hummed the Gayatri Mantra: *Om, Bhur, Bhuvah Svah, Tat Savitur Varenyam*…purred it in reverence…this sacred of all sacred Vedic mantras that had gotten me through my studies, that had grounded me in earthly energies, removed barriers and provided a well-lit path. I sang it out in gratitude because it had rooted a modicum of its "sound of light" inside of me, confirming my voyage on this planet as being on course—bumpy or not.

I roamed beyond the sprawling site's main attractions. If there's anything equal to the Roman Forum, it's Hampi. Hours went by, at times without seeing a soul. At the Stepped Tank, I was blown away by its mathematics, like the Taj Mahal. I looked down into it—its concentrated solidness. To me, its stability provided a counterpoint to the precariously balanced boulders encircling Hampi. The tank had been a ritual bathing place, and it was nearly intact—made of gray stone with its apex penetrating the earth, an upside-down pyramid. Its open base, now its top, was at ground level, forming a square. Steps, used as seats descended into the ground in a series of tiers and numbered in rows of fives and tens. Several rows of steps iterated the pyramid composing its sides. Each layer cascaded to where the water had once been but was now empty.

To my delight, the ancient people of Hampi had carved their initials to mark their seats. My heart wrapped itself around the tank's romance. I searched for *my seat*, for *my initials* carved centuries before. Were any AKs there? How could there be? And yet I thought it possible if only I could remember who I had been—Who? ...here...then...lost so many years before.

Avinashilingum College for Women Coimbatore, Tamil Nadu Southern India

Ganesh stared benignly down at me from a poster hanging above the dean's desk. I waited for ten minutes before tiny Assistant Dean Gana swept into her office. She ignored me and peered up at the poster, crossing herself vigorously bowing several times before Ganesh, touching the poster in reverence. *Fitting*, I thought. Ganesh is the Hindu god of intellectuals, the perfect patron for Avinashilingum College for Women I was about to teach at for a week.

Gana and I chatted about how I had gotten there to Coimbatore at the tip of Southern India. How my friend, Cathy, had set me up with a visit to Dean Fatima, who had been a friend of Cathy's aunt during the mid-century while she was a nursing instructor. I had taught at the college level, so I'd agreed when Cathy suggested

I offer my services pro bono at this college of home sciences for women. I loved to teach, and now this stint was fitting into what I'd learned at the Kalachakra Initiation—to extend a hand and give back to others.

Assistant Dean Gana filled me in on the young women studying at the small college. Each woman was from a family interested in promoting the education of their daughters. "What is it that you can teach these girls while you are here?" she asked.

"I've taught kindergarten through graduate school. I'd be happy to teach them about creative and critical thinking," I said.

Gana sized me up. "That will work fine. You can also help the upper-level girls with their resumes. They will need to be firmed up."

"OK," I said. "I can do that," and I thought it would be interesting to see what the women wanted to do with their lives. After a while, Gana went to the door and called her young assistant, Amrita. She handed me over to her to be taken to the guest-house.

"Please follow me," Amrita said, walking briskly through the small quadrangle which was fenced in from the outside and contained a series of classroom buildings plus a dorm at the far end. At the guesthouse, she unlocked the door into a large entryway. My first-floor bedroom was spotless, spacious, carpeted, and sparsely furnished with a bed, chair, and table. A large window opened up to a small, walled-in courtyard with low shrubs that would afford me some air. No screens covered the windows, same as in Lucknow. Also, no sari-clad women with baskets of cow excrement balanced on their heads. No screens meant mosquitos, and Amrita said, "Here are mosquito coils to burn during the night."

"Thanks." I was still taking malaria tables but wasn't going to take any chances.

"Dean Fatima expects you for dinner at her living-quarters tonight," and she took me to the front door where she pointed across the quadrangle to the Dean's home.

Dean Fatima was about seventy, less than five feet tall, gray-haired, plump, and talkative. She immediately went into her back room, coming out with a welcome gift, a packaged sari. "Here," she said, opening the package. "I will help you put this on." And with the help of her maid, they wrapped me in yards and yards of green and white cotton material. We stood together laughing as the maid took a picture.

Fatima and I ate dinner, a vegetarian dish followed by lots of sweets. The TV ran in the background, and the Dean watched it intently, occasionally glancing in my direction. I made conversation, she smiled and grunted in reply. At the end of the evening, we went over my assigned duties.

Along with teaching daily classes to the upper-level students during the week, Dean Fatima said she also wanted me to visit the science labs and review the department's curriculum. They wanted to make sure it hit critical concepts for better instruction. Further, she suggested I spend my afternoons counseling the girls for advanced degrees. I could see Dean Fatima and Gana were determined to put me to work. But then again, I figured it was an opportunity to share my experience with the Dalai Lama, the most profound teaching I'd had in my life. We could dig into the essence of selflessness and service.

When dinner ended, I thanked Dean Fatima for the meal and the sari without realizing I'd made a drastic mistake. While she and the maid had been engulfing me in an ocean of the sari's twists and turns, I had taken no notes on how to wrap the dress. And it wasn't until I had arrived in Cairo weeks later when it became necessary for me to unpack and wear the silk sari that I realized my blunder.

All the students were eating breakfast with their hands. I gulped. Had I scrubbed mine before I'd walked across the courtyard to get breakfast in the dining hall? Was there a sink nearby? I didn't see one, so I went to the kitchen to ask for a fork but got a spoon instead. Taking the poor battered utensil, I sat, set it next to my plate, and followed the other's example. I broke chapatti, scooped up rice, and ate with the tips of my fingers extended carefully.

After breakfast, I went over to the classroom, where I introduced myself and asked the students to tell me their names. About fifteen women stared at me blankly but complied quietly. Then, I gave them an overview of how we would spend the week examining creative and critical thinking ins and outs.

"Well," I said, "before we begin, what questions do you have for me?" Silence in the room. Time drifted by. I waited patiently. Finally, a young woman who had introduced herself as Surita raised her hand to ask, "What is creative thinking? Why is that important?" *Good*, I thought. *We're getting somewhere.* And I lectured out definitions and history about famous inventors such as Alexander Graham Bell and Tesla. No further questions, I launched into a brainstorming session which, in all honesty, fell flat. Brainstorming requires fluent and flexible thinking. But it was OK. I went on to a mini-debate.

Then I tried a quick lecture on critical thinking the same way I did at home with my students. The young women still just listened passively. "Take a side. Where do you stand on women's voting rights? What's your opinion on whether women all over the world should have the right to vote?" Big pause in the room.

A hand went up, "Ma'am, we have the right to vote. I don't understand."

"Yes, India is the largest democracy globally, but women in other countries do not vote. What's your view, let's say if you didn't have the right to vote?"

Blank faces. "How about property ownership by women," I offered. But again, the women struggled to examine that idea critically, and the debate was lethargic. Finally, when it was over, they were relieved, and so was I.

At that point, I dropped the academics and asked them to tell me about their experience at the college. Here I met with a locked box response. Hard as I cajoled, I was unable to pry their thoughts and feelings loose. I thought back to my own unrestricted educational training in the seventies that, of course, back then was everything New Age even for teachers. Some of it had been radical.

I had worked in a special education department that had won a three-year grant to instruct teachers in Confluent Education. This innovative program came out of California and emphasized integrative instruction of mind, body, emotions, and spirit. I, along with colleagues, was immersed in Gestalt, Bioenergetics, Psychodrama, Transactional Analysis, and Psychosynthesis, some of which I applied to my everyday teaching activities. I was especially captivated by the early twentieth-century mental visualization work of Roberto Assagioli, author of *Psychosynthesis*. His work emphasized the soul as it is configured with the will and imagination. His ideas fed into my own skills, my ability to visualize. And they eventually seeped into my thesis that described how imagery was used to create original ideas.

Now, I scanned the students' faces sitting before me, and I questioned how I might reach them. I had a bunch of innovative methods in my arsenal, but which to use? Dry lectures and quick experiential lessons weren't doing the trick. Clearly, it was going to take much longer than a week to get them to open up.

But now, it was time for lunch. Before dismissing the students, I encouraged them to make an appointment for the afternoon, "Bring your resumes, and we can go over them to talk about your careers." I went back to the guesthouse, scoured my hands, and made sure I touched nothing before going to the dining hall.

Later that afternoon, I sat in the guesthouse counseling. Surita came, and we went over her resume.

"Surita, what career are you aiming at?" I asked.

"Career? No, Madam. My parents sent me here to have a chance at finding a suitable husband."

Yes, I thought, *arranged marriages here. Marriages were family affairs, not about love but about convenience. Feeling versus commitment. Probably little chance of finding a soul mate.* "Well, OK. In the meantime, tell me what you hope to major in," and we took it from there.

Other students came and shared their dissatisfaction with the academic work they were doing. I probed them. It had no meaning. As the week went on, I taught, visited the science and home economic labs talking to the instructors. I checked over a stogy curriculum, helped with resumes, and listened to more complaints. The happiness quotient on campus was low.

As I planned daily lessons, I thought about how the women's hearts were not connected with their studies. I prepared to encourage them to rethink their plights by telling them about the Dalai Lama's Kalachakra Initiation, how he had pointed toward service to others as fulfilling. But again, that might seem weak. My own engagement with my brain had taken a Kundalini awakening. And I knew many things needed to come together for something as big as that to happen here.

I thought back on my own struggles during my doctoral studies. How I'd traveled the path of Jnana Yoga, the branch of yoga considered the quest for knowledge and wisdom, yoga's most challenging practice. A lot had come together during my doctoral studies (and before), priming me for this brand of mind yoga. And of course, because it was yoga, meaning "union of mind and body," it had begun with physical activity: tramping through the woods with Dad getting grounded to the Earth. Next, Dori had led me on a transcendental course where the boundaries of reality were accepted as fluid—*very*.

But importantly, during my academic struggles, *I had asked* the Universe for help. And once I'd asked, the Universe had shown me the way—meditating, praying in the pool, the Gayatri Mantra, Shri Anandi Ma kindling shaktipat—all necessary avenues for Jnana Yoga to kick in. All practices required for tapping the underlying drivers of the Universe that worked to engage my mind/body. All opening my capacity for extreme concentration to get through those academic years, that up-mountain ascent I'd won.

Did they even have Physical Education here, the precursor to Jnana Yoga? A grounding in Mother Earth? The women probably didn't hike, but I bet they did enough walking that might trigger pranayama breathing. Still, did they meditate or tune into something like the Gayatri Mantra—all essential things needed to open the mind for "an awakening" into a higher level of consciousness? One that called for the union of the mind/body? Unlikely.

But still, the teacher inside of me wanted to get their brains and spirits into gear. It was crucial to prime them for that visceral acquaintance that connected their personal *being and doings* with the world. Connect them to their work, that collective web of sharing knowledge now that I was back in my role as teacher. That's what I saw as *my* responsibility. It would be hard. It had been hard for me.

Jnana Yoga had asked me for something that was called ortho-cognition—the ability to think about my own thinking. It asked me to transcend beyond my own thoughts and ego to connect with my spiritual self. Here's where the cobra came in, of course. Here's where I accepted and embraced the guidance of Kundalini custody that opened in me. Here's where the purpose of my life got spelled out. And even though it's tough to put into words, here's where I began in earnest to search for liberation, although I might not have known that precisely at the time. Yet, I did realize I had been taken up by an underlying drive that became a search for my true nature, one that pushed me toward liberation.

Liberation... *What is that anyway?* For me, at least, it was the release from the cycles of suffering, the bruises from childhood and adulthood. I wasn't so sure about what was happening with the cycles of re-birth involved in that concept, but the whole reason for engaging in a practice of Jana Yoga *was* liberation. That *was* the point. So, even though the path of Jnana Yoga had not been easy, it had worked for me. Here now, at the College for Women, it seemed fitting that a lesson in liberation from unhappiness, at least, was a good start. After all, I was in India where Jnana Yoga had originated among the Hindus.

The following morning having slept on it, I planned to share my own academic struggles, my heart with these women. I would teach them how to ask the Universe for help. Teach a little imagery. Open up the non-verbal side of their brains. This is how it went that day.

First, I did a brief look into my head and heart, how I'd gotten stuck in my studies. How I'd coped emotionally during my doctoral work. Then how I had asked for help—God, the Universe, Ganesh—and meditated (not the cobra part, still a secret buried in me) using a mantra and mental imagery to bring focus to my cognition, to my mind/body as a whole. I gave background on visualization, its connection to the imagination, and the will. Then starting them slowly, I said, "Let's try a small practice. Close your eyes and breathe…picture a rose…Tell me what you see."

One student, squinting her eyes, said, "Oh yes, I can see the rose. Yes! I can see it clearly. Red!" Another with eyes tight, arched her neck toward the ceiling countered, "What rose? No Madam, I see nothing at all." And yet another, "Where is it?" *Oh well*, I thought, *it would take time.*

It was stifling in Coimbatore at the tip of Southern India at the end of January. One night about ten, with no AC in the guest house, I went out to get a breath of air. I walked round and round the college's dusty quadrangle before altering my path heading toward the women's dormitory. As I approached, heavy padlocks chained the dorm's grated metal doors. My mouth palsied. I stared at the chains.

The following day, I asked Amrita about it. She said, "This is for the protection of the girls. We cannot have incidents where there is harm done to them." I thought *We cannot have incidents where the building catches on fire, and there's no escape, where there's no freedom.* But it was more than this. The women were locked up not only physically but emotionally and mentally. I'd seen that in the classroom.

On the fourth day, Assistant Dean Gana sent for me. She said, "My family is having a wedding. My niece and her fiancé will be married. Would you like to go?"

"Yes," I said, happy for an opportunity to see an Indian wedding.

"I'll arrange for the driver to take you. I also want you to give the girls a pep-talk on motivation," she said. "They need to be encouraged to work harder. You can do that. Yes?"

I was turning into a guidance counselor. Each time I met with her, she piled on more work. But I said, "Yes, of course." I realized I could stretch my skills in any direction she demanded because Gana was right. Even though motivation was the hardest thing to kindle in people, it was key. I knew only too well how difficult this would be in one lesson or even a year.

I believed that goal setting was essential to a women's success. Once I had set my sites on college, I had struggled financially and emotionally, not knowing how to connect with a collegiate system. Going to college was a long way from how I understood the workings of the world. But in the end, it was all worth it. I had kept a promise to myself. Ended up with one of a handful of degrees in my large group of cousins, none of whom had gone to liberal arts colleges. I had ended up with a satisfying career all because I had worked toward a goal that leveled out my life's discrepancies. These students in my charge needed a glimpse of that happiness—no, that bliss—that comes from goal setting, hard work, and achievement.

And I wished I wasn't so hell-bent on keeping my secret so I could tell them about my Kundalini opening. Tell them how I had sensed its flow, my cobra, an awakening within my internal knowledge that was linked not only to cognition but drive. How I had accepted it for what it was, a spiritual channel to my work on this planet. And how me sitting in the Dalai Lama's presence for ten days under a hot tent had opened that channel even wider.

At the next lesson, I launched into a pep talk. "Ladies," I said, "Here are the questions you need to grapple with throughout your life. The first and most critical is: Who am I? Consider it. The answer to that question connects your head with your heart and spirit. The answer also lets you question your circumstances to find out what your purpose is on the planet. Next, you want to ask yourself: What's my mission here? What's my job? Then, you set a goal and send its intention out into the Universe asking for help." All faces went blank. Dark-haired Surita raised her hand.

"Madam, why are we doing this? Getting to know who we are?"

"To find your personal meaning. Find your happiness to set a goal that creates a better world for yourself and for others. That's at the heart of liberation."

It wasn't possible to keep it simple. I didn't try. I touched again on the topics the Dalai Lama had spoken about, selfless service to others and the impermanence of all things. I was running out of time for such a heavy topic, and it was clear the women needed a bit more than I could give right then. But I believed and suspected—being who I was—that my presence in the women's lives might let them pick up some of my noisy curiosity and my vibes. And that that would spark a desire in them to move forward, always forward without getting too stuck. When I had finished my lesson, I thought the Dalai Lama would have been proud. As a final touch, I told the women they needed a mantra, that they needed to tell themselves that they were lovable and capable. Tell themselves that they were "Special." And I think Dad would have been proud.

I went to the wedding. It was the second day of a three-day affair. The Dean's driver dropped me off, telling me he'd pick me up in a few hours. The bride sat next to her groom on an alter in full regalia, dressed in an elegant, white sari. They were like Mumtaz Mahal and the Shah at the Taj. She was festooned with gold necklaces and bracelets that dazzled under the artificial lights. For his part, the groom wore a traditional turban decked with flowers. A cord was draped around their necks to ward off evil. A scarf tied the two of them together, a symbol of a union that, for me, had been sacred but far too fragile. I wished them well, better than well; I wished them bliss.

Dean Gana was nowhere in sight, but a warmth permeated the beautifully decorated hall. Music played in the background, and after an hour of sitting and watching the bride and groom busily greet their guests, I was escorted upstairs for dinner. The meal consisted of buttered chicken, paneer, and kofta curry doled out on a shiny green banana leaf set before me. I ate with my hands along with everyone else.

By that night, I was down to one mosquito coil and placed it in the middle of the carpet. I went to sleep. In the middle of the night, I awoke smelling smoke. The rug was smoldering. I quickly doused it from my water bottle, creating a puddle on the floor. I had almost set the room, the guesthouse, on fire. The next morning, despite all my scrubbing, a black spiral was left charred in the rug. How was I going to explain that?

When the week ended, Amrita came to send me off. Somehow, she knew about the ruined carpet. As well as charging me for rug repairs, she also charged me for staying in the guest house. Although pleased about providing free teaching, when I was done with the College, I was glad it was over. It had been precisely what I expected, a taste of the culture, one from a woman's point of view, one that my mind juxtaposed against those sari-clad women flinging animal waste against the wall in Lucknow, the woman on the sidewalk in Delhi, the grandmother begging.

I'd come to Asia to turn my brain off. Yet, for one narrow time slot, I'd reached back into my old life to give the students my best shot, only to discover I was not the teacher but the student...me getting the big lesson. An eye-full of how young elite women were treated in India—stunted in their ability to question, locked up at night, and perhaps heading for lives...well, who knew what? Cathy had been right sending me here. I felt lucky to have her as a guide. I also thanked Ganesh for allowing me to give some selfless service.

Across Southern India

I LEFT AVINASHILINGUM College by train traveling south to Madurai to the World Heritage Site of Tiruchirappalli—yet another one of the subcontinent's architectural wonders. Once there, I quickly saw the shrines, which in contrast to Hampi's natural restraint, made a show of being garishly painted. I soon split. Fatigue had set in against temples and tombs. I was developing a love-hate relationship with the country. The dirt, the lack of sanitation, the environmental degradation, arduous travel conditions, crowded buses, blaring video players, difficulty finding a decent room, a caste system that sharply relegated the poor to live in garbage-bag tents—all of it there, entrenched, depleting. Yet, I was driven forward, also gorging on India's absurd but mystical cornucopia.

Like a dream-lover, the genius loci of India argued with and caressed me. Its protagonists and antagonists, acting out their roles, brought me high and carried me low. Players holding me in their arms fast, their spirit so large, so inscrutable that the whole of India's voice roared music resembling no other place on earth—psychedelic jazz replete with antics synchronizing me with its rhythmic source. India's loci took liberties with my soul... etched melodic rhythms on my heart, stirring my consciousness... as only a lover would.

Still, identical to any passionate love affair, it began to overwhelm my state of balance. I thought of what the night goddess in Kathmandu had said about fleeing to Thailand to escape the bedlam. I, too, needed a break before I hit the last stop on my enlightened being list, the Ashram of Sri Aurobindo at Auroville.

I was now on another train to the East Coast of India to Madras to the beach. Memories of Sunday afternoons relaxing on Long Island Sound beaches, fishing, and swimming with Agnes and Biscute swarmed my mind. Again, I needed deliberate re-grounding. But this time, not in the stalwart care of the woods, but in the emotional, watery freedom of the ocean. I needed to crawl back into that liquid womb.

I picked the Ideal Beach Resort at Mahabalipurm. It was at the top end charging fifteen dollars a night, expensive for India, but staying at two-star hotels for the past three months called for a bit of a splurge. Plus, the guidebook said it had a pool. Reception gave me a large bright room. I unpacked and went to the restaurant. Fish was on the menu priced at what amounted to about 80 cents. By this time, it was February, and I had gone a long time without cooked vegetables. Starved for them, I ordered two different kinds only to be amused when the bill came. The veggies cost more than the fish. The waiters had looked on bemused.

That night, I peeled back the covers revealing scrubbed sheets and crawled into bed, falling into a soundless sleep. When I awoke, I had the sensation of having slept on sandpaper. My fingertips stroked the sheets feeling fine grit. I thought I must have gotten into bed with sand on my feet. I put on my bathing suit, intending to jump into the pool. Before I left my room, I dug for a large safety pin in my toiletry bag and used it to hang my passport and money belt inside the heavy drape on the window. With that secure, I went to the pool, peered at its iffy water, and got directions to walk the few kilometers to the beach.

Repos beach is located on the Bay of Bengal in the northeastern end of the Indian Ocean. When I got there, several Indian families were spread out on blankets. Men and children body-surfaced waist-deep in the whitecaps that rolled in from the ocean. Without losing a beat, I put on a tee-shirt to keep myself from scorching in the sun and plunged into the sea. I dove to the bottom over and over again, fingertips stroking the rippled sand, opening my eyes and my mouth to the seawater.

The Bay of Bengal was not blue-green like the Atlantic Ocean off the coast of Cape Cod, a spot I held special going at the end of every school year to regroup. Instead, the water was marine blue. I liked meeting the ocean again, its balmy breezes tangling my hair, its salty wetness washing my skin, its bossy waves tossing my body. I enjoyed my relationship to the ocean, Mother Earth rocking me in her liquid cradle.

I swam. Arms stroking, legs kicking, splash, splash, splash diving through the waves. Diving through the crest, its horsetail hissing, leaving its mark upon the sand. Lap, lap, lap. Back and forth, back and forth, visualizing a stream of healing prana pouring from the tips of my toes out the top of my head, streaming through my chakras, pulsing through each organ. Then reversing it, I flowed light from my brain out the tips of my fingers, curling elegant mudras as I swam through billions of gallons of life-giving seawater—that I hoped whales had imparted their healing soul songs to.

And I wondered: *Am I swimming in Kaligandaki River molecules? Had any flowed thousands of miles to meet me first in the Ganges… then to continue their flow blending into the Indian Ocean? Had those Gandaki packets of energy found their way to me swimming here in the Bay of Bengal? Had my skin absorbed their fuel again, those negative ions inhaled by Gome and me trekking the Gandaki's banks now mixing with this ocean's potency? Two givers of life—the Kaligandaki and the Ganges—in league with the Bay of Bengal flushing spiritual debris from my body and soul?* That crazy-minded part of me—that Dad part imagined so.

I swam harder, plunging through the waves, and I felt the same old pleasure I'd experienced praying for Karette and everyone else that time in the pool. But this was different. It was coming from a spot that had let go and forgiven. I prayed again for everyone… including Tim. Waves with foamy sprays rolled over me, transparent and warm. I melded with them, relaxation.

Out of the water, I walked up the beach soaking in the vibes. Away from the swimming area, I caught sight of a man coming out of a shack. He walked to the high-water line and squatted using the tide's cycle as a toilet. *Well,* I thought, *we are all in one great cycle of eating and shitting.* All living and dying, working, and playing, doing and being, and me? Was I any different? Who was I to judge? No. I was no different. I walked along and watched the galloping waves fling their crests, wedding bouquets in the briny air.

Shade was a premium at the beach. Only three tall palm trees cast long shadows. I threw my towel on the creamy sands lining myself up in one tree's narrow band of shade. I took out my copy of *Moby Dick*, but no book, not even this favorite, could compete with the whispers in the air, the battle of the waves, or the control the sun had over me. I sat feeding on my own obsessive quest to stop, to watch, to be.

People came and went. The beach giggled with Indian women and young girls who took off their sandals, pulled up the hems of their saris, and tiptoed thigh-deep into the surf. It reminded me of Agnes, Biscute, and me as kids playing endlessly at the beach for hours. I wondered what they were doing at home, wishing they were here with me to share the bay's glorious water. I'd have to call Agnes the next time I got to a phone store to touch base and make sure everything was OK at home.

I'd written Dori telling her about the Dalai Lama. How the full bell of his voice vibrated through the multitude and into my heart. After one more stop on my enlightened beings list, I told her that I'd end up in Madras (Chennai), where I could pick up a general delivery letter at the Post Office. I hoped she'd write.

The sun strutted across its azure field, patterning the beach with islands of shade. Twenty minutes later, I tugged at the towel's hem inching back into the shade. The sun moved; I tugged the towel. Moved again. Again, the sun was in control. The palm's trunk cast a long, shadowed spear, a sundial gnomon pushing me farther and farther across its sands, pushing, pushing, pushing...me through Time.

The hotel's over-maid came into my room to ensure that the bed was made correctly and the bathroom cleaned each day. One day, I met up with her at mid-morning and asked her how she was. She responded with, "I'm bored," and she described her job as tedious. She showed intelligence and probed me about going to the USA to escape her plight. Again, I heard the abandonment of India's little girls, this time by a culture, not a mother.

That night after dinner, I strolled the grounds; and when I

returned to my room, I walked to the end of the hallway and stepped out the door onto a small balcony. The back of the hotel was in sharp contrast to its main grounds, which were planted with hibiscus bushes and had small patches of green lawn. I glanced to my left. Several slim Indian women in saris knelt by a stream washing laundry. Sheets were pounded on rocks, rinsed in the stream, and laid out on the sands to dry. Mystery of gritty sheets solved. I laughed.

During my stay at the hotel, the Indian Dance Festival at Mahabalipuram was scheduled. It would take place in the evening on the beach, and I went. I sat in the back row facing an outdoor platform with the Indian Ocean as a backdrop. The afternoon's heat smoldered as the sun's pink light faded out of a cobalt sky.

A sitar began to play high-pitched, staccato music. Three dancers emerged from a side tent pirouetting onto the stage. Dressed in opulent saris, their bodies undulated from head to toe, their outfits swayed in an iridescent gleam of emerald, ruby, and citrine silk. Shiny black hair framed the women's faces; eyes arched in black mascara sparkled. Each woman lifted her head in angular precision—first to the right, then sharply to the left in a geometrical motion repeated in her arms and legs. Bare feet, toes pointed, the women's fingertips formed elegant hand motions, mudras, aesthetically inscribing the air with their hands.

The sun yielded. The night grew velvety. The sitar music sent out a springy buzz that stretched through the air. Each woman's body coiled and uncoiled fluidly, expressing its utter gorgeousness sung before us an intimate knowledge of feminine truths. Ocean, sky, gentle night. I felt soft. My own energy system unwound from the base of my spine to glide to the top of my head, my own personal melody spiraling with each dancer's movement. I watched this primal conversation. I felt sweet.

I thought of the silk sari I had packed away in my suitcase. *Would I ever wear it? Have its honeyed fabric caress my skin?* I could ship it home along with the one I got from Dean Fatima when I got to Madras. But for now, beauty was in the air—the dancers, the musicians, the audience, the people at the hotel cooking my carrots, the women washing my sheets, and the families on the beach playing, everyone in the whole world, beautiful. A harmonic beauty. I couldn't have felt more beautiful myself.

Aurobindo Ashram

Re-grounded by my ocean stay, I was back on the trail of my enlightened beings list. It was mid-February when I got to Pondicherry, one hundred miles south of Madras. I found my way to the Sri Aurobindo Ashram, established in the early twentieth century by Sri Aurobindo, who said, "All life is Yoga." There were two sections where to stay, and I booked the part of the ashram five miles away in Auroville built as a utopian camp for the international community.

The room was fancy by any standards. It amounted to half a circular brick cottage surrounded by a small, shallow moat that trickled water keeping the crawling bugs at bay. Every time I stepped over it, I marveled at the unpretentious engineering job it accomplished. Situated in the woods, I knew the mosquitos would find a way through the screens. I took the malaria tablets religiously despite the warnings on the label about hair falling out. Mine hadn't, and this time, I was skipping the mosquito coils.

The Auroville Ashram was built for world peace allowing all humanity to unite in a model community. I can't say I disagreed with this philosophy. Nothing was prescribed, no robes, no blood tests. Sri Aurobindo had promoted *self-concentration* as a critical method to merge self-awareness with Divine Power. It sounded akin to Jnana Yoga to me, and I liked that. But still, I wondered briefly how Monrova and Paula were making out in Pune.

I'd chosen the Auroville community instead of the ashram located in Pondicherry. At Auroville, no alcohol or drugs were allowed, which didn't quite guarantee anything. But usually meant peace and quiet, again different from what I expected at Pune, where Monrova and Paula had encouraged me to go. Now, I just rented a cottage, and I was good to go. It was more my style, although I wasn't sure what I'd find.

It was quiet in Auroville. Too quiet. The other half of my round cottage was empty. I was hoping for some company given that I had encountered fifty thousand people in Mundgod. Auroville covered a couple hundred acres of territory. I was in a small enclave consisting of sleeping buildings and a separate dining hall for guests. Little was going on, and I decided to find the action. I went to the main building, booked a massage, and got the yoga schedule. The air was cool enough, and I walked down a wide path through dense woodland, hearing several birds calling in the distance. *Where was everybody? Nary a soul in sight.* I got a sense that nothing was going on, that Auroville was a work in progress.

The following day, I went to yoga. I moved my body through the asanas and my brain through the words, but nothing stuck as exceptional. I went to the lecture in mid-morning. Aurobindo's concepts on the "Supermind" were fascinating in light of my own cobra. But somehow, transforming humanity into a divine existence gave the impression of being a far reach even though I believed in 'special within,' I truly did. I went back to the office and signed up for a foot reflexology session. My feet had behaved as geniuses trekking across the Himalayas, and they needed treating.

For three days, I followed the same routine. Yoga, lecture, massage, a long walk. I'd examined all the trees and bushes by this time, especially the hibiscus blooms growing throughout Auroville. Unlike the chrysanthemums I'd seen at the Botanical Research Institute in Lucknow, no earthy fragrance perfumed the air. Instead, the hibiscus' erotically fringed stigmas danced out of crinkled whirls of ballroom-petaled saris.

I walked round and round and round. I had booked a week. The plants and trees began to merge into a blur for me. Then one afternoon, I passed a large house with a woman sitting in a window seat. When she saw me, she called out and invited me in for tea which I accepted gratefully. We chatted. The woman poured tea, and I asked, "Is there any satsang?"

She looked at me through the shaggy bangs of her long gray hair, "Satsang? No, not here. There is no guru here to conduct that." *Strange*, I thought. I had rested up on the beach at the resort, and I was ready for more; but on the other hand, I must admit I wasn't too disappointed. "Is there a particular yoga teacher you like?" eager for another Girish who I had met in Rishikesh.

"No," she said. "They're all good. While you're here, though, you should visit the Matrimandir, the Temple of the Mother. They're still building it, but the Inner Chamber is now open to the public."

"Is there a group there to meditate with?"

"There's no group meditation there, not yet. You'll go to concentrate silently."

"Oh?"

"The four pillars of the structure are aligned with the four corners of the compass; all in alignment so consciousness can open," she said. "Matrimandir is called the Temple of the Mother because it symbolizes the universal energies of the Mother, the driving force of existence. You have to get a ticket with an entry time at the office."

"OK."

"Matrimandir is the soul of Auroville."

"I'll do that." And I remembered that the term "Mother" had also been ascribed to Mt. Everest (Divine Goddess of the Universe) and to the Kaligandaki River in Nepal (Divine Mother).

When I got to Matrimandir, Temple of the Mother, I saw the shape of a geodesic dome appearing to hover organically like an earthstar erupting from the land. After Aurobindo died in 1950, his closest collaborator, Mirra Alfassa—a French spiritual guru called The Mother—continued building the structure.

My entry was at 1 PM, a fifteen-minute slot, to "concentrate" in complete silence. I waited outside under a banyan tree for the exact moment to enter. A handful of others and I ambled up a circular walkway similar to the ramp in the Guggenheim Museum in New York. From the second-floor balcony, I entered the domed, inner chamber to a stark interior. White carpeted floors and marble walls filled the room. There were no windows and no place to sit. I concentrated.

The high ceiling overhead had an opening in the apex where a beam of sunlight focused down onto a sizeable crystal-glass globe. The ray of light fastened my attention to the sphere— precisely round, filled with light, luminous. I stood in place and concentrated on the vibes of peace, the vibes of the Universal Mother, but I wasn't getting it. Instead, I felt that I was at Disney Land.

By this time in my life, I'd spent more than a bit of time focusing, but this was different. I'd come so far from home intending to un-focus my mind, so now trying to concentrate inside an ingeniously constructed dome—something was wrong for me. Standing in its silvery, sterile perfection made me edgy. There were no flowers, no smell of incense, and hardly any people. I stood frozen, almost afraid to move, to disturb the ambiance. A stream of light pierced through an opening in the apex of the building to land on an exquisitely engineered crystal globe made by the Germans. It shimmered as it sat centered in The Temple of the Mother, yet at the same time, the place felt unoccupied of anything.

I thought of the puja under the tent during the Dalai Lama's Initiation Teachings. I could still hear the dove-like murmuring of the crowd, the Dalai Lama's laugher ringing out—the glorious clutter of people. And the monks, the monks madly rushing to and fro tossing out food; faces damp with sweat, baskets on arms, dashing about the crowd, performing the ritual to remove all obstacles, worldly or inner or secret, that blocked freedom from entering us. But here, I'd been given barely fifteen unwelcoming minutes. I concentrated again on the ray of light streaming steadily onto the crystal globe. Something felt contrived.

I didn't know how to question it, but I knew there was a question to be asked. I was inside a magnificent structure—The Temple of the Mother dedicated to World Peace. Yet, I wasn't feeling the life force of the place. On the contrary, I felt even lonelier and more disconnected, all of which made me find the expensive glass globe pointless. What vital information was I missing?

I dug in, trying to understand what was going on. Why I wasn't getting it? Something about unity with others was rummaging around in my head but lost. I thought back to the women living in the garbage bag tents, the sari-clad women throwing cow dung against the wall to earn a living, women locked in dorms, women working in dead-end jobs, women sleeping on sidewalks, women washing sheets in rivers, women begging with babes in their arms. My head was racing around. *What vital information was I missing?* I agreed with what I'd heard in the lectures about Sri Aurobindo's philosophy—self-concentration to access the divine within—I was living a facet of that existence, but here, something was lost on me.

I thought about the lepers begging under the searing sun in Mundgod. This, too, felt nearly the same as meeting with the lepers. Things were missing from my understanding of life. And I didn't know exactly what they were. And sadly, just then, I didn't much care either. I didn't want to concentrate. That felt too close to the responsibility I had left behind, plus here it felt meaningless.

Outside again, I stood in the shade under the banyan tree and took a last look at The Temple. I realized that I had not tuned into my cobra, nor had it tuned into me, during my few days in Auroville. There was no signal, nothing. I must have slipped into a space that closed me off from Aurobindo's message, which left me with far too much sterile time on my hands. I was bored.

Boredom is one of the most, if not *the* most, desperate states of mind I can slip into. I can mark the few times I've been bored. Times that impacted me deeply. Thankfully they have been infrequent, usually after a great deal of focused work with nothing concretely planned at the end to switch me from intensive *doing to* simple *being*. Somehow those spells had always been death to me, slow, unnerving death that I fought hard to drive off. Now here at Aurobindo, I got reflex therapy on my feet to help with my ennui. It sent an unforgettable blast of juice surging through my body, but it wasn't enough.

I had too much time to kill until my stay ended at Auroville, which didn't resemble utopia to me at all. The only thing I enjoyed daily was scrutinizing the job done by the tiny moat circling the base of the cottage keeping the bugs out. Finding myself clutched by boredom, I was bewildered. I wondered whether or not the ashram was in decline despite the nice lodgings and offerings of yoga and wellness programs. Feeling bored, I was confused; because the whole point of the trip *was* about simply *being*. Unwinding. Taking in the breath of the place. Flowing. Doing nothing! Yet something here didn't fit. I couldn't figure out what it was. So, I did what I always did when in a dither. I walked.

As I tramped through the woods, I thought about how I had landed in Auroville searching to visit yet another enlightened being but had found none. I grew increasingly listless. I was wasting time, and that felt mildly painful. I had booked a week's stay hoping for more. Still, I wasn't regretting Pune and its "good times." My sexual attitudes kept me boxed in, although I was feeling lonely.

My retrieval from boredom came in the morning in the shape of a tall, gangly, tussle-haired guy who pranced into the dining hall. I glanced up from my oatmeal and banana breakfast to see him pause, take in the room, and with a glance plunk himself down across the table from me. I put on a smile the size of the Great Barrier Reef.

"Can I join you?" said the English accent.

"Sure. Please." I grinned at him.

"Place is pretty empty."

"I'll say. Where you from?"

Brian turned out to be an English cabbie who was a yoga buff touring India like me. We talked over breakfast and clicked.

Finishing, he said, "I've rented a car for tomorrow to tour Pondicherry, interested?"

"You bet," I said.

Brian taxied us around Pondicherry. I don't remember where we went or what we did, and there weren't any sexual vibes (he might have been gay). Still, the upbeat babble that poured from Brian's heart never stopped as he drove us around. He told me about cabbing Mr. so-and-so political boss and Mrs. whose-what's all around London—everyone except the Queen.

I told Brian about my trek into the Annapurna Sanctuary and the Dalai Lama's Kalachakra Initiation. He was impressed. Those few hours, where Brian overflowed like fragrant bunches of yellow roses and gallons of sauvignon blanc wine that we inhaled together, were fun. Was he the enlightened being I had come to Auroville to meet? Or maybe a bodhisattva who heard the cries of the world and expelled them by his laughter and delight at life? Could be. Brian fed my inner child by being who he was, a cabby whose spirit exuded sparklers of bright light. He fit the bill with his own brand of shaktipat that I was sure he spread from Baker Street to Piccadilly along the avenues of London.

Those last few days in Auroville taught me that enlightened beings come in different shapes and sizes. They do not necessarily wear white clothing, or cashmere shawls, or monk's robes. Two days later, I packed my bag, left, and went to Madras (Chennai). I intended to ship things home, check for a letter from Dori, and buy a bus ticket to Bombay on the west coast—my last stop before leaving India.

TIME IS ONLY AN INCH

Madras to Bombay

Several rats scurried across the steps of the Madras Post Office. I carried in a box and deposited it on the counter. The weight of my winter coat, hat, gloves, bell and Dorje, hiking boots—vital for my trek in Nepal five months ago—was being shipped home. Everything except the sari, mandalas, and the singing bowls (not wanting to lose them). The package was sent off, and yes, my friend Dori had come through with a letter. Getting it was drinking an elixir reconnecting me with home. I missed sitting down and having a cup of coffee with her. I missed discussing my dreams with her. I missed her blithe spirit sharing in each other's company. She'd received my postcards and updated me on what kind of workshops she'd taken since I'd left.

I didn't stay long in Madras. The time came to finish up in India and head for Egypt. I packed my bag to depart for Bombay by bus. Like me, I'd met a woman at my hotel who was also 'getting out of Dodge' taking the bus to the west coast. We'd had dinner together one evening and had agreed to go to the State Bus Stand to depart the following day. I was glad to have a travel buddy because Indian buses weren't my favorite, but they were cheaper than flying.

The din of buses could be heard before we entered the enclosed chaotic and smelly plaza. The vehicles roared in and out spewing noxious exhaust. Dark-faced men scowled in one corner seeming to promise mayhem. My pal and I entered and stood there looking for the ticket booth. Men crowded us from all sides. I searched for women seeing two or three small groups huddling in tight knots. My throat tightened. One more look, one more smell, and I turned to my buddy, "Let's get the hell out of here!" And without discussion, we bolted through a gate, threw ourselves out onto the street, hailed a taxi, and jumped in. I can't remember how I got to Bombay, but it wasn't by bus. Travel across India for that last leg became a blur.

Bombay encapsulated India, a sprawling hive of activity. It was from here I'd fly to Egypt. I wasn't going to linger long, but I did have a promise to keep to my friend Dina with whom I had taught and had made a promise to before I'd left home. She'd asked me if I found myself in Bombay if I would check out a cemetery where her sons-in-law's great-grandmother had been buried. I'd said, of course. Now arriving in the city, I found a cheap hotel, threw my things in the room, and got ready to tick things off my to-do list.

I'm not sure how I picked that hotel in Bombay. Alone (my travel buddy had gone off to Goa), it could have been that the other hotels were full. Or maybe it was late, or maybe I was too tired to observe or care about what was going on because I was leaving India soon. But it was cheap, and maybe I was compensating for the beach resort and ashram stays. It struck me as a strange place with a narrow staircase lined with mirrors leading to the upper floors. But this time, the men running the business were friendly enough, although the room was small and tacky with no window and the bed wedged against a wall mirror.

I got out my guidebook and perused the city's map to orient myself. First, I went out and found the American Airlines office where I booked my open-jaw ticket to Cairo. I couldn't wait—the pyramids, the Aswan Dam, all of Egypt that had been on my bucket list since third grade. I wanted to see the whole country's enormous history. The flight to Egypt didn't leave for four days giving me time to kill.

Next, I got myself to a phone store, bought minutes, and stood in line waiting to put a call into my sister Agnes. I woke her from sleep.

"Hold on, I have to go to the bathroom," she said.

"No," I shouted into the phone. "I only have so many minutes, and there's a long line behind me waiting."

"OK, OK." She said and told me everything back home was

going well. The dog business was good. Family members were doing family things—Biscute managing the four kids, etc. Nothing was new or changed much. Then a surprise. Agnes said, "Hey, your friend Cathy called, and she's going to Egypt on business."

"What? Cathy in Egypt?" I was incredulous.

"Yeah, she said she's going to be in Cairo in three weeks. Wait, I'll get the name of the hotel. OK, here it is. She's staying at the Forte Grand Hotel the third week in March." I whooped for joy, hardly believing I'd be meeting up with Cathy in Cairo! It was the end of February, and I hadn't seen her since October when she'd dropped me off at JFK. What kind of miracle was that?

Encountering Cathy in Egypt would be special. I recalled the adventures we'd shared together over the years. We'd taken trips to DC to visit her folks, backwoods swimming, hiking the New England forests, enjoying the bond we shared with nature. But more than that, Cathy had a Dad who had mothered her the same way Dad had mothered me. Cathy, well, she was a mother who nurtured others certainly, but she was also Dad in countless ways— her attunement to Mother Nature—but especially her practice of always throwing "life preservers" to her family and friends, her insightful understanding of people, of me. Cathy was teaching the world how to be a mensch. She was always teaching me.

When I hung up the phone with Agnes, I thought: *Cathy and I could spend some time seeing the sites together. What fun!* But what I didn't know: it would be more than having fun. It would be that Cathy was probably the only one in Cairo (that I knew) who knew how to drape a sari, a skill I'd be needing badly.

After that, I purchased a couple of disposable cameras. I'd made that promise to Dina to find the Christian Cemetery of Sewri outside of Bombay. Repaying Dina, who'd given me support during my divorce, was a no-brainer. Dina's generosity during the breakup of my marriage to Tim had helped me to survive it. Whatever I could do to repay her, I would do. I would take notes and photographs of the headstone during the search. A picture is worth a thousand words.

That done, I found my way through the crowded streets of

Bombay, looking for a bookstore selling English titles. Bombay, like the other cities in India, is filled with culture. And I walked past the Golden Temple, Harmandir Sahib, on the shorefront of the Arabian Sea. Built by the Sikhs in the 16th century, the temple shimmered in gold leaf. The building spoke of India's wealth, richness, good fortune, blessings, and advantage in contrast to so much of what I'd seen during my journey throughout the country. Lavish and meager. A sign posted outside welcomed all the world's people, and I felt it honestly expressed Indian ideals.

The clerk at the bookstore pointed me to the back corner where they shelved books written in English. *The City of Joy* was long gone, and as for *Moby Dick*, I was almost ready to float Ishmael away on the last page with him in Queequeg's coffin. I needed a guidebook to Egypt plus a good general read. It was quiet and cool in the store.

I browsed among a good selection of fiction until one title jumped out at me—*The Unbearable Lightness of Being* by Milan Kundera. I'd never heard of it, but it drew me, or rather it grabbed me. I read a few pages and liked the philosophical bent examining the idea of eternal return. This is where everything in life keeps repeating itself by juxtaposing two polar opposites—responsibility and personal freedom. Maybe it was a modern take of what the Dalai Lama had said about reincarnate cycles of life.

I read more. Its message appeared to express my own life at that moment. After all, I'd recently finished, quit, sold, and divorced a good decade of my life and turned my back on a load of responsibilities, at least for a year, sending myself into a vacuum of freedom. The book called this a "lightness of being," except with one significant difference for me. What I was experiencing, right then in my life, wasn't *unbearable*, no, not at all, it felt more than bearable; it felt rich. I recalled the helicopter ride out of the Annapurna Sanctuary feeling ever so light. And I remembered leaving Mundgod with truly a "lightness of being," feeling Special.

I got curious. Why was the "lightness of being" unbearable for the characters? I dug into the book's pages. Kundera decried rules and morality—everything needed to run society smoothly—exposing these boundaries as useless. He caught me off guard.

After Dad and Mother had given me the Harvard course in Anger Management 101, I happened to like rules, the sense of order they gave me. Wasn't I already breaking enough rules having a cobra?

If I bought this book which seemed to question what I now felt as my tidy sense of being, where was it going to take me? Its viewpoint—life as meaningless— felt a strong tide pulling me into discouraging waters. But still, I had the uneasy feeling that my travels were somehow being examined by it. I was hooked by the tension it created in me, and I bought it.

Back at the hotel, I was going out to dinner when I passed a young man dragging a woozy woman dressed in what appeared to be a half-slip up the stairs. I caught the guy's glazed eyes squinting at me in cocky puzzlement. Then, a shock ran through me. I was in a flophouse! I stopped in my tracks and reversed myself back into my room. I packed my bag, proceeded back down into the lobby out the front door into the street, and thumbed madly through *Lonely Planet* for another hotel. It was hard to laugh at. But I had a funny feeling maybe the book I'd bought was right—I was already repeating history just as Kundera suggested. Stupidly, I'd done the same thing in Spain at age twenty while traveling as a college student looking for cheap digs.

Keeping the Promise

I pocketed the two disposable cameras, went to the train station, and bought a round-trip ticket to Sewri. This was the town where the Asker's great-grandmother was buried. It was about a sixty-minute ride outside of Bombay.

Once on the platform for local trains, I was utterly lost. My guidebook for this out-of-the-way jaunt was of no help. Primarily, everything was written in Hindi. After riding the rails throughout

India for four months, I had a foreboding about entering any old car that might fill up with men. Departure time was in two minutes. I searched the fast-thinning crowd for a woman who could help me, but there were none. Then to my right, a man dressed in a business jacket stopped and looked quizzically into my confused face. "Do you need help, Madam?" he asked in English.

I pushed my ticket toward him and said, "I'm going to Sewri."

"Sewri?" he seemed puzzled but said, "Please come with me. You cannot take any car; you must take the women's car." I followed along after him rushing down the tracks past several coaches. He stopped and pointed. "Go here. You will be safe. It takes about sixty-minutes. The Sewri sign will be written in English."

Relieved and grateful, I got into the car designated for women. Twenty pairs of eyes stared at and ignored me simultaneously. I put myself in a seat and breathed a sigh of relief, thanking my guardian angel.

Sixty minutes later, the train pulled to a stop on a high, raised platform. A sign read Sewri, and I got off. To my dismay, I was in a small, busy city, not the smaller burg I had been expecting. The truth was, I had no idea where the cemetery was located. Unlike other places visited over the past months, a map of Serwi was not in the guidebook. I stared over the platform at a narrow street lined with small shop-fronts displaying the wares of various merchants.

I scanned around. There was no station master to help. And there were no other women who looked like me. I thought of the mean kid I had encountered at the bus stand at that godforsaken park outside Keoladeo Park. And my anxiety told me to jump back on the next train to Bombay. But I couldn't do that. I was being propelled forward by my debt to Dina. And as irrational as it was, I knew by now that every time I got agitated, I needed to push forward. And this time, I had a promise to keep.

I threw my shoulders back, took a deep breath, charged down the long flight of stairs, and dashed under the tracks toward the crowded street, not knowing where I was going but nonetheless going. Men began to stare at me. I felt totally alone, out of place, nervous, and vulnerable. I knew I'd have to ask for directions, but I hadn't anticipated what a lost cause that might be in this non-tourist town.

I was in a swarm of stalls piled with cauliflowers, bananas, root vegetables, clothes, and trinkets as far as the eye could see the length of the street under the platform. At one end, a vendor was buried behind an enormous mound of silvery sardines with dried olive-yellow skins glinting in the sun. The smell of incense drifted in the air while a boil of voices conducted the morning's business. Confused, *which direction would I take?* An old man walked by, and I called out, "Sir?" stopping him to ask where the cemetery was. He stared at me blankly, then lifted his boney, brown arm to point down the long row of shops, saying, "Clock, clock."

"Clock? Clock what?" I asked. "Cemetery, Christian Cemetery?"

He pointed vigorously and moved away briskly.

Not understanding him but thinking there might be a clock tower by the cemetery, I walked in the direction he had pointed. Soon, I came to a stall operated by a tall gray-bearded man, wearing gold, wire-rimmed glasses watches laid out in neat rows in front of him. His hands held a wristwatch as he deftly turned a small screwdriver into its back. He had a particularly sophisticated manner the other vendors lacked. As I approached, he peered over the top of his glasses to look at me questioningly. Was it possible that he spoke English?

"Hello." I ventured.

"Hello, Madam," he said in a low voice.

"Do you speak English?"

"Yes."

"Thank God," I said, breathing a sigh of relief. "I'm here looking for the Christian Cemetery. Can you direct me?"

"Of course, Madam. It is right up the street. Not far. You walk up this way," he motioned to his left, "for 700 meters, and you will see the entry on the right-hand side of the road. Not far. Ten minutes."

"Thank you," I said and walked along the row of stalls, grateful for his help. When I got to the end of the commercial activity at the train station, I walked up a hill lined with whitewashed residential buildings. I walked for ten minutes. The morning was glaring. *Was I headed in the right direction?* Sweat beaded on my forehead, and dampness pooled under my armpits. I was trying to translate meters into miles but figured if I kept walking, the chances were I'd find the cemetery or someone who could help. As I stood in the shade of a tree, I blotted my forehead, sipped water, and wished a taxi would come by, but none did.

I continued my trudge up the hill, finally reaching an archway flanked by two whitewashed pillars bearing the name Christian Cemetery Sewri over a wrought iron gate. I let out a big sigh of relief as I entered, only to see a vast burial ground filled with thousands of gravestones. Again, I had expected a backwater cemetery with a few graves, and I shook my head in disbelief.

A small office stood to the entrance's left. When I stepped in, a tall, iron-haired Indian greeted me. "Hello," he said, "Can I help you?"

"Hello. My name is Anya Kru. I'm here from the United States looking for a gravesite. Friends of mine want information on the burial site of their great-grandmother."

"We can help you, Madam. I am Ruban, the caretaker here. Please have a seat."

I sat, relieved that he was there, and the place was organized. I had expected to wander through the cemetery, a small cemetery, quickly finding the grandmother's gravesite. I had her name. But here, that was not going to be the case, given this graveyard's scope.

"When was she buried?" Ruban asked.

"Oh, I don't know, but her name is Margret R. Owensmith."

"Madam, that does no good. You see, this is a big cemetery." He pointed out the window bobbling his head slightly. "See that. Thousands of graves we have. We need the date of death to find the section she is buried in."

"I'm not sure when that was," I said.

"You can see our records…" he pointed toward a wall stacked haphazardly with large, dusty, canvas-covered journals that had dates numbered on their spines. "That is where you look to find the lady's name. There in the journals, you can find the exact quadrant of the cemetery she is buried in. But to help, we need to know when she died."

I'd arrived with little information to go on. I turned my head and stared at the piles of death records. I opened the cap of my water bottle and took a long drink.

"When did she die?" he asked again.

"I don't know. I wasn't told."

"Well then, there is no use to wander here."

His face was stern. It made me reflect on how death had echoed its motif throughout my trek this past year —Kathmandu's Pashupatinath, the vultures, the burning Ghats at Varanasi, the Taj—now landing me here to wander through this massive cemetery without a clue. I felt with this task, not having an accurate death date that I'd been tossed under a Wheel of Time, one that didn't even belong to me. I didn't know a thing about this woman. But now, her death, or at least its date, was in my care.

"OK, OK," I said. "Let me guess. I need a minute." I gulped more water. Then I wracked my brain tracing back through the generations. First, the son-in-law's age? OK. Thirtyish. Estimate the age of his mother. Yeah. I'd met her at the wedding. OK, fiftyish. Now, guess the age of her mother before her, and then her mother before her. Next, I calculated the deaths stretching my brain through generations reckoning a birthdate of great-grandmother Owensmith and then the year of her ultimate demise. Doing all this, I placed her death somewhere between 1924 and 1928. I said to the caretaker. "Let's try these dates."

Ruban went over to the shelves tugging at the journals, releasing a small dirt devil which enveloped my sinuses. He placed the twenty-four by twenty-four-inch square books on the table in front of me. I opened the first one to see handwritten inscriptions of names along with death dates written next to sectors in the cemetery. I thought: *When was the last time anyone had looked at these? Breathe, Honey, breathe...* and I ran my fingertips down rows of inked letters marking souls departed, my fingertips searching the records of the dead. Nothing was alphabetical. I glanced at the caretaker; no help there.

Yet, I took heart. As a child, I'd been the one who'd spot a four-leafed clover in a meadow or bits of sea glass on the beach. Dad had claimed a photographic memory, and right now, this minute, a 20% inheritance from him was what I needed to pop the Owensmith name into view.

Another deep breath. I turned the pages quickly skimming them. The fan overhead creaked keeping the room cool. I got steely. If it took all day or the next, I'd do this. I could find a room here in town. After all, I'd been proven unfussy about my digs. If I had to go into the cemetery and search plot by plot, I'd do that, too. I'd promised Dina.

I turned the pages—Philips, Jordan, Das Silva, Northrup, Miquitta, Aqrawal, on and on. Names of Christians who had come to this stark land never to leave, finding a resting place in its arid sod. Five minutes went by, then ten, then fifteen, me turning the manuscript's dry pages. I glanced at the other journals looming on the shelves. The caretaker appeared slightly amused, yet he remained at his desk politely busying himself.

I kept at it, sipping water, scanning. Then there it was: Margret R. Owensmith—her death date in 1926 along with the plot and quadrant number she was buried in. I fell back in my chair. Dina had done so much for me. I was going to be able to do this small thing for the Askers.

I pocketed the cameras and walked up the rows of headstones toward the Owensmith gravesite. The markers were simple and elaborate, some with carved angels and polished crosses comparable to those seen in the States. The sub-continent sun filtered through numerous Ashoka trees, aptly called the sorrowless tree, making the air strangely calm. My breath slowed for the first time all day. A sense of peace overspread the graveyard and me.

The Owensmith burial site was in a quadrant far into the cemetery. Shards of sun and shade lit the headstone. The marker was several feet tall and bore several inscriptions with different dates. I took out a disposable camera and snapped photos from different angles. I had a small pad, recorded the names of those buried along with their dates. There, under Margret R. Owensmith's inscription, was a birth and death date of an infant. It was buried on top of her.

I looked away. A grounds man walked by. I had come a long way to see this. The sun, the shade, the stillness pooled. I stood there rereading the inscription. And I meditated on the repose of the woman and the baby buried together. What had she been like? Had she been happy here? Why had the infant died? A few Our Fathers and Hail Marys slipped from my lips as I finished up the visit sketching the gravestone and snapping the last frames of the camera.

When I got back in the office, Ruban looked up from his desk.

"Done? Would you like a coke?"

Sure did. I was emotionally spent. I dropped into a chair and drank the coke savoring its sweetness. The caretaker and I chatted about my success and findings. But I began to be agitated. Something was disturbing my well-being, telling me something was wrong. Something was telling me I had to go back to the gravesite. I tried to dismiss my uneasiness telling myself everything was OK—I had the pictures and the sketches.

Abruptly as if possessed, I grabbed the second camera, jumped up, and ran back into the cemetery. I snapped the entire second camera at the gravesite, hastily shooting front, back, sides, longshot, short shots shooting the roll entirely. Back in Bombay, with both cameras developed, sure enough, I discovered the reason for my distress. All the pictures on the first roll were blurred. Only the second held an ancestral memoir for the Askers that enabled me to keep my promise.

In a way, I wasn't surprised at what happened that day. That day—when the "angel" got me to the women's car, the watch-repairman pointed the way, my visual skills kicked in, and something made me jump up to run back to the grave—was just one in many where I would slip into alignment with the harmonic rhythms of the country. Its order and disorder, its magnetic hold, and, of course, my own excitement where I was at "home" in India's Universe.

Carnal Satisfactions

A TRAIN, A bus, a taxi. I was glad I'd packed lunch in my little stainless-steel containers for the sixty-mile journey to the Western Ghats. With two days left before departing India, I took in one more UNESCO World Heritage Site, The Ellora Caves. In Bombay, I'd skipped yet another offer by Sri Sathya Sai Baba's devotees—a celebrated guru in India—to stay at his place and hear him speak. I must admit that when I was at his Ddharmakshetra temple, a radiant light had flashed from the marrow of my core outward through my skin. Still, I'd been told he was a phony using sleight of hand to conduct his so-called miracles. So instead, now, I was heading for the Caves. It was my last sightseeing stop in India.

Considered a natural museum, the Caves were carved from the mountainside, a dark taupe, purplish basalt. It was one of the largest rock-cut monasteries in the world dating back to 600-1000 CE reflecting Buddhist, Hindu, and Jain religions. And the title "Caves" was a misnomer. Yes, the Caves had bats tucked into ceiling crevices. Still, hundreds of columns and arches, plus massive figures of elephants and other cherished animals, fill thirty-five chambers. Also, after looking around, the word "monastery" didn't fool me either. Most of the monastic prayer halls were filled with erotica. I turned a corner greeted by an outrageous Shiva Linga (think penis that could keep the human race going forever). Other sensual statues of gods and goddesses expressed stark sexuality evidently held sacred by the community.

This was my sendoff to Egypt. It took me hours to explore Ellora. Upper levels contained beds for pleasuring, the monks' entertainment (all this from the guidebook). Sex messages, a historical record of carnal satisfactions, carved not so subtly in the inner rooms, were easily read even after thousands of years of abandonment. Hmmm. I reflected on my celibate status. You'd think I would have connected with someone during the past four months, but no.

I am always desperate for a swim. One last thumb through the guidebook, and I found an expensive hotel that offered pool access to non-registered guests. This is where I'd spend my last day in India before my 11 PM flight to Egypt.

The fifty-minute bus ride drove past broad sidewalks lined with dozens of black, plastic garbage bag tents—shelters resembling the ones I'd seen in Rishikesh. This time, instead of living on the banks of the Ganges under trees, families were sleeping on the pavement. Their tents, that same flimsy plastic, wedged up against a construction site of glistening expanses of newly poured cement sidewalks.

At the pool, I swam and refreshed to get ready for the next leg of my trip. I had always wanted to go to Egypt. It all began in third grade with *My Weekly Reader*, a current events-based magazine for kids. In the *Reader*, my imagination flew from one end of the globe to the other. Each week, I waited for its arrival to soak up the news from all over the planet. People. Places. Maps. Visuals. And the funny thing was, I was captivated with the construction of dams built around the world, monumental structures. When I read about the Hoover Dam, I wanted to see the Hoover Dam. When I read about the Aswan High Dam to be built across the Nile River, I wanted to see the High Dam. I became obsessed with the world's architectural fetes. A young engineer budded inside me, one that couldn't be actualized given my gender, family background, and no way to get support for that academic direction. Still, the *Reader* fed my hunger to hit the road that began with Dad and Mother. And my eight-year-old brain begun to keep a bucket list, putting Egypt and the Aswan High Dam at the top. I wanted to see it all. Every bit of it.

Sitting by the pool, I put aside Moby Dick and dug into Kundera's *The Unbearable Lightness of Being* to get to know the characters. There was a cheating husband, a soulmate of a wife, two friends—all entangled in some kind of a desperate love story. The theme had overtones of eternal return that sounded like reincarnation. Although linked to suffering, I wasn't sure whether or not it was related to reincarnation and liberation like the Dalai Lama was talking about. Whatever, the plot was an entanglement. It purported that life was an unbearable responsibility—something I had met face to face with, dealt with, and during this time in my life, wanted to escape from. Well, for at least one year.

And though my life had been a clumsy combination of pain and joy, I'd managed to "bite through," so the book grated on me. I had embraced rules for civility, for their security that had kept my personal chaos at bay. The book's ideas didn't fit with what I wanted right then in my own life. I was after the *lightness of being* implied by the title. Worse, the theme hinted that life was meaningless when I had learned, while in Mundgod, it was not. Nonetheless, despite the complex characters and philosophy it put forth, I read on, swimming, reading, swimming.

Later that afternoon, the bus ride back to my hotel went by the same freshly laid sidewalks from the morning. The concrete must have dried. The newly erected black, plastic tents populated the pavement out the window—homes for men, women, and children. I thought *There's a good example of "the unbearable being"—if ever there was one—the unbearable darkness of impoverished India.*

During my stay, an aperture in my consciousness had opened, one privy to the suffering of others. Still, in pity, I turned my head away. And sorry to say, my mind pitched into the past, imagining my fingertips brushing the tops of grasses as I walked to the pond using imagery to retrieve a sense of balance from a world gone stupid—people living on sidewalks, pieces of humanity falling apart.

It was almost midnight in Bombay's Sahar International Airport. I dashed toward my departure gate past the women's restroom. A young woman sat out front, the toilet wallah. Our eyes locked, which made me instantly remember an old, silly urge from my teenage years—one to relieve my karmic debt, or so I had thought. I flashed back to that day in New York City when I had used the old restrooms located in the pit of Grand Central Station.

Not quite dirty but shabby and in need of renovation in the sixties, the women's restroom was where indigents hid for the night. While waiting in line to pee, I mulled over the toilet maid's foul job. I thought my own karmic debt (whatever its accumulations had been at that point) might be lightened by doing her job, spending a day in her shoes scrubbing the toilets sat upon by thousands of women, swabbing out shit-clogged commodes and spit stained sinks. Doing that might produce some kind of insight…an empathy for others to serve not only in repayment of all my past transgressions but also to keep in balance the things I'd been gifted with— "You're Special, Honey."

On that day in the women's toilets at Grand Central Station, without me even knowing it, I guess something else was going on, too—a knowledge that I couldn't quite put into words just then but embedded in me. A yearning to connect with everyone, feel for everyone, know everyone, love everyone, tolerate everyone, be part of everyone: "me" the toilet scrubber. So, now after four months of *being* in India and *facing* the toilet wallah at Sahar Airport, I got it.

I dug into a pocket, held out my remaining rupees, while the wallah—her eyes reflecting a complicit understanding of my small redemption—rose to smile, hands extended receiving… mirroring mine, giving yet receiving, as she and I met in Namaste: "I salute the God within you": I/Thou…I/Thou toilet lady…I/Thou the toilet *ladies* of the world—you and I are one! And I realized that when I had entered India, I had entered its people; and now, as I departed India, they departed with me—their beauty and their pain.

PART IV

EGYPT

CHANCE. YOU CAN define it in different ways: possibility, odds, accident, freak, fortune, or fate. When chance is defined as possibility, it implies either a random event or that actions have been set for its occurrence. Chance is the backbone of Amor Fati, which translates into "love of one's fate." That is, loving your life, whether it holds suffering or happiness—whichever, it doesn't make a bit of difference; everything is blameless. Everything is worthy or at least necessary to produce the singular fingerprint of your soul waiting to enact its karmic design. So, with an abundance of possibilities, I have to say that Chance, inescapably, embraced me in Egypt.

*

MELTING ICE CUBES

I LANDED AT the Cairo International Airport on a warm March morning. The plane approached the landing strip, skirting the Sahara Desert. Outside the window, a watery, marine blue snake, the Nile, coiled up the country's fertile spine shimmering. India had been bone-dry—with fixed fields—but Egypt was shifting sands. My excitement grew.

A taxi took me into town. I found my way to the Ismailia House Hotel, a backpacker's place chosen from *Lonely Planet*. Once up the rickety elevator, I was given a spacious, clean room without much ado. I was tired but content. Egypt had starred at the top of my bucket list for almost forty years.

I didn't linger in Cairo, only two days, enough to take in the Egyptian Museum to see King Tut's paraphernalia. The exhibit contained the jewelry, furniture, chariots, food—everything he needed for the afterlife. I'm not sure I'd ever seen anything glitter quite so much.

To begin my jaunt, I took the overnight train to Aswan. This time not a sleeper, but first-class "sitting," which ended up being OK. There was a mix of people, including families, but different from Indian trains, it felt less frenetic. No wallahs hauled chai up and down the aisles, and there was no throwing of clay cups out of windows. I was sorry I missed the scenery along the Nile River, but it was cheap and fast. It was spring by now. My plan was to work my way down from Aswan through Luxor, snorkel on the Sanai Peninsula, then end up back in Cairo just as Cathy was arriving from the States. This would take about three weeks.

Once in Aswan, I arranged a trip to Abu Simbel and the Aswan High Dam. At four the following morning, a caravan of three taxis drove through the barren but stately Sahara Desert, heading toward the edge of Sudan. Dust clouds streamed behind the cars as we raced through an imposing history. Emptiness. A vast cloudless sky, warm and dry. After several hours of this, a cluster of camel herders blurred by the blank car window, ripples of heatwaves rising from the desert floor, backlighting them with a rising sun.

Several hours later, we reached Abu Simbel. Four colossal statues sat on thrones facing South. Simply put, the massive sandstone monument built in 1264 BC reeked of nobility. And although I don't know whether reincarnation is possible, the sixty-foot monoliths that included Ramses II and his wife Nefertiti drew me back in time. Knowing the history of the place, how it had been cut up and hoisted to its present location, I imagined Nefertiti sitting there on her throne morphing into Jackie Kennedy, who essentially was responsible for rescuing the gem.

And again, I imagined that Nefertiti (and her husband) should thank Jackie Kennedy for keeping them from drowning. Kennedy, in the sixties, had put forth a successful international effort to save the ancient monument from sinking into Lake Nasser, which was going to be created by the building of the Aswan High Dam. But before that, under the supervision of Polish archaeologist Kazimierz Michalowski, the giants had been cut and raised 213 feet and reconstructed on a bluff overlooking the newly formed lake. That's where I was now, gazing at the statues, their serene faces gazing toward the horizon.

My imagination took over. Could the two rulers possibly have imagined the hordes of tourists who'd come to snap photos thousands of years later? Impossible. But still, here, another love story had played out, in the desert, surviving Time. What were the chances unless, of course, Nefertiti had re-incarnated as Jackie Kennedy? Why not? And with this love story writing itself in my head, I was taken back to the Taj Mahal. I heard chisels clinking against stone, felt the vibrations of rock shattering under the hands of artisans, inhaled fine silt sifting to the feet of carvers as they sealed the passion of husband and wife into an eternity of stone. Here it was Nefertiti and Ramses II…a Jackie and Jack…a tapestry of love woven by the hands of Time.

The visit wasn't long. The group and I passed through a small door at the base of the statues. Bas relief carvings showed battle scenes, and kings adorned the walls. Further, inner recesses held statues of kings and gods. The guidebook said it was penetrated by sun rays on certain days in October and February, the King's birthday and coronation day.

On the way back from Abu Simbel, the caravan stopped at the Aswan High Dam. Well, a dam is a dam, is a dam. Even though it was nothing much of a dam, it did not disappoint. Unlike the Hoover Dam, engineered with vast slabs of curving concrete, the Aswan High Dam spanned two miles built as an embankment dam. It was a mountain filled with compacted soil, earth, and rock. It did its job to hold back the Nile, Egypt's life-giving plasma. It had been built to blend into the surrounding desert, and it did. A gridded concrete panel resembling the baleen of blue whales marked a fitting touch to its métier. Forty years on my bucket list. The Aswan Dam. Tick!

Back in Aswan, a dream awakened me. In one scene: an ice cube melted. I chuckled. Dori didn't need to be here to interpret the dream with me. It was apparent that the imagery alluded to the release of sexual repression. I giggled to myself, but I also knew better than to dismiss the dream as meaningless.

I wanted a day to settle in with a swim and to read. *The Unbearable Lightness of Being* had gotten unbearable, and I'd ditched it. The main character, in love with the love of his life, was still an incorrigible womanizer. Each character lived a consumptive relationship giving into love's magnetic pull while believing their affairs were random, senseless flukes. I fast became weary of Kundera's take on humans as inept in love and life—ruled by the whims of Chance. But, despite my own experience with Tim, or maybe because of my inexperience, I still believed. Anyway, the book's downbeat tone was more than I wanted to swallow at that time. Done with it, I don't remember, but I might have tossed it into the Upper Nile for the crocodiles to digest. In its place, I found a copy of *Death on the Nile* by Agatha Christie in my hotel lobby. Its setting was in the Old Cataract Hotel that I found out had swimming privileges for non-guests, so off I went.

The Old Cataract Hotel is right out of the Victorian era. Walking in Agatha Christie's footsteps, I entered the three-story sienna building framed by two stately Medjool palm trees. The reception was a series of arched doorways painted with red and white bands heralding Muslim designs. Chandeliers hung from the ceilings. I bought a day pass at the desk and turned to see a busboy strolling through the lobby. I called him and asked, "Could you show me one of the rooms, please?" I was curious.

"Certainly, Madam. Come this way." We went down a short hall where he opened the door into a large bedroom. Gauzy panels of heavy puce brocade curtains draped the windows filtering the morning light. Furnished elegantly in an old-fashioned manner, the walls were gold-colored, and a chandelier hung over a four-poster bed. I thought of the hotel room I'd had in Pokhara, the one sitting under Mount Machhapuchhre (The Fishtail) honored by the Nepali. And how the Fishtail had mirrored its sharp snowy summit in nearby Lake Phewa, its glassy waters on that clear day I'd arrived. Magic. Now, in contrast to this room, I remembered that room's unforgettable shower, which to my laughter had drenched the entire bathroom, flooding the toilet, sink, everything when turned on.

"This room is lovely," I said, thinking: *So romantic*, recalling the melting ice cube dream. "I bet these rooms are expensive."

"Yes, Madam." I took a last look, thanked the busboy and went to the pool.

The pool was on a bluff overlooking the first cataract of the Nile. Feluccas sailed beneath a small forest of palm trees which lined its banks. Another busboy hurried over to give me a towel and set me up with a chair. I swam, read, and relaxed. The spring air was warm, and I was lulled back to the roaring twenties when life was Gatsby-ish. It was easy sitting there drinking a gin and tonic, nibbling my lunch, soaking in the spell of the Old Cataract, reclining over the Nile. My eyes followed the pearl-colored feluccas that drifted along the gray-green river, wishing I had someone to sail with. The busboy came by holding a tray and smiled eagerly.

"Hello, Madam, fresh towels for you?" his eyes flashed at me—more than polite eyes. They gleamed and danced—a lascivious belly dance. *He's hitting on me*, I thought.

"Thank you," I mused, polite but not inviting. Several times during the next hour, he came by fluttering his eyelids to ask: "How can I help you?" offering to get me another drink or two. I was flattered. He was young and apparently hoped to be naughty. I'd been celibate for my entire trip, and this was the first time a man had hit on me. I wasn't looking for a lover on this trip, but I was amused, or maybe more so aroused.

It was clear, this busboy was offering a one-night stand—the service variety. If the dream I'd had the other night was pointing toward a sexual encounter, it wasn't going to be with him. There was no "chemistry," no nothing. During that time, no matter how horny I might have been, it was too risky to start jumping into bed with just anyone. AIDS abounded. Later that afternoon, taking a ride on the Nile in a felucca alone, it occurred to me that a companion might fit nicely into the romance of it all. I was alone and felt it.

Luxor

I THUMBED THROUGH my *Lonely Planet Guide* and found a reasonably priced hotel in Luxor, one with a roof-top pool. Seventh Heaven. From its location, I could easily visit Karnak and the Valleys of the Kings and Queens, then back to the hotel to swim in the afternoons. I checked in and went to my room, not sure what I had expected. The room was a dismal prison cell, not quite the COPD room on the Circuit in Nepal, but not a place I'd enjoy. But then the hotel had a pool, and I went to the roof to check it out.

The pool was drained, a pit of peeling paint surrounded by a ring of lounge chairs disgorging stuffing. Was this a trick? The sides of my neck got hot. I stalked out of the hotel, hoping against hope that other Luxor hotels had space. I grumbled as I walked along, not quite sure where I was going. Shortly, a horse-drawn carriage came up alongside me, and I stopped. A young, dark-haired Egyptian man smiled and asked, "A carriage ride, Madam?"

"No," I said and stormed on, but he must have read my face. He cocked his head and said, "Can I help you?" I stopped. I heard something in his friendly demeanor, and it occurred to me he was a local who might know of a hotel. So, I said, "I need a new hotel. The one I have won't do." He didn't need the whole story.

"Yes, of course, Madam. Come with me. I have a small hotel for you right up the road. Perfect. You will like it, I assure you." His face, his voice, both sincere. "Come, I take you." And he signaled for me to get into the carriage with him and the driver. Clean-cut enough, somehow, my inner radar was telling me this was OK. I wasn't getting any bad vibes, certainly no sexual vibes from him like the busboy. He simply seemed to be offering help. Maybe he got a commission every time he brought a tourist to that hotel. That was it, certainly.

I didn't have to mull this over, analyze the situation ad infinitum;

after all, it was mid-morning; what could I lose? I sized him up again. *He's up-front*, I thought, and his voice was…was what? Whatever, I didn't become suspicious; instead, I climbed into the cab feeling both ridiculous for getting mad over a room I hated and for needing rescue at the same time.

"This hotel is run by a German couple. They will give you a nice room. I assure you," he repeated soothingly. "My name is Amsu."

"Does the hotel serve food?"

"Maybe breakfast but no dinner. But don't worry. You can come to my mother's house for dinner. It will be our pleasure to feed you." Things were looking brighter. I was getting a home visit thrown into the deal. I felt this guy was really OK.

The hotel was small, clean, and quiet. It had an open rooftop lounge that overlooked the Nile. I was delighted with its atmosphere and booked a room for several nights. Amsu and I went back to the other hotel, gathered my things, and returned where I settled into my new digs. He'd been polite start to finish. Feeling upbeat, I went out for a long walk only to find Amsu waiting for me in the lobby when I returned. He asked, "Please, will you come to meet my mother? She will cook us dinner tonight as I said. We do not live far."

Well, he had served as a sort of prince-in shining armor by rescuing me. It would be rude to refuse his invite. The hotel owners evidently knew him, making the whole thing feel legit. "OK," I said, thinking that after all, he lived close by. But later that evening, when Amsu picked me up, and we walked to the ferry crossing, I realized his mother lived on the other side of the Nile. And I hesitated. But then, seeing myself as a representative of my country (Mother telling me to "Be a good American girl!"), I convinced myself it was OK and went along.

Once on the other side of the Nile, we walked about a half-mile into a forlorn cluster of small houses. The light faded out of the sky. No one was around, Amsu chatted cordially, yet I felt a modicum of anxiety. But once at his house, things eased up. His mother sat on cushions spread out on the floor and gestured for me to sit.

Her face was lined with age making her look more like his

grandmother than his mother. She had a meal spread before her on a round, low table—lamb, mashed fava beans, lentils, falafel, sliced tomatoes, and stacks of pita. A savory smell wafted throughout the room, and we ate. Amsu's mother spoke no English. He translated my stories of where I was from and where I had been into Arabic. I was feeling more at ease but cautious. I still had to get back over the river.

After the meal, I was invited to smoke the hookah. This is where I drew the line. I'd grown up seeing Mother's fingers stained yellow with nicotine from rolling her own cigarettes. In her more sensible moments, she had raged against her addictions, programming Agnes and me that smoking was "a dirty habit." I guess that had sunk in. Neither of us smoked, and I didn't now.

Amsu's mother smoked; he smoked. I plastered a smile on my face as it occurred to me that he might be a gigolo. Does a gigolo take a woman to meet his mother? I'd never been good at figuring out people's motivations that weren't direct, so it was possible I'd missed cues somewhere along the line. No alarm bells had kicked in, but after this, I thought it was time for me to leave. I'd been polite being a "Good American Girl" repaying the kindness Amsu had shown me, but, now, I'd had enough.

As the smoke billowed in the room, I said, "Amsu, it's time for me to go back to the hotel. Please thank your mother for her hospitality. Let me offer you a gift to pay for this delicious meal."

"No, no, not at all. You are our guest," he insisted.

I said my goodbyes to his mother, and Amsu walked me back to the ferry through the deserted village under a dark night. I had a plan in mind to beat him silly if he tried anything. But he didn't. At the crossing, I thanked him again profusely and tried again to offer money for dinner, but he refused. On the ferry, I waved goodbye, never to see him again. The ice cubes clearly didn't melt here either.

Walking into Time

In Egypt, Time hovers a palpable thickness that draws exponentially from the past to settle into personal spaces, the one I found myself in now. Like Hampi in India, the Karnak Temple complex radiated its own unique vibrations that drew me in. Entering its space, a grand esplanade greeted me lined with Ram-headed sphinxes—no need for red carpeting. At the far end, the Hypostyle Temple stood with massive columns. Carved with hieroglyphics depicting religious ceremonies and battles scenes, they mirrored papyrus reeds that thrived along the Nile's swampy banks. Still deeper inside, the interior glyphs recorded histories of kings and queens. The air in the temple was still.

The whole of Karnak, built over 2,000 years ago, was constructed to represent the Universe. It had been dedicated to the gods Amun, his wife Mut-the Great "Mother," and their son Khonsu. As I wandered through, one relief caught my eye: a woman under a multi-branched tree, the tree of life—akin to the giant banyan tree I'd stood under in Auroville. Here again, The Mother symbolism permeated the ages, along with the tree of life. It made me think how important Mother had been in my life…giving me a certain grit that might not have been instilled without her.

Being there in Karnack, I was pushed back in Time. Mother, Dad, Agnes, Biscute, my family, and friends with me walking beneath the forest of papyrus columns carved by ancient hands. Again, I could almost hear stone being chiseled, practically inhaling dust drifting in the air floating forward in time to meet my present moment. Had I walked these halls thousands of years before? Been a sculptor here? Or a painter? A commoner worshiping among the mob? It felt very familiar.

I walked deeper into the Temple's core. The chambers got smaller and smaller, eventually reaching a narrow, dark room exclusive for the king and a few select priests. No one was there but me. I imagined myself sliding through the narrow neck of a winged hourglass, slipping backward into a previous life, slipping through eternity, toward a rendezvous. I had sensed this before—a homecoming—when I'd arrived in Kathmandu, then again when I'd re-grounded on the Tibetan Plateau, and yet once again in India, in the chaos of it all. But here, inside this sacred temple in Egypt, it had a different twist. A past life flickered on my shoulder, thrusting me toward a future one. And something in me wanted this lunge into the future. Karnak was doing that to me.

Later that evening, back from sightseeing, I went up to the hotel's rooftop lounge and nestled myself in. Palm trees swayed along the road's edge. Muffled voices rose up from pedestrians passing below. I watched the great, watery coil of the Nile reflecting a blue sky, watched its fertile currents being delivered to the Mediterranean. The warm fingers of the evening caressed the remnants of the spring day. I sighed.

No pool, but a perfect spot, thanks to my anger, my inheritance from Dad and Mother, their life-long row that became my Harvard course in Anger Management 101. Just blow off steam, problem solve, get what I needed. All lessons lodged in my reflexes becoming shadow parts which I owned, valuable emotional currency to deal with issues. Now, settled in this intimate hotel, I lounged under the billions of stars shining above its open roof-top balcony and me.

Gulls flew overhead. The last bit of light dropped below the horizon closing the day. And without knowing it then, only realizing it later, the anger which had gotten me to that hotel had been in league with Chance. Chance had worked its precision throwing the dice where the lusty face of Time was about to uncoil my personal destiny.

The Valley of the Kings is the most exclusive burial site on the planet, and I was drawn to the graveyard like a nomad to water.

I'd spent a lot of my journey in a state of thanatopsis fascinated by death and its undertakings—Pashupatinath Temple, the vultures on the Annapurna Circuit, Keoladeo Park, Varanasi, and the Christian Cemetery at Sewri. Now, at the Nile's ferryboat crossing, I paid the boatman a coin and mused a bit about the meaning of this ride to visit the underworld.

Dori would have had a lot to say about this process of crossing what we'd see as the River Styx, the mythological boundary separating the world of the living from the abode of the dead. She and I would have analyzed it like a dream. Was my subconscious kicking up a message, some kind of upheaval going on down there in my personal vault? Egypt *did* keep digging into my psyche, but as I stared into the swiftly moving whitish-gray water passing beneath me, I put it aside.

Once on the other side, I walked into the Valley of the Kings. This mountainous area sits under the control of the Sahara Desert, and Mother Nature had taken a vacation when it came to greenery here. Scree and rubble engulfed the site, an excellent place to hide bodies for safekeeping. If I had wanted to do a painting of the sun-bleached limestone hills that hunched over the West Valley, first I'd have mixed a whole lot of white paint with burnt umber. Then I'd added touches of sienna accenting the hillocks to capture this famous terrain. But I didn't have my oils with me. Instead, with guidebook in hand, I took in several tombs that penetrated deep into the Valley's slopes. Yes, all of them had been plundered by grave robbers—they'd been used between 1539-1075 BC—so that today, each was guarded by heavy, screened gates flanked by a couple of half sleepy guards who punched my ticket.

The entrance of Queen Tawsert/Sethnakt's tomb led to several hollow shafts where mummies once lay. Its well-preserved wall murals reenacted ancient everyday life in a flat, two-dimensional style typical of Egyptian art. The figures—kings, queens, Horus god of healing plus other gods— were stained sienna, ochre, and turquoise. Hieroglyphics depicted funerary texts and bas reliefs of ankhs, scarabs, papyrus, egrets, snakes, and, of course, some graffiti.

Next, I went into the tomb of Horemheb. A steep flight of steps led toward a false burial chamber. The only thing to see beside his red granite sarcophagus was unfinished wall paintings, unfinished according to the guidebook because he experienced an untimely demise. Then on to Amenophis II, ninety steps going far into the Earth into the burial chamber. Stars covered the ceiling.

The last tomb belonged to Ramses III. It was not fully excavated but had several chambers and side passages open to the public. Again, the walls showed scenes of everyday life. This time two musicians playing harps to the gods while the royals hobnobbed with Horus. Ra, the sun god, rode his barge through the netherworld.

Surrounded by all this death, my thoughts went back to my morning's rummaging. I asked myself: *Was I heading for a symbolic death of an old Self?* Something stagnant holding me back from more fullness in my life? My eye kept catching the tombs' walls painted with pharaohs wearing headdresses adorned with single cobras rising from their crowns—their guides. The cobra was emblematic of a steadfast, strong ruler. In some way, crawling into those burial chambers in the ground, seeing those cobras reminded me of my personal guide that had taken me on this journey.

I walked deeper into the passageway, taking in what had been Ramses' day in ancient Egypt—stepping in the same dust the tomb builders probably had. It didn't pay to be claustrophobic, which I wasn't. Although I was aware I'd trekked under the heads of the Himalayas and at this moment was traveling into the belly of mountains that had once held, and probably still held, the bones of Egypt's royalty.

If the ceilings had caved in on me just then, I don't think it would have mattered much. I had a hard time shaking off a sense—and this sense was quite whimsical—that I was trekking through an umbilicus connecting me to the earth's core. A sense I was tethered by a power bigger than myself. And I wondered what was going on in my subconscious.

Was I being pushed to let go? Drop a layer of resistance, old worn-out habits finished so that I was ready to hop on board Ra's barge? Slip into the netherworld with a new me opening up to a broader life? It felt possible…did that kind of change even matter to me? I had promised to return to everything I'd left behind—*had promised* in exchange for this one year of freedom. So, it didn't matter which way it went—which way Chance tossed the dice—because even though I was shrouded by death, I felt quite alive.

It Wasn't Accidental

My favorite place in Luxor at the end of the day was the rooftop lounge. Perched in a cushioned chair, I curled my feet under me to gaze over the balcony at the Nile flowing along the fringes of the Sahara. The setting sun layered melon-colored hues on the Western rim of the desert. The air was balmy, and I got up to stretch and thought about how far I'd come. My world at that moment was clear of responsibility, of longing, of effort; everything left behind. It was the spring equinox, a turning point in the Universe. The moon would be full that night.

I heard footsteps coming up the flight of stairs behind me. Till then, I'd been more or less alone using the lounge. I turned as a man crossed the threshold of the doorway. He was in his forties, tall, slim; a shock of curly, brown hair framed his face. Our eyes met, or maybe they touched. Behind his thick wire-rimmed glasses, his eyes were the same gray-blue-green of the Atlantic Ocean off Cape Cod. My eyes fluttered, skidding wildly into a quick flirtation. Sounds muted. My breath stopped. Maybe the river had even stopped for all I knew. Did my neck go red? I grimaced inwardly. Had he noticed? I was no flirt. My heart pounded in my chest. Then, in a split second, I regained some control, smiled, and said, "Hello."

He said, "Hello," then his hand reached up to his mouth with a quick, "Sprechen Sie Deutsch?"

"No, I don't. Do you speak English?" I was hoping.

"Um, a little, yes," he said softly.

"My name is Anya."

"My name is Henrik," he parroted carefully.

"Oh, where are you from? I'm from the States."

"Oh, ja. Where from? Deutschland, Um, Germany." He knitted his brow, pulling out the words.

"Yeah, that's right. This hotel is run by a German couple."

"You? Where are you from… in the US?" he echoed me in a heavy accent his eyes darting around struggling to drag English words out of his head. Looking up into his face, I struggled to keep my heart from beating out of my chest.

"I'm from a small state called Connecticut."

His eyes lit up. "Connecticut! I've been there. Connecticut!"

"You have?" I was surprised. The balcony felt warm.

"We, my buddy and me. We travel to Boston, then New York… through Hartford." He grinned, showing well-kept teeth. I smiled back. There was a strain in his voice, but mostly I heard a convincing resonance that drew me in.

"Right through my home state," I said, my grin getting bigger as I tried to tamp down a pull building inside of me. One I couldn't put my finger on but felt like being in a small boat heading for the brink of Niagara Falls. Then, anxious to keep the conversation afloat, I asked, "Where have you been here in Luxor?"

"Ahh…I been here one day. Where have you been?"

"I went to Karnak. It's spectacular, and I took in the evening show." A flip-flop was taking place in me. This time not in my brain but someplace deeper that hoped for some…for *his* companionship… at least for a bit. "The shows are in all languages, and I think the German one is on Thursday." The collar of his shirt was pulled to one side to reveal a pulse on his slender neck.

We gazed at each other blankly. Henrik's fingers went to his upper lip stroking one side. I felt his eyes on me. *Those eyes. What's behind those eyes?* And I thought: *Eyes, the color of the Atlantic Ocean, but not on a sunny day. On a day when overcast skies will only accept a long walk on an empty beach.* I tried to keep my eyes from fluttering, only it was proving impossible to close them down.

"My English is not so good," he said.

"Better than my German, which is nil," I said, trying to sort out certain messages. *Why was I so fluttery inside?*

Cooking smells wafted up from the streets below. I could see he was thinking. His mouth drew down at the corners. He stared at me then asked, "Ah, Mrs.…?"

I interrupted, "No, no! Call me Anya. I'm an American. No formality needed."

"Do you know of a place, a restaurant to eat here? I need tonight..." He searched for vocabulary, "Did you eat?"

"Yes, I've had dinner already. Luxor is pretty sparse on restaurants. There's a small restaurant not far from here up the street. Another place that's better about a mile, two kilometers, up the road." Again, he knitted his brow, squeezing more English out of his brain.

"Tonight, I find a place. Can you show me where the other place is tomorrow?"

The air stood still. "Sure."

Then he paused and said, "Would you go with me?" Something in me smiled. The language barrier was definite, but not the chemistry.

"Yes," I said. And thought, *Oh, yes!*...

Back in my room, I lay on my bed. A date tomorrow! I got up to examine my collection of shabby clothes. What would I wear? The black and white dress bought with the sari had pantaloons that would cover my gorilla-esque hairy legs gone un-shaven for months. From Nepal to Egypt, I'd resisted shaving my legs or underarms and had kept my shoulders hidden (and worn skirts and pants below my knees) per cultural standards on the subcontinent. But I was an American woman inculcated with anti-hair ideals, and that kicked in fast. Even my eyebrows had only occasionally been plucked to avoid regrowth of my usual Freda Kahlo unibrow.

Hurriedly, I dug through my toiletries, searching for the small three-inch mirror I'd broken out of an old makeup case before leaving home. I started to pluck my eyebrows. As I worked, my eye caught the glass. At that moment, I realized Henrik had breached my hold on reality. That uncontrollable eye fluttering, that heart-pounding, I'd been struck by "the thunderbolt"! *The thunderbolt!...* like the one Mario Puzo described in *The Godfather* for his character Michael Corleone. When Michael's reality, in an instant, had capsized after he had glimpsed a woman and spontaneously had felt an overwhelming desire for her.

My hand trembled. The mirror reflected a reversal of roles, me the one caught up, shaken by a shift in my psyche—at an alchemical level. Something inside of me, my whole body, some dream buried unimaginable, had been roused by this man. Was I even breathing?

The following morning, I didn't see Henrik at breakfast before I went off to the tombs. I was giddy about having a date. I tried to calm my rising excitement. *Had Henrik, sleeping a floor below felt the same? If he had, where might this take me? Take us?*

Later in the afternoon, when I got back to the hotel, I did yoga and rested for a few hours before showering and dressing. Then, I put on the black and white dress with the pantaloons and went to the lobby to wait. After an eternity of sitting, thinking that he might not show up, Henrik bounded down the stairs smiling widely.

At the restaurant, we ordered. When the food came, I watched Henrik's hands, nails smoothly trimmed, turn his utensils to cut his food. Our conversation struggled, and I avoided using slang. "What do you do for work, Henrik?"

"I'm a chemical researcher," he said.

"A scientist," I nodded to let him know I understood.

"Scientist, ja, I work in a lab on medicines," further explaining that he ran medical research for a small company in Northern Germany.

"I'm a teacher. I'm taking a year off from work. I recently finished my doctorate and got a divorce. So here I am." His eyebrows shot up.

"Doctorate?" I could hear he was impressed. And I was impressed. Here was a guy, also with a doctorate, who liked a smart woman.

"I have a divorce, too," he said.

Good, I thought, *you're single*. My eyes outlined the contours of Henrik's face, his full lips. And the angles of his shoulders that showed through his shirt.

As we talked, he paused and hesitated, his English creating a barrier. He wrestled his way through the conversation but soon became apologetic.

"Don't worry," I said—listening to a whole different dialogue going on in the backroom of my mind—one that made me blush. Henrik's genuine smile plus his shy sensuality were getting to me. To help, I chattered about books I'd read: *The City of Joy, Death on the Nile,* and *The Unbearable Lightness of Being.*

"Ja, I read that," Henrik said.

"You've read it?" *Huh!* I puzzled.

"Oh, ja, sure," he shrugged frowning. "It was a lot of Nietzsche, a lot of how do you say it? A lot of .... hurt?"

"Yeah, I thought so too."

I continued to fill in the gaps in conversation and told him about Nepal and India and how I had gone to the Aswan High Dam. He looked at me quizzically.

"Oh, I'm interested in that stuff," I said and told him how it had been on my bucket list since third grade. "I also build things."

"Ja, me...I put in the last tile in the driveway before my wife serves me with divorce papers." My backroom conversation snorted, wondering why she'd ever let him go. At the end of the meal, Henrik asked, "Have you been to the Valley of the Queens?"

"No, not yet."

"Would you like to go tomorrow?"

"Yes, I would, and I haven't been to King Tut's tomb yet either."

"Ja, Good," he said nodding. "We go." I felt his warmth.

After the meal was done, Henrik and I walked back toward the hotel. The sun cast a glow, a last nightly heartbeat conceiving the nacre of a pearl. Street vendors along the way sold spices. We stopped to look. One vendor handed Henrik a spice. He crushed it, held it to his nose, then turned to me the seeds beneath my nose. I inhaled. Those blue-green eyes. Horse-drawn carriages took passengers along the broad street. I thought of my solo felucca ride and asked Henrik, "Would you like to take a carriage ride?"

"Ja, sure," he agreed.

The clacking rhythm of horse hooves carried us along the palm-lined banks of the Nile. Henrik's hand hung from the carriage catching the breeze, and we sat shoulder to shoulder, knee to knee but not touching. We'd been talking for several hours in English, and he began to stammer with uncertainty telling me about the family dog. "Ahh," he said, inhaling deeply, "Would you say pat or pet for the dog? What word is right?"

"Pet. You'd say pet. But don't worry about pronunciation. English pronunciation is different depending on where you live in the States. You can pronounce words this way or that…depending on where you come from," I laughed and began to sing "You say potato, I say potahto…tomato… tomahto…" from the song *Let's Call the Whole Thing Off*.

And even though I couldn't remember all the lyrics, it broke the ice of the language barrier; and he laughed at my silliness. Then, when the carriage stopped, Henrik stepped out to reach up for my hand. That nano-second, his touch, cascaded my emotions into turmoil. Something in my unconscious loosened. I'd been celibate too long.

Later that night, in my room, alone, Henrik's voice still echoed in my chest. This chance encounter was playing with my heart. Was this meeting some kind of fate or foolishness? As I sat on my bed, a surge of self-doubt arose.

It didn't make any sense to get involved. Was I even going to go with Henrik tomorrow? Here I was making a decision as if I had a fixed commitment. He was a perfect stranger, but it somehow didn't even feel like it was my decision. Would he change *his* mind about going with me? The language barrier? Something had changed in me, my whole focus. My ability to control my heart was at stake, and my indecision ruffled me. Here I was tripping around the world, totally independent, and I was afraid to have some fun, a simple fling. But it wasn't that simple; it was an avalanche overtaking me. I felt I was being held hostage by Chance, and I knew, somewhere inside me, the decision to meet up with him again wasn't really mine. I would go tomorrow. I greeted a new part in myself, a vulnerable part.

This was not like meeting Tim. That had been a childhood romance. It had started in high school and developed, almost defaulted, into marriage in our late thirties. Neither of us had been married. There had been no "thunderbolt" with Tim. He was intelligent and funny with a certain irreverent charm. Instead, we carried each other's histories, and it had been time to experience rubbing souls with another person. This felt different. This felt intended.

Henrik and I crossed the Nile going to King Tutankhamen's tomb. At the entrance, we descended a set of narrow steps into four small rooms. The chambers covered about 1,000 square feet. Although Tut's mummy and artifacts had been moved to the Egyptian Museum in Cairo, where I had seen them earlier, a richness beyond spacetime occupied the tomb. Artificial light bounced off the 3,000 year-old walls stippling the chamber with gilt. "Awesome," I said.

Henrik nodded his head in agreement. "All this gold," he murmured as he looked into my eyes.

Wall murals depicted the lives of Tut's world, and one had twelve baboons that represented the hours it would take him to reach the afterlife. His empty sarcophagus lay in the center of the main chamber. The rooms were cramped compared to the other tombs I'd visited farther up the Valley, and it was hot.

As we examined the tomb, Henrik grew quiet, and he drifted to another part of the room, turning his back to me. I couldn't figure it out. I felt a seductive pull between us, but well, after all, I didn't know him. I could see damp spots appearing on the back of his shirt, so I gave him space.

Once out of the tomb in the open air, all was okay. Henrik and I talked about the opulence of Tut's tomb as we made our way to Hatshepsut's Temple, a woman pharaoh. Once there, Henrik and I peered down into a small metal grate that encircled a stub of dry root. A sign outside the temple read: "This tree (in the form of a root ball from southern Africa) was brought from Punt by Hatshepsut's expedition, which is depicted on the temple walls." The pharaoh's accomplishments included this first known successful transplant of a non-native tree.

"This thing can't be thousands of years old," I said. "I don't think plants can last that long in the desert."

"Not possible. Maybe plastic," Henrik joked.

"I've studied plants. It can't be the same one."

"I studied plants. Not possible."

I stared at him. "You studied plants?"

"Ja. When I was in high school working for a pharmacist in town. He picked wild plants, put them in jars with names. I learn them all."

My brain flew open. The dead tree's holdfast threw up a bond between Henrik and me. That part bonded with nature, with plants. Staring into his face, someone I'd met just days before... when *my heart* had set a place for him to sit...well, now *my head* invited him to sit and more.

Later, we found a small place for lunch. As Henrik sat across from me, a breeze tousled his wispy, dark hair. And it lifted the worn, emerald-green fabric of his silky shirt. His eyes amplified. I watched his wide smile, his neck, his length. Flies buzzed around us, and he picked up two straw fans from the table to wave them off. Again, I took in his hands. Next to the café lay a massive broken statue strewn in shambles on the sands. Henrik glanced at it and said, "You think Jack-in-Beanstalk?" We giggled.

My time in Luxor had run out. Cathy would be waiting in Cairo. I felt torn about leaving for the Sanai Peninsula to snorkel. And I knew Henrik was going north to see Abu Simbel. We had dinner again; he took in the German evening show at Karnak, and each night I went to my room alone while Henrik went to his also alone. We had visited for scarcely three days. When it came time to say goodbye, he and I discussed each other's travel plans: how I was ending up in Cairo to meet Cathy while he would be returning there as well. Then Henrik surprised me, "I want to meet you in Cairo." I went quiet for a moment, taking this in. Did I want to be involved? Was I already involved? I gave him Cathy's hotel information before leaving.

A part of me never expected to see Henrik again. Yes, there was chemistry, but I also didn't want to regret that I had thrown myself away on an impulsive romance. Or worse, picked up a venereal disease. Yet, he had said he wanted to see me again, and I began to long for that. He had promised. Would he keep it?

Singing Bowls

The way I feel about water is almost holy. Wet, life-giving, cleansing, washing away of sins, a baptism into rebirth. I had always loved its silkiness washing over my skin. It didn't matter if I was swimming in a mucky, root beer pond in upstate New York when I was a kid or in the surging ocean waves off Cape Cod. I could never wait to get back into the water again; it renewed me. Having left Luxor and having met Henrik, that wasn't what I needed now. But,

I had never really snorkeled, and because I'd read that Egypt had a world-renowned diving spot on the Red Sea—the Blue Hole—I had planned a trip to Dahab to snorkel the reefs.

Taxis through the desert, a ferryboat ride across the Red Sea, another cab, and I arrived in Dahab directly north of Sharm El-Sheikh on the Gulf of Aqaba. On the first morning, I stood outside the white-washed beehive buildings of my hotel and begged the scuba divers for an invite to ride with them to the Blue Hole, their endpoint for the day. They agreed.

Once there, I put on my rented flippers and mask and carefully walked about twelve feet before slipping into the turquoise water of the Hole to snorkel. Fishes of every shape and color—a virtual spray of flowers appeared before me: yellow striped, green and pink, dotted, spotted, blue, neon orange, black and white. Bodies armored in spiny battle arrays, streaming dorsal fins, filmy tails, googly eyes, and tiny hinged mouths that puckered and pouted and puffed.

The fish flowed in and out of delicate corals clinging to the sinkhole's sides formed out of carbonate bedrock during the ice age. Suddenly, a small, dusty-rose octopus slid from under a rock, holding me rapt by its antics darting among the coral. As soon as it spied me, it was gone, squeezing into a crevice.

I swam along the Hole's rim, wanting to catch a glimpse of its bottom, said to drop over three hundred feet. I'd been warned about strong currents, knew about the strength of rip currents, respected the ocean, and didn't have the nerve to breach the edge of the Blue Hole's circular perimeter. I extended my arms to pull myself through the light-filled saltwater. I drew the sun-rays into my toes up through my chakras, praying it through my arms, then releasing it from my fingertips to form mudras caressing the sea. All to become one with the underwater festival.

Hours went by in and out of the water. I floated suspended above the pinkish-yellow utopia. Henrik's face glided handsome against the background of the reef, his smile, gray-marine blue eyes, everywhere around and through me. On the beach, well, I could have pitched a tent and lived there forever to drink up its vibes for the rest of my life. I thought of Cairo.

At noon, I went into the water again, swimming toward the opening of the Blue Hole to explore its depths. The scuba divers emerged from the marine-blue abyss. It was other-worldly. Snorkeling the Hole, I'd become an explorer in a parallel universe, one where the child in me grew yet more secure finding joy.

I spent loads of time underwater during that week. But at night, tucked into my strange bee-hive hotel in a room with no windows, I had time to reflect on the past several months I'd been on the road through Nepal and India. I rummaged through my backpack and took out the singing, brass bowls and mallets I'd bought in Pokhara, now far away yet still close. I imagined its main street lined with shops selling sundry handicrafts, including the bowls.

I sat on the bed, placing the smallest bowl in the palm of my hand running the mallet around its rim. It sang out sweet, a sound soothing my heart. Henrik invaded my thoughts again, as he had at the Blue Hole. I felt something more than a physical attraction to him. He'd proven as cautious as I, as far as advancing our encounter into bed. Plus, I hadn't given him the go-ahead signal either. Maybe I was still battling shyness and caution, a wound from Mother, maybe not confronting some personal villain. When single, I'd had few one-night stands in the past, relegating them to no fulfillment, to nothing, to never again. Henrik, though, was electric, the angle of his chin, his eyes, his touch, the lines of his body through his emerald shirt. With him, I'd felt a biochemical dance and felt his electricity…*had he felt mine?*

My hand ran the mallet around the bowl's rim, which took me back to Pokhara one more time—to the store where I had bought the bowls stacked high brimming in every imaginable size. The shopkeeper had come over, "Namaste."

"Namaste," I'd replied.

Namaste, Henrik. I greet the God within YOU!

The shop owner picked up a bowl in one hand, took a wooden mallet in the other, and gently struck the side of the bowl.

I had been struck...

The sound sang into the air entering my chest—a clear wawawawawa—the same subterranean intonations of the monks at Taksindhu Monastery...

...by a thunderbolt...

He handed me the bowl and mallet and signaled how to make the bowl sing, and said, "You do...open your chakras."

... opened me...my heart...wide...

I took the bowl into my hands, felt its curved bottom, coolness against my palm

... the carriage ride...your touch...

I rolled the mallet round its rim. Wood against metal rang out caressing me in pure sound—the Gayatri Mantra all over again, casting a spell into me.

...you... casting a spell...on me...

One by one, bowls to ear, I struck them, listening, each voice different, heartfelt or not, deciding, wanting more than one.

...deciding...wanting...wanting...

I struck them over and over again—whales, wolves, the wind vocalizing, crying to me.

...your voice...echoing to me...crying to me...

I tried to decide which ones to buy as a round-faced man came into the shop, picked up a large bowl, and ran a mallet around its rim, giving voice to its cosmic song—ranggggg, rangggg, rang-ggg—then drawing the bowl to his face, hovering it next to his lips which puckered and pulsated the sound back and forth playing the bowl—a Stradivarius, eerrr, eerreng—pulling vibrations in and out, changing pitches hypnotically, finding and sending the kiss of sound into the air.

... your lips, your kiss... finding mine...

I sat in Dahab, rolling the mallet along the rim of each bowl, letting them hum their voices into the room, into my heart. The sound (it was said) was that of the Universe manifesting. *Was there a place in Henrik's heart for me?* Would I dive in headfirst if he contacted me in Cairo? Well, if he didn't, it was only human. I felt nervous yet more awake than I ever had with a man. Somehow, as my head struggled with the whole thing, it didn't matter. In Luxor, Chance had thundered away the armor around my heart.

Finishing up in Dahab, I was on a bus to Cairo heading for the Ahmed Hamdi Tunnel under the Suez Canal. Anxiety took over me. I loved dams but hated tunnels. Being from the East Coast of the USA, I had experience driving through the Lincoln and Holland tunnels in New York City. Until I'd learned to avoid them, I had held my breath, imagining its narrow sides closing on me in a vice grip. Now, as we approached this tunnel's entrance, my breath got shallow, and my chest tightened. I clamped my eyes shut, tucking myself into a fetal position in the seat. I could hear the bus laboring below ground pushing through one long mile. It finally carried me up and out into Cairo to meet up again with Cathy. And if promises were kept, possibly Henrik.

Cairo

The taxi dropped me off in front of the five-star Forte Grand Hotel on the busy outskirts of Cairo. Cathy's company had chosen well. I was aware, after traveling all day from Dahab, I was a bit of a bag lady. I expected resistance when I walked to reception to ask for Cathy's room. I smoothed my hair, straightened my black and white dress, and tucked in the straps of my dusty backpack to make it look close to a regular suitcase. The male desk clerk glanced at me politely, said, "Room 422," and pointed to the elevator. Despite my ne'er-do-well appearance, being a Westerner, I fit perfectly into this hotel.

It had been six months since I'd left for Kathmandu when Cathy had dropped me off at JFK. Now she was in Egypt on business along with two men from her company. When she opened the hotel room door at my knock, we bear-hugged.

"Look at this! I can't believe it!" I said, glancing around the room, recalling my stays in hotel rooms that ranged from unheated dorms to flophouses. The room itself had two twin beds, but out the window in the courtyard below, a double swimming pool glinted up with two blue eyes. In the distance, as if a mirage, the Great Pyramids of Giza stood rooted on the edge of the Sahara Desert. Luxury. All those scanty accommodations during the past six months, but now I'd landed a sleep at one of Earth's power points—the Giza pyramids—same as I'd done in the Annapurna Sanctuary.

Cathy and I went to dinner. She updated me on family and friends and learned about my trip. When dessert came, I smiled across the table at her and teased, "I have a German boyfriend," waiting for her reaction.

"What? What do you mean, boyfriend?" she asked.

"I met this German guy up in Luxor, and well, he'll be here in Cairo soon, and he said we'd meet up again."

"Meet up again?" Her tone was serious.

"Well, who knows," I said dismissively as if I didn't care.

She stared at me. Cathy is an old soul. One you don't get around readily, one you don't fool. Cathy—deep brown eyes, no, penetrating brown eyes under those thick glasses, with skin that had never explored a drop of make-up—wide awake. As far as clothes, the thrift shop was her favorite venue. When we met in graduate school, I sensed pedigree, smarts, and compassion with a capital C—think the "Giving Tree" personified. We spent a great deal of time tramping through the woods examining wildflowers, not afraid of mosquitoes.

Whenever I needed help, Cathy was there sober and capable, a straight-arrow persona hitting its mark every time. We'd known each other for so long, Cathy had access to my unconscious cutting through my stonewalls. Now, sitting in this elegant dining room and fed a drop of knowledge about the twist my love life had taken, not even the entire story, her eyes told me she was processing the whole thing—analytically, emotionally, spiritually—at all levels of consciousness, which she did effortlessly.

The whole story got spilled out, thunderbolt and all. I babbled on about the carriage ride and visiting the tombs with Henrik. Pleasure overspread her face. When we got back to the room about ten o'clock, she bent over to pick up a note that had been slipped under the door. Reading it, she turned to me chuckling. "It's for you! Your thunderbolt calling!"

I read the note. Henrik had arrived in Cairo the same time I had, and he'd called the hotel to leave a message asking me to call him back. My hand shook a bit. I looked up at Cathy and said, "I'll call him tomorrow."

Cathy stared at me in disbelief. I looked away.

"Look," she said, "We were just talking about thunderbolts, right?"

"Yeah, but…"

"Well, he probably arrived in Cairo not long ago, and he's put a call into you first thing. So, call him right now."

"It's late."

I could see a take-no-prisoners look which was meant for me. "No, it's not too late! It's been a week since he saw you, and he's thinking of you!"

"Well…"

"No, That's how guys work. It's visceral with them. He's not going to be able to sleep unless you call him." Her voice was getting higher pitched. I stared at her. I felt pushed over an edge and wanted to put it off.

"I don't know, I just…"

"Just what? No. You're out here in Egypt, you meet this guy… you like him, he likes you obviously, so don't refuse him a date. Who knows where this is going to take you? Just call him!" Her tone was growing insistent, necessary.

I had cold feet. I wanted and didn't want this. I couldn't figure out exactly why or what I was resisting. After all, the thunderbolt had hit me, and truth was, I felt caught up in a fierce attraction for a perfect stranger. But still, I dug my heels in, a thousand excuses banging around in my skull, trying not to remember all the wasted attempts at romance that had piled up in my life.

Cathy saw that I was running away from this relationship precisely as I'd done in the past. She knew my reluctance and fault finding when it came to men. "Look, it's time! Put Tim behind you and see this guy," she said. "Believe in the moment."

I thought of Tim, that last day in the house, me prepping it before the realtor came. Coffee perked, apple pie smells wafted from the oven filling the kitchen with aromas of home. Then Tim arrived to pick up the remaining items from the basement. For the last time, we sat on the back porch—close friends in many ways—someone I'd married because, well, that's what people do, get married. I looked into his warm brown eyes. He'd read every word I'd written for my course work, and I thought that I owed him more and started to explain. "It's not that I didn't, don't love you...."

He interrupted me, "I didn't cheat on you," he blurted out.

I looked at him thinking he'd cheated himself. He was a good guy; I knew that. And I had to admit Tim had provided support during my doctoral studies, but now I was finished. It had been painful for me living with Tim. I didn't have a lover or even a friend to do things with. He didn't understand my needs, what my soul desired. I had felt alone in my marriage and realized my assumptions about marriage hadn't included charity for his addictions or what I thought of as his indolence. I didn't know if I would find happiness or love again. I didn't care. It hadn't taken much persuasion for a divorce. Too many demands on him caused him emotional arthritis. I was moving through a door I felt would take me into a completely different space in my life. Nothing mattered anymore. "OK." I said, "I just wanted to...."

"I always loved you. It was your friends, Cathy and Dori pushing you into this, wasn't that it?" I stared at him, putting his failures on them. He hadn't taken into account a marriage devoid of sex.

"No," I stammered, taken aback at his vitriol, him thinking I didn't have a mind of my own. Just then, the realtor knocked on the door.

Did I believe in this moment? Had I been waiting for this moment? What did this moment mean? Or, hold? Why was I so hesitant? Cathy was ushering me over a crazy barrier I'd built around myself, pushing me to override the sense of failure I'd felt with old boyfriends, with Tim. A boundary I'd created and perpetuated and didn't want to cross.

Here I was on a journey greedily devouring a big dose of self-determination, having released myself from all the entangling strings snarling up my brain, body, and my heart …wanting to re-member myself…and now, I was fighting off a relationship that promised… what?

My head controlled my heart. A mounting resistance fought off everything that comes with a relationship—love, heartbreak, fulfillment, abandonment—love's trickster nature. Agnes was already on her third partner. Yet, some real missing parts in me were asking to be filled. I was still young enough to have a child if I had wished. It was as if I'd learned nothing in my time treading on the planet trying to find love like everyone else. *Why shouldn't I get involved?* I thought of Henrik's eyes, his voice, and smile, and I recognized a sense of "Special" inside me.

"There's the phone."

I picked it up.

Henrik came on the line. "Hello?" he said.

"Hello. Henrik? It's Anya. I got your note."

"Ja, Hello." He cleared his throat.

"How are you?"

"OK. I am here in Cairo. Do you want to meet tomorrow? Have you been to the museum?" I could hear the stammering in his voice mingled with gladness threading across the telephone wires.

"Yes, but I'd love to go again."

We made plans to meet at ten the following morning in front of the Cairo Museum.

I hung up, Henrik's pleasure pulling at my heartstrings. And in an instant, I slipped back to Fatehpur Sikri, where I'd tied a string while whispering into the smooth, marble filigree to make a wish: "Find true love, solve these desires haunting my heart."

In the morning, before leaving for the museum, Cathy told me to invite Henrik to dinner at the hotel that night. The museum plaza was jammed with people. I waited. I was wearing my faded blue rag of a dress but pretended that I had bathed in Chanel No.5. Several minutes passed. Then Henrik came rushing out of the crowd rewarding me with a smile.

The Tut exhibit was filled with the tomb's contents—unimaginable luxury: jewelry, statues, food containers, furniture, canopic jars. We strolled through the rooms admiring what we'd missed in Luxor. The rest of the day was a movie script. We walked through open-air markets, talked to the merchants, bought small scrolls of hieroglyphs, and stopped at an open oven with roaring flames to eat freshly baked bread. I was riding a roller coaster not strapped in.

"Cathy says to come to dinner tonight at the Forte Grande."

"Ah. I don't have...how do you call it? Right clothes?" he said.

"Don't worry. Please come. If they kick us out, they kick us out."

We hopped a bus and rode it randomly through Cairo. Getting off, I reached up to touch Henrik's shoulder lightly. A current charged between us—a touch he later said felt as if he had been branded.

That night, Cathy and I met Henrik in the lobby and went to dinner. Cathy did her mensch stuff, taking up the situation where I could not. During dinner, she exuded motherly warmth as if she were meeting, approving of, and coaxing a man who wanted to form an alliance with one of her daughters. Henrik, on his part, drew her in with his own brand of charm. As we ate our way through a couple of courses, I couldn't help sneaking glances at him, the way the corner of his mouth lifted when he smiled, the way his body moved. We ate. Cathy knew more about men than I had guessed, a capable guide. I watched her conduct a serious transaction on my behalf.

Late in the evening, we both realized that Henrik was struggling with English and getting tired, so we brought dinner to a close. Henrik wanted to pay, but Cathy refused and put it on her business tab. Although it wasn't obvious to me at that time, Cathy had arrived in Egypt at precisely the moment to help untangle my emotional snarls. To give me a push down a path, not merely for my love life but for my spiritual growth.

Before Henrik left the hotel, he and I agreed to meet the next day to go inside the Great Pyramid of Cheops. He also had plans for the three of us. "I want to take you both to the Cairo Opera House. They have there, Uhm, *Die Lustige Witwe*...umm... *The Merry Widow*. Come? But I worry about no proper jacket."

"Yes!" We nodded enthusiastically.

Cathy said, "I'll borrow a jacket and tie for you from one of the guys I'm traveling with."

Great Pyramid of Cheops

The Great Pyramid of Cheops towered 454 feet above us. Tickets punched, Henrik and I entered a narrow tunnel leading up to the pyramid's center, the nucleus of ancient Egypt. Soon, the shaft's ceiling dropped below five feet, and we bent like reeds angling up the passageway chiseled four and half thousand years before. I stroked my fingertips along the limestone blocks holding up millions of tons of stone and mortar.

To relieve the tension from being cramped, Henrik and I snickered back and forth.

"I hope you're not claustrophobic," I laughed.

"Claustrophobic?" he asked.

"Yeah, that means the space is too narrow and small, and you get anxious."

"Uh, no. Not claustrophobic. Hoping no earthquake," he joked.

After stooping for more than a tenth of a mile, Henrik and I reached the center of Pharaoh Cheops's tomb. Seven other tourists were there looking at the massive granite sarcophagus that had once held his mummy. Henrik and I inspected the vault. The seventeen-foot ceiling was supported by granite blocks that framed the room now stripped bare of its riches by grave robbers. The stone coffin, in the middle, was seven and a half feet long and three feet high. Its size had necessitated it be brought in and placed in the chamber long before the pyramid's construction was finished. That sarcophagus wasn't going anywhere, ever. The builder's tremendous effort and smarts made sure of that.

We looked up, we looked around, there was nothing much to look at. The tomb's walls were naked of hieroglyphics or the paintings seen in Tut's chambers. Yet, being there with Henrik inside the Great Pyramid of Cheops—one of Earth's most potent power points (it being set in alignment with the two smaller pyramids outside, and with the constellation of Orion's Belt, plus with the polar star Alpha Draconis) a place of death and afterlife—I felt Special. So alive.

My imagination, which never abandons me, was working overtime inside the pyramid, boosting my ego like always. At the same time, I was aware it could work against me to make me think I was engaged with life when instead, I was in a fantasy world hiding from life. It didn't matter then. Nothing did. The Wheel of Time pivoted backward and forward, and there was nothing I could do about it either. It wasn't random, or without rules, I didn't think. Instead, it was Time's own perpetual progression, its iterations, its interferences in my life that had drawn Henrik and me together, or so I thought. It felt like a dream. I stood there in that rare and timeless space with someone whose spirit drew me like stars in the heavens. And I spiraled my cobra out into the Universe, entwining his Kundalini with mine.

"It's pretty empty, isn't it?" I asked.

"Ja. Empty and monumental. Everything stolen sold a long time ago."

"Probably everything melted down. Maybe a past never to be re-found."

I smiled at Henrik. He grinned back. We snapped a few pictures—me in the blue, thread-unwinding dress worn at Fatehpur Sikri when I'd hung its string on the wishing filigree. *Had the Universe delivered?*

Henrik and I crawled out of the pyramid into the hot sun. I turned back to take in the magnitude and consequence of the blocks that had enclosed us. For a moment, nothing stood beyond but the Sahara Desert, its eternity. Then in an instant, I was back inside the bowl of the Annapurna Sanctuary, its mountains interfacing with the grandeur here at Cheops, and me, with this man at my side. Henrik fell like a shooting star into my soul.

The solar boat was next. Discovered in pits behind Cheops in 1954, the boat's pieces were reassembled and housed in a six-sided concrete museum perched behind the Great Pyramid. It had been used to carry the bodies, but more importantly, the souls of Egypt's dead kings down the Nile on their way to their entombment to heaven.

Inside the museum, suspended platforms ringed the craft. Its cedar pieces were from Lebanon and spanned 141 feet by 20 feet wide. The once-living material gave off an aura that cast a spell, a life force captured lingering in the wood. It was easy to imagine it sailing among the papyrus reeds fighting the currents of the Nile River.

Henrik had drifted away from me to walk to the opposite side, moving into his own space. In the short time I had known him, I could read his body language. *Was he struggling with the language again or something else?* He felt complicated, the type of guy I was drawn to, intelligent, funny, and complex, a Tim. But there was something very different between them. Henrik felt strong and capable; Tim hadn't. Still, Tim hadn't slipped in and out of emotions hard to pin down. We walked over to the Great Sphinx.

I was lucky to have traveled to Egypt when I did. That year, few other tourists visited its historic places—Abu Simbel, Karnak, inside the Pyramid of Cheops. And now, sitting at the base of the Great Sphinx, that famous enigmatic beast, I felt lucky. I was there with Henrik, two tourists drinking in a memory. Still, I realized I was there with an equally puzzling guy.

The afternoon sky was warm and dry. Henrik took out a bag of peanuts from his daypack and popped them into his mouth, offering me some.

"Can you imagine the Sphinx's human face on a lion's body coming in and out of the sands over the ages?" I asked. We read stuff out of our guidebooks. A few kids roamed the area and came closer, smiling shyly. As they got closer, Henrik offered them peanuts.

"Do you have kids?" I asked.

"Ja, four. Three girls, one boy," he said.

"Really?" I'm sure he heard the surprise in my voice.

"Oh, well..." he began to explain. "We, my wife and me, we were dating... having troubles, but she got pregnant, so we married. The first daughter, then the second was coming. Then two more. Then enough— I had a vas, vas...?" His brow scrunched to search for the words.

"Vasectomy," I offered, yet puzzled by hearing such personal stuff.

We sat there for an hour in that ancient astronomical crossroads. Sat under the polar star hidden in the bluest of blue skies, shining its spell toward the earth. Henrik continued his story. "So here we were. We tried, but it was not working out. We would argue, and things got worse. Then the final straw. She throws my bookcase to the ground. Books all over...a mess..." his face grimaced. I imagined his wife's anger. I imagined all the kids. Henrik spoke gently, describing it all. I took it in feeling consolation.

As we talked, an internal monologue ran in the back of my

head. I asked myself what the odds were that Henrik and I had slipped through some sort of numinous time shaft cycling through spacetime to moor once again in a shared narrative. That was in my research, how the mind draws on past time to access future Time for ideas; so why couldn't it access the past for a former relationship? I liked that, the idea of tapping into a previous lifetime…one where I had unfinished business, one which embraced this man. I didn't think 'thunderbolts' fooled around. And I didn't think Kundalini did either. My running dialogue played with the idea that Henrik and I were drawn together to reiterate a mutual history once enacted in the deserts of Egypt.

Cathy had off from work, and I had told Henrik that she and I had hired a guide to ride camels across the Sahara Desert. I invited him to join us. After riding for about twenty minutes, my camel went lame. The guide said, "Get on with her," pointing to Cathy. Ignoring him, I asked Henrik, "Do you mind if I join you?"

"Come," he said and reached down, pulling me up on the camel. I clutched his back feeling his muscles under his shirt. My vibes struggled to stay in my own body, but I was beginning to feel like Mata Hari.

We road across the rosy-beige sands of the Sahara Desert past desert ruins. The sun glared overhead. At one point, we stopped before a low, pre-dynastic pyramid made of mud bricks and stone. A group of Japanese fortified safely under umbrellas came running around the corner from behind one of the crumbling pyramids to stop and snap pictures before running back to their bus. We burst into laughter at this incongruity. We rode on. I pressed myself against Henrik's back ever so lightly. When we parted, Cathy and I told him we looked forward to the opera the next night, and we'd meet him at the Opera House with a jacket he could wear.

The evening of the Opera came. For that day, Henrik planned to visit the City of the Dead. I rested all day at the swimming pool and shaved my legs. I didn't have any makeup and went to the hotel's gift shop to buy some, but none was available. Instead, I bought a small magenta, blown-glass perfume bottle wanting this symbol of femininity to remind me of my moments in Cairo.

Cathy came back to the hotel with a borrowed jacket and tie for Henrik. But, a touch of food poisoning kept her in the toilet, so she opted out of going to the Opera. Getting ready, I took the sari out of its package. I admired its wide border—a pattern of purple, green and red horses marching among turrets reminiscent of the Taj Mahal. My fingertips caressed its red, gold, and shimmery black surface.

"It's beautiful!" Cathy exclaimed. "You need a petticoat."

"I don't have one. Do you?" I asked.

"No. Let's skip it. But you do need a belt, or it won't work." She dug one out of her suitcase and put it around my waist to attach the sari. I put on the choli, the fitted flame-red bodice with sleeves to the elbows. As we oohed and ahhed at the silky touch slipping through our fingers, Cathy tucked one end of the material into the belt. She commenced wrapping the acres of fabric around my body—her decades of living in India where she'd seen them wrapped kicked in. She wrapped and wrapped, getting all but six feet of it arranged.

The remaining yardage puzzled us. I wished I had paid closer attention when Dean Fatima and her maid had wrapped me up at Avinashilingum College. Cathy and I wrapped and rewrapped the remaining yardage, unable to drape it properly over my shoulder. It was getting late. My anxiety level rose. I had an hour taxi drive into the city to the Opera House. Our hands flew around the few remaining yards of silk. Still, finally, after exhausting all options, we stopped. Cathy dropped onto the bed to figure what to do. "Why don't you…" she began…

I took a breath, grabbed the remaining material, threw it about me in a cyclone only to have the last piece of silk fall into place. It draped gracefully over my shoulder. We shook our heads. My midriff was bare, and we discussed keeping it covered as much as possible. Unfortunately, I had no decent shoes—no glass slippers— that went with the occasion; consequently, I put on my sneakers. I'd keep my skirt long to cover my feet as much as possible. When it was all done, and I looked into the mirror, I felt a goddess—Cleopatra going to meet my Antony.

But like Cleopatra, who had her problems entering Rome, I had mine entering Cairo. The taxi cab driver turned the ride into a public van picking up and letting off everyone hailing a cab along the side of the road. I was chagrined. I was out of time. When the taxi reached the Opera House, I was angry I mistakenly insisted on being let off at the wrong entrance in the back of the large building. Draping the jacket and tie over my arm, I ran to the front but stalled to a crawl, not wanting my whole dress to fall into a pile of autumn leaves around my ankles.

As I slowly rounded the corner to the front, the plaza was nearly empty. Everyone had gone inside except for one loan figure shoulders drooped. Henrik thought I'd stood him up.

"I'm sorry, I'm sorry. I didn't know it would take so long…the taxi…," I handed him the borrowed jacket and tie. "Cathy is sick and can't come."

"OK. OK.," he said and struggled to get into the jacket. It stretched across his back and rode up his wrists. He spun the tie into a quick knot at his throat as we hurried toward the entrance. He handed in the tickets and mumbled something in French to the ticket-taker. We got to our seats moments before the opera started. I breathed a sigh of relief, although it felt like I was sitting next to an enigma.

I didn't understand a word about what was going on in the Opera. Still, I certainly pretended to have a good time, occasionally turning toward Henrik and smiling. He looked straight ahead. I wasn't sure he'd recovered from me being late. When the break came, I excused myself to rush to the restroom, where I hid in a stall to recover. Regaining equilibrium, I smoothed my sari's silken layers, ensuring they were secure, inching them down to cover my sneakers. I wasn't afraid of losing my shoe like Cinderella had, but I was worried someone would see them. Leaving the stall, the other women in the ladies' room turned in my direction to exclaim at the sari's beauty. "Oh, it is magnificent!' one said. I caught myself reflected in the wall's full-length mirror. I was surrounded by women nodding an endorsement as I cocooned in my sari's satiny folds.

After the opera, Henrik took us dancing to a rooftop restaurant. We ate a bit. They played *Stranger in the Night*, and when we got up to dance as I stepped into his arms, I'm pretty sure our feet hardly moved an inch across the floor. A trance. It hadn't been the best of nights. Me being late plus all the talking in English nonstop once we left the Opera. Wanting to ease his strain, I said, "Henrik, why don't you stop talking in English. It's too much. Talk to me in German. It doesn't matter if I understand or not. I will." That worked for a bit, but he was reluctant. Despite the magnetism between us, at the end of the evening, he put me in a taxi back to the Forte Grande, promising to come out the next day.

In the morning, Cathy had recovered from her stomach bug and went to work. Henrik arrived in the late morning and came up to the room. We sat looking out at the pyramids. He'd brought a book of poetry.

"I want to tell you something," he said.

"OK." His face was serious.

"In Luxor, that night we met, later I was reading a poem. Can I...?" he asked.

"Sure. I love poetry. Read it to me."

"It's by Derek Walcott." Henrik read: "Love After Love"

"The time will come
when, with elation,
you will greet yourself arriving
at your own door, in your own mirror,
and each will smile at the other's welcome,

and say, sit here. Eat.
You will love again the stranger who was your self.
Give wine. Give bread. Give back your heart
to itself, to the stranger who has loved you

all your life, whom you ignored
for another, who knows you by heart.
Take down the love letters from the bookshelf,

the photographs, the desperate notes,
peel your own image from the mirror.
Sit. Feast on your life."

(Walcott, Derek. Love After Love. Derek Walcott Collected Poems 1948-1984, Farrar, Straus & Giroux, 1962, p. 328.)

"That's beautiful." *A love poem.*
"Do you know him, Derek Walcott?"
"No, but I want to hear it again." He reread the poem. His voice was filled with tenderness. Heat built in my body. My breath uneven.

Henrik went on, "I felt such feelings, how do you say, coming between the two rooms, yours and mine that night." He glanced again at the book. And I realized that the thunderbolt had hit him too: his nervous system had responded equally as mine, responded to a stranger who had come knocking at his door, reshaping his trip in Egypt, ripening it for both of us.

"I felt them, too."

Then, when his eyes, mysterious marine-blue eyes, lifted off the page, they met mine bridging what space was left between us; and he leaned over, stroked my cheek to kiss me. My mouth on his, I reached up, taking his hand, strong and magnetic, then his arms were around me with mine holding him as he picked me up to carry me to the bed.

Later, searching for a room together, we went to the first hotel I'd stayed at. The Muslim receptionist stared at us, a glint in his eye flipping through our passports—one German, one American still gave us a room.

What gives a relationship birth? During the next couple of days, Henrik changed his ticket back to Germany, and he and I went back to the museum, walked the streets hand in hand, smiled into each other's smiles. Each morning, we ate hard-boiled eggs, gazed into each other's eyes, laughing, yet fooling no one in the hotel, I'm sure. Love-making is a private thing, yet universal. Between us, I felt an indisputable current renewing two narratives, both ancient yet not.

One afternoon, Henrik went out shopping for his kids, and when he came back, he handed me a small package, "Here, I bought you something." Surprised, I opened it to find a small, pedestalled alabaster dish. Walking to the window, I held it up to the light, which penetrated its golden-white smoothness. I turned to him, "You make me happy." I said and dropped more deeply into his aura.

"I want you to come to Germany," he said.

My heart jumped a couple of beats. This was becoming more than a fling. It was becoming a possibility. I held my breath and said, "Well, I have plane tickets to Greece...."

"Greece?"

"Yes. I was in Greece twenty-five years ago during my college years, but I missed Delphi, and I want to see where the eternal flame had once burned. After that, my plane tickets take me to Budapest where I'm meeting Cathy. She'll be there on business again in three weeks."

"Then come after that. Ja, that is good," he said.

"OK. Yes, I'll come. Because I was going to Poland, I'll let my mother's family in Poland know there's been a change in plans."

Henrik took out a small pencil from his pocket, tore a piece of paper out of his journal, and began to draw a small map. It was of a car traveling along a dotted pathway to a house in northern Germany, a map for me to find him.

"Give me the name and address of the hotel in Budapest. I will contact you." I got it from Cathy and gave it to him before we parted. Our time had run out in Egypt. Henrik flew home. Cathy flew home, and I flew to Greece.

When Egypt was over, I felt caught in a web of life—strong yet fragile, at times whimsical, but still with a silky sensation of fullness. It was a bigger dose of that old, familiar feeling I get when I'm swimming, breathing rhythmically through a continuum of water that asks, no, urges me to open to my healing light coiling my Kundalini, that now shimmered through my body, now throbbed through my heart chakra, now carried me into the future. That memorable year, autumn in Nepal, winter in India, March in Egypt—had offered me an inescapable spring.

Yet Another Eternal Flame

The Temple of Apollo at Delphi once housed an eternal flame considered a major oracle located at the world's navel. Muktinath Temple skipped through my mind. And I could see its modest blue flame flickering in that remote shrine on the Tibetan Plateau. Still see it questioning me, as I had questioned it before starting my trek along the Gandaki River.

I was with a young woman, Pia, a smoker, down from Israel, who I'd met at my hotel in Mount Parnassus. She, like me, wanted to see where the eternal flame had once burned. Hoping to see an actual flame, our hotel-keeper directed us to an area where he thought one burned. We walked up the ancient way where green lichens turned the pink rock into mountains of sea mist. Once at the site, Pia and I peered into an empty crevasse. No flame burned. But I did feel palpable energy coming from the earth.

Undeterred, we found our way to the Temple of Apollo. Several columns remained standing set on a dais surrounded by blocks of stones. But it was the flame Pia and I were after. I thumbed through the guidebook. It said the Oracle was built on a point where two fissures emitting gases crossed beneath the earth.

Here, the Greeks had chosen a woman, the so-called "oracle," who made predictions. Sniffing those gases all day frenzied the woman-oracle, who in turn babbled out prophecies to ancient rulers—ambiguous at best and open to interpretation. *Smart, girl.*

Keep those ancients on their toes, I thought. Pia and I sniffed the air. We smelled nothing.

But here, as well as in Muktinath, the message for the Greeks had been essentially the same: Know thyself. And that made me recall what I'd recently learned, sitting satsang in Lucknow and Rishikesh, hearing the sat-sangee's pain, re-examining my own, how hard it was to 'Know thyself!'. That Self-examination of *thy mind, or thy heart, or better yet thy soul*—never mind *thy fellow human being*—was acutely taxing.

There was Henrik. And I recollected how, during those last few days together, he'd not slipped away, withdrawn into his own world the way he'd done at Tut's tomb or the Spirit Boat. Yet, those moments still puzzled me. But, now, in this vacant, sacred temple, I admitted I couldn't possibly know much of anything about what went on inside another person's head. Not mine, and certainly not Henrik's. He was a stranger in the night to me. One who wanted me to come to Germany to visit him in his home. And frankly, right then, thinking about him, I actually didn't care one iota about any big question in life that usually rumbled around inside my head. I'd pushed them aside. It was my heart, not my head, that was pulling me forward in Time. I felt thankful for the past six months—greedy moments I'd stolen from duty. When Time had given my spirit flight like those Siberian Cranes at Bhaktapur who challenged the Himalayas to soar free.

No sweet odors of intoxicants escaped from beneath the Temple of Apollo to make Pia and me rave. We left and walked up to the Olympian Track, the site of the first games. It was April; the air was cool, the sun bright. A row of stone bleachers lined one side of the track, 4th Century archeological ruins, perched on a hillside encircled by pine trees releasing veils of pollen. Lebanon cedars cut dark green minarets across the skyline. The same wood used to build the Egyptian Spirit Boat that was seen by Henrik and me. The other side of the track was overgrown with weeds that stretched about six hundred feet in front of us. Something called from inside me, and I said to Pia, "Let's run!" —which tripped a switch, and we raced across the field, pumping our legs tearing for the finish line—running madly into the past.

For those two minutes, it wasn't me anymore. I imagined wings attached to my ankles, and I soared back 2,000 years, inhaling primordial air, hearing the roar of the crowd, an ancient athlete in me lifting through space touching back in Time. I slipped into a different reality which, in truth, wasn't what I wanted at all, not right then. Right then, what I really wanted was only the moment I was in, a reality that might include Henrik. At the end of the raceway, Pia and I sputtered, gasping for breath laughing wildly.

I glanced at her young face—pretty, framed by black hair, large dark eyes—and knew both of us undeniably raced toward a future, a flame burning somewhere, somehow for each of us…bidding us realize ourselves yet more fully.

I had several weeks to kill in Greece before meeting up with Cathy in Budapest. I went to Loutra Edipsou to soak in the thermal springs then on to Crete to chill out on the beach. Once settled in at a Plakias hotel nestled on the island's south side of the Mediterranean Sea, I swam in Crete's many bays watching the sunlight flood through the surf surging over me. At night Greek music played in the café, but I had no one to dance with.

I sat on the volcanic rocks overlooking the Libyan Sea as waves crashed in. I hummed the Gayatri Mantra into their depths. I searched the blue for Henrik's eyes. Fishermen went by in boats, and we waved at each other. I climbed the hills and walked along miles of fields of flowers—this time familiar: Queen Anne's lace, thistles, red poppies, and copper lupines. I drank in their shapes and colors as they drew me closer and closer to home by their presence. Walking the fields, I took Henrik with me, discussing the flowers.

One evening I sat out on the beach. The moon was full—an ivory rose petal quivering in the sky. Henrik. I pictured him, his enigmatic eyes looking at the moon at that exact moment. Envisioned me in his arms, his hands, so strong, stroking me, a pulling tide loving me again. Yet, my new love felt fleeting. There was no stillness. I'd just regained a treasure-trove of equilibrium, re-nourished and re-grounded my body, mind, and spirit. Now, the scales had tilted, and I was being asked to drop my heart armor. I couldn't help but feel that my relationship with Henrik threatened to toss my heart aside like an old Valentine card after its initial delight. Still, he'd invited me to his home in Germany.

I was conflicted. Love had always sucked up my brain, making me other-directed while losing myself. I thought of the poem Henrik had read me at the Forte Grande: "In losing love, you will have found it." Still, I felt tender, aware I was feeding largely on his memory, not his actuality. I could be alone, had spent a lot of time alone even in my marriage, but did I truly want to be alone? I didn't know. A push-pull inside kept me off-balance. Work invaded my thoughts. But what I did know was that when I out walking, I'd find myself searching the sea and the shoreline rocks for the gray-blue-green of Henrik's eyes.

A couple who I'd seen staying at my hotel came strolling up the beach. I had overheard them speaking both German and English, and as they approached, I said, "Hello!"

"Hello," they said. "Lovely moon this evening."

"Yes, it's lovely. Can I ask you how to say something in German?"

"Of course, how can we help?" said the man.

"How do you say 'I love you' in German'?"

They smiled warmly and said, "Ich liebe dich."

I repeated, 'Ich liebe dich.' Is that right?" Then several times more to make sure I got it.

"But," the woman said, "If you want, you can add the punch line...."

"Oh? What's that?" I asked.

"Try this: Ich liebe dich, mein Schatz."

I repeated her words and asked, "Means?"

The woman and man laughed, "I love you, my darling, my treasure."

I strolled the beach repeating the phrase. *If I am going to Germany, this is really all the German I ever need to know.*

Budapest

I sat in the tub at Hotel Korona, re-reading the letter from Henrik. It had been waiting for me when I arrived at Cathy's hotel in Budapest. The edges were getting wet.

> Dear Anya,
> I want you to come to my home in Stade to stay with me. Come by train from Budapest to Hamburg where I will pick you up at the train station. Call me to arrange the details. I have planted a rose for you. Red. I long for you.
> Henrik

Cathy came in and sat on the toilet seat lid and said, "Let's get that laminated if you're going to do that!"

"No," I said, "then I won't be able to..." and kissed the letter. I was excited and anxious about this invite. In a way, I hadn't expected it.

"He's pretty persistent, isn't he?" Cathy said. We were both impressed by Henrik's intelligence, charm, and now his persistence. Still, I felt a struggle brewing inside of me.

"Oh, I can't do this," I said to Cathy.

"Sure, you can. What are you talking about?"

"I don't know; it's that I just hadn't expected him to follow through."

"Didn't you read his body language?!"

"Of course. The time we spent together was wonderful, but...."

"He's just what you need in your life right now, and you know it."

I had wanted to see Henrik again but had not dared to hope for it. Had not believed. I was good at dreaming up a scenario in my head that made me happy with no real attachments to the world. I could do that easily, a weird skill that had preserved me from painful events and relationships. Now I was aware that I might be repeating old habits, pushing away what I expected to be an unpredictable relationship. Where there was going to be hurt at separation.

"My folks are expecting me in Poland," I said.

"Let them wait!"

"I'm just being practical."

"Practical? You've just met this cool guy who obviously really likes you… you like him, right? And you're being *practical?* Do you think *love* is practical?"

"He lives in Germany.…"

"So, what? There are planes," she said. "It's like this, like I said to Emma when she was in high school and her boyfriend dropped her; love is fickle. It's a mad flowing river. You can't direct it or schmooze it to your likings. Or decide where it's taking place. It controls the situation; it controls you, and you've got to flow with it even though there're lots of boulders in the stream that may hurt you. Go!" Her tone was stern.

"I don't know. What if…"

"What if nothing! You need love whether it's satisfying or painful. You need it to give you the stuff necessary to live your life. Stop being afraid and go!"

She was right. Here I was retreating, battling against love and being loved. Henrik swamped my thoughts, usurped my ability to think straight, made me feel more than who I was already. In Cairo, I had crashed over an obstacle that I'd had no intention of breaching, yet I'd been without a lover too long, and Cathy saw this truth.

Her words floodlighted a scared child lurking behind a tired wound, touched some old hurt surrounding men as it had with Tim, his abandonment of me as a woman. I was wary. And I felt a tangle of unsortable knots, my own vulnerability and desire. I wanted to go, and I didn't want to go. Was it reality or a dream? Meeting Henrik had felt as if the relationship had come through the ages—as if I'd met up with a soulmate—but something was pushing me back.

"Look!" she said. "The Universe is asking you to *be here now*. Isn't that the journey you're on? So why are you fighting this?"

"I think…"

"Stop thinking and start feeling! Stop fighting against yourself!"

Yeah, I thought. I *had* unwittingly landed in Budapest, unable to get a flight directly from Greece to Poland with my open-jaw tickets. And now Cathy and I, plus this invite from Henrik, had all converged precisely at the same time, with Cathy pushing me toward the unknown filled with its excitement. It didn't feel unplanned.

No cobra flowed at this time that I could sense. As far as I could tell, it provided no direct backing in this affair. But I knew it was there. Chances are cobras don't get involved in the business of love directly, or at least, mine didn't. Still, then again, chances were it *was* involved—relying on a best friend, Cathy, a mensch, to interfere and push me over the finish line, the one drawn in Luxor.

Although I wanted to retreat, I was beginning to think it would be more painful not to meet up with Henrik once again. I was from the States; he was from Germany. It couldn't last, a lover, who in reality, lived thousands of miles away from me in so many different ways. Yet in others, not an inch. He felt right for me, we saw the world the same, or so I thought. I called him. I'd have to trust Henrik.

Panama

When I got off the train at the Hamburg train station, Henrik handed me a red rose. The large banner reading "Welcome, Anya," was put side, and he took me into his arms kissing me. Others on the platform grinned. Tired and unsettled, not knowing what to expect, I handed Henrik my backpack along with a galaxy of dreams lodged in my heart, ones he'd just made me more confident in.

Henrik's house was the exact picture I'd seen in a fairytale book—white stucco walls, red-tiled roof, a sky-blue door—an image I'd held dear from childhood, one of warmth and security. Once inside, it didn't take long for us to go upstairs and coil into each other's bodies, my skin reading his, his de-coding mine.

Later, he drew me a bath, steamy water strewn with mint and thyme and the petals from his garden, petals from his apple tree fully bloomed in May. Inhaling the fragrances, I soaked the journey out of my bones. He came in to help me dry off and crooned sadly, "You shaved your legs." I tilted my head at his disappointment. "Oh, well," he said, "Here in Germany, we want hair on women's legs. Sexy."

"Auh! It's an American thing!" I said, "No problem. I'll grow it again…a whole forest…for you…mien Schatz." His eyes lit up. I was hoping to make up for my error, and when he murmured back, "Mien Schatz," I knew I had.

The next night after dinner, Henrik and I curled up on the sofa with a children's storybook, *The Trip to Panama* by Janosch. *Odd*, I thought, him reading me a kid's book. But then again, I owned and treasured an extensive collection of children's books not used for teaching but because they captured how I saw the world.

Henrik read first in German then translated into English—a friendship between a little bear who fished and a little tiger who picked mushrooms. The two of them yearn to wander off searching for "Panama," which they considered the most beautiful place in the world. It was one filled with hope, where new people can be met, people who change the way you embrace your everyday life. Henrik's voice, strong German tones…strong yet soft…entered my heart, making it feel breakable. He read on. After exploring here and there, the little bear and tiger returned home, only to find that "Panama" was not out there on the road somewhere. Instead, the contentment, the hope they were looking for, actually happens at home.

When he finished, our eyes met. "I loved that," I said. *Panama* had touched a 'Be here now' place in me like I'd felt in Nepal and India, becoming a citizen of the world. I knew the choice I'd made by coming was right. The man who sat beside me had managed to preserve *the child*, a Special one, within himself. My heart melted, but more than that, my spirit melted into his.

Later, I went upstairs to get the singing bowls to show Henrik how to play them. He took one in his hand, rolled the mallet around its rim, and smiled as the sound rang throughout the house. "I like this very much," he said and picked up the next bowl striking its side…errrr, eerrreng. The wave of sound carried me back to India, sending a kiss of sound into the air, sending me back to Mundgod, where once again, my mind's eye caught a glimpse of the leper's eye. And I remembered parts lost, that I'd lost love, only to find it here again in a fairytale cottage.

Henrik went off to work; I read and puttered around the house cleaning or cooking chicken soup. The lilac bush was in bloom. I had found Henrik staring out the kitchen window absorbing its color, the deepest magenta. Later, I searched under the sink, found a vase, filled it with blossoms for the living room.

He had a garden which I weeded. Weeds are only weeds to the uneducated eye. I gathered a few tiny weeds plus the veronicas I had pulled out along with some short, delicate grasses and put them in a small glass jar next to Henrik's chair where he read. When he came home and saw them, he said, "You find gardens growing in concrete sidewalks."

In the afternoons, I'd take the old bike Henrik had gotten for me, one not used by his kids, and I rode the flat fields around the town. One afternoon, he pointed out a large indoor pool complex which was only a five-minute ride away from his house. I went swimming, and of course, to pray in the pool. It didn't take long before I got him to go with me, although he was not a swimmer as such. The strong glasses he wore made him keep his face out of the water, but after seeing me do kick-turns, he agreed to join me, and I taught him the crawl, (well barely).

Also, during that time, I remembered things at home. I hoped Tim had taken care of the income taxes. I called him to check.

"Germany? What are you doing in Germany?"

"Visiting a friend, I met in Egypt."

"Oh! Well, I'll get the taxes done eventually. But all hell broke loose back here while you were gone. My brother's been having an affair for the past year and left Thelma for a married woman. She needed all kinds of medical tests, and she was distraught. When are you coming home?"

"After I see my relatives in Poland. I'll have to call Thelma."

A few days after my arrival, Henrik invited his ex-wife, Teresa, and his children over to meet me. She came marching in, blond, blue-eyed, pretty, with her three daughters in tow. The children's faces were a combination of their mother and Henrik.

Bringing ex-wives and girlfriends together in America wasn't the norm, not so early in a game. But I was in Germany, and maybe it was all one big family here. We had tea. Teresa spoke some English reluctantly, and I felt I was getting the once-over as if they were purchasing a new car or puppy. When the conversation slipped into German, Henrik and his ex-wife's tone were flinty.

When my inspection came to an end, Teresa asked, "When are you leaving?" Taken aback, I thought there must be a translation problem going on. I looked at her inquisitively and decided she wasn't rude. But instead, she was actually asking how long I was staying. I said, "When I finish weeding the garden." They turned to Henrik for a translation, and all laughed uncertainly. For my part, I understood that his family was here to stay. It meant our relationship was serious, and his family would become part of my family.

During that visit, I had noticed that Teresa was calling Henrik by a different name. When they had left, I asked, "Why is Teresa using a different name for you?"

"Ja, well, I'm going to a therapist. He helps me with my stress. I want to live happier…"

"I'm glad you have someone to talk to. It's always good to hash out your problems."

"So, I tell him I hate my name. We talk. And, I change it to take my middle name."

"Sure, why not? I get it," I said. He'd made an identity switch. I was with a man who'd turned over a new leaf. I was impressed.

Henrik smiled coyly as if he was going to tell me more, something confidential. He leaned closer and said, "When I got back from Egypt, my therapist teased me. He asked, 'And how does Anya pronounce your name?' and he hummed my American pronunciation of his name, "Henrik..." We laughed.

"Tim and I went to a shrink too, but it didn't help," I said.

"Yes, well. He and I talk. We sort out problems that are not good in my life, my past marriage, other things." Then he paused, "Before Egypt, I had a dream, and I described to him where I go down into a pond to find a pearl in the mud," he beamed at me, "and we, he and I, laugh that there is something good to come of all this strain with my life."

A drenching rain went through, and when it had cleared, Henrik and I went out and sat on the terrace. A rainbow formed in the sky. Henrik leaned over and held me. And he said, "It's a door for us to step through. I am soaked with love for you. Shall I run to the top of the house and raise a flag?" I just melted.

The following Saturday, Henrik and I went to pick up the kids to take them to a water park in a nearby town. He also wanted to show me the house he'd built for his family. He was proud of having made it brick by brick, paver by paver, and told me that when the last paver had been laid in the driveway, Teresa had him served with divorce papers. I had a rush of sympathy seeing that his ex-wife had moved on since their divorce. Her new partner lived with her and his children in the house that Henrik had built. He told me initially he'd seen him as a rival but was OK with it now.

The two-story house sided against a vast, flat meadow. Teresa and the girls met us in the living room with the dog. Every so often,

Henrik would grab one of his daughters for hugs and a prideful jostle. Each kid had a small bedroom with a bed, closet, and desk. I felt awkward parading through the house. Henrik's son, Richard, a towheaded, slight boy resembling his father around the nose and eyes, came into the hall. Henrik wrestled with him, both laughing, yet I thought a hesitancy hung between the two.

After the tour, we piled the three girls into the car and took them to the water park to play in the waves. They'd learned English in school, and I tried to engage them in simple conversation, but that didn't work too well. They kept their distance from me, chowing down salami, bread, cheese, and carrots, alternately playing in and out of the waves. I couldn't help thinking that I was missing something, that something was getting lost in the language or a 'cultural translation.'

On May 14th, we walked hand in hand on the dike, love in love, heart in heart looking at the full moon. She rose beautifully, golden, shimmering in the water. And I sang to him. This time *Moon River*, having met as drifters who had wanted to see the world. And Henrik said, "I've known you for two months."

As May fell into June, Henrik and I established a routine. He went off to work, and I amused myself doing yoga or weeding the garden, or bicycling into the town. At the library, I used Henrik's card to withdraw some English language books to read. I went to the bakeshop and practiced what little German stuck in my head: "Guten Tag. Ich möchte sechs Brötchen kaufen." The ladies smiled back at me and, without a word, filled my order. At the grocery, I mulled over how to use the weighing machine in the produce department then gave up, unable to read the instructions. I waited until a woman entered the area and asked, "Do you speak English? I need help."

"Yes, I speak a little," she said and showed me how to use the machine. I'd traveled through remote Nepal and the whole sub-continent in Asia to encounter no language problems, yet here I was stuck.

Henrik and I took turns cooking dinner, stuffed cabbages on my watch, boiled chunks of beef or pork on his, meat he'd leave overnight on the stove. I'd say, "It's not safe," recalling my food poisoning experiences, but he ignored me, convinced the meat would do us no harm, and it didn't.

Henrik had a print, *The Lovers of Vence* by Chagall. When it slipped from its frame, he took it apart to fix it. He took a strand of my auburn hair and placed it over the bride's hair before replacing the glass. And I thought *This man is of my measure. A full cup. Complex filled with…I begin to think of him as my husband.* And that night, I sang him love songs.

The summer went on. Some days were gray and overcast typical of Northern Germany. When it rained, Henrik curled up with a book, seeming to enjoy the heavy rain drumming against the windows, losing himself to the pages for hours. He read me another children's book, *Freunde* by Helme Heine. This time it was about three good friends—Franz von Hahn (the rooster), Johnny Mauser (the mouse), and Waldemar (the fat pig)—who, always playing and working together, come to realize that when night falls, there are times friends have to be apart. But it was alright, because, in the end, true friends always find each other, even if it's only in their dreams. A rooster, who would crow, lived over the fence in Henrik's back yard, and I began to call out to him, "Hello, Franz von Hahn!" making Henrik and me laugh.

One day Teresa came over with her clippers to cut some lilacs. When she was gone, Henrik had noticed a shift in my demeanor and asked how I felt about her coming to cut flowers. I said, "Tell her to keep her hands off the lilacs!"

Henrik was also willing to be dragged away from his books, and I taught him yoga. "My back feels better," he said. He, in turn, gave me a few German lessons, but usually, it was to no avail. I found it to be a tongue-twisting language. I had few skills and little confidence in the foreign language department except for Polish which had stuck in my head from childhood.

Henrik's house had two rooms downstairs. He cleaned one out and put in a table and chair. He got me writing paper and pens and an old typewriter and said, "Write!" which I did. I wrote and read him stories about my childhood which he relished.

His daughters frequently came to the house after school. One day, his youngest daughter, Klara, joined us on the raised terrace at the back of the house. Henrik peeled an orange feeding her sections one at a time as if she were a little bird. The plum tree had ripened, and Henrik handed her a basket and said to her in German, "Go up, pick the plums." She scrambled up the tree, grabbing at the fruit while Henrik snapped photos. When Klara came out of the tree, we ate the fruit, its purple juice dribbling down our cheeks. He told me he was scheduled to take her and her brother to Art Camp later in the summer, but Richard had refused to go. So, he'd arranged for me to take his place.

My clothes had become quite shabby. So, one day, I took the car and went shopping. I found a sexy, pine green blouse I thought Henrik would like and other things to fill out my wardrobe. On my way back to the house, I passed a farm market and stopped to see what they had for sale. At home in the spring, I would have gone to nurseries to fill the car with annuals for my gardens and window boxes. Now here in this market, my favorite tuberous begonias were on sale. Their petals glowed intensely a fiery fingernail polish orange-red. I couldn't resist them. I bought two along with several other plants for the garden. Back at the house, I placed the begonias on the terrace ledge. When Henrik arrived from work, he stopped to take them in. He stroked their soft petals. "Schon…beautiful," he whispered. "Ich Liebe dich, mein Schatz," I said.

We both became 'Schatz.' A warmth, a pleasure, a kiss. Henrik would come home from work during his lunch hour, I'd make sure I was wearing that green blouse, we'd make love. He'd go back to work his hair tousled only to have his colleague comment on him having been in a washing machine asking: "Was she a blond, brunette, or redhead?" The walls of the fairytale cottage echoed in laughter. But the strange thing about the blouse was that he didn't want me to wear it in public.

The honeymoon of our lovemaking also awakened something in the neighbors. The guy in the front house had the nerve to comment to Henrik on our inhibitions. Henrik picked up the mattress and moved us to the back bedroom. Our ardor was transgressive.

When we found a place to swim at a public lake, the hungering in our bodies made us ease away from the other picnickers. Hand in hand up the path, we found a cluster of large boulders, drew a circle of invisibility around us, shed our clothes, and fell onto each other, not caring if we were hidden or not, feasting on our lives, washed in lust. "Schatz!"

The summer light in Northern Germany lingers into the evening ever so slowly drunk by the transparent night. One such evening, I found Henrik on the terrace spraying the scruffy apple tree that struggled out from its spot in the bricks. He glanced at me and said, "Fungus." And he moved the container's wand back and forth like a caress, one you'd give a child you cherished. And I recalled the apple trees that grew in my childhood back yard, the ones I'd wait to bloom each spring, their delicate, fragrant pinkish-white petals, the trees I'd climbed, the ones I'd loved. I watched Henrik waltz around the tree, a slight breeze taking the spray through its branches.

"Uh, huh," I said, "Rosaceae," …the rose family where the apple tree belonged. A tree that symbolized the archetype of the Great Mother combining Virgin, Mother, and Elder. But more so, the apple represented the process of the melting of matter and sky to produce the apple as a celebration of that union.

"*Malus domestica*—keeping it alive."

"Yes...Ja," I said, And I wanted, at that moment, to stay right there, wanted to watch the buds of the tree move through summer—their relationship with Time drinking in light—to bloom, move through pollination, fertilization, then see petals cascading while the floral tube breathed itself into bulbous fruit, apples bearing seeds. Stay right there.

When he was done, Henrik and I sat on the terrace. The mellowness of the evening brought out a hedgehog grunting from the back garden, searching for insects. After watching it snuffling around, Henrik decided he needed cash, and we strolled into town to the ATM. When we returned, walking back up the drive, Henrik's body bent low, his fingertips stroking the topmost tips of tall grasses growing in the crevices along the way. I stopped. He stopped and turned as I stared at him, more so through and beyond him glimpsing eternity just long enough for my heart to catch a flash of joy and pain, held in the slant of his head, the tilt of his jaw. "What?" he said. "Nothing..." was all I could say.

Art Camp

The following week Henrik, Klara, and I arrived at Art Camp for a week's stay. Klara had pouted for most of the drive. The camp was filled with women; some married, others divorcees, all with their children. Plus, there was me, an American, unable to speak more than ten words of German, who'd snagged the only eligible man in the group. It was not going to be boring.

The group painted large tempera pictures, sculpted in soapstone, and did paper-mâché. Klara was given a room down the hall from us where Henrik could easily check on her. One night, a bat flew into our room through a screenless window. It swung around the room, a pendulum back and forth, in and out of the high corners. I enjoyed a couple of decent screams before Henrik went after it with a pillow jumping up on the bed and batting it toward the open window ushering it into the night. We screamed in laughter as others knocked on the door to check that we were OK.

Art Camp became strained. Klara withdrew from the other children. It didn't take long for the other women, brows furrowed, to corner Henrik telling him they were concerned Klara was neglected. Not being able to talk to Klara, my hands were tied.

Near the end of the week, the language and cultural barriers tightened. One night at a picnic, an issue arose where a young, dark-haired divorcee in the group stepped into the bushes to strip off her shirt and pants. At the same time, we all watched her change her clothes. I'm not sure about the others, but I gawked as she exposed her breasts in front of all the women and Henrik. Was this culturally acceptable? I hadn't seen any nudity on the beaches we'd gone to. The other women chatted with her sounding as if nothing unusual was happening. It wasn't long before she asked Henrik to take her to the train station which he agreed to do. "Will you take care of Klara?" he asked. Confused at what was going on and not thinking on my feet, I said, "Yes, of course." And off they went leaving me with Klara and the others.

When he got back, I asked, "What was that all about?"

"Oh, she just needed to go to the train station."

"But, stripping in front of everyone?"

"Oh, well," he shrugged. "Nothing. I bought us ice cream at the station."

I didn't know what to say to him. Jealousy and I don't mix. Usually, I applaud other women's achievements and beauty because I had my own. But right then, I was miffed and couldn't figure out why Henrik's actions made me feel like a teenager.

The obligation to visit my relatives in Poland was at the back of my mind. Henrik put me on a train to Krakow. After visiting with my aunts and uncles, I was back in Germany in his arms. But it was getting close to August. I had been gone almost an entire year, and financially, I needed to go home, get a job, and buy a house. But my heart was refusing to leave.

I told myself I could get a job in Hamburg at the American School. And that I could learn German. But I had to admit I couldn't possibly master that difficult tongue without total immersion. As much as I tried, I couldn't even wrap my tongue around the pronunciation of Henrik's last name that eluded me with its tongue-twisting umlauts. My lips and tongue were left searching the Rosetta Stone, unable to decode German, and I wasn't sure if this time "asking the Universe" would help. I felt I wasn't getting any help in that department anyway. My cobra rode silently—nothing visualized, nothing intuited. Actually, I was too preoccupied with being in love to check in anyway.

Reality was calling me back home. Practicalities kept creeping into my head. I'd always operated my life on that basis first. That's how I'd survived. And I was only too well aware that USA Tax laws gave me only so much time to re-invest the money from the sale of my house. I had to put it into another property, or I'd pay mega taxes to the government. To buy another home, I needed a teaching job. And I knew those began in September in the States. It was the end of July, and jobs would be posted. Was a relationship that crossed three thousand miles of the Atlantic Ocean, true love or not, going to plunge me into financial ruin? I didn't think so. *I had* won the blessings of the Gods for a year—from Kathmandu to Stade—a shower of synchronicity. But by this time, going home was inevitable, or I'd incur a major financial loss.

My heart was conflicted, yet I stopped refusing. I booked my last open-jaw ticket for the first week of August, and Henrik took me to the airport. We embraced, cried a bit, kissed, and I went through the gate home.

In honesty, Henrik had not offered me a home in Stade. Yes, he'd carried me over the threshold of his home the evening I'd arrived in Hamburg. However, he had not offered me marriage or a child that I would have liked. He'd made it clear. No more marriage for him. No obligations beyond what he shouldered already. He was not free of financial commitments to his ex-wife or family and felt overcommitted. He would come to Connecticut in October.

When I landed in New York at JFK and got through customs, a tear rose in my eyes. After one year on the road—one year that had seen me trekking the Himalayas, sitting at the feet of the Dalai Lama, losing my heart in Luxor—I exited the terminal and got down on hands and knees, and kissed the ground. Oh! "Panama!"

Arriving Full Circle

Chance. You can define it in different ways: possibility, odds, accident, freak, fortune, or fate. When chance is defined as possibility, it implies either a random event or that actions have been set for its occurrence. Chance is the backbone of Amor Fati that translates into "love of one's fate." That is, loving your life, whether it holds suffering or happiness—whichever, it doesn't make a bit of difference; everything is blameless. Everything is worthy or at least necessary to produce the singular fingerprint of your soul to enact its karmic design. So, with an abundance of possibilities, I have to say that Chance, inescapably, embraced me once again, this time in Connecticut.

*

It was easier coming home than I expected. It was August, work was calling me, and I applied for several job openings. After all, I had promised to return. And although I'd been refusing this at first, in fact, teaching was my worldly assignment, my karmic design.

I got three job offers. It seemed potential employers read my aura: This woman will slave for you in a highly organized yet creative way. I had never been apologetic for being an independent, strong woman, and I wasn't in my interviews. When my first choice hired me, Cathy, her daughter, and I jumped up and down on her orange and yellow plaid linoleum kitchen floor. It was a dream job in a heavily wooded part of the state, the area where I wanted to buy my new house. Everything that had been cast aside the previous year now came back abundantly.

The day school started, I drove to work, having come full circle—had a job, was buying a house, had Henrik in my life. I was pleased to find the school system was an international crossroads (Papaji lingered in my memory). Students had backgrounds from China, Japan, the Philippines, India, Bangladesh, Puerto Rico, South America, France, England —a place of multiple creeds, races, and cultures.

The teaching job stretched across several grades and schools, so being spiritually asleep was not an option. Thinking back on the Dalai Lama's lessons, I saw my mission was to organize and educate (or enlighten as best I could) my corner of the world. I felt as though I'd found nirvana. Unlike other teachers, I controlled a substantial budget, made my own schedule, and was given carte blanche to develop and implement programs to stimulate higher-level thinking skills. The other teachers and the town folks? Well, everyone seemed to smile. By landing in this school system, I'd arrive at a place and time to implement that unique equation I'd learned in Mundgod: Knowledge + compassion = wisdom. It was a job assigned to me by the Universe. And I was ready to begin the labor of renewing my community.

As the months unfolded, I felt guided, protected, and humble. Cobra synchronicity surged through me. I taught my students how to manipulate the world of knowledge, not just their minds, but I also guided them toward a desire to know. I bonded them with Mother Nature taking them, and groups of others outside to know the plants.

The school system was loaded with psychologists, and we tested students galore. I made sure the atypical ones (found by those testing programs) were brought to my attention to be included in my work despite seeming "unqualified" to other eyes. I intended to open minds and hearts—*to do* and *to be*— hoping they'd find insight every day, both true to themselves and stewards of the planet. To do my job, I used the newly rooted energy brought from the Annapurna Circuit, the Dalai Lama, Hampi, the Taj Mahal, and from a hotel balcony in Luxor. I felt completeness. The world was real.

Love Letters

Letters poured in, a virtual Niagara Falls. I wrote my heart out; he wrote his heart out—letters reaching across the waves roiling endlessly in the Atlantic Ocean. Letters recounting daily doings, teasing, supporting, encouraging…loving—You're Special!

Me: *Dearest Beloved Schatz, I miss you so. I walk in the woods, and I think of you. The gentians are glorious in their purple dresses waiting for you to come in October. An orb spider built a large silken web by the front door—here's a sketch for you to see. In the morning, as I go to work, I say, "Guten Morgen, Frau Orb Spider." She's quite reticent but acknowledges me with a twitch of her leg, "Guten Morgan, Anya." (Yes! She speaks German! Anyway, after several days of watching, I came home to find that she had woven a huge egg sack, so beautiful, so hopeful, so very filled with life. I regret not staying and watching her for six hours or however long it took her to weave her future into its fuzzy ball there in the tomato plant.*

My heart aches for you, Henrik. When I woke up the other night, I was in shock, realizing you were not there. I'm waiting, waiting, waiting. Thank you for the call. I love you till the end of time! Love, love, more than love. Anya

Him: *My Beloved! I sit here in the garden and think of your golden eyes! The hedgehog has come out asking for you, the apple tree still holds its leaves, the tops of the radishes have reached fifteen centimeters. My friend Helme came, and we had a good walk on the dike. He is so enthusiastic about the house which takes so much of my time fixing this* and that. The kids are busy with school. I take them to the wave park. We have a full moon over here, my love! Are you looking up? I beam my love over to you. I kiss you tenderly, I blow on your back. You get goose-bumps. I cover you up. I bite your shoulder. I melt into your arms! I love you forever! Henrik

P.S. Franz calls for you!

As love letters melted from my fingertips onto the page and flew to Henrik, I felt the connection between Henrik and me grow stronger across the separation.

Me: *Dearest Schatz! My Henrik! This house is driving me crazy. I'm so unhappy with finding all its problems.*

Him: *Schatz, I'm sitting in the garden and looking at the grapevines. The drawing below is not very artistic, but it reminds me of you! One of my favorite plants: Tendril of Vitis vinifera around a stem of Allium spec. Coiling and supercoiling around you, around us! Wished I could save the blue grapes for you! Henrik*

I never told Henrik about my Kundalini opening. Each day together, we had shown each other so much of who we were, abandoning our guards, yet there were parts we hid—me, well...and he, some corners buried deep. Of course, living so far apart didn't help. Still, how do you describe the prana that spans time and space between lovers? Its color, its texture, its spiritual electricity? I found the words the afternoon I got lost in the woods.

Alone, hiking a new trail in a four thousand square mile reserve, somehow, I got turned around. I must have been daydreaming about Henrik when I realized I was not going back to my car. I walked in circles, not recognizing the terrain or the rocks or the trees along the path. A small panic rose in me. It was getting late.

The sky was overcast, making the woods free of shadows. I stopped and looked around. There was still time before the light fell out of the sky. This was not like me, not to be able to find my way back along a trail. First, one direction, then another, still not seeing the broad track that led to the parking area. I stopped. The plants were unfamiliar. *"Breathe, Honey, breathe...."* I let go, just walked, let my boots take me along the narrow dirt path I was on. Five minutes later, a fork in the trail, I turned toward what felt like the direction of the road and walked for several minutes to reach the parking area. Relieved, I was puzzled at my lapse of orientation and drove home.

When I arrived, a message from Henrik waited on my answering machine: "Schatz, are you all right? Should I be worried about you? Call me." There it was, a telepathic energy field. A psychic nerve that stretched three thousand miles across the Atlantic Ocean. Henrik sensing my fright, communicating mind-to-mind—no, soul to soul.

Henrik came to Connecticut in October. My friends and family warmed to him quickly. We met up with Cathy again, and he met Dori. Biscute cranked up the barbecue feeding us hotdogs and hamburgers. Each morning I'd go off to work getting rides with other teachers to leave him my car. He'd go shopping for jeans for his kids, pieces of string in his pocket that measured the circumference of his daughters' waists. I was getting ready to buy, and we shopped for houses. On the weekends, we'd pack a lunch—arguing over what type of sandwiches to make, then thankfully making up quickly. We drove through New England's autumn flames and walked to a waterfall marveling at the leaves on the trees, me just as much as he.

The reading of English books had paid off. Henrik was speaking English more or less fluently, now trying to pin down pronunciation and becoming a stickler. "How do you say 'vee'?" he asked, meaning "we."

"OK, Schatz," I said, putting on my teacher's hat. "Watch my lips..." and proceeded to curl my lips into a "wwwoo" sound. He mimicked me, pursing his lips but only to produce a different "v" sound.

"Maybe a bit of phonetics will help," I mused. "Let's try this. Put

your top teeth on the bottom edge of your bottom lip…like this.…"
I opened my mouth pointing to my teeth resting on my bottom lip.
"That's how the "v" sound is made, "See?"

"OK…?"

"But, the "w" sound is made by puckering your lips into an "O" like this…" and I circled my lips. Henrik tried the "v" shape with his teeth, then puckered for the "w" sound. We went back and forth between the shapes of the sounds without getting anywhere.

"OK, stop!" I said, reviewing my options. "Look at my lips." I reached out for his hand to draw him close to me. I couldn't help but inhale his scent. "For the "w," I said softly, "do this.…" I arched up on my tiptoes, putting my lips close to his saying, "It's like you're pretending to.…" And I pursed my lips in the 'weee' sound, drawing myself closer and closer toward his lips, saying, "Wwwe, wwwwe," closing my eyes…as did his finishing my sentence. I'm not sure he ever got the pronunciation of "we" right, but, for sure, he'd mastered the linguistics of kissing.

Henrik returned to Germany. More letters:

Me: *Dear Schatz! Sunday Morning Baroque is just starting on the radio. I miss you very much. I wonder if you had a good trip home. How is your back from all that sitting? I can still hear the echoes of your voice in the living room, the porch, the bedroom, but the house is empty without you. Your fragrance lingers in my bed. Will I ever wash the sheets?*

Yesterday late afternoon as darkness fell on me, I walked the boardwalk, nothing stirring, not a plant, not a duck, only a chickadee "deeeeing" out its song asking for you. Everything resting in the deepest of sleeps, somewhere safe, somewhere warm. I miss you to the ends of the Universe. You are my Universe. I love you, My Stars! And yes, my Dearest, we will meet at the moon again, always meet at the moon with me. I promise to Love You Forever and Ever. Anya

Him: *Hello, My Love! I think of you! Oh, sweet desire! Memories! My soul is with you in CT. A perfect day for you. We just took a little nap on the blanket under the yew. I dreamed of you. Enjoyed your warmth and loving cells beside me, hear the birds singing in our dreams.*

We woke up with a chickadee loudly complaining about his colleague in competition. I reach over and hold you tight. I kiss you slightly on your left ear, and you feel how I love you. I get up to fetch us some tea. Coming back, I read you a little story in German, and you listen and hold my hands. Or maybe slightly stroke my back. Happy without any wish. Then we watch butterflies and birds and flowers. Have you any idea how much you ignited my desire? I'm trembling for YOU! Oh, sweet desire! Oh my wunderschone Anya, how do I love YOU! Henrik

Each Other's Arms

When Christmas came, I flew to Germany. Henrik and I fell into each other's arms. The kids came mid-afternoon on Christmas Eve, almost dark, the long nights of northern Germany setting in. Henrik filled the house with candles, including putting them on the live Christmas tree. The kids chatted to Henrik in German, opened their gifts, hugged their father, and rode their bikes home across town.

Henrik bustled into the kitchen. He had wanted to cook something traditional for our first Christmas and had bought a duck that was roasting. Its smell wafted through the room. I stood watching him fuss over vegetables. Finally, he took the duck out of the oven; it was brown and dry. Once plated, we dug into the bird's flesh only to chew into mouthfuls of buckshot which we spat out, giddy by the foolishness of it all.

In those darkened northern Europe afternoons where the light fades quickly from the sky, we spent a lot of time in bed. And later that week, Henrik came home from work announcing it was time to buy new dishes and a mattress. So, we went to Ikea and loaded up the cart with kitchen stuff before going to the mattress department. Once there, I immediately plopped myself down on the mattresses testing them. Henrik stared at me, "What are you doing?" he asked, perplexed.

"Testing for firmness," I said.

"I'm not sure you can do that."

"We do this in the States; otherwise, you won't know if you can sleep comfortably on it. Come on, lie down, Schatz."

He looked around to see if anyone was watching me, and as a matter of fact, other customers had begun to stare as they walked through the department.

"I don't think you can lie on the mattresses," he repeated.

"We have to, Schatz. Besides, these are samples. Chances are no one's going to buy them and take them home."

It wasn't long before the salesman came over smiling. Henrik turned to him, talking in German. The salesman jabbered back and waved his arm nonchalantly. "Ja, ja. You can lie on it. It's OK. Go ahead and try it out."

We tested several mattresses together. Bemused customers passed by grins on their faces. Soon Henrik became unflappable, testing the mattresses, chuckling at his own shift in decorum. In the end, we chose the mattress to die for—one layered with horsehair, linen, and cotton. The salesman assured us not only was horsehair used in violin bows to make captivating music, but this mattress would perform through a symphony of eighty years or more. Henrik loaded it on the top of the car, and we drove home.

Letters.

Him: *Mein lieber Schatz! I feel so sorry we spent part of our very special time still strained from house problems and work. Precious hours lost! I still hear your sentence in my ear: We will find a solution for our being so far apart. How do you feel about the house now? Can you live there? I think about selling my own house, all its problems.*

This morning at the pool, I managed my first whole lap crawling! I'm still filled with you...whatever I'm doing: yoga, swimming—everything reminds me of you. Living on memories: Anya in the carriage in Luxor, in the tomb, in the hotel room under the net, reciting verses. Seeing your eyes at night just before we fall asleep. Do you know that's the first and last I want to see every day for the rest of my life? Thousands of tender kisses ...surrounded by apple blossoms, dreams, rainbows through which we step, magic fluids of love. Your Henrik with deep Love.

Me: Dearest Beloved Henrik! I walked around the lake after school today. Winter still holds on. The sky was alabaster pink, blue, and golden in its sunset. It reminded me of the bowl you bought me in Egypt. How I love it and you. Some birches are still bent from winter snows frozen into backbends, the yoga of a winter scape. I'm glad you continue doing yoga for your back. When you get here, I'll massage away your stress. Come soon, My Darling. I love you forever and forever. I love you till the ends of the Universe, my energy stretching to yours. Have I told you that before? Let me say it again—until the stars go out! I love you! Anya

I sent him three Valentine's cards starting in January.

Him: *Mein Dearest Anya! I love you, my little Valentine, my soulmate and my seducer, my life-changer, my presence, and my future. Ich liebe Dich von ganzem Herzen ! ! !*

Me: *Oh, Schatz! Is this what heartache is made of? I love you, my Stranger in the Night"! Yours Forever! Anya*

Him: *Let me tell you. ...Oh, Schatz! Spring is coming! The first snowdrops are in bloom! And I put some lilac twigs in a vase. They sit there just tiny, tiny buds, but now there are soft green leaves and even green grapes of lilac buds. They look just wonderful. I spent last weekend with the kids away from all the stress at work. We walked in the woods and saw a deer, and found a huge bulk of frog eggs in the ditch. Fascinating! When they went home, I sat in the garden. We have a nightingale. He sings so beautiful. I haven't heard anything like this yet. Except for my LOVE whispering into my ear! I long for you and look forward to you. 12 more days till your spring vacation. I kiss you on your mouth, feel your sweet lips, see your deep eyes. I melt with you in love. Henrik*

Henrik came to Connecticut in April. I drove to JKF to pick him up. One glorious day fell into the next. We went back into

New York City to the World Trade Center and gawked out the Windows on the World, then to see the Brooklyn Bridge and the Metropolitan Museum of Art. Back home, we walked the woods endlessly, admiring and examining the spring wildflowers. On one trail, Henrik asked, "What are these," pointing to a small, white rue. I told him. He said, "Ranunculus," fixing its family name in his head. Then saying, "At home, I bought Caryophyllaceae, pink type; Primula; Sedum red and yellow; and bulbs of Begonia. I never bought them before…but just for you, Schatz."

We visited my friend Zoe and her boyfriend, who lived one town over. She, like me, had divorced and traveled the same year I had. And she'd also met a tall, handsome guy, Sven, from Denmark. He was now visiting her, and the four of us had dinner. Sven occasionally broke into German while speaking to Henrik. Finally, at the end of the meal, he said, "Why don't the two of you come to Denmark next summer when you're in Germany? Anya? Zoe here will be in Denmark with me." Henrik and I agreed.

When school let out in June, I was on a plane to Germany for our second summer together. Chronic happiness and desire created a gravitational hold pulling me passionately into Henrik's orbit. Soon after I got there, he said, "I've planned a visit to my hometown for you to meet my mother and sister." This relationship was serious if I was meeting his mother.

We packed the car and drove the autobahn to southern Germany. When we arrived at Henrik's old home, we were greeted at the door by his sister, Lenore, who also lived there. "Guten Tag," I said.

"Hi!" She ushered us into a bedroom where Henrik's mother lay bedridden. Her hand was draped over the side of the mattress dipped into a bucket of iced water. Henrik bent over and kissed her forehead gently.

"Guten Tag," I said.

"Hallo," she said warmly, smiling up, face pale haloed by gray hair.

The conversation began about the drive down and the weather. Henrik translated. I shared where I lived, my job, and how I'd met Henrik in Egypt. The conversation went back and forth between German and English. I sat by as Lenore switched to German and chatted with Henrik on their mother's condition—perhaps discussing the hand in the bucket. I didn't know. But my mind wandered off, and it made me think of my own European mother—Mother immigrating from Poland. And I recalled her own brand of medicine if that's what it was, involving an incident with a cow.

As told to Agnes and me, Mother had saved a cow from choking. She'd been out in the family farm fields tending the cows when one began thrashing its head about. She went over to see beet juice pouring from the animal's mouth. "I was scared," Mother told us. "I knew what a disaster if the cow died. I put my hand into the cow's throat and pulled out a half-eaten beet. Slime ran down my arm. That and relief."

I glanced around the room—its plain painted walls, an old bureau, a braided rug on the floor. I tried to avoid looking at his mother's hand dipping in and out of the bucket, but it *was* strange. Henrik seemed to take it all in stride—maybe some local remedy for arthritis. But as strange as it was to me, it didn't matter. I'd lived with Dad, who ate squirrel-brains-road-kill.

After the visit, Henrik and I walked fifteen minutes from the house up into low hills covered with grapevines he wanted to show me. He rubbed his arm then swept it up over the vineyard as if giving a blessing. "This is where I'd come as a child," he said, his eyes glistening and a small muscle in his jaw pulsing. It was clear the spot was important to him. That the place had played a part in his youth. I wasn't totally clear why at first. He mumbled something about coming here to destress when things got tense at home. Something about his father, who also took to bed soon after World War II and stayed bed-ridden for a long time before dying. He bent over, picked up a handful of dirt, and let it sift through his fingers. Then I got it.

Henrik was bonded with the place. The grapevines rooted in the brown soil of southern Germany—its genius loci—the same way I was bonded with the pond below my childhood house. Both of us bonded to the Earth for serenity, security, the arms of the planet holding him, holding me. Then he went on telling me about his stress. "I had a different language, dialect here," he said. "When I went north for University, I had to learn all over the dialect of the north. It was hard."

I understood what he was trying to tell me. He'd experienced what I'd undergone when I'd left my home struggling through college—a culture I'd found alien. But here, standing in among the grapevines with Henrik, I saw we both shared a poverty of sorts—I wasn't sure of exactly what—but I also saw that the Earth had been a haven for both of us. Maybe particularly the plants, the security we sensed in them, or actually knew a steadfast growth emerged every spring, every year, never letting us down.

Henrik, like me, was addicted to the healing stability Mother Nature gave—a parent, a mother, easing out bad dreams real and imaginary—feeling protected. Both of us cut from a similar piece of need. With parents who just might have been labeled flawed, but who for us were the norm. Parents living their lives, not trying to figure anything out, instead just living their lives.

We drove home along the winding road that skirts the Rhine River. Castles perched on the hillsides made it matchless against rivers I'd seen. Unlike the Kaligandaki—barrenness shouldered by subtle forces—the landscape here abounded in fertile greenery, alive with loud, compelling energy.

Henrik and I stopped for the night at a hotel converted from an old tavern that was romantic by any standard. I thought of the monk's chambers filled with erotica at the Caves of Elora. There I seduced Henrik by pretending to be the maid delivering clean towels. But the following morning, an argument broke out. I was in the tub using a washcloth he had designated as his. He came in, looked around, then down to ask me for it back. I demurred, saying, "It's soiled now, Schatz, grab the other one."

"Give me that one."

"Please…" but coldness in his eyes made me quickly reach up to hand him the washcloth I'd been using. Something in my mind pivoted. I couldn't figure out what.

Later that summer, after seeing his mother, Henrik and I went to Denmark. We took up Sven's invite to visit him and Zoe at his home on the North Sea. His house was a modern, open-space A-frame he'd built himself. Zoe said that every morning they would swim, or as it may be, dip quickly into the North Sea's icy surf.

They put us up in the spare bedroom, took us out, showed us the beach, and then we went back to the house to prepare for dinner. Sven, a much older man than the three of us, took us to the garage and pointed toward a large basket of fish. "Henrik," he said, "You're in charge of cleaning them. Here's the knife." And we left him to his task while I was assigned to peel potatoes in the kitchen. But I knew from the initial look on Henrik's face that I had better check on him soon.

By the time I returned, scales were scattered like buckshot, blood splattered the table from slashed fish heads, and guts were piled in a slimy heap. The corners of Henrik's mouth were turned down; his eyes didn't meet mine. "Hey, can I help?" I asked, trying to retrieve him from the task. He glowered, stabbing at the fish. A cold twin in him had emerged. Sven came out to check. Immediately reading Henrik's body language, he said something quick in German— "Gut! Das ist genug" and then in English "OK. Good, that's enough for now," which put an end to the carnage.

"We're all going for a walk on the beach together. Come on. I'll get Zoe." And Henrik and I went into the house so he could change his shirt.

Henrik rushed into our bedroom, tore off his shirt, and grabbed me kissing me and unbuttoning my blouse. Dumbfounded, I said,

"Are you crazy? We don't have time. They're waiting for us." He gave me a sharp look, turned on his heel, pulled on a clean shirt, and stalked out of the room.

Joining Sven and Zoe out on the beach, Henrik separated himself and walked parallel to us on a high ridge. Bewildered, the three of us walked on. Zoe asked, "What happened to him?" I couldn't tell her I'd refused to make love right after he'd been retrieved from cleaning the fish. That either the bloody assignment or my rejection had made the bottom drop out. I felt insane as I watched him sullenly distance himself from us.

I heard Sven saying, "Let him be; he'll come out of it." Which eventually, he did after about an hour. When it was over, Henrik slipped back into the conversation as if nothing unusual had happened.

On the drive back to Germany, I tried to address how he had felt only to get a sharp look that cut me short, making me sweep the matter under the rug. But as those episodes—arguments over soiled washcloths, and sandwich types, or chopping up a thousand fish, and others about seemingly nothing at all—began to thread their way through the tapestry of our love lives, its fabric started to fray. In one moment, exuberance, in the next melancholy taking me with it. My childhood had been filled with chaos, so I was used to it, but that had been for reasons I could understand.

Transits

Henrik and I continued to transit between Germany and Connecticut, those three thousand miles of Atlantic Ocean that separated us. In the fall, Henrik came for Thanksgiving. We joined Cathy's family to feed him his first turkey. We surrounded him with family, friends, and merriment. All the fixings were there—stuffing, mashed potatoes, gravy, cranberry sauce, and a juicy turkey.

On the way home, he looked grim. Eventually, he asked, "Why

wasn't the whole turkey carved at the table?" I explained the logistics of a heavy, hot turkey being brought to the table. How it had become routine for Americans to just cut it up in the kitchen, not do a Norman Rockwell Life Magazine cover. But I could hear his disappointment like he'd been robbed. Silence fell in the car. We drove along. Then he said, "You are never saying what you feel, what you mean."

"What?"

"You need to tell me how you feel," he said.

"What is it you want me to say?"

"How you feel. You don't tell me! I can't feel that you forgave me for Denmark, and it's a big dark cloud over our relationship."

Taken aback, I said, "OK, I will then. For one thing, you need to tell me how *you* feel. Why do you get into such moods that make me feel I've done something wrong?" He looked at me blankly. I went on, "That I've hurt you in some way! Denmark? Over nothing!" I was driving, couldn't see him fully, glanced at him, saw an empty look on his face, his lips pursing.

"You misread me; you're criticizing me," he said.

"No! Look," I said, "What I want to know is what…what happens to you when you…slip, when you pull into yourself like in Denmark. Can you tell me that?" I asked.

"It's nothing. I'm OK."

"But it's not OK with me. I can see you're hurting. You told me you're going to a therapist…."

"No. I stopped. I don't need that anymore."

A heavy silence suffocated the car. I didn't know what to say.

After Henrik returned to Germany, I called my friend Karette, a practicing therapist by then. I spilled out my despair, told her about his emotional rollercoaster. Told her about Denmark. "Karette, being with him confuses me. It can be the smallest of things that throw us off—stupid things—washcloths, and it's gotten to a point where I have no idea what we are even arguing about! It makes me feel crazy. He closes off to me. And it sounds like he stopped going to his therapist." She sympathized with my gloom, "OK. Let me hear it all."

I vented my upset. How things that didn't matter to me became issues for Henrik. How they cast him into a dark mood. "I feel I can't just live a normal life with him. He's so sensitive." But, as much as I tried, I couldn't pry a diagnosis out of her. She was too professional for that.

Letters:

Him: *My dear Love! I just came back from a walk into the winter wonderland! It's just fabulous! Sunny and bright. I took you out with me, told you tales. I'm so grateful to you, so deeply nourished and content. Thank you so much. And yet, I'm in quite a crisis! New Year's thoughts made clear what's been building up since weeks and months: there is something wrong in my life! And instead of resting, I just collapse. And, when you come, just being unable to just melt in eternal love and joy with you.*

This house gives me headaches! Still not fixed and still cold. I should have taken a flat which I could leave whenever I want to. All this money. All this working for taxes. I feel quite desperate! I could just cry, Runaway. Pack and travel. Of course, I would miss you and the kids. What happens now is I find a deep loving feeling for myself, a slightly aching heart, a sadness, and a smile with tears. Coming closer to my own mirror.

My soul speaks out to your soul, merges into yours. I feel so connected to you; the heart waves are extending, seeing you in deep love. Getting to know you more and more, goodbye to images of you, welcome Anya as you are. I love you forever and a day! I wish us time and space and patience to grow together, let love and passion, let grow curiosity about each other. My soul mate, you touched me so deeply. Henrik

Me: *Dearest Schatz! I don't know what to say to you. I'm without words. If I could, I would hold you in my arms and caress you ever so tenderly. Sing to you. You, for me, are so special. How do I let you know this? Yes, you need rest and to find peace in your heart.*

My house too gives me pains; I'm still upset I bought it. Work? My

Henrik, you must learn to be both bold and take things with a grain of salt. Realize that "before enlightenment..." or any kind of rest, for that matter... our job here on the planet is to "chop wood and carry water."—the job, the kids, your family. Simply that. It's the moments together that open us up to each other and the world. Please let me help. How can I? Please feel me through space and time, and patience so that we can grow together.

And I'm sorry for your aching heart. I kiss it deeply to its depths. I kiss you and kiss you and kiss you a thousand times over and forever. This year will be our happiest yet. We will see a thousand new birds together. I love you more than I can say or write. And I shout my Love for you across this Atlantic Ocean, which keeps me from you. Do you hear my love, Beloved Henrik? I LOVE YOU FOREVER. Anya

Our second Christmas came, and I flew to Germany. Henrik's kids visited, he lit the Christmas tree, and we exchanged gifts. I had brought the children books and lots of kites for the wind that constantly blew across that part of Germany. His oldest daughter seemed in a funk. I asked her what was wrong. She told me she'd had a disagreement with her father. I told her to listen to him carefully and to be patient. I reminded her that he had mega responsibility at work and home. Then I caught myself. Here I was starting to make excuses for Henrik.

Henrik and I spent the week going to museums. He'd also bought tickets to the Hamburg Opera for later in the week. When we arrived, we found our seats that had an obstructed view. He asked, "Is this OK?" "Sure, no problem," I said telling him that Cathy and I at times bought similar seats to Broadway musicals.

Before the opera night, I'd asked him for opera notes to read. "No," he said. "You don't need that. I'll tell you what is happening."

"No, I'd like to read the plot. That way I can absorb it. Operas are often complex."

On the way to the opera, he proceeded to give me a sketchy summary that garbled in my ear, a summary I didn't quite get. But it didn't matter, not then; because once it started, I just enjoyed the opera—its pomp, the arias, the costumes, the scenery—and besides, I had prepared for the evening.

Before we had left to go to Hamburg, I had put on make-up, polished my nails rose red, and bought a pretty, new hat. When Henrik saw me come down the stairs before we left the house, he'd looked away in what seemed like distaste. I felt deflated, unsure. Now at the opera, he sat detached; and I cut him slack thinking he was engrossed or embarrassed about the seats. Then, after we returned home and got into bed, he turned his back to me. I was bewildered.

The letters continued back and forth:

Him: *Hello, Mein Schatz! The end of a long week at work! And a successful one! I'm finding success at work with a new project I'm working on, connections with companies and the University. I can't wait to see you in April! I found the begonia bulbs from last year for planting this spring. I am trying to get Richard to come more often, but he resists. I see the girls. I look forward to you; just three more weeks till your spring vacation. Be there in April... I call you; I miss you; I love you, sweet and tender! Millions of kisses! Forever Your Love, Henrik*

Me: *My Dearest! At night, I have bats that fly around the house. During the day, I can hear them in the garage under the eaves: Mumble, mumble, mumble. I found a great oil painting class after school. It has an excellent instructor, and I've set up a small studio in my house. How are the children? Have you checked with the school on Richard? I know the systems are different, but I think it would help to have him tested. I LOVE YOU FOREVER. To the ends of the Universe, I promise that to you, my most beloved One! Anya*

Him: *My Dear Anya, I'm lying under the plum tree. Chickadees playing and singing, dashing in and out. New songs. Sparrows arguing. The sunshine right through the flaming-red petals of the poppies. Another terrific spring day. The week will be hectic with symposiums and lectures on the road. I'm not really content, not feeling at home while my love is so far away. I miss your tenderness very much! A few weeks! Love, Henrik*

Me: *Can I keep up with my Beloved's letters? Love that is poured over me again and again in torrents of sunshine. I think not, but remember, always and for a day, how much, how very much I love you—from that first moment I saw you in Luxor…before I even expected…before my heart knew…before my very being began to sing your name…well! Forever, Anya*

Yet every so often, the current of our relationships dimmed or even short-circuited. When Henrik came in April during my school vacation, I took him to Cape Cod, at a time of the year I'd never been there before, off-season. Here we were in one of my favorite places on the planet, and it turned out to be cold and dreary with nothing in bloom, few stores open for shopping, and few other visitors. Walking on the beach was no fun, with a sharp wind cutting in from the Atlantic. I could see he was not happy, nor was I. We huddled in the studio I had booked, one that had turned out to be shabby and cramped. Soon, we left. I did everything wrong that week.

On the drive home, Henrik's eye caught a sign for the Whaling Museum in New Bedford, and he wanted me to stop. I said, "Not this time," just wanting to leave the whole thing behind and feeling exhausted. Back at the house, I lit a roaring blaze in the fireplace, trying to save the last few days of his visit, ward off the disappointment we both felt over the Cape, the exhaustion of the joy we'd been expecting. We held each other, watching the fire flare, eventually reduced to embers glowing red then dark, holding each other still more tightly.

Gdansk

In our third summer, Henrik planned a vacation for us, this time to Poland. We'd drive through the northern part of the country to the beach at Leba then on to the reconstructed Old Town of Gdansk. Because I spoke enough Polish to get by, it was my job to find us a room for the night. We found a possible place, and I went up the stairs and knocked on the door. A barking dog appeared from around the back. The animal advanced, teeth bared, snarling, and snapping at my legs. I lurched back, my heart pounding. I whirled, running down the stairs heading for the car, hoping the dog wouldn't chase me.

Shaken, I yanked open the door and jumped into the car. "A dog almost bit me!" I cried. Henrik's face was expressionless.

"Buckle your seatbelt," he said and drove off, his face stony.

We sped away. I felt stunned... an unbearable distance between us. What was wrong with him, with us? I stared straight ahead, swallowing my feelings, reminding myself that he'd actually done nothing. We were on vacation; it was all right.

Henrik's mood improved during the drive to the beach at Leba. We walked for miles on the white, sugary sands that squeaked beneath our feet and ate ice cream. But in Gdansk, the winds shifted again.

Before exploring the rebuilt Old Town, Henrik went off to find an ATM machine to get Polish zlotys, leaving me to wait. Time passed, and then more time passed. As I peered at the corner where he'd disappeared into the buildings earlier, his long body dragged into view, shoulders sagged, jaw taut, aura pallid—and I realized that my lover had collapsed back into his double life.

I inhaled deeply to try to pull all the shrewdness I could muster from my core, hoping to talk?... no, laugh? ...maybe charm?... him out of his doom. Hoping in part, at that moment, to channel

Karette's counseling brilliance, which, of course, I didn't have and never would—an ability to combat someone's unrelenting anguish—to rescue the day, rescue my relationship with my beloved, who'd turned himself—before my very eyes—into Sisyphus, punished, rolling a baffling rock (that I didn't understand) uphill, only to have it smash down on him time and time again.

I was confused by the Universe. The one I knew took care of me. I wanted it to be orderly when I knew damn well it was not! I knew it to be just like this: filled with the Dads and Mothers, with Indian students locked in their dorms, with families existing in garbage bag tents on the sidewalks—crazy, stupid, pitiable, random—just as much as it was filled with the hotel owners in Delhi praying for vomiting and shitting guests, the Dalai Lama teaching compassion, the bodhisattva-Brians driving cabs in London—sane, wise, benevolent players—rational people keeping the place harmonious as best they could. But I didn't cry. Not then.

I said lovingly, softly, cooingly, "Mein Geliebter Schatz?" only to slide backward from cold eyes. "Did you get your money?"

"Ja," he growled.

"Can you tell me what's happened?"

"What? Nothing!"

My head spun a whirly-gig, unable to figure out what to do. Something must have happened at the ATM. "Well, tell me what's bothering you," I begged. His cheeks were sallow; he shrugged, mumbled something incomprehensible, and turned to walk down the main street of Gdansk. I stood there. In a moment, he was back muttering, "I'm OK," only to turn on his heel to walk several paces ahead of me into the Old Town. I followed.

As Henrik and I made our way along cobbled Dluga Street, spaced about twenty feet apart, I looked at the restored buildings of Old Gdansk—tall, narrow, colorful, charming houses—reminiscent of Amsterdam. The tourists' voices bubbled around us. People gazed and pointed into the shop windows loaded with amber, carved souvenirs, and weavings from the mountains of Zakopane. It was more heartache than sadness I felt. More grief than chagrin.

More slipping back into my childhood, needing to run into the woods to the pond. No bitterness. Yet, it was more than all that. My love had turned out not to be an anchor but a sail.

I felt lost. I didn't believe that Henrik was 'OK.' I knew I wasn't. There had been a wedge growing between us. At home, concern swarming around me after what had happened in Denmark, I had called Karette to air my troubles. "There are times I feel a whirlpool is controlling my life," I told her. But again, being professional and not directly involved, she had resisted giving an opinion, but others had not. A fellow teacher who gave me rides to work when Henrik was in Connecticut tried to wake me up. "Isn't going back and forth to Germany too long a distance for a relationship?" Puzzled, not seeing his angle, I naively said, "Oh, no. It works."

Henrik walked ahead of me, frozen in brooding that gave him, nor me, no apology. I'd been swallowed by something I couldn't understand. My brain, which usually assumed the attitude of a glass half full, even overflowing, now drained away. What was *this*? Something that didn't make any sense to me, threatening to take us down, the edges of our love eroded by unfathomable emotional currents that I didn't know how to swim against. Find a mooring? I didn't know how.

I trailed along after Henrik trying to remain tender. I watched his stiff back, a brittle tone telling me to stay back. The tourists around me ambled along in and out of the shops, bags full of gifts. There were swarms of amber jewelry, globs of honey-pieced sunlight glowing in the shop windows. I began to feel miserable, pulled into my own gloom. After twenty minutes of this, something in me snapped, and I grew impatient with his temper. I went from repulsed to doing an about-face. A part of me, that Special part, told me I was still OK despite my aching heart. And I wanted to shop—Henrik could find me if he so chose.

I turned into a store that overflowed with amber. One chunky amber necklace, two pairs of earrings rimmed with glinting silver, a few extra pins for gifts, and I felt better. Outside Henrik was waiting, standing not far away. And I thought, *I'm sure glad I'm not pushing a rock uphill only to have it constantly crash down on me*, but then again, something inside me had crashed that day.

Driving back to Germany, again, the mood swung. Henrik and I shared stories of our childhoods, and we were happy. Once back at his home, our loving routine resumed. Yet, I felt sands shifting beneath my feet that threatened to topple me over. Uncertainly, I spent an evening bringing up the incident in Gdansk.

"Schatz, what happened in Gdansk?"

"Nothing happened. I told you that day I was mad, and it wasn't at you," he said. "This dwelling on stuff."

"But…" *I'm feeling helpless…he told me he was angry…?*

"Don't reject my feelings now," he said.

He…feels rejected? I'm the one who feels rejected… "We're not communicating clearly," I said. "I feel…" *I can't get inside his head…* "I'm worried when I see you…."

"There is nothing to worry about. It's intimidating when you talk for me and say 'we'…."

If only I spoke German… "Listen…"

He grabbed my hand and held me tight kissing me. And it was just like that, I let it go—one moment loving, then a transformation into someone I didn't recognize, someone I even didn't want to know. I felt his strength so that I wanted more—his tenderness, his laughter, his love that filled my soul. I pushed my concerns to the back burner—both of us did—and we got through the rest of the summer without incident. When he was working around the house, I'd find him and sing him little love songs.

Fall Letters:

Him: *My Beloved! The plums turn blue in the garden, one is eaten a green one (delicious!). The apples make a ruin on the terrace! The Buddleias grow butterflies a plenty. Birds are singing a sea of flowers. The sun is hot, above 30 C! Almost unbearable, but it is time for harvesting, and Klara is up with her basket. Richard and I have taken up fishing. Can you check the Bargain News you have there to see if you can find some waders for me? I'd like to try fishing in the river. I need to escape from all this stress piled on my shoulders. Kids not working strong in school, finances, and workloads at all hours and weekends. I need to rest when I come. Hold you in my arms and kiss you a million times over. A million, million kisses and more. I love you. Yours Henrik PS: I had a dream I send to you here to decipher.*

Me: Dearest Schatz! Let's see. Here's a letter from you in my mailbox. What fun. I tuck those millions and millions of kisses into my heart and send them back to you. Of course, I'll look for waders for you. And I'll get you a fishing pole and the gear as well and have it here for you when you arrive. Oh! I'm sorry to see that you are sad and strained by money matters and responsibilities. I know how you feel and would like to take some time off. And forget everything. I did that, remember? My trip to Nepal? I wonder what's going on in all these dreams! Your dream, Schatz: I think it's about a very vulnerable feminine aspect of yourself that needs taking care of. And, I think it means, if you nurture this feminine part, it becomes a member of your family, your Self. My dreams lately have been quite strange, as well. In one, all of my furniture and belongings were stolen from my house by a woman and a man. I see the stripped white walls. The man, in my dream, cut a circle of skin deeply into his lower left cheek. I miss you, miss you terribly. I'm sorry for your aching heart. I kiss it deeply to its depths. Love forever. Anya.

October came. Henrick visited again. I found waders, bought the fishing gear, and took him to get a fishing license. Henrik spent a lot of time fishing the Housatonic River and the lakes and streams in the surrounding areas. As the week went on, he ventured out, alone, further and further away from where I lived. I spent days painting in my studio, lost in my own thoughts. One day blurred into the next, with the end of the week arriving quickly. All too soon, I was putting him on the limo in Danbury to send him back to Germany.

A Stonewall

Cobras have a way of informing, letting you know what's happening—the truth—even if you don't want to hear it. This time, mine used a form of nonverbal communication—tears—an equally profound nonverbal language that informs, gives evidence.

*

Everything changed over Christmas. I was in Germany again with gifts for Henrik and the kids. Henrik was preoccupied with work. I was left on my own a lot. Stonewalling seemed to simmer below the surface of all our interactions. On one walk around a nearby lake, we discussed a poem that I had shared with him. One about losses in my life, including not having children. I felt him slipping away from me and stopped to ask, "Henrik, what's happening? How are you feeling?"

"Oh, me? I'm fine. But you, you aren't."

"What do you mean?"

"That poem…"

"I was just trying to share with you how I was feeling. Did you think I was blaming you?"

He looked away. "I feel criticized by you."

"Are you OK? I'm concerned that you're depressed," I said.

"Don't put that load of crap on me! Your unresolved mother stuff."

"What?!"

He said nothing looking away.

"What are you talking about?" I asked? "We're having a conversation…." But he turned and walked on, saying, "We have problems, a distance problem, so we don't succeed in partnership as I need it for talking and establishing a partnership. I've got problems, obviously. Yours are deeper, more hidden."

I ran behind him grabbing at his sleeve. "Look. I'm sorry. I love you, but we've got to talk. We know we do."

"It's so difficult to understand somebody else. A different culture and language. We never made a serious attempt to live together. You make all the decisions. I regret that I introduced you to my mother. Let's go!"

I felt helpless. A stonewall. Unable to reach him, I retreated into my own unhappiness. Henrik and I kept our distance. Back at the house, when Klara came, I set her to chopping vegetables to cook soup. Henrik spent still more late hours at work.

The night before I left Stade, I crawled under the covers with a book, absorbed in a plot where a man betrays his lover. Sobs broke from my throat. Cries from deep down, so far down spilling from my inner space, I wasn't sure where the bottom was. Something wrong took over my body. A dam, waiting for this moment, broke, releasing a torrent, a lament—something robbed, something dead, or something run away. Choking breaths wrenched my body burning tears from me. Some truth, one I couldn't grasp, had seized my body. Henrik came into the room. He frowned and asked, "Why are you crying?"

"I don't know," I blurted through my tears. His eyes bore down on me, his face an unreadable fortress.

"What's wrong with you?" he asked again, his voice remote.

"I don't' know!" I wanted, expected him to comfort me, take me in his arms, but he turned away and went back downstairs. The next day, our parting at the airport was tepid at best.

Living the Opera

At home, I put that last night in Stade aside and embraced work's routine that got better and better as the job went on. Henrik would arrive in April, and I thought we should find a way to sort out our growing differences in the freshness of the spring. Until then, I dove deeper into my work, finding creative ways to teach, plus I continued my evening painting classes.

In the class, the instructor played music in the background. One night, as much as I tried to ignore it, a song in Italian began to haunt me. I put in my earplugs, now a mainstay from my Nepal dog barking days. The following week again, the song played low in the background pulling at my heartstrings, rousing a dread I couldn't put my finger on. When I'd had enough, I went over to the instructor and asked, "What's the name of that song?" "Songo," he said. And the following day at school, I dug for its translation.

The song's English name was: *Time to Say Goodbye* by several Italian songwriters (Quarantotto, L., Sartori, F., Peterson, F., 1996). It was recorded by Sarah Brightman & Andrea Bocelli with the English lyrics by Sarah Brightman, which included "…all the light is missing, … the door you've opened…Close"… The Derek Walcott poem came to mind—the poem Henrik had read me at the Forte Grande Hotel in Cairo… its words: "Feast on your life" —now felt eclipsed by this "Goodbye."

I felt, well, it wasn't a grenade that went off in my heart, but more a slow landslide that occurred. My subconscious mind was making it clear a small crisis was brewing, and a reckoning was needed. The time had come to face reality, to understand what was true and what wasn't between Henrik and me. When he arrived, I knew I'd try to find a way to patch up the relationship because I wasn't ready to let go.

Spring letters:

Him: *Buenos dias, dear Anya! Thanks for your letter. Last week I went on a camping trip with friends. A very brisk wind blew so loud we had to put on heavy rain gear to break the wind! As we hiked, we ran into a cloud of birds migrating, and it looked like a locust plague! Unbelievable! But beautiful, too. But strange thing, I just didn't come to a rest. Being in this quiet world with actually nothing to do, I feel an* uneasiness deep inside of me. I think all the time that I have to go back to work where I have a lecture to give and have no desire to work it out. There are more meetings than I can stand. Very intense and, as a whole, not too optimistic for the future. Coming from a draining world and going back there isn't easy. Talk to you soon. I will see you on April 9. Here are my flight numbers. Love, Henrik

Me: *Dearest Henrik! Thank you for your letters. I run to the mailbox when I get home from school hoping to find one. And there! My heart leaps to you! I'm getting ready for the spring plantings mulling over seed catalogs and planning the begonias. And thinking about what to cook for you when you arrive. All is not well in my heart which loves you very much…cherishes you…sees you in all the flowers and the grasses… When you come to Connecticut, we must have a good honest talk… about your stress, about everything…I love you forever. I love you; I love you. You live in the sound of my soul. Anya*

That April, like any spring in New England, was damp and chilly. Henrik came during my school break. As the limo approached, I caught a glimpse of him, shoulders bowed and head turned away. When he got out of the van, I came and gave him a hug, only to be met by eyes that were stones. "Hi, Schatz," I said, reaching to kiss him.

"Hello!" he grunted and turned to get his bag.

"Are you OK? How was the plane ride?" I asked.

His back was hurting him, he said. It had been a long flight. It was dark by then, and I sped home only to get stopped by a cop. My clean record got me out of a ticket. Once home, Henrik immediately went up to bed, where I joined him, stroking his back gently. We lay in bed as strangers. Anxiety froze in my throat. But then again, his back *was* hurting him, so I let him be.

In the morning, Henrik said he needed to walk alone. He disappeared down the road for several hours. I milled around the house, washed clothes, rearranged stuff in the garage, pretending to keep busy all the time watching for him to return. Dinner was strained.

He left his dishes on the table and went to watch a movie on the TV. I cleaned the kitchen and joined him searching for conversation.

"Schatz, I bought tickets to the New York Metropolitan Opera for Saturday just before you leave. I'll drive. Do you feel up for going?" I asked.

"Sure, why not?" he said and turned back to the TV.

"OK," I said, hoping to break the ice, wary not to say the wrong thing that would send him into a funk. But that night again, love-making eluded us. His body language shut me out. I felt him slipping away from me. But I said nothing, thinking of all the other times I'd tried to bring him back, feeling undercurrents steadily dragging me beneath the surface of our love, getting me lost.

We hiked up Bear Mountain, a 2,300-foot peak in the Appalachians. Henrik distanced himself several feet in front of me. I dragged myself up the mountain, watching my boots strike the trail. When we reached the top, we sat on a boulder overlooking the valley, ate our lunch, and made small talk about how the trees were still bare of spring leaves. It was like talking to a neighbor.

For the next several days, we retreated into our separate corners. Henrik took the car to go shopping for his girls while I stayed home to walk the roads around my neighborhood, trying to quiet my heart. In the three years with Henrik, I'd let his moods strip me down emotionally, them making me feel as if I had to handle him with kid gloves. And that was precisely what I was doing those past couple of days: not shopping with him, getting ice for his back, cooking foods he liked. But truth be told, my heart was tired of his sulks, and he wasn't making me happy. His rollercoaster emotions carried me along with him into what felt like some personal black holes, yet I loved him.

When he got back from shopping, Henrik called the limo to make a reservation for his return trip to the airport. Listening, I heard him slip and use his old name, the identity he'd cast off many years before.

On Saturday, I drove us into New York City to the Metropolitan Opera. It was April 17, 1998; we'd been together three years. Madama Butterfly was playing, and we listened to the singers unravel their story of tragedy and deceit. Later, at home in bed, I was overcome by fear that I was being cheated on. I didn't want to know this, yet I knew—but still, he had come to Connecticut. Hurt from the last few days churned inside me; so, I confronted him:

"Why aren't we making love?" I choked out.

There was no answer.

"Do you have another woman?"

"No!"

Anger unclogged my throat. "You have another woman!"

"No!" he said, not looking at me.

"What's wrong with you?" I pleaded. "Tell me!"

"I'm tired…my back…"

He was lying. "You've met someone else!" I accused.

"Leave me alone!"

Something in his voice tore me. "You're lying! You've been cheating on me, haven't you?"

He stared at the wall.

"You…you've betrayed me!"

"Ja, OK, I met her. Ja, I have someone at home."

"How could you…?" *I was begging…*

"You don't see me anymore! I see your difficult times, but you don't see *me*!" he said.

Shocked, I kicked away the covers shouting, "Get out of this bed. Go!" my body bent in rage. Without a glance, he left the room. I was too stunned to cry. I lay there, unable to move as if my existence was draining out of my veins. The truth humiliated. I'd thought I was above the rest. I'd been so preoccupied with my love for him, I'd ignored what was really happening. I lay there hunched into the covers wanting them to smother me to sleep. I stared at the ceiling, being pulled deeper into the 'goodbye' that had been brewing— still fighting it, still smelling his scent on the sheets.

I took him to the limo to return to JFK. We stood waiting on the sidewalk as the van pulled up to the curb. The afternoon was overcast, holding back its rain. I felt cold.

"Why did you even bother coming?" I asked.

"I had a ticket."

I shook my head in disbelief. "Saving money?!"

Other travelers rushed from the parking lot, bought tickets from the driver, hugged, kissed, and got into the limo. One woman paused to look at us, standing apart, rigid. I looked away down at the cracked pavement. I didn't care if I was overheard as I scattered our dirty laundry on the sidewalk. I was alone and felt it.

The driver came over eyeing us. "Pay for your ticket, Sir?"

Henrik dug his fists into his pocket. "Yes," he said, handing the driver a few bills then turning away to heft his bag into the back of the van. "I need to go," he said, "I don't know…thank you…." My throat tightened, scared I'd never see him again.

"I don't want to be thanked by you!"

He went on, "I don't know how to say…this life…how do you say? … is dead to me." A blade tore my heart. The limo driver glanced at my face. My eyes were on Henrik's back as he got into the limo. I stepped closer to the window, lifting my hand; he glanced at me, nodded his head, and was gone.

The Letter

My world went spinning those days after Henrik left. Yet, each morning I drove to work, and each afternoon, I drove home, tears streaming down my cheeks. A week after he had left a letter arrived. My fingers trembled digging into the envelope, wishing for a reprieve, a reversal of fate. It read:

Dearest Anya,

The plane to Germany had engine problems out over the ocean. We had to turn back to the airport. Flying back to you. Facing death? I was just benumbed. Revolting thought of 2 women circling in my brain. Nobody else, not even my children. The woman in first line and more

vivid you. The other one Hedy, whom I got to know 2 years ago whom I met again some months ago who took part of an empty space. I don't know what we can do at this point and what we can share not being lovers. Thank you for your love which nourished me so deeply. Thanks for your hatred and resentfulness which made me clearer. So often times I feel treated unlovingly or even rejection. I, many nights, I lie wide awake.... I still feel so very close to you, I feel so sorry, my heart burns, and I feel torn apart. I wish we can be friends, very best loving friends!
   Love,
   Henrik

    I stood there numb. I saw his hands writing the letter, reaching out, quieting the singing bowls that played in my heart for him. So much had lurked around corners, stuff I'd only glimpsed in part, stuff I should have paid closer attention to. Why had I worn blinders to the kaleidoscope of his emotions? Why hadn't my intuition kicked in, warning me off this hurt? But it had. There, in the painting class, that song had held up a musical mirror— "goodbye"—a message only my subconscious understood. And then there'd been that hysterical crying the night before I left Stade. My cobra had indeed kicked in—from the start, even before the start.
    As I dug back, it was clear, my cobra hadn't just given me a sign but the whole story of my conflicted love affair. In India, before leaving for Egypt, I'd bought that book—Kundera's *Unbearable Lightness of Being*—where I'd been given my whole story. Characters involved in depression, deception, and betrayal, all there, giving me a glimpse of my future, letting me know love *is* random and haphazard without rules—stuff I didn't believe just then. But there was more, Henrik had even told me while sitting before the Sphinx— his bookcase, thrown over by his ex-wife. So, now I knew it had not been out of meanness but revenge, all those kids and...all there. *But why? Why this journey?*
    Over the ensuing weeks, I went back and forth between relief that he was gone, sick at heart from his moods, yet I wanted to be with him forever. Everything we'd had rolled through my mind:

Riding camels across the Sahara Desert, standing inside The Great Pyramid of Giza, testing horsehair mattresses, flame-red begonias, his bond with nature, to each other—the mysteries of a thunderbolt—opening, yielding, transforming. I still wanted to be loved by him, sleep by his side, and listen to his breath for the rest of my life.

Don't Flee

I cried for two months. And cried some more, even though my head said, "Good, he's gone!" trying to jerk me back to reality, but it was of no use. My heart refused to give in. I felt alone and abandoned, wondering if he was lost to me forever. At one point, I called his tape to see if he'd disconnected it, disconnected me. The line was busy, and I was glad that he was home— feeling his presence on the other end. I took solace from that scrap, still trying to wrap my head around it all. My body ached for him, but mostly heartache infected me. I contacted Karette, who gave me solace.

"Your letter made me cry," she said. "I wish we lived closer, so I could be with you to support you."

"I've never felt lonelier in my life. I want to crawl inside a box and die. I called him, and he said I never understood him, never listened to him. I cry and cry and cry."

"Anya, we pay a fierce price for closing up. This happened to me after the death of my dear friend Ivy. But you've got to remember it's your odyssey, yours, for you to find your whole truth."

I sighed. "Truth was, Karette, he drove me away. He was always saying I was rejecting him, criticizing him when I saw the reverse! He drove me crazy! It was like some old angers he had buried inside of him that were directed at me, punishing me. Why would he do that? He loved me. I'm the one who should be angry at him!"

"This breakup with Henrik completely threatens your survival at many levels, especially your heart. Anger is the most primal of survival energies, so of course, you must get angry to survive. Not just at him, but all other threats to your existence, now that it's opened up."

"It hurts. He loved me. I loved him. That was a choice I never made."

"I know. It could be that Henrik was not ready to join you in the oneness you wanted to share with him. Sure, it was your destiny to meet, but the chance of separation was also embedded in that destiny. You've got to claim what is yours. Recognize your needs and meet them. Recognize your wants and ask, no beg, for them. And then you will eventually detach from them but not until you process it all."

"The whole thing has burned my heart. I don't have any words for this pain…something stolen…something…." I cried. "But really, he'd never promised me anything, yet I wanted, expected him to fill that part of me that…." I sobbed, "He was my soul mate…isn't that a promise?"

Outside the window, the sun was setting. It reminded me of that first afternoon when I'd reached the Annapurna Sanctuary and had watched the sun travel below the summits of the highest mountains on the planet. And I tried to taste again all the beauty and nourishment I had experienced there. Karette was silent, letting me think and feel. Then she spoke again, "Look, this guy Henri Nouwen explains what happens in our hearts in his book *The Inner Voice of Love*. He said there's a deep hole in our beings, like an abyss. We will never succeed in filling that hole because our needs are inexhaustible. Each of us, you, have to work around it so that gradually the abyss closes."

"This relationship was more fantasy than reality that's for sure. And I was enjoying it. It was filling a hollow spot in me. I wanted the wonderful parts of him, not the demons that plagued him."

"No matter what your anguish, don't be tempted to flee from it. Don't be tempted to get distracted by the world's doings. Avoid the extremes. Don't become totally absorbed in your pain, and don't stray far away from the wound you want to heal."

I nodded in a silent agreement. It was almost dark now, and I reached over to the switch on the lamp by my chair. "I'm trying to think positive. Work's going well, summer's almost here, and I can't stay home. It's too hard. It feels empty here. I signed up for a vision quest in Colorado. I need the mountains to help me get through this," I said.

"Yeah, OK. I understand but look at it this way. The gift that Henrik gave you is to dissolve all opportunities to divert yourself from this wound. His betrayal—inadequacy, whatever it was—has caused you to become so open and raw that avoidance is impossible. Here you were, the most energetically conscious, hard-working spiritual person I have ever met, and you had at least one more major hurdle. You knew it was there. Yet, the timing was not right to go there. And now it is."

Mission

It never was an option for me to hide away in the murky den of depression licking my wounds even though I may have wanted to. I still had several weeks before the end of school and the vision quest booked in Colorado. So, I began the process of healing at home—walking in the woods, doing yoga, meditating, swimming. I began to accept I was guilty of creating and existing in my own fiction. Part of me felt a fool that I'd believed in dreams with him, but another part still didn't want to let it go. Two things kept me steady. The woods and work.

Work was medicine for me. Each morning, I put on my grit mask carrying out my duties. It was spring, a good time to introduce my students to the ways of Mother Nature. I dragged them outside into her green lab to examine her ecological game-plan for the plants. I taught how she arranged things mathematically in her world—flower petals, the margins of leaves, tree branches. We enjoyed her sense of humor displayed in the maple tree's branches thrown skyward like the arms of an umpire calling a touchdown.

On another day, I spotted a fragile, blue-green scab on the bark of a tree. "See that? That's called a lichen. Can you guess the job it does for Mother Nature?" Blank faces stared up at me. I explained the symbiotic relationship of alga to fungus that judged air freshness by denoting air pollution in its own right. Young faces beamed. My students loved consuming facts no other kids knew. But, at the back of my mind, while I pointed out the tiny, breathing mandala that we examined, something chortled wordlessly: I/Thou the lichen, hoping I'd connected Mother Nature's soul with theirs, just a little.

Later in the day, the parent of two kids who'd been in the lichen group stopped me, her face lit up. The lichen lesson had grown a runner sprouting ah-has elsewhere in someone's consciousness. And my vital signs began to return, my soul restore...one lichen at a time.

Along with bonding my students with nature, there was yet another balm I extended to them—which in turn helped me to get through the end of that school year. It was the one I'd received in childhood from Dad. I made sure each student in my care received that incalculable message, one often not taught in school or home, that *they* were Special. I sent it tacitly but strongly, casting each a life preserver from my Kundalini to theirs, kindling sparks of future flames while helping to re-ignite my own.

Vision Quest

It was dark the first night. "Tell us your life story. You've got five minutes each," said Root, the leader of our Vision Quest. One guy, Hansen, in my group of three, began. He told us how he'd been sent off to a fancy prep school and raped by the older students until he finally fought back. This candid telling, his un-disguised reality held up a mirror to the remaining blocks still stuck in my psyche. My wounds murmured back—listening to Hansen was nearly the same as encountering the lepers in Mundgod. I shared Mother's—no, our rape story—for the first time dispassionately. Then touched on Henrik only briefly. After that, the other man in our group spilled out his story. Vulnerability, weakness, violence, sorrow. Each one of us, in turn, stripped our psyches naked, primordial griefs spilling into the night. After that was over, the public confession of my wounds, I thanked Hansen profusely, feeling a release.

It was July. When school finally ended and summer had arrived, I'd hopped a plane to Telluride, Colorado, to the Rocky Mountains finding my way to this Vision Quest. Eleven other men and women were there. I needed the forest to heal, go back to the mountains to re-center. The leader, Root, was a practitioner of shamanic journeys, an experienced therapist who knew the ways of the trickster lurking in the human mind, and who believed in Mother Nature's therapeutics.

That first day, Root had us introduce ourselves using names we'd chosen for our vision quest—monikers for healing. Mine was: *She Who Sees Through Purple Eye*. In prepping for the quest, we'd been asked to spend an entire day (sunrise to sunset) in the woods at home, and I had. Usually a joyful task for me, that day was buggy like none I'd ever seen. And my left eye was bitten by a mosquito that made it swell, turning it plum purple. My quest name, given me by a bug.

Next, Root introduced us to his chief assistant Sol and others who'd be helping him, and he oriented us to the week. First, there'd be a shamanic drumming ceremony in camp. Then the group would engage in a sweat-lodge purification ceremony which was central to our quests. After that, we'd hike into the mountains to find a spot to sleep alone outside in the woods for three nights.

After dinner, Root and his crew built a large campfire and began a drumming ceremony. The tongues of the fire leaped into the chilled air toward the star-filled night feathering its blackness. Each face was lit. We'd been asked to bring rattles from home that we shook to join in with the rhythmic beats of the drums. The cadence built. Various clatters and pings of seeds and beads and sands whispered below the strikes on the drums.

It wasn't like the session Karette and I had experienced with Ruth Inge Heinz during our doctoral workshops—the intensity of that taking us into the underworld. Here it was different. My wrist flicked my rattle, and my body absorbed the pulsing drum beats, a slow-building urgency, its sound entering my body…bumm, bumm, bumm…twack… bumm, bumm, bumm…twack … the drum's voice driving me along, singing and praying its way up my spine, coiling with my heartbeats, falling into a light altered trance, a sense of wellbeing, of inclusion that took me along, not quite knowing where I was going, yet moving. When it was done, Hansen's face, sitting across the fire, appeared softer than it had the night before.

After the drumming, others went off to bed. A woman named Billie Rae and I sat looking into the dying fire. The logs disintegrated, falling into a pile of glowing embers. We exchanged our stories, me sharing my heartbreak over Henrik this time, thunderbolt and all. She said, "Hey, Sister! Funny how this guy does you a big favor."

I gave her a look. "What?"

"Yeah, he holds up the mirror of the Self—so you can see *you* reflected."

"He said I rejected him when the fact was, I felt he rejected me, the love I'd given him—no choice!"

"See, it's all about energy. Thunderbolts are energy things, monster twisters containing the juice of life that can knock you off your ass, making you vulnerable. Yeah, they're the ignition of sexual union that validates our egos—that tries to get them to heal so we can go ahead and merge with our soul mate. But, well, we're all vulnerable, and that's especially noteworthy for us females. This guy made you fall head over heels into your unfathomable feminine, and then! He cheats on you, right? And it hurts, right? So, on the one hand, your ego is being validated; but on the other, the job was too big for him just then, right?"

I thought of what Karette had said. "The way I saw it," I told

Billie Rae, "He kept falling short—couldn't pull himself together. Or maybe, I kept falling short. I couldn't help him. Like I'd fallen into quicksand."

"Sure! You gotta get this message sunk into your brain: When it comes to living and loving, it's especially dangerous being a woman. But there's no choice."

"I thought he was my soulmate!"

"Soulmate stuff? Huh! A soulmate helps you to learn about your self-worth. You gotta embrace *you*, all of you—strong, competent, intelligent, and all the feeble helplessness that makes up the feminine mystique. Look! We're defenseless. Dependent? Powerless? Yep! –that's how we're connected as one. And, it's hard to know what you don't know about love—it's liabilities, its dullness, its darkness because it pulls more than it pushes. So, give it up, Girl! You gotta let go!" I took in her words. Billie Rae put hope in my heart.

Yet, as I went to bed, I felt exposed but steadier. Billie Rae had offered the same unflinching support I got from Karette. And I realized for the first time that no matter how Special I was, I was still a woman, which made me just as susceptible as any other on the planet. Susceptible to suffering—like those sari clad women in Lucknow, the woman on the sidewalk by Roop Kala, or the women sitting satsang trying to figure out how they'd gotten themselves in such messes and how they were going to get themselves out. I was no different. With one whack, Billie Rae had wiped yet more fog off my inner mirror. And I knew I needed to re-think, to rebuild.

Stripping emotional toxins was at the heart of that Vision Quest. The following night, the group loaded into vans and drove to where a round hut (a wickiup) used by southwestern Native Americans was set up as a sweat lodge. It was covered with black tarps and blankets. Nearby a campfire was being tended by Sol and several other of Root's assistants. Large stones were piled next to the fire, waiting to be heated, then placed in the firepit inside the lodge where they would be doused with water to create steam. As I stood on the open field, a billion eagle-eyed stars stared down out of the blackness of the Universe, lookouts brushing us with light.

Root added a few more words about the purification ceremony we were about to undertake. He instructed us on how to enter the sweat lodge. First, all of us women turned our backs to the men, who were turned away from us. We shed our clothes and crawled into the wickiup sitting to one side on towels we'd brought with us. Next, the men entered sitting opposite—twelve of us forming a tight circle around a pit of orange embers smoldering in the center.

Once settled in, the lodge's flap closed, swaddling us in quiet. Billie Rae was to my left and Hansen to my right, just past the doorway. All eyes locked into the embers. Next, Sol and the others with shovels entered one by one placing smoldering rocks into the center pit. They poured water on; steam filled the wickiup.

Outside, Root began to drum and chant while circling the wickiup. Mesmerized by the glow of the fire and warmed by the hotness of the steaming rocks, I let the drumming enter my chest and felt my brain waves sync with the rhythms of the drum's heartbeat.

Minutes went by, the chanting slowed and came to a stop, and Root entered the lodge and sat. "You'll begin this sacred ceremony expressing your anger. You're to dig into your pain, hurts, your bitterness. Look for the wretched in your life and speak it out. Your voice is your tool. Find it so you can discharge the venom buried in your muscles and joints, your body. You'll do this in unison all at the same time. Remember, go for honesty…remember just like Eric Hoffer said, 'We lie the loudest when we lie to ourselves.' Got it?"

Anger. At first, an indistinct muttering, grievances here and there, then continuous slow drilling of voices built, an undertone to an impending rumble. Billie Rae's voice rose above the rest cursing her mother, then across the fire, a male voice called out in anguish, then Hansen swore names… yells and cries from others, an anguished vent. The voices shouted, cursed, and tangled, blistering the walls of the sweat lodge. A rip current erupted in me. I cried out wounds from childhood and those inflicted by Henrik and Tim, swirling my emotions through the lodge thick and dirty with the others. I spat it out—anger, a truth that belonged to my life, choked it out, a rusted tool, wanting to rid myself of it —yelling from a corner of my soul no longer wanting to hold its poisons, hidden soiling my life. Together the group wailed, each congregant howling for thirty minutes—a chorus of rage, bloodshot, ugly... and good. A boil lanced. Left to heal.

The flap of the lodge opened. More rocks, water, steam hissed. Root came in. "Now it's time for you to grieve. Remember all the losses, all regrets, all the sorrows that have piled up in your life. Find what has saddened you deeply ...abandonment, cruelty, heartache. It's there. Find it and grieve it." He left, and we began—low moans, a hesitant breeze preceding a storm. The steam swirled; the temperature inched up.

Sweat dripped from my temples, gathering into the corners of my eyes and lips. It rolled down my back, between my breasts to my belly into the creases of my thighs, its wetness pooling. Low pleadings grew steadily...Father! Mom! divorce...hurt...broken...why... Why! lost...taken...cancer...no, no, sorry...NO! Why? Why?... Why!"... torrents of laments.

My ears filled with cross-talking, overtalking, sobbing en masse, a roar of sorrowful entreaties, ghosts emerged from the past. Hansen held his head and wept. I grieved for the loss of camel rides through the desert, a touch that branded, a love that soared, apple trees and grapevines and bats spinning through open windows. I grieved for mattress testing, eating duck filled with buckshot, and I grieved for "Panama" —pouring out my heartache—love given me that had restored my soul. And done with all that, at last, I circled back round to Mother...lost...and to the loss of Dad, of course. And to Tim, the loss of his...of him...of what I wasn't sure. But I did remember that I had wept silently through the divorce proceedings, and he had too.

Root entered the sweat lodge for the third time. He shoveled a hot stone into the fire pit, threw on more water that hissed a geyser of steam into the air. "Forgiveness is your next challenge," he said. "Look into your heart and into your life and search for people and things that require compassion. Who and what in your life can set you free? Who gets a pass? Who doesn't? Look deep. Are you included in this? Now, forgiveness," and he left.

Together, breaths of hot air were inhaled, sighs exhaled, shoulders rose, backs straightened. Histories—lodged in muscles and joints (hurt, spite, hate, self-cruelty, grievances) —were abandoned. A low cooperative mumble commenced. Our words fused—a collective voice—declarations, assurances, pardons… OK…OK…OK…forgive…forgive…pardon…I…father… beg… You! Mother…me…I'm sorry…forgive! But this time, our cries rang beyond the limits of the bowl that held us—that black tarp womb—becoming a singular voice carrying our collective mercy into the Universe. Us begging to re-gather pieces of our lives stolen or lent or lost, us wanting to cut loose anchors to go on.

Across the circle, hands stretched out to the fire pit, palms opened, then turned back to touch on hearts. I had forgiven Mother long ago. But this time again, taken by the heat and the collective force of pain mingled with pity, I gathered strength letting go of bitterness—a residue—craving repair for myself still holding on for so long. And, with yet more clarity, I thought: *I forgive you, Mother.* And then I forgave myself— I/Thou Mother—I forgive You/Me closing a circle in need of wholeness.

The flap opened, Sol and the others placed more rocks into the fire pit, dousing it with more water. Steam huffed up, and I gulped it down, although I was beginning to feel dry. The devouring orange embers glowed luminous forming a radiant mandala beneath the stones, a flower of life blossoming in the center of our wounds. Root's last instructions were to express thankfulness. Having just rid my heart and mind of so much, I gave thanks for Mother, Babcia—their grit that I had—and for Dad, a soul-father. Thanks for Agnes, Biscute, Dori, Cathy, Karette—all bodhisattvas in their own ways. And Tim. I felt gratitude for his love. I felt love for his love so generously given.

And around me, Billie Rae and Hansen and the others—a wave of gratitude—I heard chants of recognition, acknowledgment, admiration, praise—family, friends, lovers, themselves. Around me names mingled with tenderness pouring out louder and louder, some laughing, some crying yet more. And I gave thanks for the past, the present, and everything stretching before me waiting. Thanking my own shift of reality, my cobra, a guide that had set me on a path in sync with my *doings and beings*. Thanks for the energy system in my family that fed my core bonding me with Mother Nature making me believe in myself. I was filled with gratefulness for my job, creativity, imagination, for that year of freedom, for that year I had lived.

Spellbound by the embers, red eyes pulling me in, once more, I was in the Annapurna Sanctuary twirling like a top absorbing its powers as it absorbed me. And I thought of Gome and the sat-sangees at Lucknow, and the women locked in their dorms and the lepers and the grandmothers sleeping and begging on the streets of Delhi, and of meeting up with Cathy in Cairo. I gave thanks for the strength I knew I had that could help break me from my heartache and despair.

Each voice quieted to a hush. I gave final thanks to those who sat with me in the lodge, those who'd feasted an intimate Thanksgiving—all in alignment—a Norman Rockwell magazine cover.

When it ended, outside in the cool night air, I felt good. The stars blazed overhead. My skin felt free—cleaner than it had ever been. Free. Detoxed from wounds new and old. No towel was needed, no shower, no hug. Nothing was needed. For two hours, twelve of us had sat upright—in a ceremony Root said honored the feminine spirit—congregants in a chorus of fury, pleadings, clemency, and gratitude, and, perhaps comprehension or maybe, at least, anticipation for healing. I was one of those. Now cleansed, I felt the spirit's grace and merely needed sleep and to dream again.

She Who Sees Through Purple Eye

I tied my tarp to two small bushes getting my site ready to sleep three nights in the Rocky Mountains. Being out there alone in the woods was the heart of the Vision Quest. I pulled out my sleeping bag and mat from my backpack, unrolled them, and placed them under the tarp next to my supply of water. There were no cell phones, books, paper, or pen, and no food. I'd be fasting.

The group had hiked the mountain to reach a meeting point where Root and his crew would stay. Once there, he'd directed us to spread out, find a spot to sleep away from others, and then come back for approval before setting up camp. He told us Sol and his crew would covertly monitor our sites during the days out there alone.

It was now mid-afternoon, and I settled into my site. I'd found a large open outcrop surrounded by towering spruces and aspens; several massive sheets of granite nosed from the earth. One gigantic boulder balanced at the very top of the area I had chosen. It reminded me of Hampi—now far away in India but still close, the beauty of its coral-colored rocks dancing one atop the other. But this boulder was different...forceful. Poised, it oversaw my space—solid and personal.

I spread the contents of my backpack out under the open sides of the tarp-tent. I glanced around and wondered if mountain lions prowled the area. I wasn't worried about that, but I was getting ready to sleep basically under a bush. I knew the mountains were allies of the oceans and, in their own right, housed a share of violence coupled equally with beauty. Still, my bond with nature was strong, and I'd chosen this exposed site because I liked it, the idea of sleeping under the stars where I could smell the scent of spruce and feel the solid Earth cradle me in her arms. Mountains. Sun. Air and three gallons of water I'd hauled up the trail.

As night came on, the sky took on a pastel glow, fading the faces of the aspens and pines into a rich gray-green. I sat in a lotus position by the tarp and placed a three-inch-long white string Root had given each of us on my knee. I emptied my mind of words, focused on my breath, and watched the string. Root said when we no longer could see the filament, we were in a moment between day and night, a special moment of equilibrium. A yin and yang instant, between the familiar and the unfamiliar, confidence and fear.

I focused on the strand. One time zone slipped into another. I was back at Fatehpur Sikri, pulling a string from the hem of my blue dress, tying it into the marble filigree, then wearing that same dress while walking the markets of Cairo with Henrik. I felt the earthfall of granite beneath me as I watched the string's whiteness weaken into gray. Watched day blend into night. I was suspended on the edge of this today and that tomorrow as the night pulled at the day, letting those cherished moments slide into the past. I'm not sure if it was gradual or a snap, but the string became invisible, and I rested in the dark glad that it was soft and warm.

One by one, stars awoke aloft wrapping me in silence. I took off my hiking boots, scarred brown leather, their sight replaying my trek across the roof of the world. The dust was long gone; still, I couldn't help but hear the churning of the Kaligandaki River and see two lone figures moving through the spirit of the land, me and my guide Gome. Pressing boot on trail to find nothing more trustworthy than the rock beneath. That's where I'd met myself. There and in the truth of the Dalai Lama's sweeping laughter that had opened me up to something larger than myself, and there in the gray-blue eyes of a man facing me inside the Great Pyramid of Giza. Those recollections stumbled into the night, and I got up to crawl under the tarp to sleep, only to see a bonfire of stars overhead.

In the morning, I did yoga. The salute to the sun standing tall; then downward-facing dog to the earth, drawing the heat of the rock up through each chakra—root, sacral, solar plexus—expanding it there at that third wheel of vitality, the ring of fortitude that had always lived there. I drank water and walked around the clearing. Lichens and plants grew out of crevices on the stone's surface.

A small skull lay in the grasses, and I placed it—a symbol of parting—at the foot of my boulder bed.

Fasting made me slow down, and I sat listening to the birds, hearing warblers and a raucous jay in the ocean of trees. Then I walked up to the boulder balanced at the top of my space. My eyes searched its crevasses carved by eons of wind and water. And I stroked my fingertips over its slatey surface, its coarse stamina, paying attention to each of my inhalations and exhalations. Then, counting and breathing, I imaged my cobra, lustrous and serene, rising over my head. For a long while, with my back against the stone's mineral toughness, I meditated, letting the cobra's light swim through my body—from toes to head, purging yet further preoccupations from the sweat lodge.

As the shadows changed on the rocks, I was reminded of Repos Beach in India, playing with the sundial palm tree being pushed through Time to spiral onto Chance's hook. Here now in the mountains, I stretched out to yield to the warmth from the rock backing me. And I felt the bedrock gather me into its arms, a touch familiar and strong. I was in good company.

The hours slipped by. Root had said to spend time calling in our personal power animals from the four corners of the Earth. They, he said, were a support system needed when we felt weak and drained of courage and no longer able to deal with the hardships and trials thrown at our lives. Unlike a spirit animal that guides a person on their life's journey to teach them lessons (like my cobra), a power animal is different. It brings messages of boldness that smooths the path and assists in doing the work destined for. Work imbued with emotional depth and peace. Power animals are protectors. They possess specific survival skills that can be drawn on for duties and responsibilities. It was now time for that, and I dug into my backpack for my rattle.

I found a depression in the granites to sit facing North—facing that massive boulder —and I focused on my breath once again. I shook the rattle sending out its rattlesnake call. Lungs filled, emptied, filled, emptied. The boulder blurred. I felt myself taken into its belly, its core—hard, strong, something that had survived through the ages, now serving to announce a power animal.

It didn't take long for my imagery to kick in and the sense that a bison was staring at me. Its sharp horns shining in the sun, its full, dark brown shaggy mane, its eyes polished with unyielding determination. I scratched through my brain for its meaning. A herd animal, endurance and resilience for the long journey, and a message that survival rested in being part of the community. I watched its enormous head sway as my imagination fused its humped body into the boulder.

I turned to the East and waited. Lungs filled, emptied, filled, emptied. A bumpy-skinned toad hopped out of my mind's eye. Often thought of as supernatural creatures, toads are associated with dark, mysterious forces. Yet, a toad is capable of adapting and regenerating. And that was the message now, one of blending in, working behind the scenes—wait, watch, and observe during this time of change. A time of shifting into a subsequent stage of life, different now because part of the journey was done. Lungs filled, emptied, filled, emptied.

Facing West, I closed my eyes, opening only to a slit, waiting. I shook the rattle. This time, a rabbit formed in my mind's eye—abundance, prosperity, creativity. I smiled. Soft, warm, timid, clever. Breath in, breath out, breath in, breath out. I sipped water…offering it to the rabbit, nourishing the lifecycles within it and me.

Finally, I turned to my site's South side, where the slabs of granite pushed down into dense, shaded woods strewn with fallen trees covered by moss blankets. Lungs filled, emptied, filled, emptied. Rattling, I visualized a blue whale plummeting in and out of clear seawater, singing soulful songs that penetrated the miles. I wasn't quite sure then what the whale's survival skills were. Still, I knew I'd been brought the music of the Earth. Later, I discovered that whales meant compassion, solitude, and unbridled creativity. It was a creature that plummeted the depths and coped by coming up for air every now and then. I understood that. I'd done that in the past.

And I imagined the whale's sounds traveling up my spine—like the Tibetan monks at Taksindhu Monastery trumpeting harmonic messages on their six-foot-long horns throughout that night long ago. Imagined the whale's moans and sweeps and calls filled the spruce and aspens that trembled in the current of a breeze.

As night approached, the fasting and emotional work made me ready for sleep. I re-tied my tarp tent to the bushes suspended about two feet off the surface of the rock. I crawled under and reached into my pack to take out a zircon purchased in Rishikesh. I'd brought it as a ritual offering, part of the vision quest. I put the stone in a small crevice at the base of my sleeping pad. And I focused on it only to recall the puja in Mundgod (the monks distributing food), the act of worship during the Kalachakra Initiation, its purpose. How when it was over, all of us sitting under that tent had shed our red head and armbands, symbolically ridding ourselves of all negative thoughts to invite a sense of compassion, open our hearts to everything the Initiation had to offer a readiness to serve all sentient beings, moving from I to Thou, a most profound connection.

It was time to focus my purpose for being here, ask a favor of the Universe. I'd done that before, of course, but what I wanted now was to be free of my heartache, the sorrow I felt at the loss of Henrik. I had everything else I needed, a job, a house, a car, family and friends, a sense of being Special, but my heart hurt. It was as simple as that, and of course, not as simple. Because, still, I wondered, would I go on seeing Henrik in every full moon, every blade of grass?

The light washed out from the mountain. When I could no longer see, I closed my eyes, once again visualizing each animal helper I'd called in that day, clutching the warmth of the bunny closest. Then I reached back into the past to touch upon those power points I'd encountered during my year-long trek. I walked there, again, in the mountains of the Himalaya, in Varanasi with its grievers, and in the Taj Mahal in love's embrace. Again, I heard the Dalai Lama's voice transmitting compassion for all humanity, and I felt the rush of Time inside the Great Pyramid of Cheops. I let each impression imprint a restorative foothold in my heart. Then supported by the solidness of the rock, I felt my body soften against its hardness, felt my jaw slacken, felt myself letting go of expectation. I fell into a deep, dreamless sleep.

In the morning, the zircon was gone. I suspected a woodrat had taken it—yet another power animal tough and fearless—this one now well-heeled. I drank water and spent the day repeating my sweat lodge grievances and appreciations over and over again. I spoke them out to the aspens and pines, trying to forgive Henrik, surrendering as much as I could, accepting the hurt as part of myself. After all, I was *She Who Sees Through Purple Eye*—given that name and came with a wound to heal.

I went on this way throughout the day. I visualized myself cutting the psychic cords that bound me to him. And as the afternoon came, I was given a few more glimpses that the relationship was over for good. Despite loving me, Henrik's life had been driven by something else—something I couldn't understand—a harshness toward himself that had turned on me. There had been an emptiness filled by another woman to help crowd some abyss inside himself. Foolishly, I'd been in bed with Henry VIII, expecting loyalty and getting disposability. Instead, he'd thrown away the pearl he'd found at the bottom of his dreams. Still, I believed his pain. Pathetic.

The fasting had amplified everything. I took in the pulse of the Earth, even more finely, feeling the tendrils of Mother Gaia reverberate around me and into me. The edges of the aspens trembled in the breeze, the blades of sunlight glinted over the toughness of the granite slabs, the boulder at the top of my spot stood tall—all took me in. My cobra rode high. My power animals floated through my mind giving me support. And I saw myself picking up each part of my heart, shattered glass, and gluing the pieces back together, hoping it would hold.

I thought: *He thrived on the separations between us, so he could savor a gloom buried somewhere in him… Broken. Just broken. The whole thing broken.* But there was also *my part*. The part where the Universe wasn't finished with me—my heart, or was it my soul?—that part of me tied to Henrik. This was something, more than something, a path the Universe had delivered me. Something I was getting.

Henrik's love, or rather my love for him, was a dictator in my brain. A moment-to-moment thing, an intense focus that took my all. Took it like my doctoral studies had; the practice of Jnana Yoga had demanding so much from me. *This heartache…huh!... is a form of yoga*, I thought, *not Hatha or Jnana. No! This is different!*

This yoga—this "union," this "connection"—that characterized my bond with Henrik had a different intent. This yoga attended to my heart, but more importantly, it attended to my soul—it was Soul Yoga. Where the space between my heartbeats and my breaths met Henrik's—met their fervor and playfulness, their understandings and mistakes, their cuts and mendings, openings and closings—and where now my heart, broken as it was, was a matter for my soul to heal.

Although I didn't think that Soul Yoga existed as such in the Yogic tradition, nonetheless, I was certain it defined my bind with Henrik. Not named exactly, but maybe Soul Yoga was explained by Sage Patanjali in the yoga sutras. That's where he had classified the last three parts of the eight-fold path of yoga as Antar practice, Antara being Sanskrit for the heart. He'd said those final practices gave a practitioner insight beyond an easily perceivable reality, allowing for a sharper vision to recognize your true self. So, now sitting here in a space, a sacred circle of the Earth I'd created for three days, I was searching for my own vision. And it dawned on me that once again, the Universe had taken me on a quest, not for my brain, but this time for my heart. No! my soul. Possibly binding me forever. A journey of the soul to fulfill a life's mission—Antara Yoga!

Did my relationship with Henrik prepare me for this practice, this Antara Yoga, this *heart questing?* Had my cobra guided me to this soulmate trek that once it had begun, I'd accepted it with such abandon? That *was* its job, after all. First the head, now scraping away false identities to fall headlong into authenticity. So, I shouldn't have been surprised to find myself in Henrik's arms where Chance had placed me, my Kundalini. That exquisite consort of light that played within me doing its job opening me up to more of who I was to be. And as this occurred to me, I knew it would take time, and action, this re-stitching of my heart.

I visualized a silver, sentient cord tying me to Henrik. That mad idea that our breaths had spanned eternity hand in hand, and I slashed at the cord with a mental saber, slashed and slashed and slashed severing it, releasing him to the stars. In a way (just like that telepathic time I'd been lost in the woods when he'd felt my distress), I fell into a moment where I joined him in what I suspected was his deepest anguish. His feelings that our relationship was like a hostage crisis. In pushing me away, Henrik had been trying to explain something to me about himself, something in his own sense of Self, that I didn't understand. Couldn't possibly understand— coming from the abundance of my own self-worth. And I wondered if it was possible for me to love myself again, to get over the torment, to find again the Self-respect needed to surrender to the journey of being a woman.

By the end of the Vision Quest, well, the mountains were generous to me—their prana salving my wounds old and new, regrounding me with tears and dirt and stars, letting me see that there are love stories in life and, of course, there are tragedies. I was simply living mine. Chance had played a hand. At times, turning me topsy turvy, and at times cleansing me while steering me toward unfinished soul work.

Once on the plane, I felt a feeling shaping itself into a small mantra. It was an old, familiar life preserver that said: *You're going to be OK, You're Special,* and I believed it.

Cleaning Drawers

People's lives move through many dimensions of spacetime. Mine did too. During that painful time, I surrendered to my grief, letting the hurt run its course. I started to clean out my psychic drawers one by one, discarding what was no longer needed, letting go.

I guess I was someone who would love Henrik forever. I don't think that made me a fool; it made me human. But I was aware that to bounce back, I couldn't merely accept what had happened. I had to embrace it. Deep in the beatings of my heart, tucked in its enigmas, there truly lived a love for Henrik, who just maybe, maybe, I could add to the teachers in my life whom I'd loved and who had shaped my spirit. Gatekeepers like Dad, Mother, Tim. All who had wounded and gifted me at the same time who (even like me) were a bit broken, yet serving to make me more whole. People who were placed on my life's path to teach me lessons—karmic ones— to help me learn about myself, the world, and others. Help me learn to forgive.

Forgiveness sounded right. That powerful session in the sweat lodge in the mountains. And what Karette had said about Henrik not being ready to join me in my life. It *had* been our destiny to meet, but the point might have been for *me* to serve as *his* gatekeeper just as I'd been served by others in my journey. From that, a residue of wishes, sincere—and yes, loving—still lingered. But I also realized he, too, had served in the growth of my soul, the wholeness I perceived as Antara Yoga. That sounded true to me, but admittedly, it took a long time before I no longer found Henrik in the grasses in the meadows.

I kept cleaning those psychic drawers. Another one held Tim.

Disposing of, clearing, accepting. Tim, who had loved and supported me, had made me face the realities of everyday life—its worries, its failures, its heartaches. Although, what appeared to be an unfavorable marriage, in the end, I guess, it too had been a push for growth. Tim had heralded me through my doctoral process, making me live a life that demanded a wholeness of spirit, one where I had needed to ask the Universe for help.

As I threw out the remains of that drawer, I remembered that after the divorce, Tim had given me Teddy Boon to stay with the rest of my collection of dolls. And that one day, while straightening Teddy's tie that Tim had made, I found Tim's wedding band tied to the inside of the collar. I was grateful I had not been remiss in paying him back. I'd settled thousands of dollars on him from the sale of the house, but he'd been luckier than that. Lucky that I had been a dreamer—or more likely, I had a clandestine cobra guiding my life—which, I believe, had saved his.

The final drawer I circled back to held Mother—her wounds, her desire to drown her pain, her weakness as a mother. And I realized how long, how many soul years, it could take to slog things like that out for anyone. I took those parts of her that were me—the cook, the canner, the seamstress, the gardener, the parts that went it alone and could brave the crossing of the Atlantic Ocean—and absorbed her grit and productivity into my Self. As time went on, I loved her more for all that she was. Some circles finally close.

As I let go, I understood that my whole life had gone in a direction that was uniquely mine. That each experience, each person, each joy, each cut, and mending had been an opportunity to grow. With Henrik, my heart had been lost, but somewhere on the way, some things were won. I'd won me.

Yet, I must admit, there were things I didn't win. I'd lost love, and sorry to say, I never found another man to fill that seat in my heart, that unavoidable space that wants, looks for and hopes to welcome the I/Thou of a beloved stranger. Never found. A reflection of my soul in another's eyes, never found.

I didn't expect another thunderbolt, but a part of me yearned for a relationship, longed for someone to complete that circle of me as a woman. Other teachers at school had found husbands on match.com, so I set up a profile and went out with a few men. One whose wife, after five kids, had let herself go and another on an overnight boat date who, in the end, wasn't for me. Soon, I ended my subscription to Match. I realized it's true that some circles never close, are never meant to—regardless of thunderbolt strikes unequivocally authorized by the Universe.

Did the thunderbolt experience ruin me for the rest of my life, making me look for the same thing? Thinking back on Henrik, I had to admit there was a small measure of relief my heart was no longer wrenched by someone else's torment. My life with him had begun to become an act of stuffing my emotions away, not facing them. Maybe our long-distance relationship had fit flawlessly into his emotional system. It could be he *wanted* to yearn, wanted me out of reach so he could savor the ache of separation surrounded by the gray, overcast skies of his home. It was an eggshell—our relationship—strong yet fragile. Truth was, I'd been happy but blind. Finding love for me had always felt comparable to unraveling a Gordian Knot. What had unraveled for me during our relationship was existential loneliness. I knew there was someone on the planet who…well…anyway.…

I wasn't scared of being alone, not having a husband or kids of my own. I learned long ago that I didn't fit into the mold of wife or motherhood, being too independent and constantly pushing those roles to the back burner. And maybe I was afraid of getting into a lockbox relationship that worked against everything my soul was asked to do in this world. For my whole life, I'd refused to give in to most social demands imposed on women expected to not fully become who they were meant to be. I knew I alone was answerable for not losing my sense of Self-worth, my Specialness, something I never intended to do.

Gradually as time went on, I left my personal unrest behind and re-found the meeting point of my personal joy and mission of service. At home, I was thankful. I entertained family and friends and planned trips abroad. The bell and doge bought on the Tibetan Plateau stood on the mantelpiece. The Shiva statue held court at the front door. The white khata scarf from His Holiness Trulsik Rinpoche lay wrapped around a mirror, the singing bowls placed below. I took time on weekends to write a book based on my research and got my paintings into several art shows. During summers, I took my 'citizen of the world' passport to Cambodia, saw Angkor Wat, and went on safari in Africa. At times, my life was solitary—a beat of quietness, a pause in space, a breath of prana—which I needed and cherished.

I kept swimming and hiking and doing yoga. The more I used the power of light streaming through my body in the pool—praying for family and friends and the world—and the more I hiked in the woods communing with plants and feeling the Earth beneath my feet and hearing her songs in my heart, the more I restored mind, body, and soul. My back never went out again, and I ended up hiking Kilimanjaro.

The memories from my trek, now so many years ago, beginning in Kathmandu, built a bedrock of well-being which made me unapologetic for being a resilient, productive, intuitive woman. One who believed, and always would, that service empowers and builds the blood of Self as it supports others. Work became my new love affair.

I presented at national and international conferences, won a teacher-scholar grant to travel to Japan with other US educators visiting schools, businesses, and cultural sites. My life felt good; it felt right. I was not simply surviving at work but thriving from breath to breath—each communal moment inhaling me as I inhaled it.

My cobra, its Kundalini alignment with the Universe, made work run effortlessly. It eavesdropped on my daily actions, and I let it. After all, I was hooked to a spiritual channel (one I'd asked for), so why not let it deliver the goods when I needed help, like in the past? If things got out of whack, a quick thought popped into my head to correct the course of action. Or often, that old synchronicity—that magical stumbling the Universe had provided me during my year-long trek—persisted, where I'd bump into whomever or whatever was needed to make things right.

Hard meetings with angry parents? Encounters that stepped over emotional avalanches on steep mountainsides? Simple. I regarded myself as a public servant in the marketplace, ready to bring about a harmonious outcome. In those onerous meetings, I'd visualize my cobra spiraling its diaphanous, golden energy. I'd let it enfold, ever so gently, along with everyone else's, energetically connecting our humanities into one for a positive outcome. Nobody ever suspected.

And the Dalai Lama's message of service—knowledge plus compassion equals wisdom—that karmic seed he'd planted now thrived. And I realized that the whole of the Universe was contained within me and I in it. And that, in a way, my Kundalini awakening was more ordinary than you'd think. It was not some super-intuition where I could easily pick the winning Derby horse or make a killing on Wall Street. Instead, it was beyond me just wanting to know. It was about the doings in my own life, individually, and my being engaged with the people in my community, bringing out our best.

That was how I read my spiritual liberation, a waltz between *being* and *doing*. My spirit, my cobra, its detachment—its magnificence, its silent energy organizing my prana around each day—a *this is it* day, this is *the only moment there is* day—supporting my intentions with determination. My life moved into yet another dimension, letting me be soft as well as hard. I felt free in my work, stronger and more awake.

And it became clear to me it didn't matter what service I was performing. Those linear constructs that drove most days—constructs I knew were underpinned by a random flow of reality—also led me to a *fullness of being* because I met them with light. And the toilet wallah, the one I'd met at Sahar Airport when I was leaving India, came to mind, making me understand that the year I'd pressed Go! had borne consequences that had multiplied my acceptance of *what was* and *who I was* in the larger picture of things. So that now, whatever I was doing no longer mattered, whether the janitor scrubbing out the school's toilets filling soap dispensers or the teacher polishing young minds growing synapses—it was all the same, worthy and blameless. I felt utterly liberated to work at my essential *doings*—I/Thou…I/Thou toilet wallah, I/thou teacher, I/Thou human being.

Alignment Postlude

I got the journey I wanted and more. Each morning when I arrived at work, the school bell sang out its mantra—Eerr-rangggg—bringing me into alignment with my Self, my community, and the Universe that delivered the quest I was destined for. It occurred to me how that thread, the one I'd unraveled from the hem of my blue dress to tie around the wishing screen in India, had granted my wish *to find true love* twofold. Not only had I met Henrik, but I'd met my destiny in teaching, where I found a place of zeal bringing me home to yoga within myself, a union of effort and surrender. A place from where each day I tacitly cast life preservers to my students: From my Kundalini to theirs, kindling future lights of compassion. You're Special! It felt good.

One afternoon, driving home, it had rained. The sun broke out to create a double rainbow. I stopped along the side of the road to watch its fire strike each bead of rain reflecting their sparks in two arcs, shimmering necklaces over the Earth. And I smiled, re-witnessing that teahouse with its thin walls in the Himalayas. Remembering how my trek had taken me to places beautiful and heartbreaking, where my body was strengthened, my spirit ignited, and my heart—well, once unlocked—was allowed to sing its narrative, losing some things while gaining others.

As I watched the rainbow curving its brief flow through Time, I knew each moment is its own moment with room to grow. And that during my trek, each mountain, each river, each Taj, each Pyramid, each sari-clad woman and leper I'd seen had also seen me and belonged to me forever. My heart had known—after that precious inch of Time—I'd end up right back where I'd started, chopping wood, carrying water, and I had. That afternoon, when I reached home, and the garage door rattled open, I repeated my daily mantra: *Thank you, God, for this Earth, this job, this house, this family, these friends…this humanity. Thank you.* And I inhaled the kindliness of the path I was on and the kindliness of the moment I was in.

Post Script

Love flows through a web of spacetime, sometimes tenuous, sometimes self-willed, to embrace us with unfinished business. Several years after Henrik and I had split, he re-opened our dialogue with an occasional Christmas or birthday note. When the era of email arrived, I received these lines:

January 9, 2000

Dearest Anya!

I'm with you ever so often. Today, cleaning the house, I found a strand of your long hair sitting on the window sill!

Love,
Yours Henrik

Epilogue

June 10, 2021

Dear Henrik,

Just the other day, I found a box in the basement that contained all the letters you had written me and copies of some I had written you. I read them. It wasn't easy. But what I saw in those pages was, well, I have to admit…love.

Our relationship, in the end, was painful for me; but as I read on… Clearly, all this doesn't matter anymore, not at all!

Still, with those letters, my heart softened against that residue of regret and loss lodged so long ago, and yes, that I'd let go of. Yet, I wanted to write and thank you.

That was the year the Universe took me by hand to escort me down a path I was to take---a journey that belonged to me---a journey for my soul. One with you in Luxor where we met.

So very simply, thank you for those few years in my life that you gave me...YOU! Thank you for Egypt. Thank you for the romps in the woods and on the beach, the horsehair mattress, our mutual bond with the Earth, and for you being in my life, in my soul.

You know, in those letters from 25 years ago, I vowed to love you forever throughout this Universe, and I want to tell you that I do.

That note I emailed you after Zoe died, asking to be informed of your death, (Really!) was merely a message from one person to another who has shared a moment that was precious to say: Remember, Henrik, here

TIME IS ONLY AN INCH

in this Universe, you are loved; no, you are LOVED FOREVER. I promised you that, and I do keep my promises.

With a Smile for You Always,

Yours,
Anya

Recognitions

Many are in my gratitude for supplying the lifeblood of this book. First, applause, of a very loud kind, goes to my writing partner Kay Carlotta Baxter for her steadfast weekly appointments during the four years it took to write this memoir. Her level-headedness, personal talent for straight thinking, and hikes in the woods meant more than can be expressed here. Ironically, COVID-19 helped too, not only delivering time to get the job done but allowing for the book's refinement to the point where the effort of writing met the joy of offering it to the world. My beta readers deserve a standing ovation for their warmth and astuteness to detail: CF, VV, CAC, and SD, who supported me across the finish line. A heartfelt thank you goes to everyone I encountered during that year when I experienced the most "Special" space and time of my life. Each individual stretched me in new dimensions and helped me soar in directions, never to return to the same relationship with the world. Each person in this book lives inside me forever.

References

Gershwin, G., Gershwin, I. *"Let's Call the Whole Thing Off"* (1937). *Let's Call the Whole Thing Off* recorded by Fred Astaire & Johnny Greer with his orchestra (1937).

Houston, V., & Snow, S. (1996). Gayatri mantra the sound of light. On *Gayatri Mantra: The Sound of Light* [Cassette tape]. Warwick, NY: American Sanskrit Institute.

I Ching, the Chinese Book of Changes (Wilhelm Trans., 1950 86-9). Bollingen Series XIX. Princeton University Press.

Quarantotto, L., Sartori, F., Peterson, F. *"Time to Say Goodbye"* (1996). *Time to Say Goodbye* recorded by Sarah Brightman & Andrea Bocelli. On Angel Records (CD., 1997. 4:04). The English lyrics (by Sarah Brightman Lyrics at azlyrics.com. Chelsea Music Pub. Ltd.)

Walcott, Derek. Love After Love. Derek Walcott Collected Poems 1948-1984, Farrar, Straus & Giroux, 1962, p. 328.

www.ingramcontent.com/pod-product-compliance
Lightning Source LLC
Chambersburg PA
CBHW030133170426
43199CB00008B/48